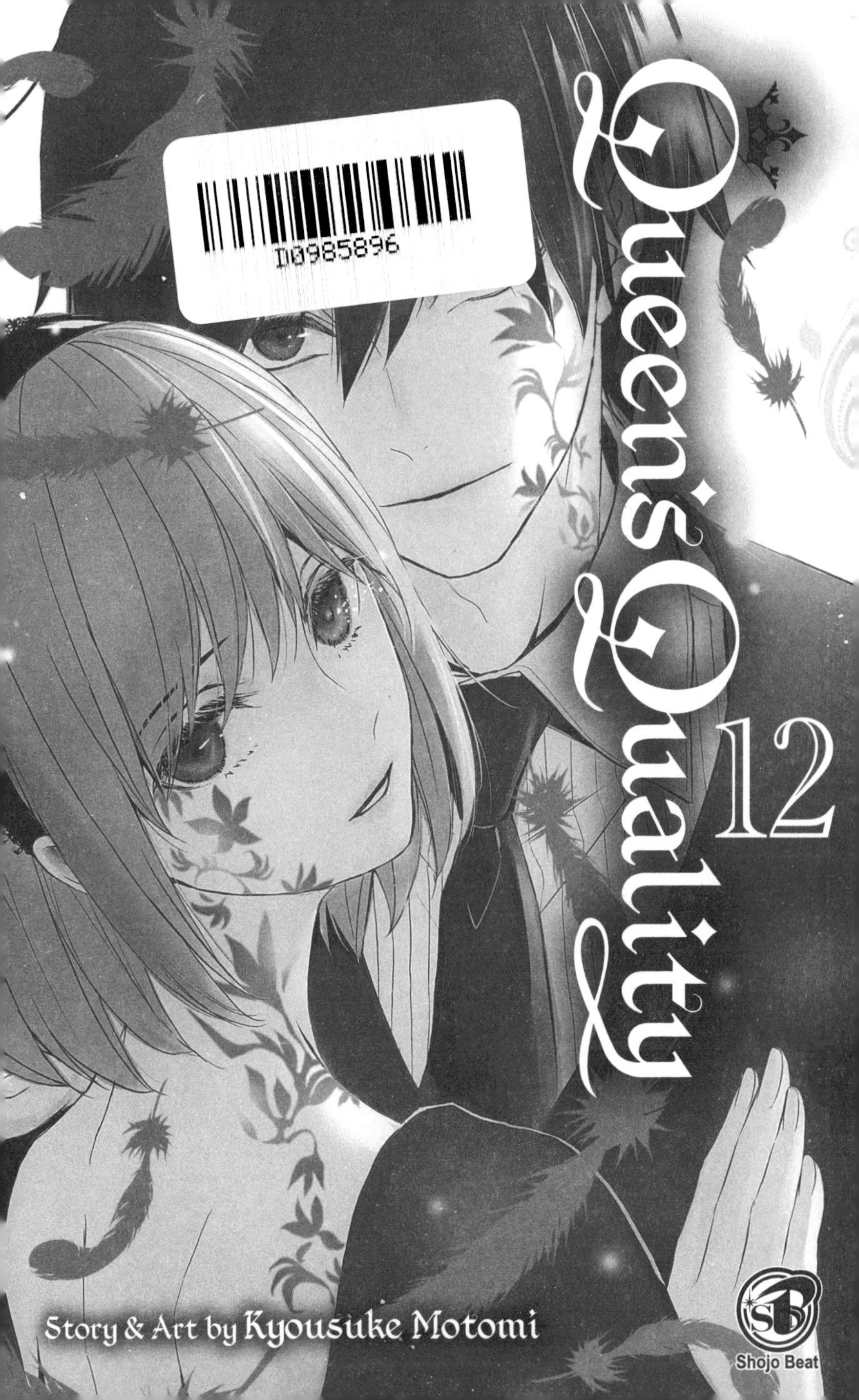
Queen's Quality
12
Story & Art by Kyousuke Motomi
Shojo Beat

Queen's Quality

CONTENTS

Chapter 53........... 5
Chapter 54 26
Chapter 55 65
Chapter 56........... 107
Chapter 57........... 129

12

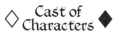
◇ Cast of Characters ◆

Fumi Nishioka

An apprentice Sweeper with the powers of a Queen, this second-year high school student dreams of finding her very own Prince Charming.

Kyutaro Horikita

A mind Sweeper who cleanses people's minds of dangerous impurities. Although incredibly awkward with people, he and Fumi are now dating.

Ataru Shikata

A former bug handler who uses bugs to manipulate people. Saved by Fumi and Kyutaro, he has joined the Genbu Clan.

Miyako Horikita

The prior head of the Genbu Gate Sweepers. She can be both strict and kind, and she watches over and advises Fumi.

Koichi Kitagawa

The chairman of the school Fumi and Kyutaro attend. He's a Sweeper as well as being Kyutaro's brother-in-law.

Takaya Kitahara

One of the Genbu Clan, he was originally a member of the main Byakko Clan. He's an expert with suggestive therapy and is actually Fumi's uncle.

◇ Story Thus Far ◆

The Horikitas are a family of Sweepers—people who cleanse impurities from human hearts. After seeing Fumi's potential, they take her on as an assistant and trainee. Within Fumi dwells the power of both the White and the Dark-Gray queens, both of whom have the ability to give people immense power.

Fumi and Kyutaro are finally on the same page emotionally and are now in a relationship! Soon after, when it becomes clear that a snake is dwelling within Kyutaro, Fumi defeats the snake and attains the powers of the True Queen. Kyutaro makes a deal with his snake and brings it to meet the one hiding within the Seiryu Clan. Kyutaro allows his much weaker snake to devour some of his wishes in order to give it more strength and to protect Fumi.

MONTHLY BETSUCOMI SALE DATE NOTICE ON TWITTER AND INSTAGRAM

CHAPTER 53

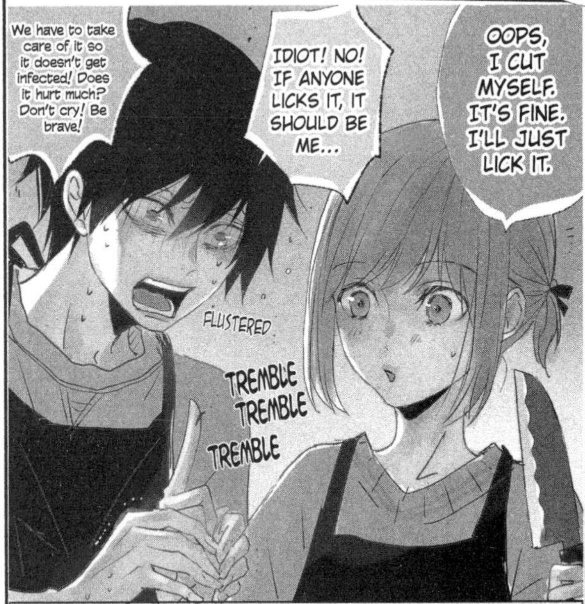
OOPS, I CUT MYSELF. IT'S FINE. I'LL JUST LICK IT.
IDIOT! NO! IF ANYONE LICKS IT, IT SHOULD BE ME...
We have to take care of it so it doesn't get infected! Does it hurt much? Don't cry! Be brave!
FLUSTERED
TREMBLE TREMBLE
TREMBLE

KYUTARO'S FINE WITH SEEING HIS OWN BLOOD, BUT HE'S THE SORT WHO GETS BOTHERED BY SEEING SOMEONE ELSE'S BLOOD (ESPECIALLY IN EVERYDAY LIFE).

IT'S MORE THAN A SIMPLE MATTER OF GETTING RATTLED BY SEEING OTHER PEOPLE'S BLOOD. KYUTARO GETS WORKED UP BY ANYTHING HAVING TO DO WITH FUMI. HE PROBABLY CARRIES BAND-AIDS AROUND JUST FOR HER.

LET'S SEE... WHAT'S UP IN *QUEEN'S QUALITY* THIS MONTH?
* KYUTARO SURE LOOKS LIKE HE'S ABOUT TO FAINT WHEN HE SEES HIS OWN BLOOD HERE.
* HEY, QUEEN, AREN'T YOU TOO STRICT WITH THE SNAKE?
* THE PIGGY MOSQUITO REPELLENT IS GLARING AGAIN THIS MONTH.

REALLY, THIS CHAPTER'S SUBJECT IS A LITTLE TOO SERIOUS TO POKE FUN AT.

I SEND OUT TWITTER UPDATES LIKE THIS EVERY MONTH. YOU CAN READ SOME OF MY OTHER MUTTERINGS THERE TOO.

@motomikyosuke

I'VE STARTED AN INSTAGRAM ACCOUNT TOO! (KYOSUKEMOTOMI)

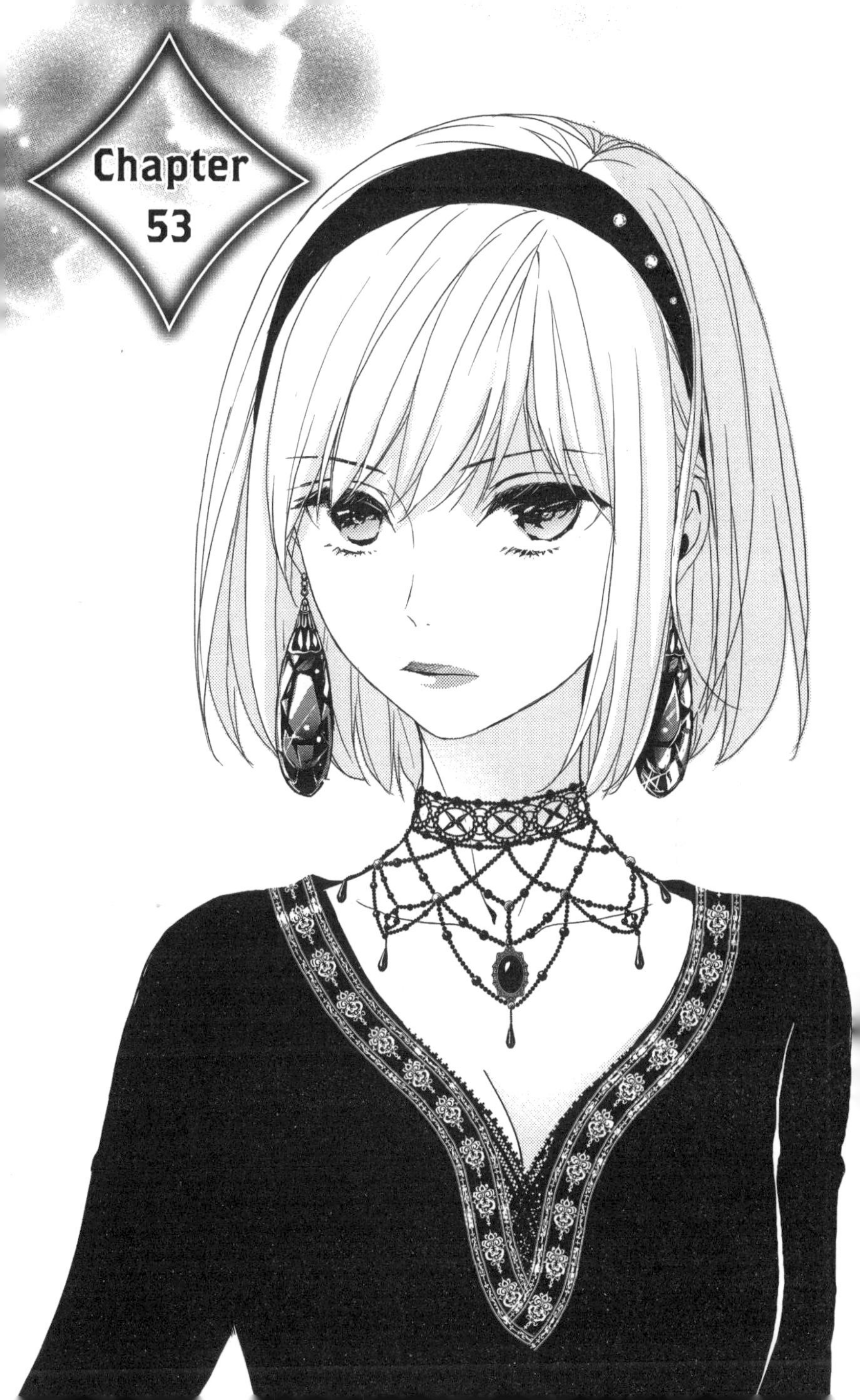
Chapter 53

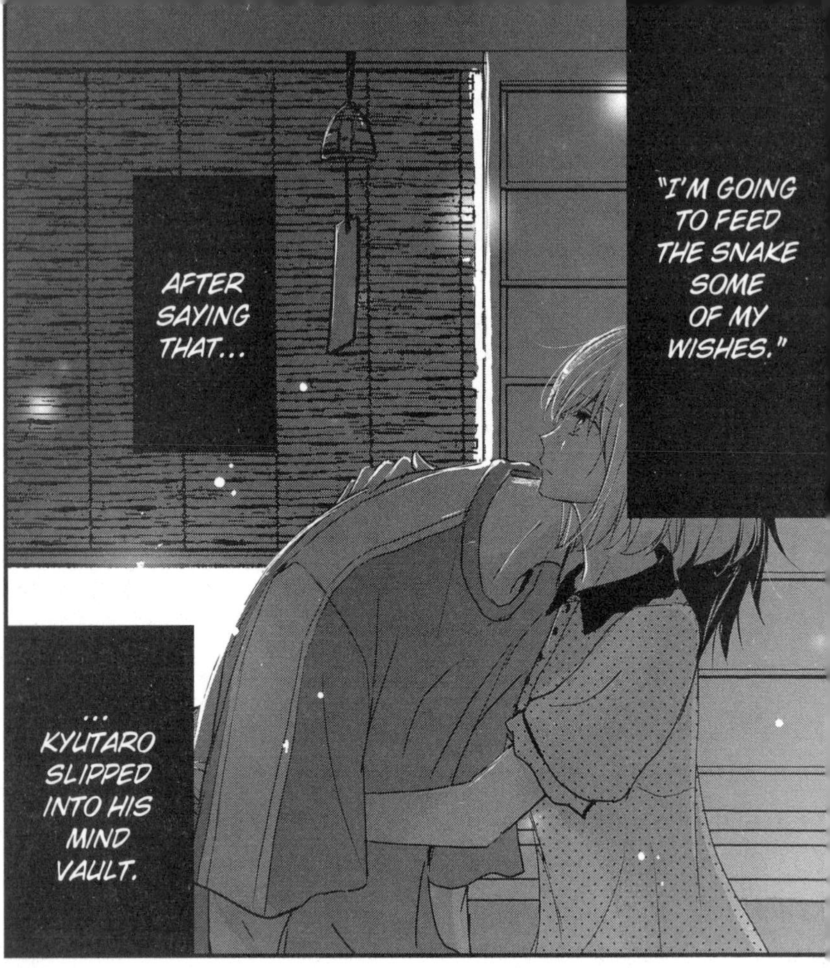
"I'M GOING TO FEED THE SNAKE SOME OF MY WISHES."
AFTER SAYING THAT...
...KYUTARO SLIPPED INTO HIS MIND VAULT.

Hello, everyone! I'm Kyousuke Motomi.

Thank you for scooping up volume 12 of *Queen's Quality*. We're now deep into the Seiryu arc. The art is getting ever darker!! I haven't held anything back in this volume. I hope you enjoy it.

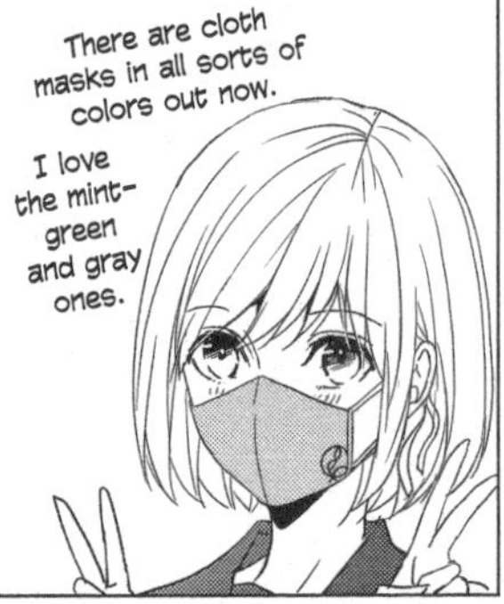
There are cloth masks in all sorts of colors out now.
I love the mint-green and gray ones.

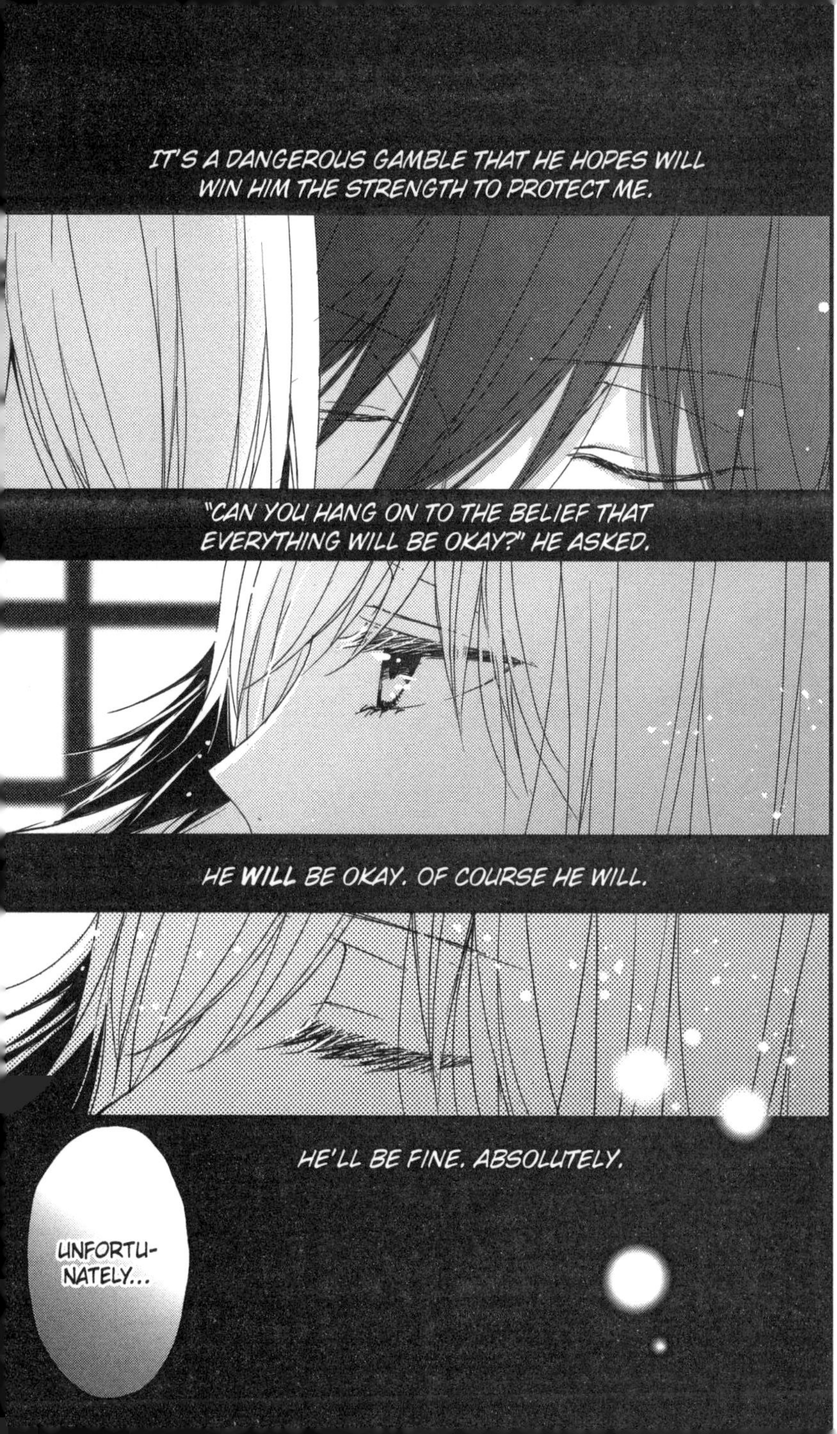
IT'S A DANGEROUS GAMBLE THAT HE HOPES WILL WIN HIM THE STRENGTH TO PROTECT ME.
"CAN YOU HANG ON TO THE BELIEF THAT EVERYTHING WILL BE OKAY?" HE ASKED.
HE WILL BE OKAY. OF COURSE HE WILL.
HE'LL BE FINE. ABSOLUTELY.
UNFORTU-NATELY...

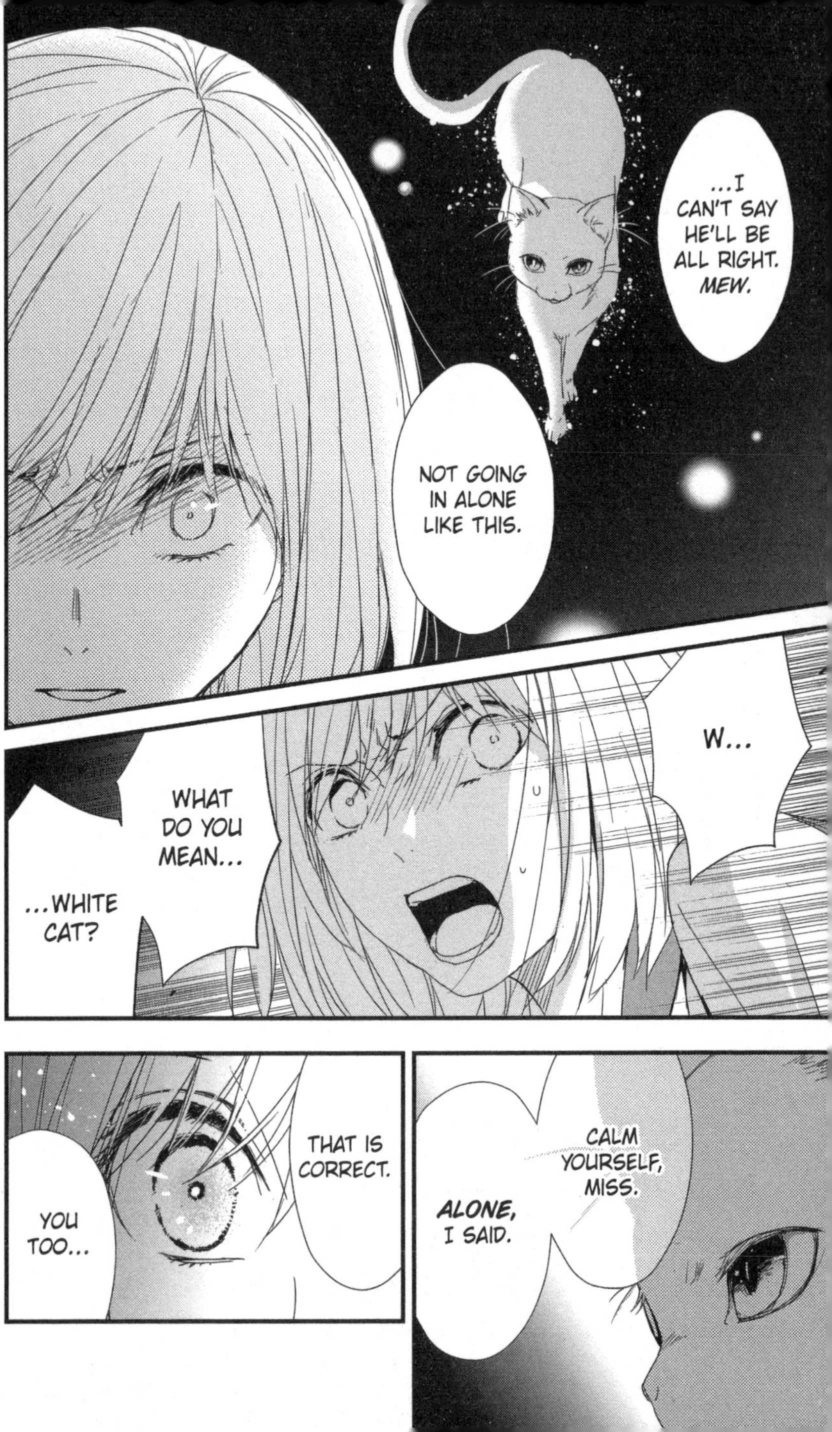
...I CAN'T SAY HE'LL BE ALL RIGHT. *MEW.*
NOT GOING IN ALONE LIKE THIS.
W...
WHAT DO YOU MEAN...
...WHITE CAT?
CALM YOURSELF, MISS.
ALONE, I SAID.
THAT IS CORRECT.
YOU TOO...

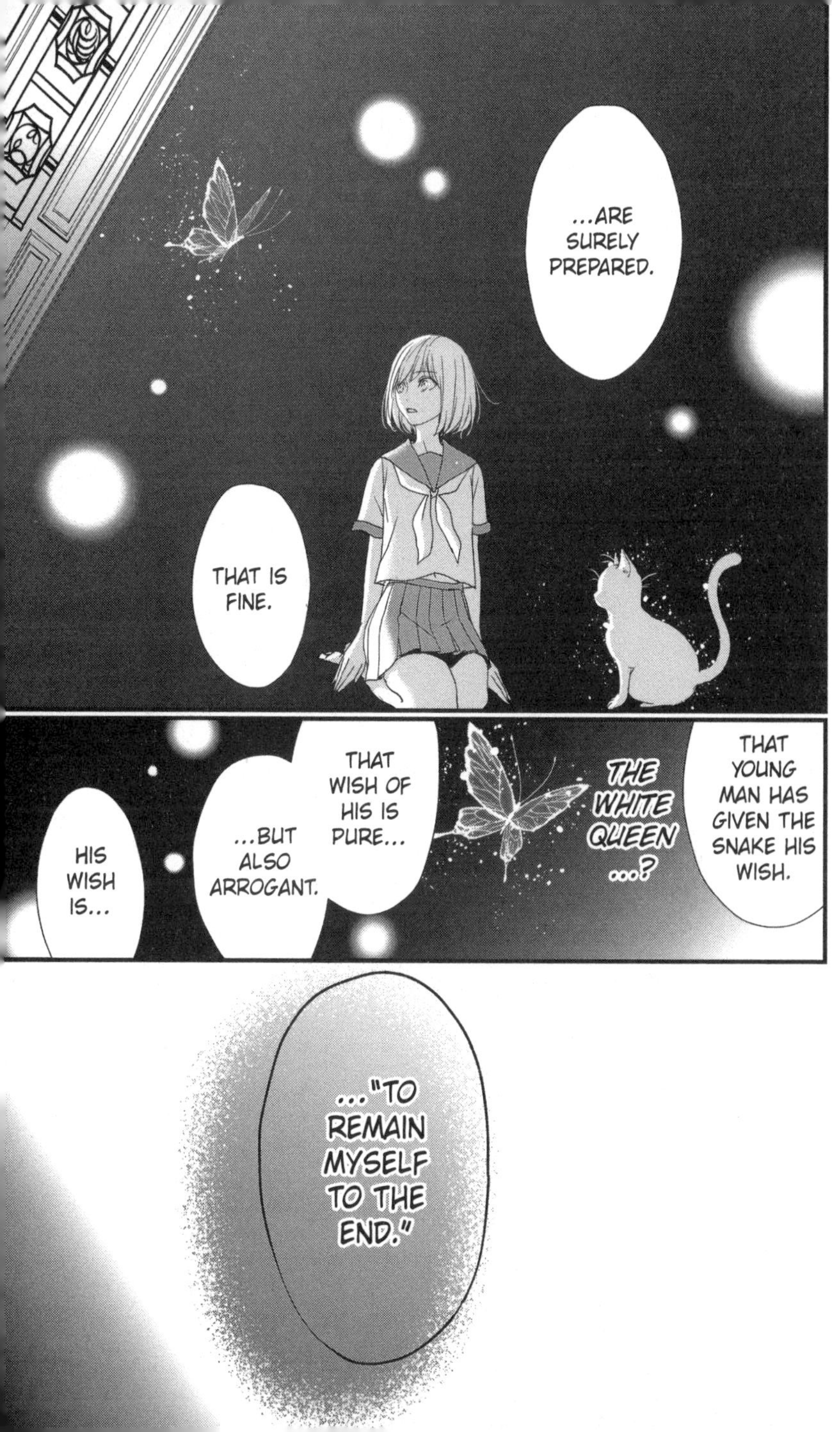
...ARE SURELY PREPARED.
THAT IS FINE.
THAT YOUNG MAN HAS GIVEN THE SNAKE HIS WISH.
THE WHITE QUEEN ...?
THAT WISH OF HIS IS PURE...
...BUT ALSO ARROGANT.
HIS WISH IS...
..."TO REMAIN MYSELF TO THE END."

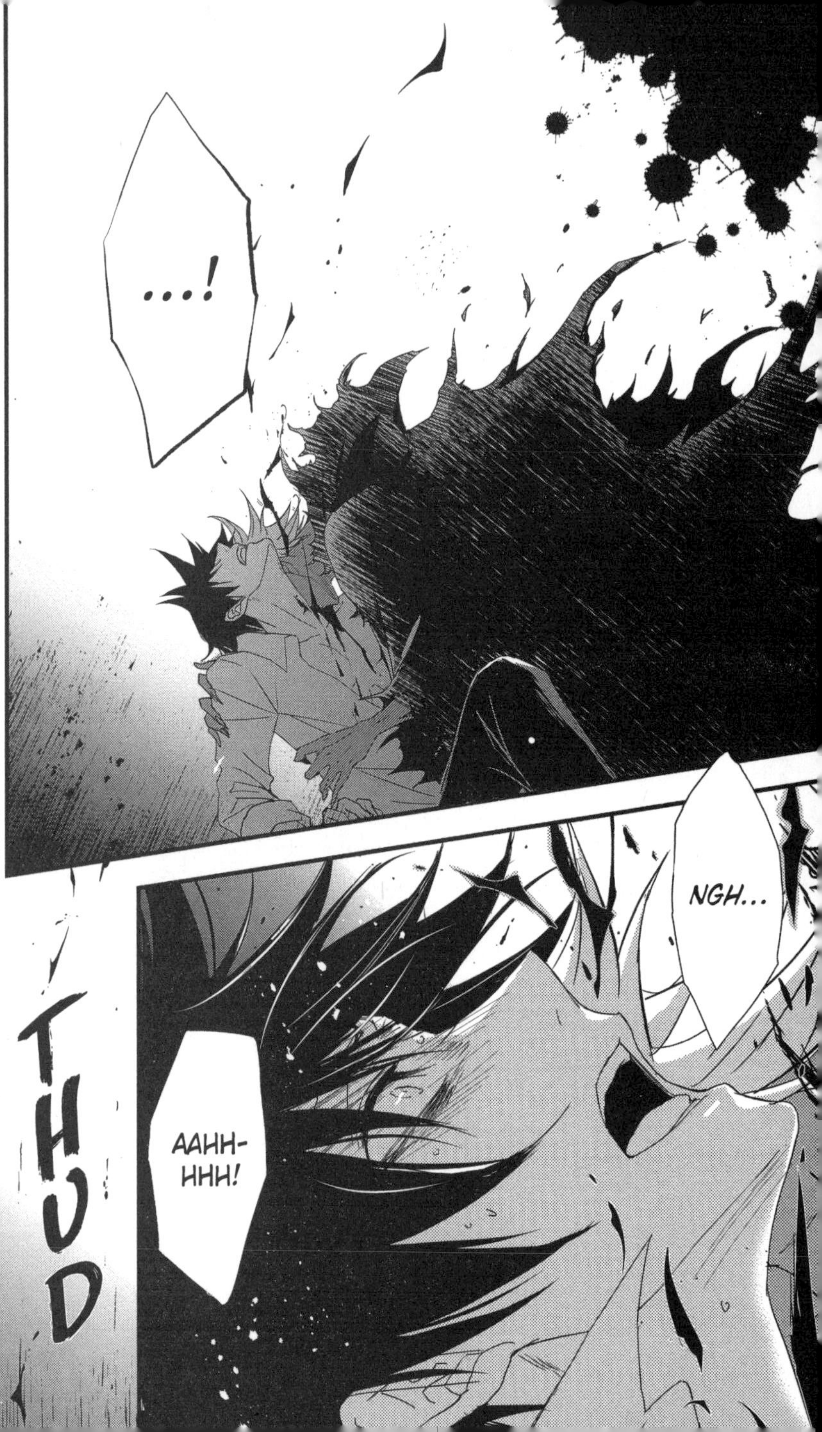
...!
NGH...
AAHH-HHH!
THUD

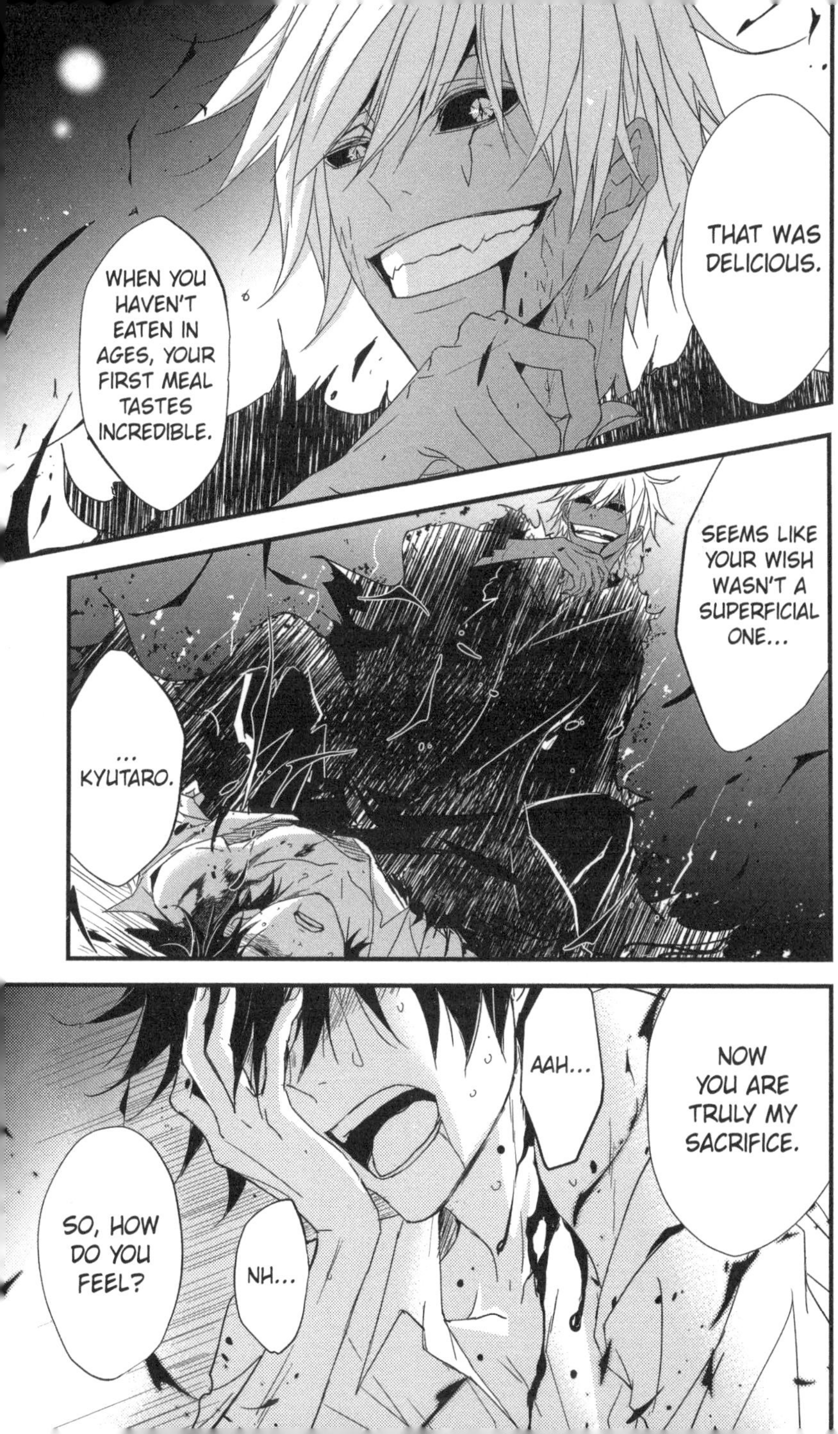
THAT WAS DELICIOUS.
WHEN YOU HAVEN'T EATEN IN AGES, YOUR FIRST MEAL TASTES INCREDIBLE.
SEEMS LIKE YOUR WISH WASN'T A SUPERFICIAL ONE...
... KYUTARO.
NOW YOU ARE TRULY MY SACRIFICE.
AAH...
NH...
SO, HOW DO YOU FEEL?

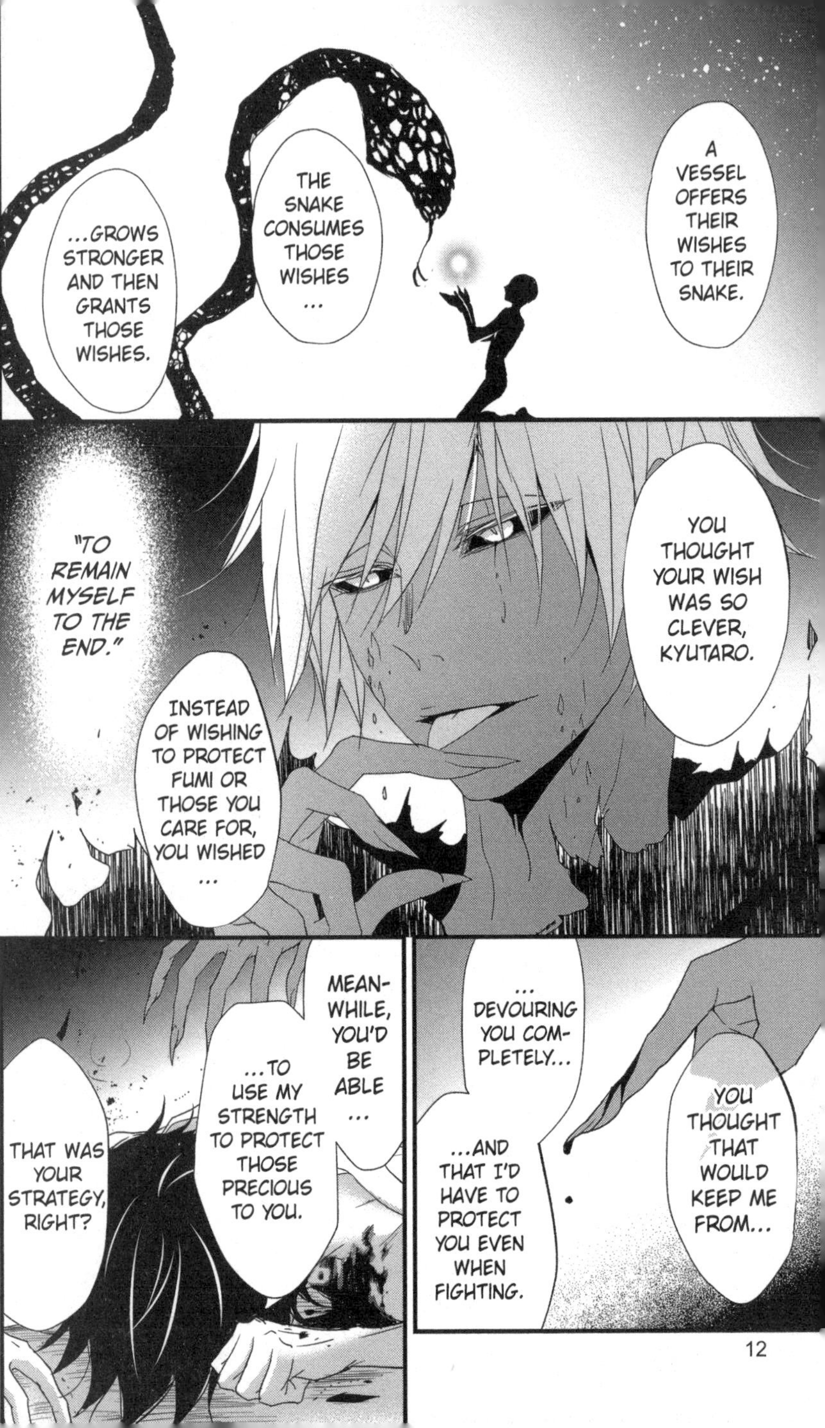
A VESSEL OFFERS THEIR WISHES TO THEIR SNAKE.
THE SNAKE CONSUMES THOSE WISHES...
...GROWS STRONGER AND THEN GRANTS THOSE WISHES.
YOU THOUGHT YOUR WISH WAS SO CLEVER, KYUTARO.
INSTEAD OF WISHING TO PROTECT FUMI OR THOSE YOU CARE FOR, YOU WISHED...
"TO REMAIN MYSELF TO THE END."
YOU THOUGHT THAT WOULD KEEP ME FROM...
...DEVOURING YOU COMPLETELY...
...AND THAT I'D HAVE TO PROTECT YOU EVEN WHEN FIGHTING.
MEAN-WHILE, YOU'D BE ABLE...
...TO USE MY STRENGTH TO PROTECT THOSE PRECIOUS TO YOU.
THAT WAS YOUR STRATEGY, RIGHT?

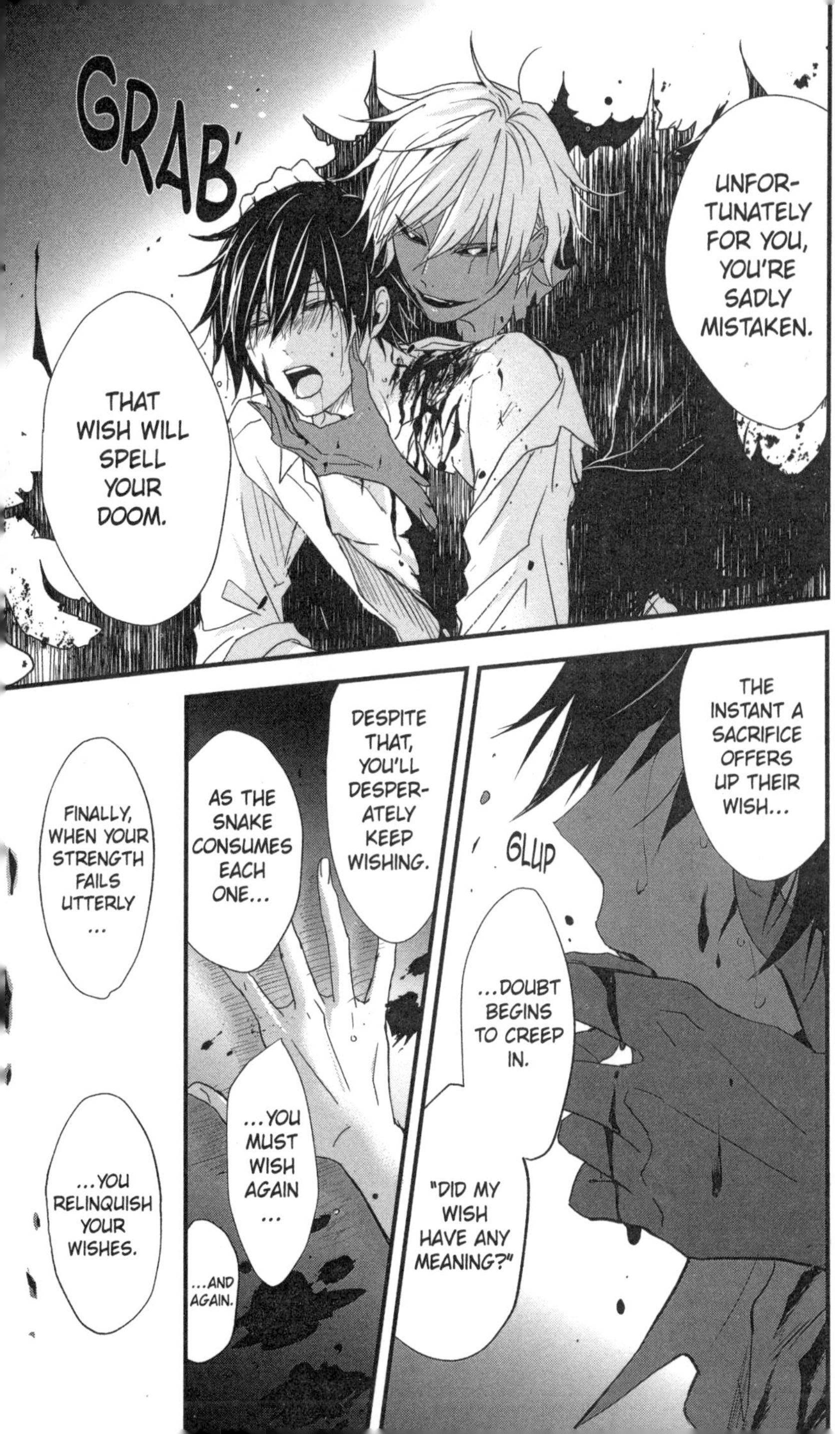
UNFORTUNATELY FOR YOU, YOU'RE SADLY MISTAKEN.
GRAB
THAT WISH WILL SPELL YOUR DOOM.
THE INSTANT A SACRIFICE OFFERS UP THEIR WISH...
GLUP
...DOUBT BEGINS TO CREEP IN.
"DID MY WISH HAVE ANY MEANING?"
DESPITE THAT, YOU'LL DESPERATELY KEEP WISHING.
AS THE SNAKE CONSUMES EACH ONE...
...YOU MUST WISH AGAIN...
...AND AGAIN.
FINALLY, WHEN YOUR STRENGTH FAILS UTTERLY...
...YOU RELINQUISH YOUR WISHES.

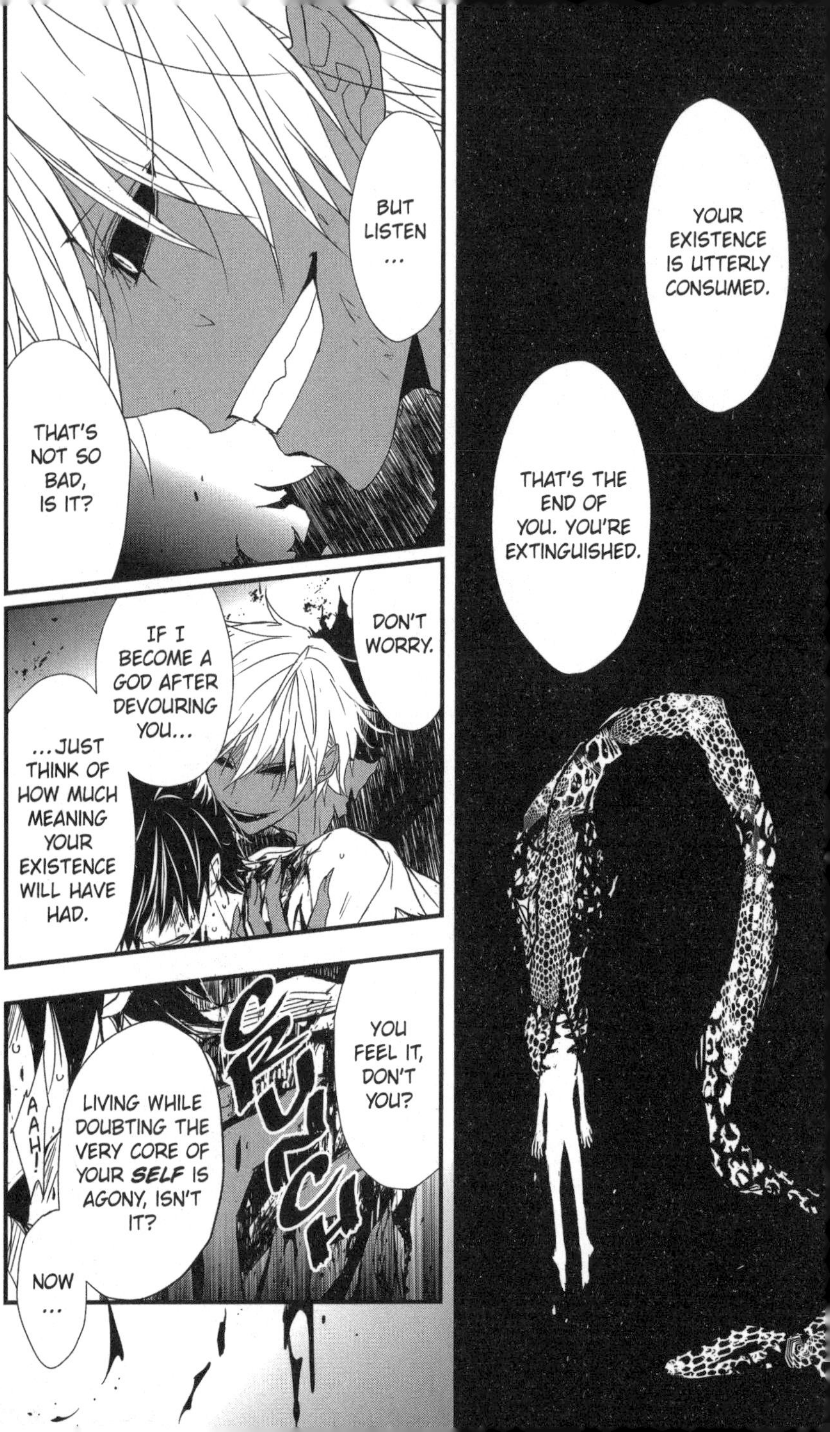
YOUR EXISTENCE IS UTTERLY CONSUMED.
THAT'S THE END OF YOU. YOU'RE EXTINGUISHED.
BUT LISTEN ...
THAT'S NOT SO BAD, IS IT?
DON'T WORRY.
IF I BECOME A GOD AFTER DEVOURING YOU...
...JUST THINK OF HOW MUCH MEANING YOUR EXISTENCE WILL HAVE HAD.
YOU FEEL IT, DON'T YOU?
LIVING WHILE DOUBTING THE VERY CORE OF YOUR *SELF* IS AGONY, ISN'T IT?
AAH!
NOW ...

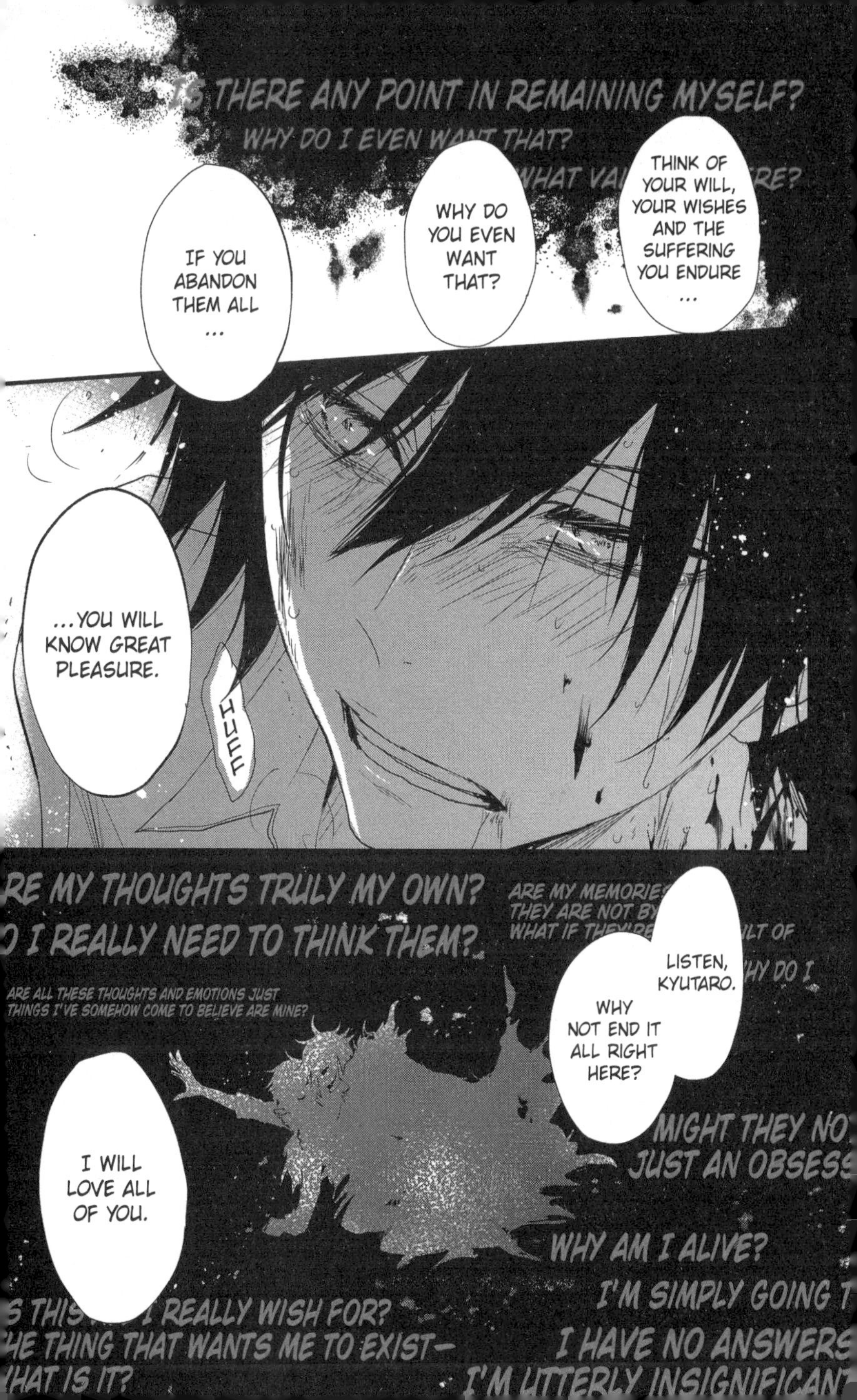
IS THERE ANY POINT IN REMAINING MYSELF?
WHY DO I EVEN WANT THAT?
THINK OF YOUR WILL, YOUR WISHES AND THE SUFFERING YOU ENDURE ...
WHY DO YOU EVEN WANT THAT?
IF YOU ABANDON THEM ALL ...
HUFF
...YOU WILL KNOW GREAT PLEASURE.
DO I REALLY NEED TO THINK THEM?
ARE ALL THESE THOUGHTS AND EMOTIONS JUST THINGS I'VE SOMEHOW COME TO BELIEVE ARE MINE?
LISTEN, KYUTARO.
WHY NOT END IT ALL RIGHT HERE?
WHY AM I ALIVE?
I HAVE NO ANSWERS
I WILL LOVE ALL OF YOU.
WHAT IS IT?

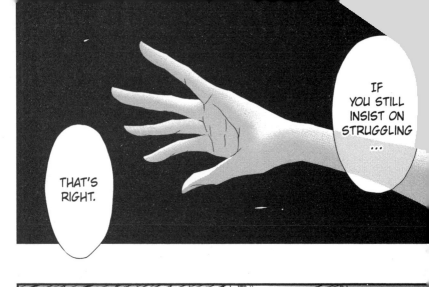

IF YOU STILL INSIST ON STRUGGLING...

THAT'S RIGHT.

...!

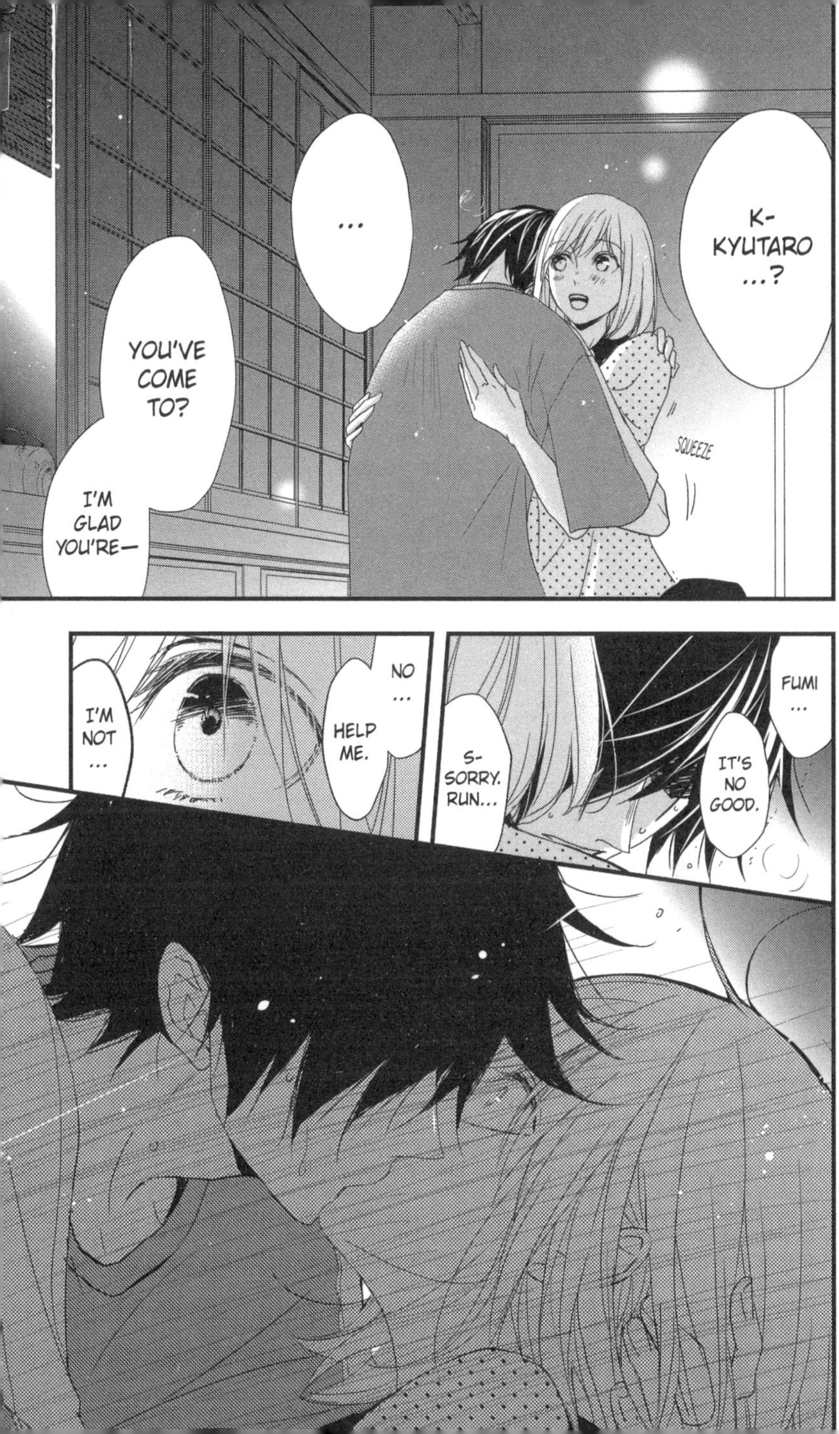
K-KYUTARO...?
...
SQUEEZE
YOU'VE COME TO?
I'M GLAD YOU'RE—
FUMI...
IT'S NO GOOD.
S-SORRY. RUN...
NO... HELP ME.
I'M NOT...

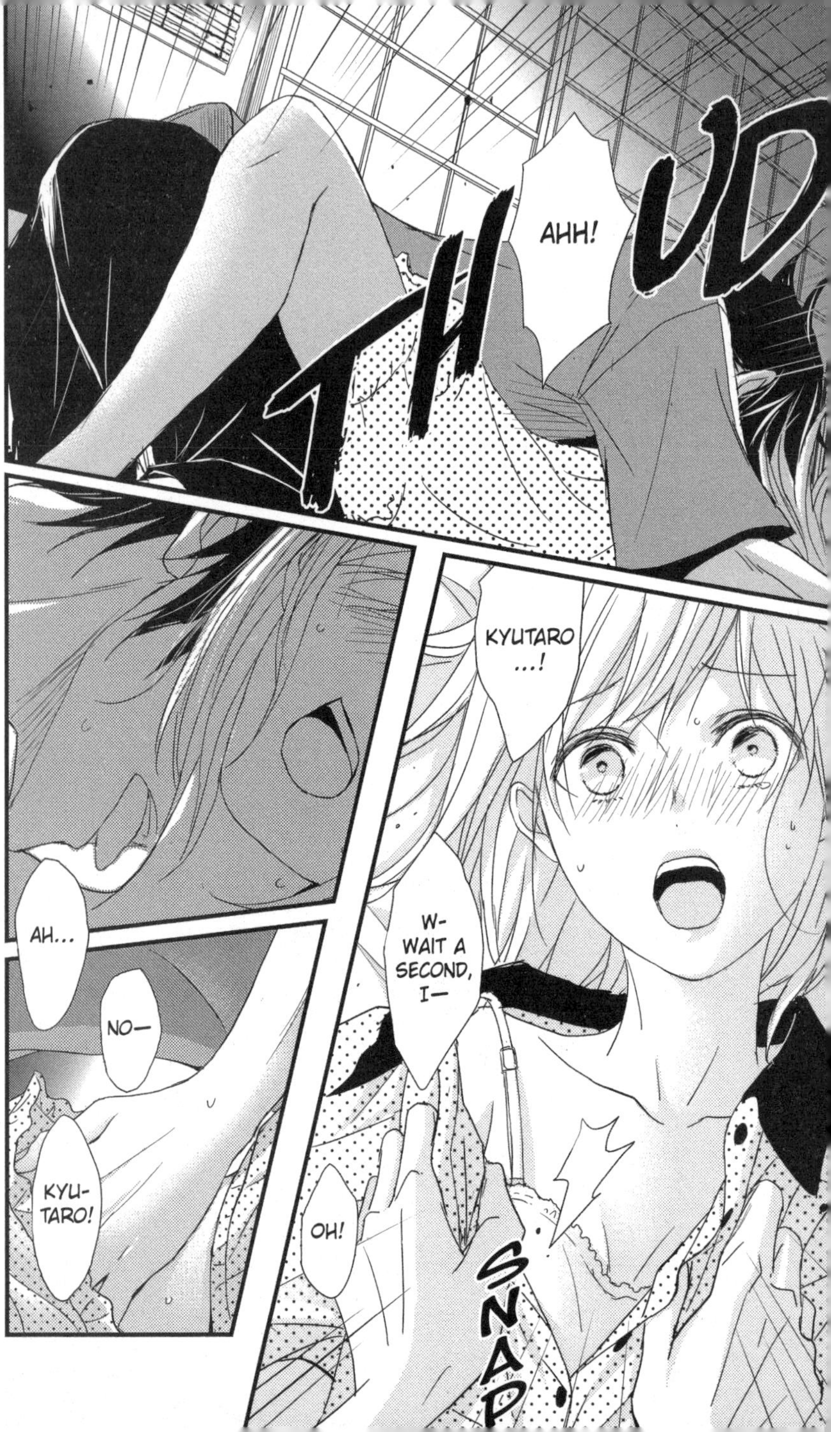
THUD
AHH!
KYUTARO ...!
W-WAIT A SECOND, I—
OH!
SNAP
AH...
NO—
KYU-TARO!

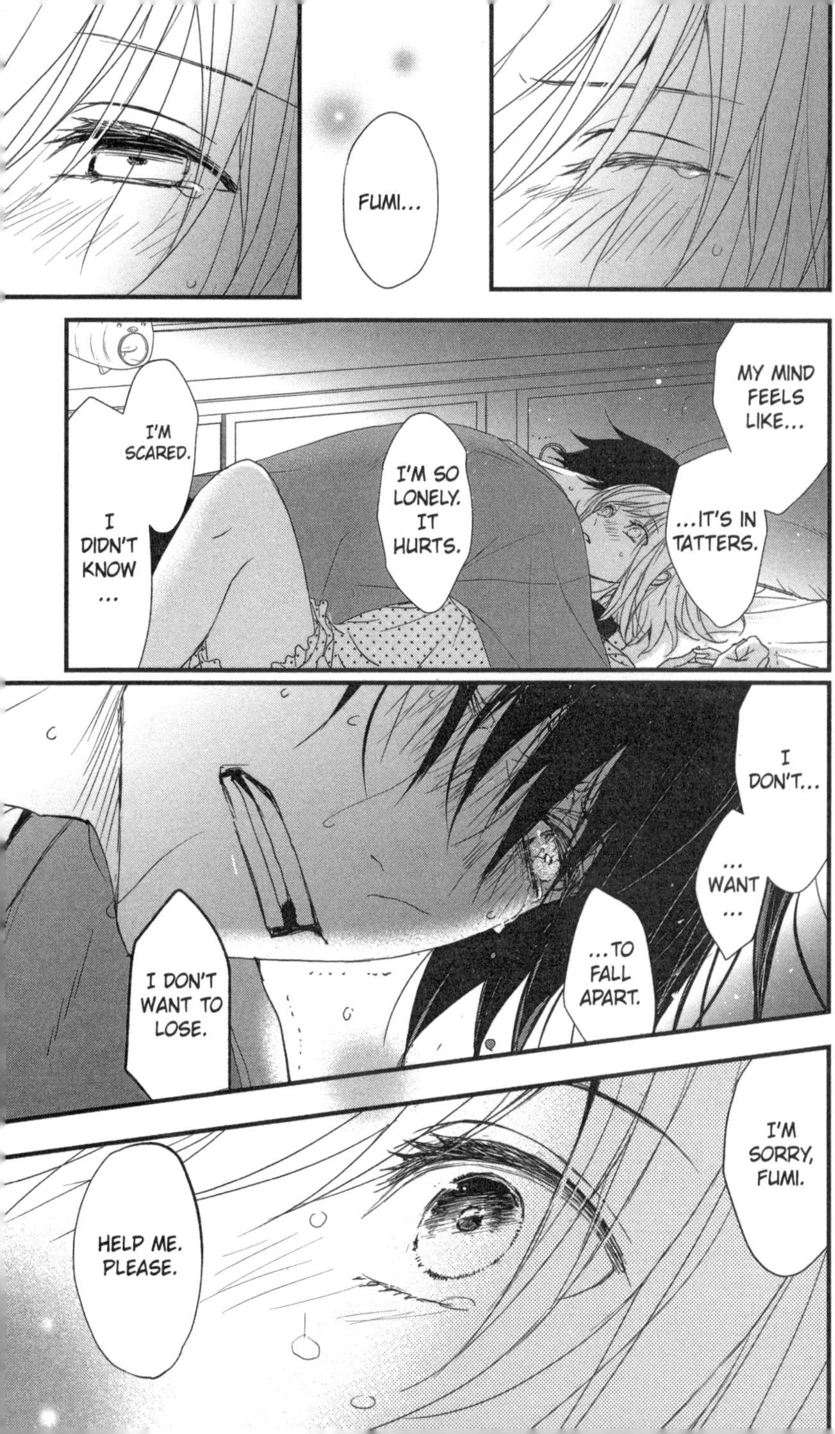
FUMI...
MY MIND FEELS LIKE...
...IT'S IN TATTERS.
I'M SO LONELY. IT HURTS.
I'M SCARED.
I DIDN'T KNOW ...
I DON'T...
... WANT ...
...TO FALL APART.
I DON'T WANT TO LOSE.
I'M SORRY, FUMI.
HELP ME. PLEASE.

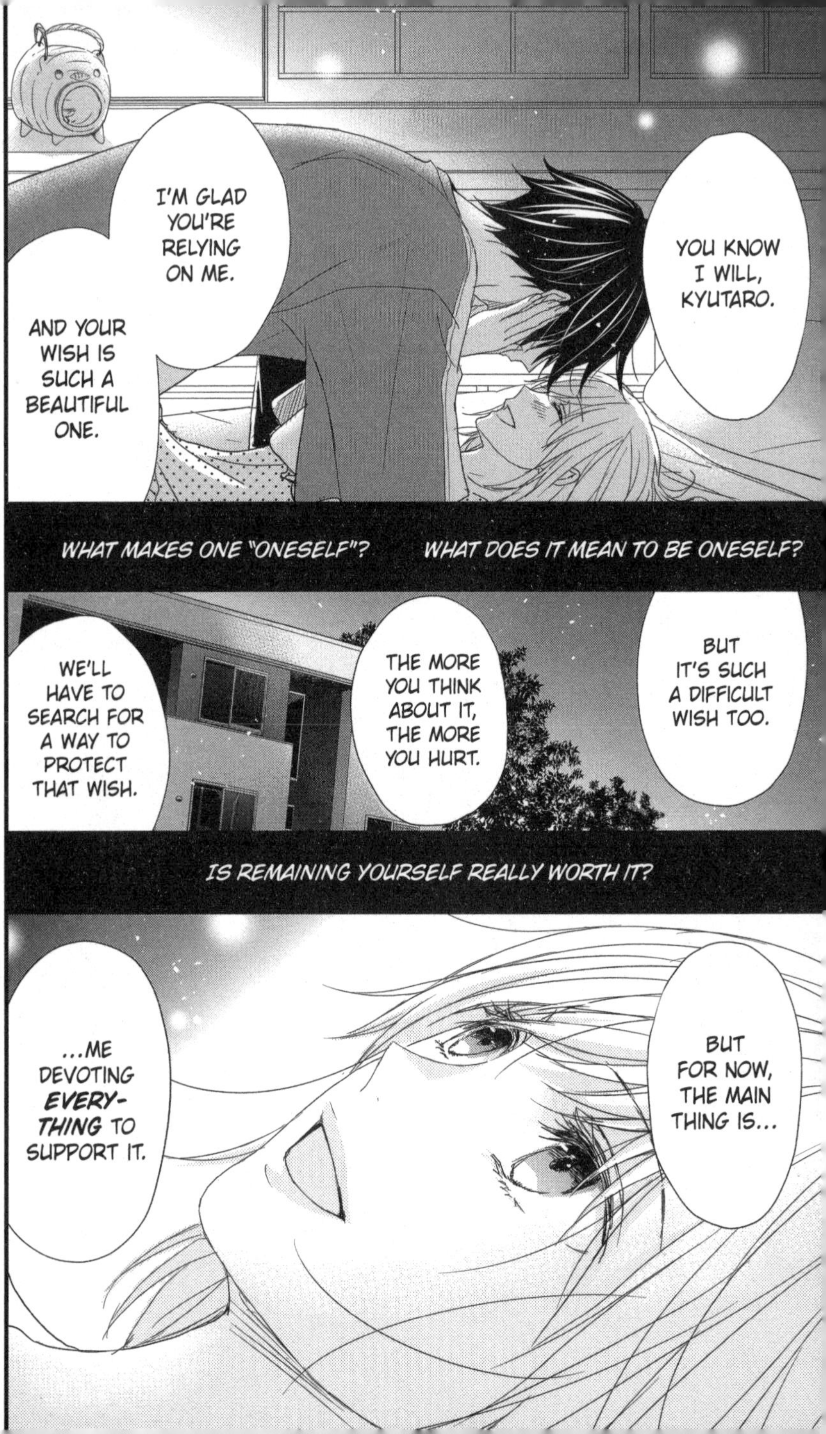
YOU KNOW I WILL, KYUTARO.
I'M GLAD YOU'RE RELYING ON ME.
AND YOUR WISH IS SUCH A BEAUTIFUL ONE.
WHAT DOES IT MEAN TO BE ONESELF?
WHAT MAKES ONE "ONESELF"?
BUT IT'S SUCH A DIFFICULT WISH TOO.
THE MORE YOU THINK ABOUT IT, THE MORE YOU HURT.
WE'LL HAVE TO SEARCH FOR A WAY TO PROTECT THAT WISH.
IS REMAINING YOURSELF REALLY WORTH IT?
BUT FOR NOW, THE MAIN THING IS...
...ME DEVOTING ***EVERY-THING*** TO SUPPORT IT.

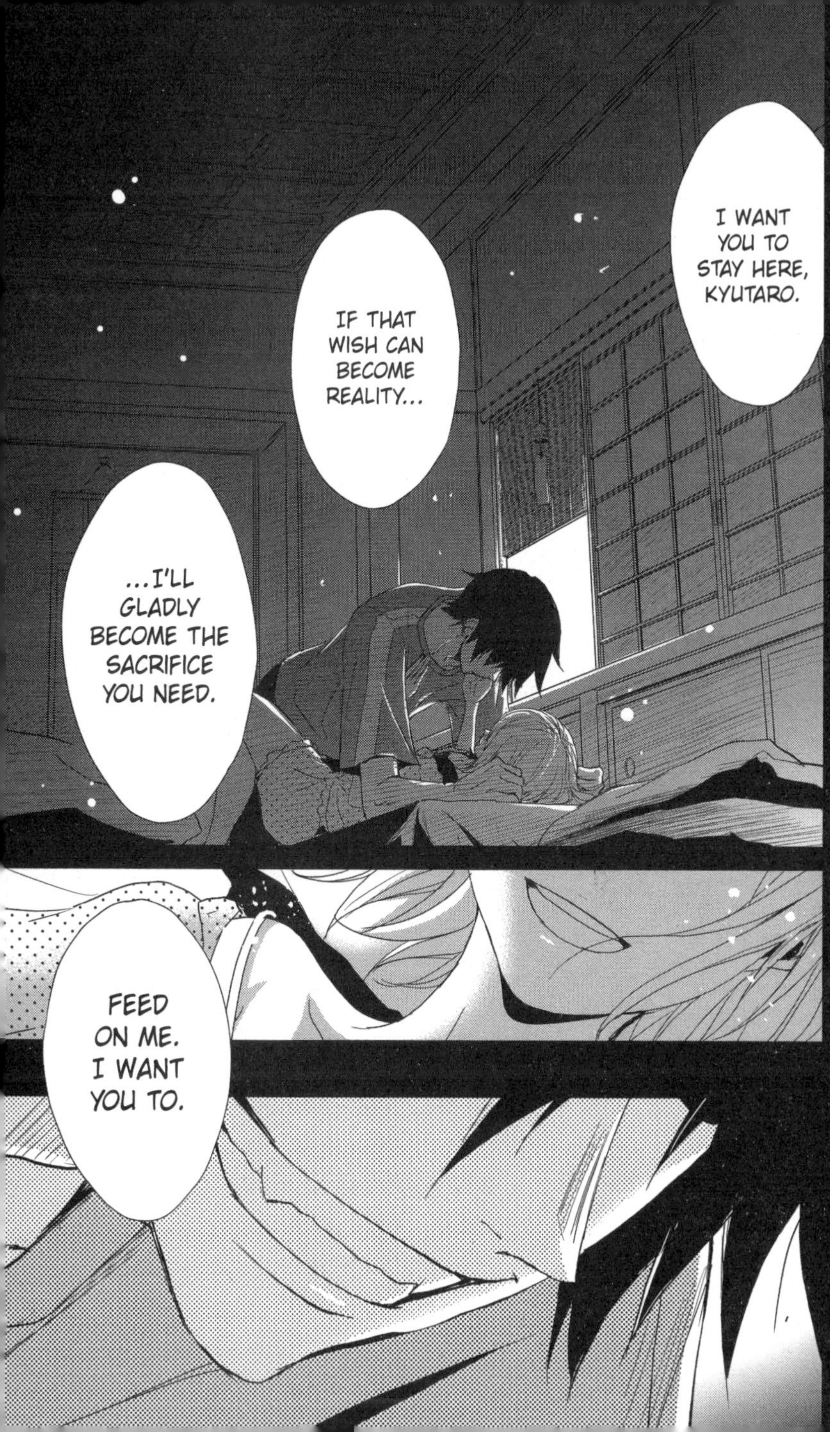
I WANT YOU TO STAY HERE, KYUTARO.
IF THAT WISH CAN BECOME REALITY...
...I'LL GLADLY BECOME THE SACRIFICE YOU NEED.
FEED ON ME. I WANT YOU TO.

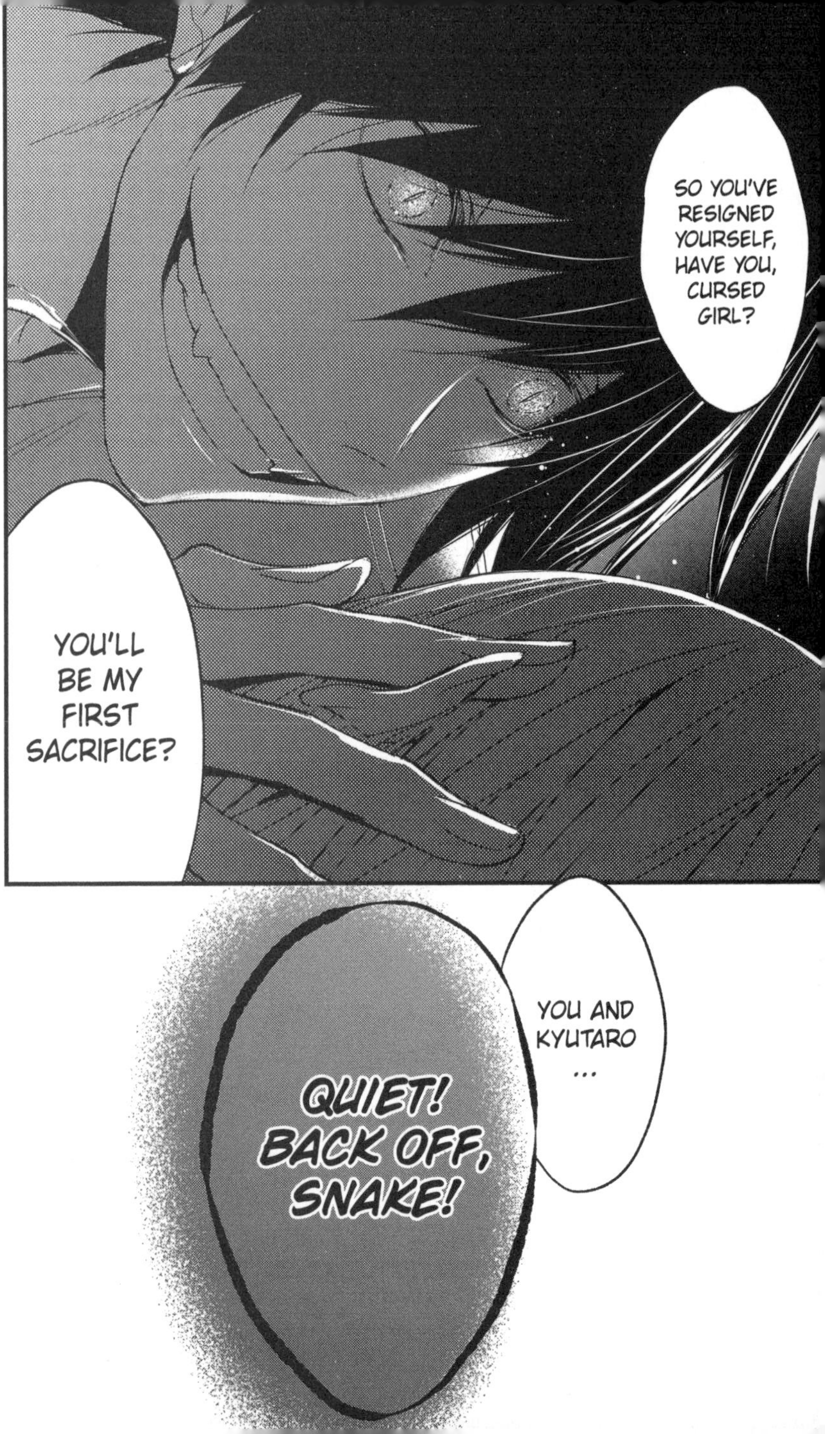
SO YOU'VE RESIGNED YOURSELF, HAVE YOU, CURSED GIRL?
YOU'LL BE MY FIRST SACRIFICE?
YOU AND KYUTARO ...
QUIET! BACK OFF, SNAKE!

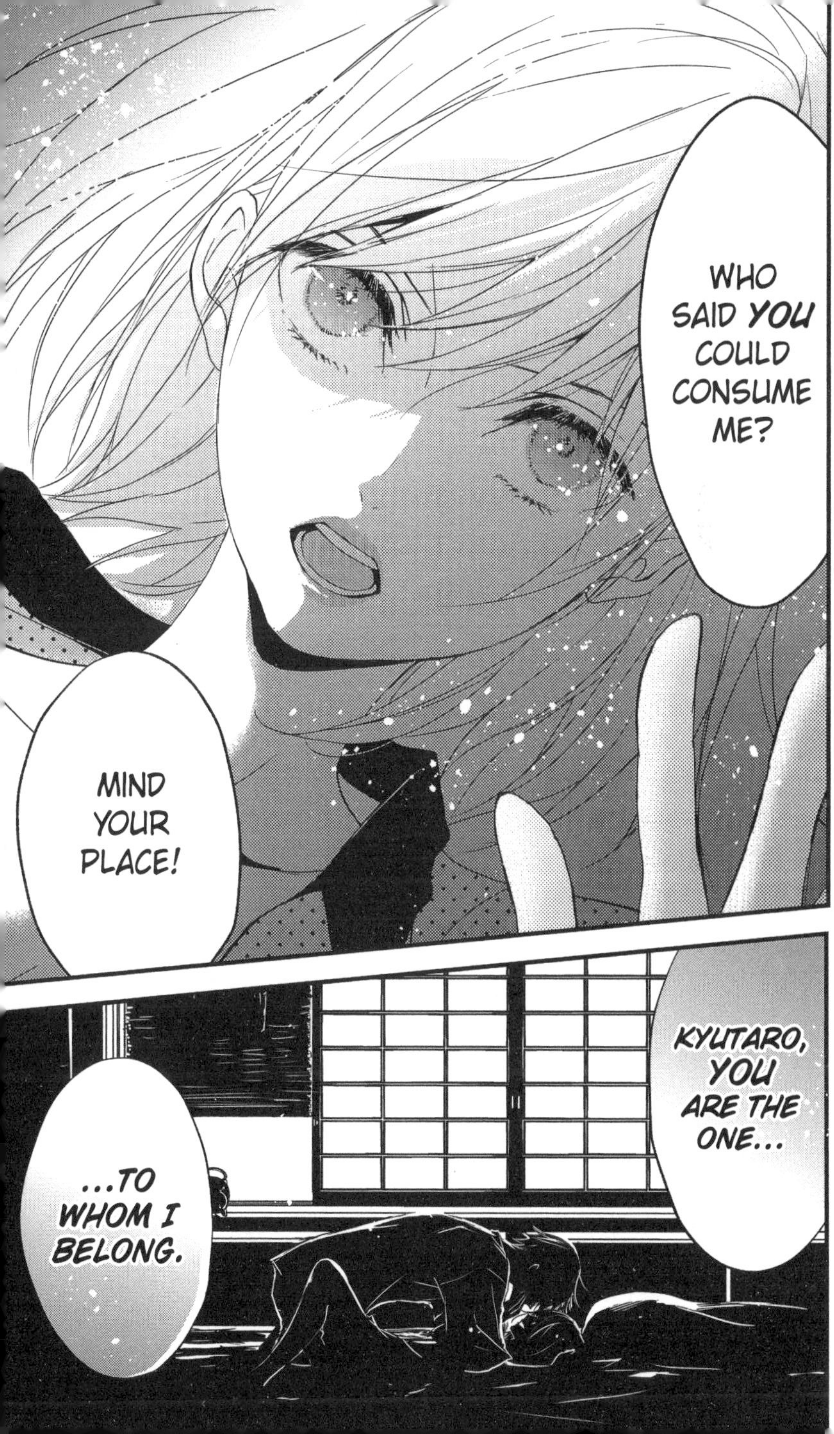
WHO SAID *YOU* COULD CONSUME ME?
MIND YOUR PLACE!
KYUTARO, YOU ARE THE ONE...
...TO WHOM I BELONG.

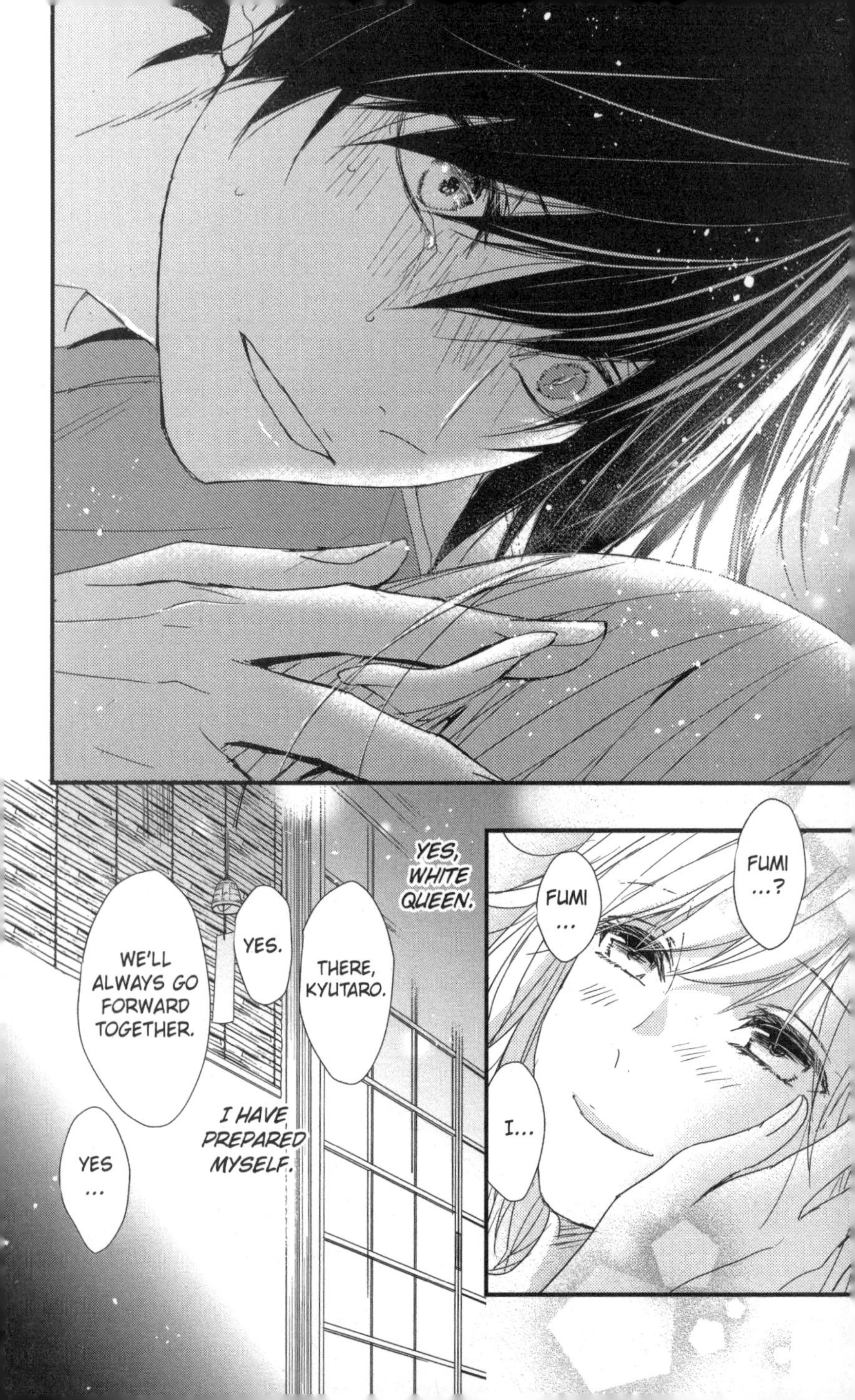
FUMI ...?
FUMI ...
I...
YES, WHITE QUEEN.
THERE, KYUTARO.
YES.
WE'LL ALWAYS GO FORWARD TOGETHER.
I HAVE PREPARED MYSELF.
YES ...

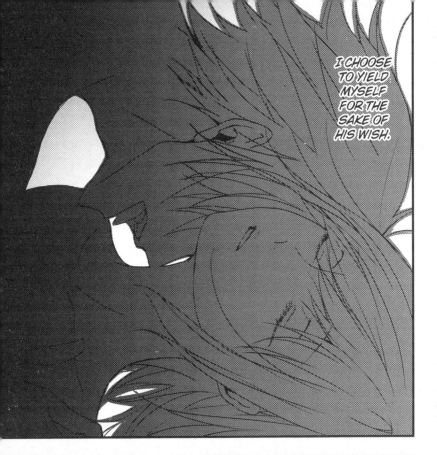

I CHOOSE TO YIELD MYSELF FOR THE SAKE OF HIS WISH.

THAT WILL DO.

YOUR WISH IS ALWAYS...

...BEAUTIFUL.

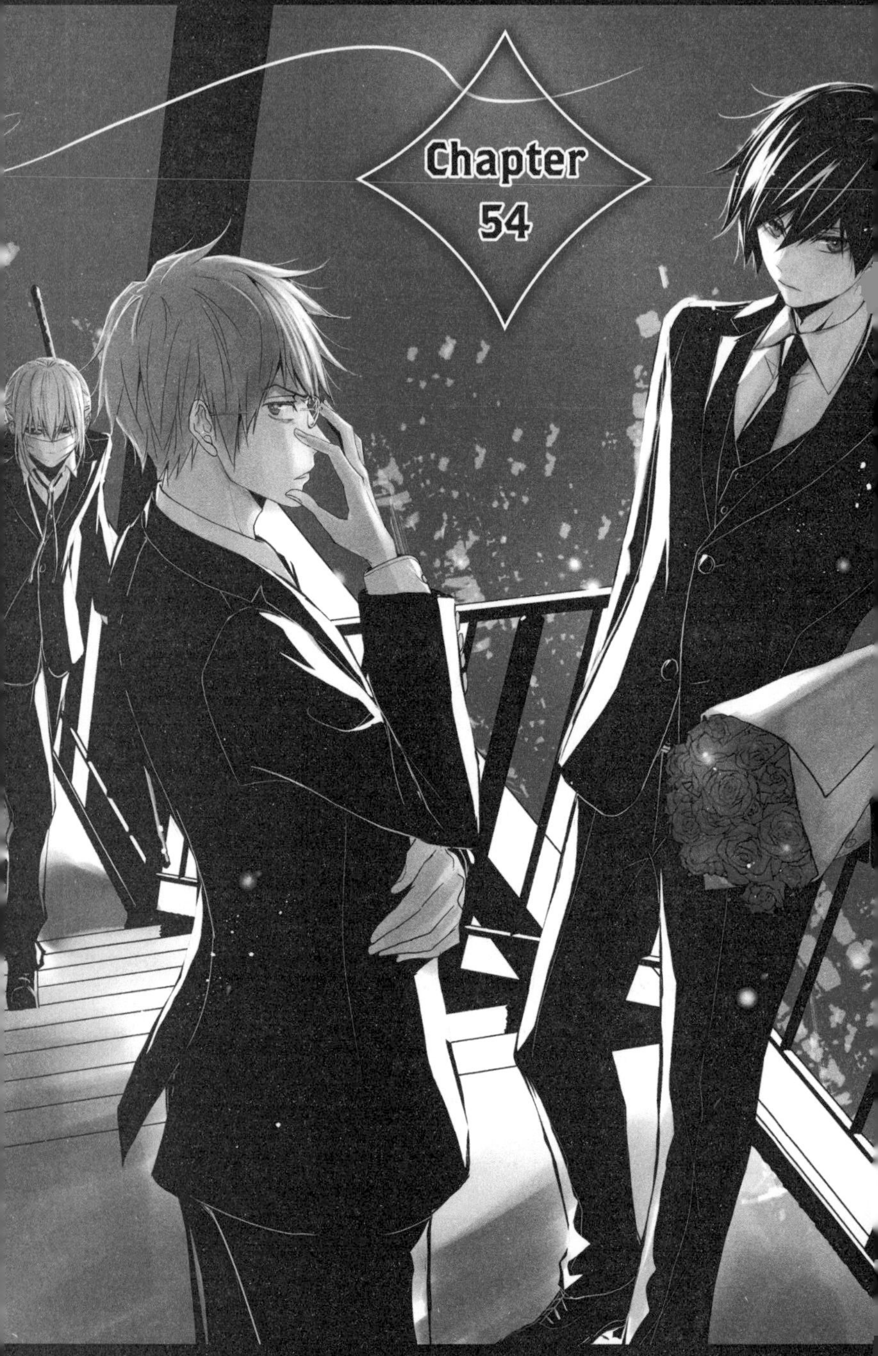
Chapter
54

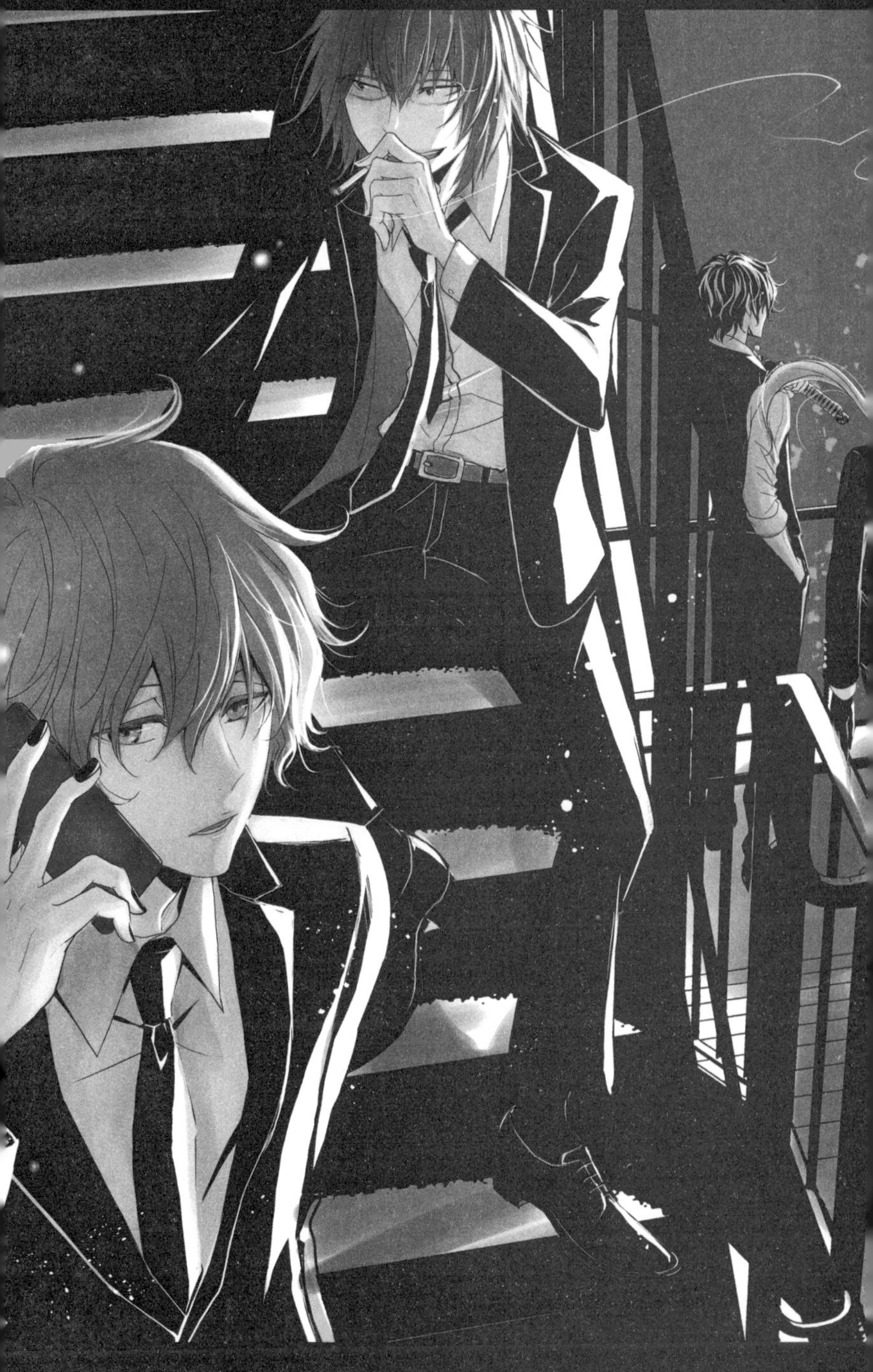

CHAPTER 54

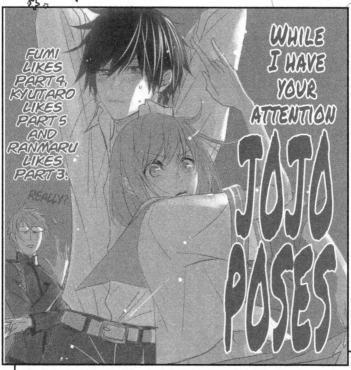

MONTHLY BETSUCOMI SALE DATE NOTICE ON TWITTER AND INSTAGRAM

WHILE I HAVE YOUR ATTENTION
JOJO POSES
FUMI LIKES PART 4, KYUTARO LIKES PART 5 AND RANMARU LIKES PART 3.
REALLY?

LET'S SEE... WHAT'S UP IN *QUEEN'S QUALITY* THIS MONTH?
1) THERE ARE PROBLEMS WITH THE WAY KYUTARO SPEAKS.
2) I'D LIKE YOU TO NOTICE FUMI'S JOJO POSE, BUT RANMARU MAKES IT IMPOSSIBLE.
3) I HAVEN'T DRAWN A CROW IN A WHILE.

IT SHOULD BE KYUTARO'S TURN, BUT RANMARU GETS ALL THE GOOD PARTS IN CHAPTER 54!

I LIKE PART 4 TOO, AS WELL AS PART 6. THE PART WHERE THE HERMES SISTER REVIVES IS VERY MOVING, ALONG WITH FF'S LAST LINES.

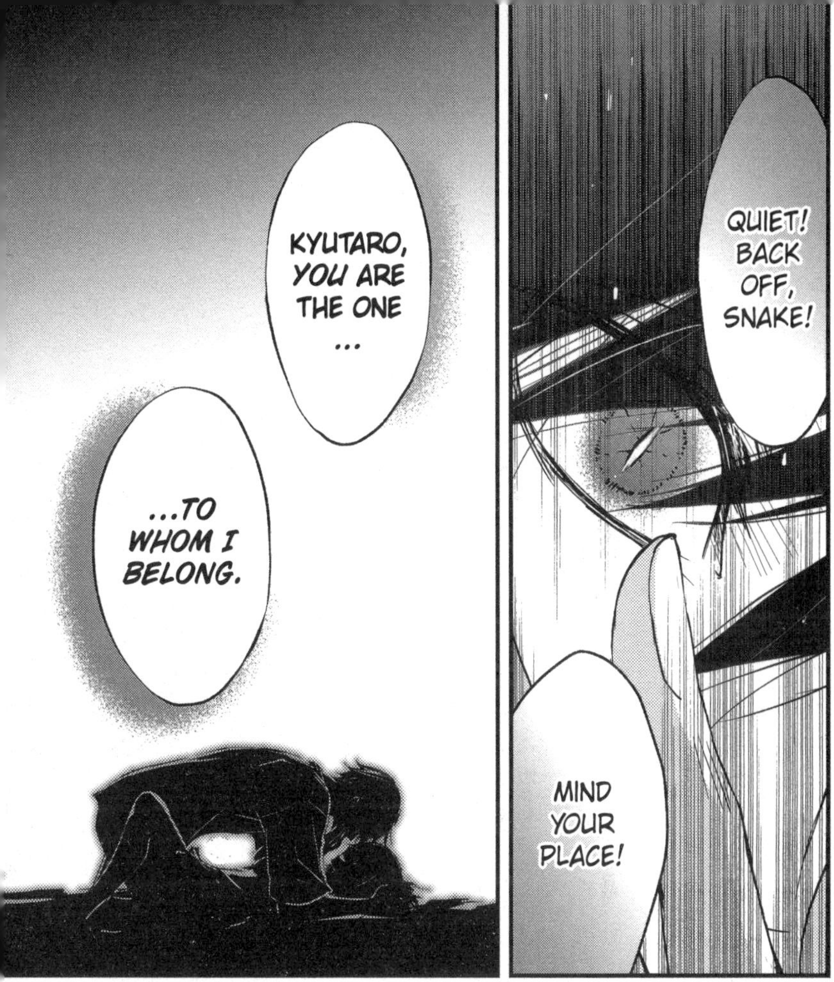
QUIET! BACK OFF, SNAKE!
MIND YOUR PLACE!
KYUTARO, YOU ARE THE ONE ...
...TO WHOM I BELONG.

What's Been Going On ①
Generally, manga artists tend to plod along and work solo. However, now that more and more people are working remotely, some manga artist friends and I decided we'd give it a try too. Under the guise of working for a company, we've started playing at "working remotely." It's worked out well, so we're continuing to do it. By setting start and end times and designating breaks, our lives have become more organized. I feel like it's improved my mental health.

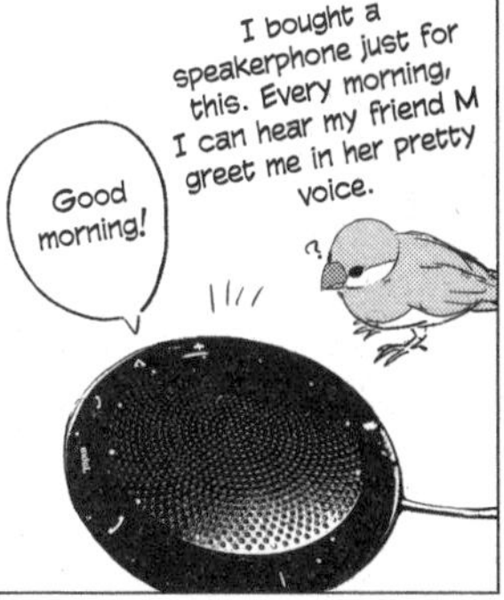
I bought a speakerphone just for this. Every morning, I can hear my friend M greet me in her pretty voice.
Good morning!
?

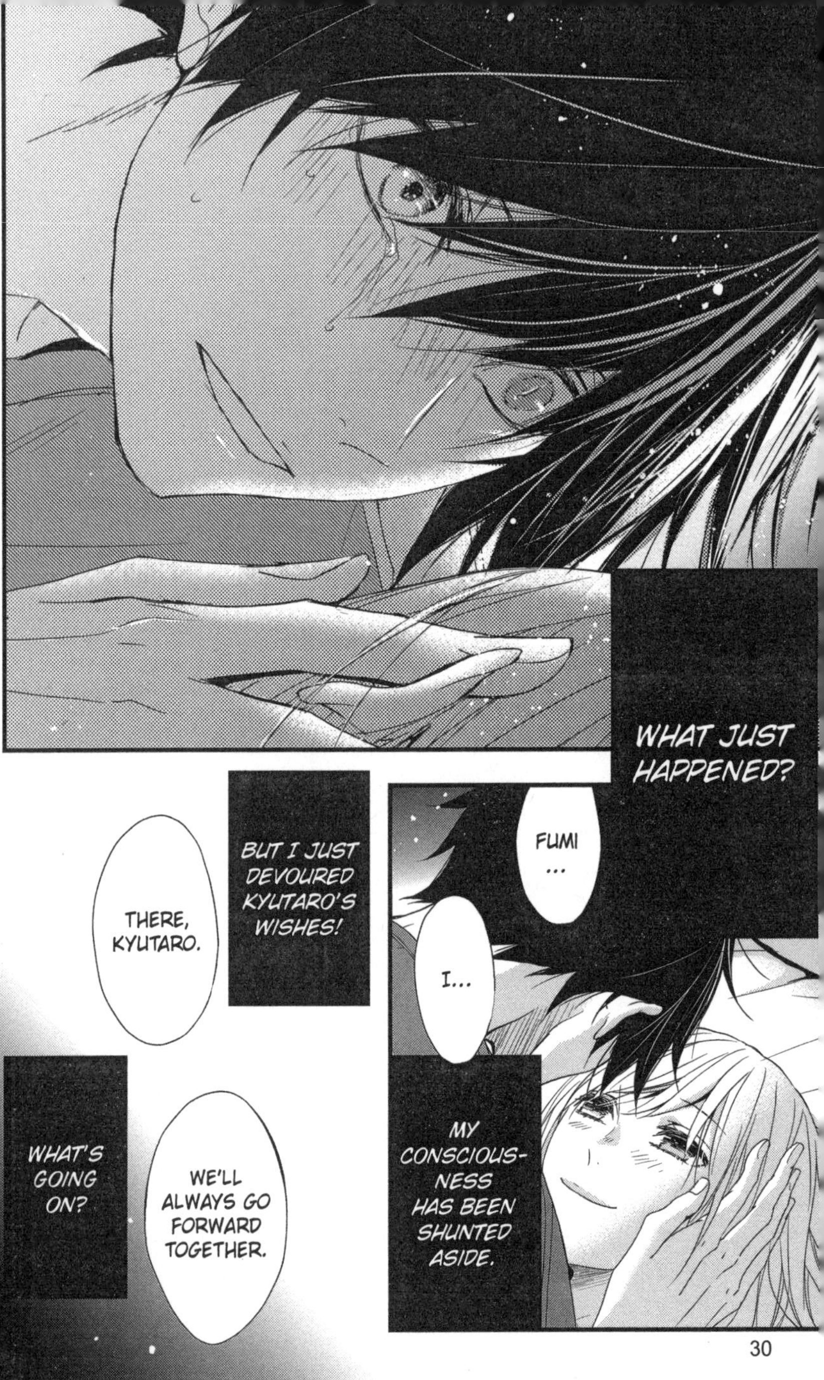
WHAT JUST HAPPENED?
FUMI ...
I...
BUT I JUST DEVOURED KYUTARO'S WISHES!
THERE, KYUTARO.
MY CONSCIOUS-NESS HAS BEEN SHUNTED ASIDE.
WE'LL ALWAYS GO FORWARD TOGETHER.
WHAT'S GOING ON?

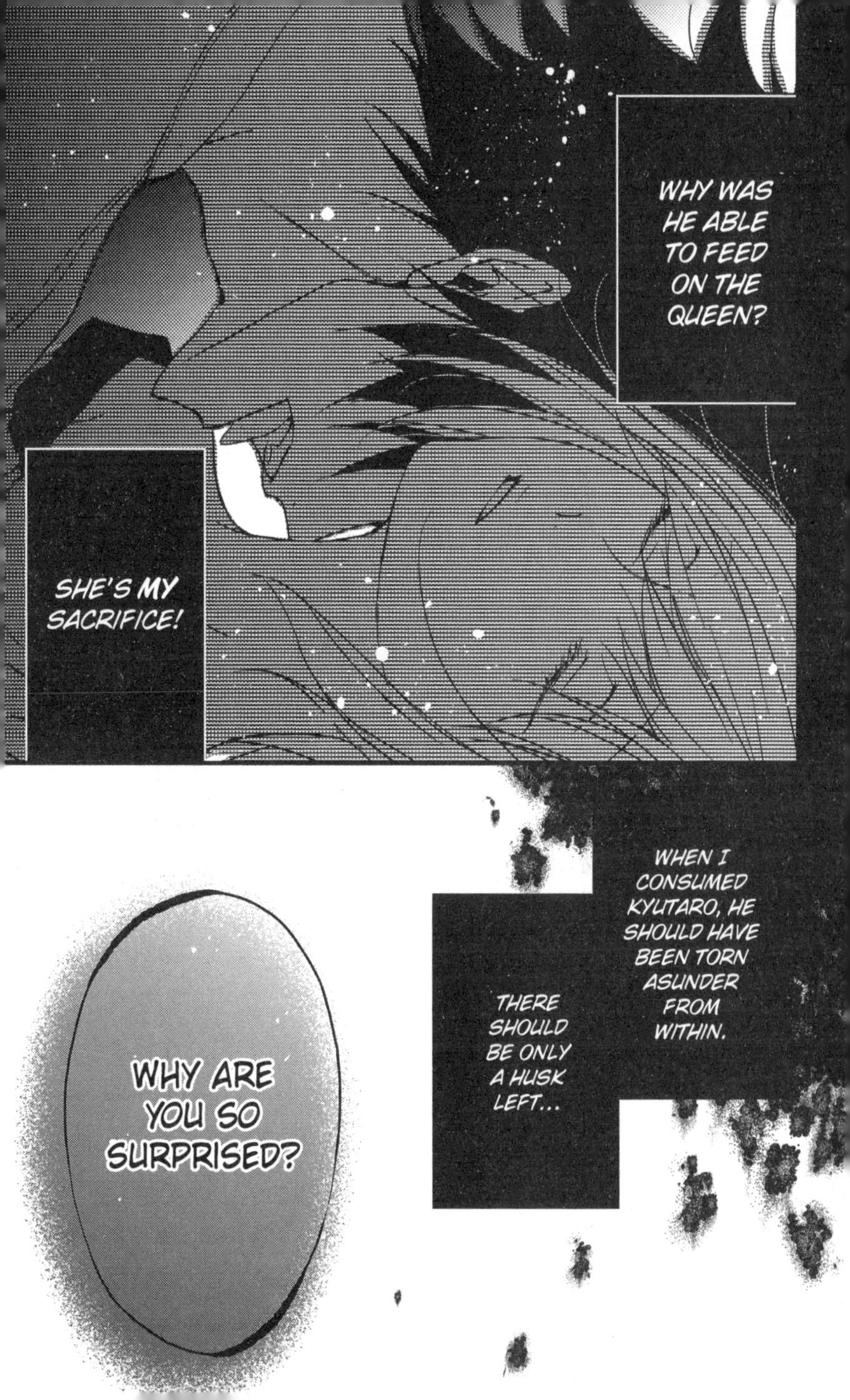
WHY WAS HE ABLE TO FEED ON THE QUEEN?
SHE'S **MY** SACRIFICE!
WHEN I CONSUMED KYUTARO, HE SHOULD HAVE BEEN TORN ASUNDER FROM WITHIN.
THERE SHOULD BE ONLY A HUSK LEFT...
WHY ARE YOU SO SURPRISED?

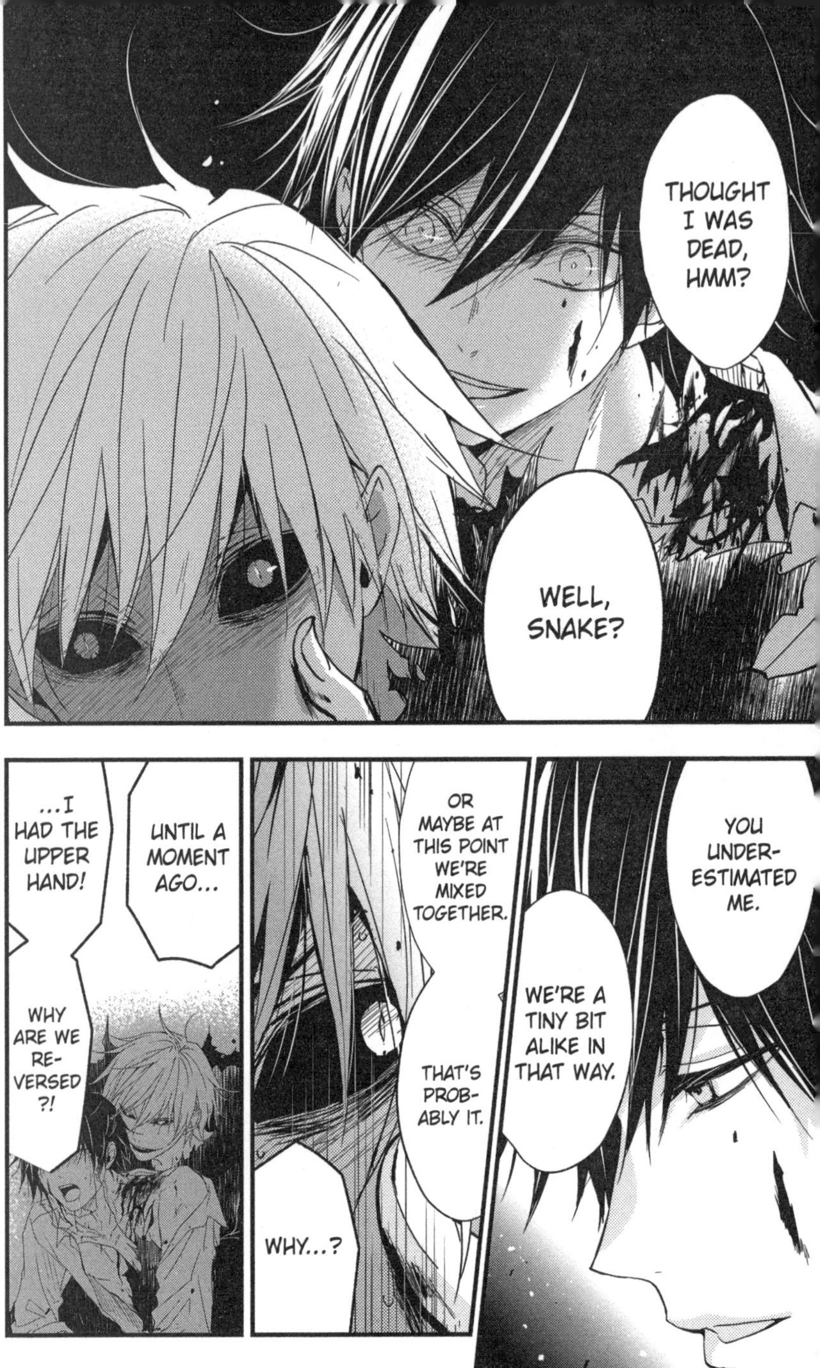
THOUGHT I WAS DEAD, HMM?
WELL, SNAKE?
YOU UNDER-ESTIMATED ME.
WE'RE A TINY BIT ALIKE IN THAT WAY.
OR MAYBE AT THIS POINT WE'RE MIXED TOGETHER.
THAT'S PROB-ABLY IT.
WHY...?
UNTIL A MOMENT AGO...
...I HAD THE UPPER HAND!
WHY ARE WE RE-VERSED?!

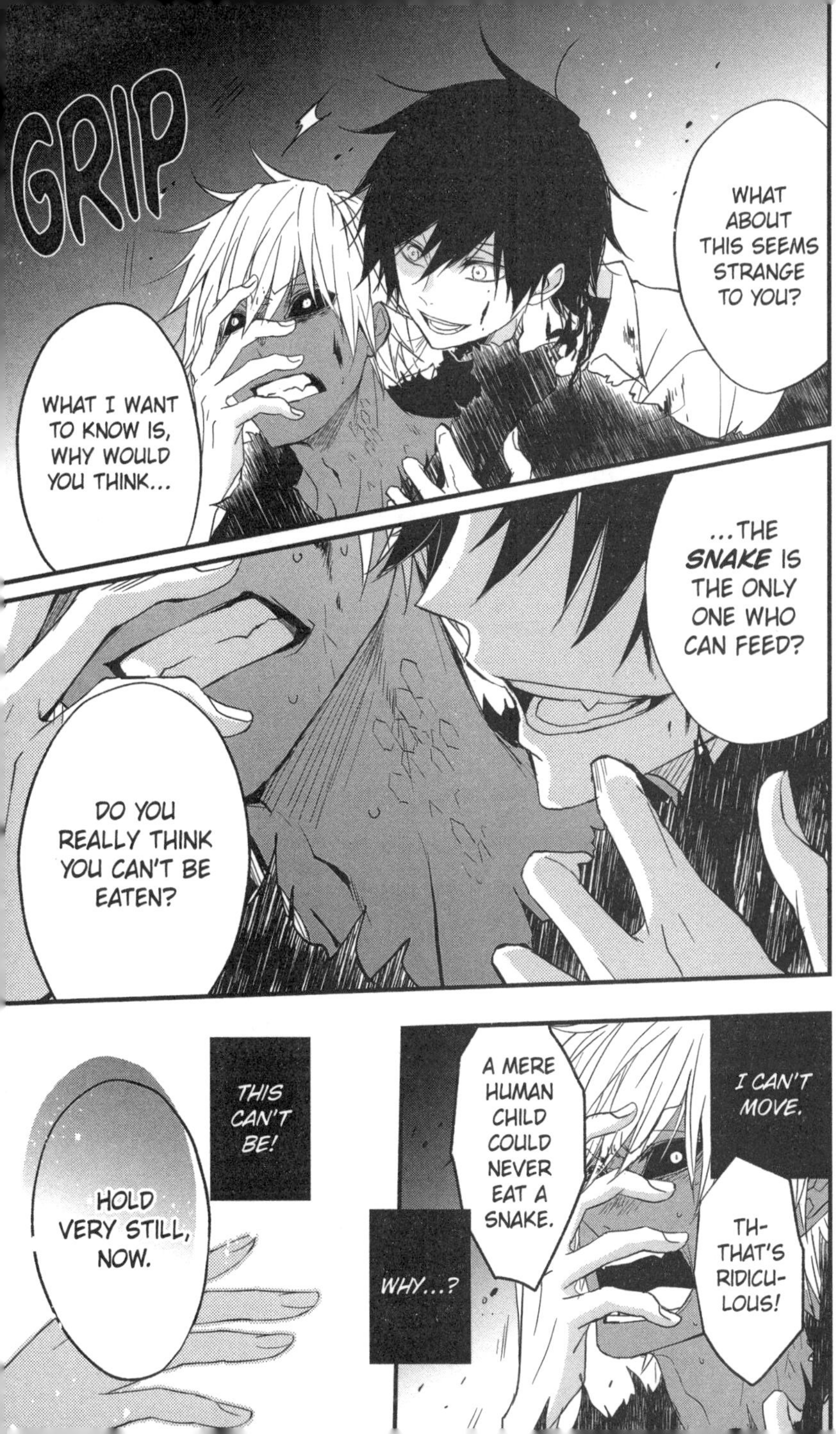
WHAT ABOUT THIS SEEMS STRANGE TO YOU?
GRIP
WHAT I WANT TO KNOW IS, WHY WOULD YOU THINK...
...THE SNAKE IS THE ONLY ONE WHO CAN FEED?
DO YOU REALLY THINK YOU CAN'T BE EATEN?
I CAN'T MOVE.
A MERE HUMAN CHILD COULD NEVER EAT A SNAKE.
TH-THAT'S RIDICULOUS!
WHY...?
THIS CAN'T BE!
HOLD VERY STILL, NOW.

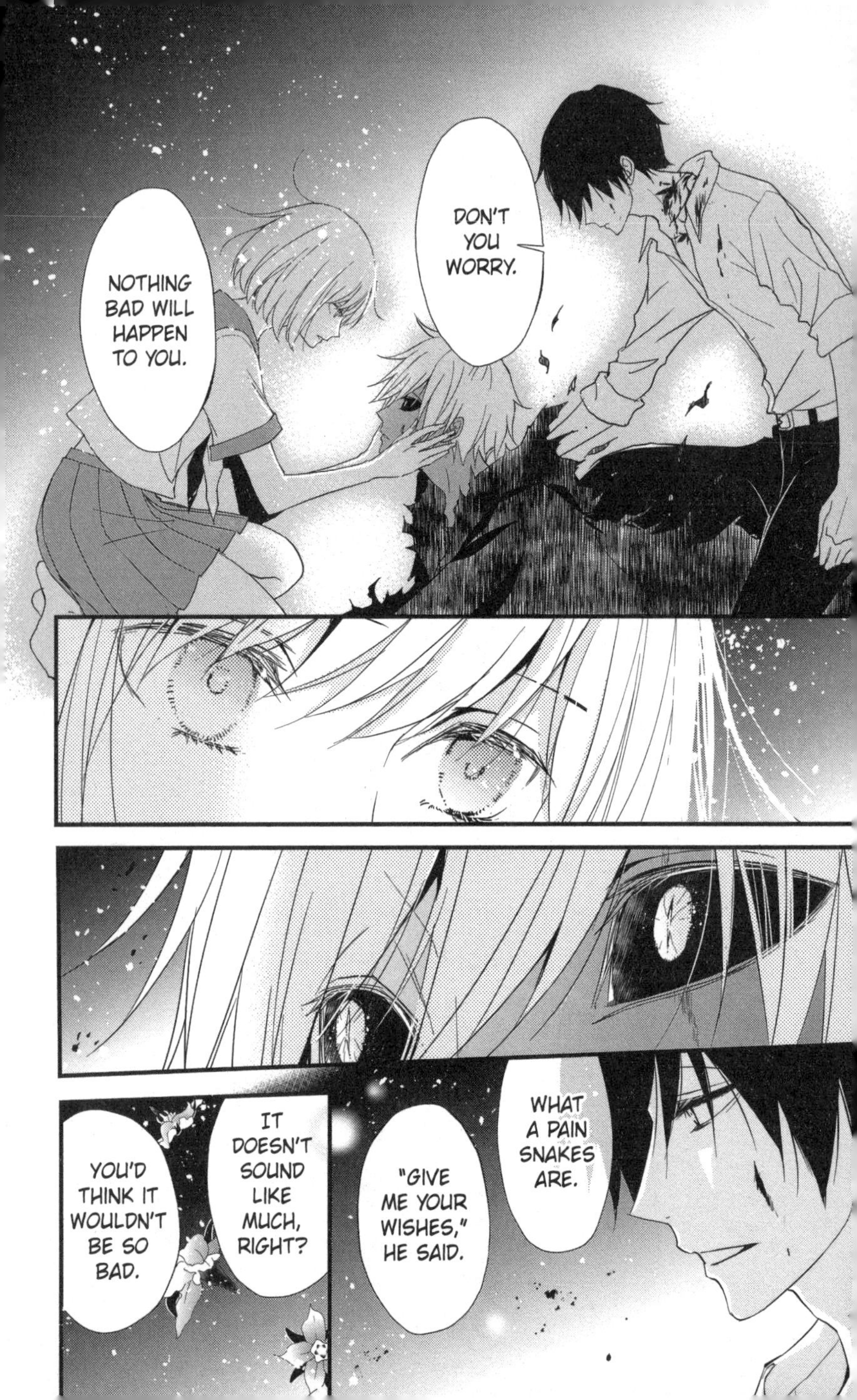
DON'T YOU WORRY.
NOTHING BAD WILL HAPPEN TO YOU.
WHAT A PAIN SNAKES ARE.
"GIVE ME YOUR WISHES," HE SAID.
IT DOESN'T SOUND LIKE MUCH, RIGHT?
YOU'D THINK IT WOULDN'T BE SO BAD.

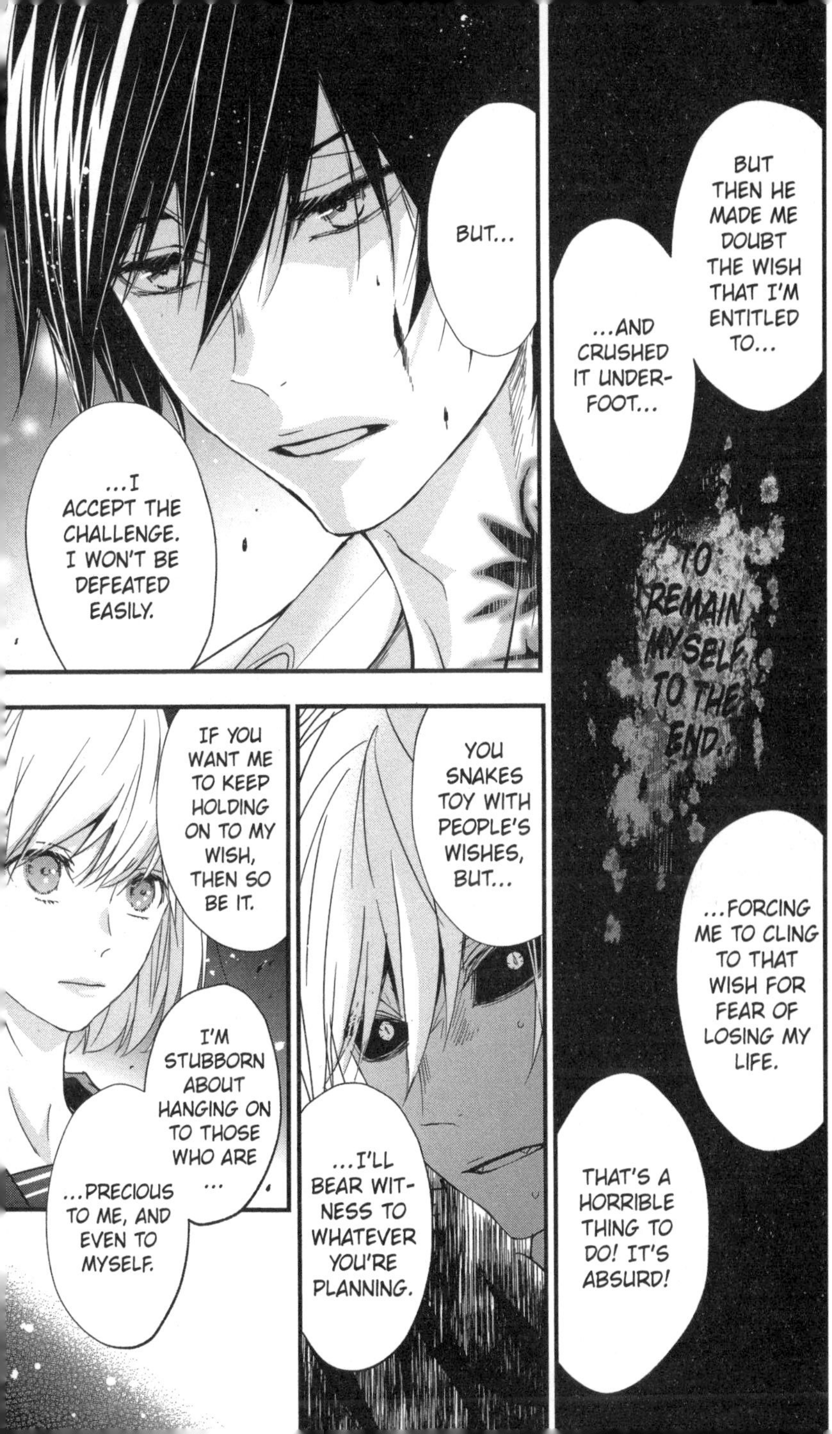
BUT THEN HE MADE ME DOUBT THE WISH THAT I'M ENTITLED TO...
...AND CRUSHED IT UNDER-FOOT...
TO REMAIN MYSELF TO THE END.
...FORCING ME TO CLING TO THAT WISH FOR FEAR OF LOSING MY LIFE.
THAT'S A HORRIBLE THING TO DO! IT'S ABSURD!
BUT...
...I ACCEPT THE CHALLENGE. I WON'T BE DEFEATED EASILY.
YOU SNAKES TOY WITH PEOPLE'S WISHES, BUT...
...I'LL BEAR WIT-NESS TO WHATEVER YOU'RE PLANNING.
IF YOU WANT ME TO KEEP HOLDING ON TO MY WISH, THEN SO BE IT.
I'M STUBBORN ABOUT HANGING ON TO THOSE WHO ARE ...
...PRECIOUS TO ME, AND EVEN TO MYSELF.

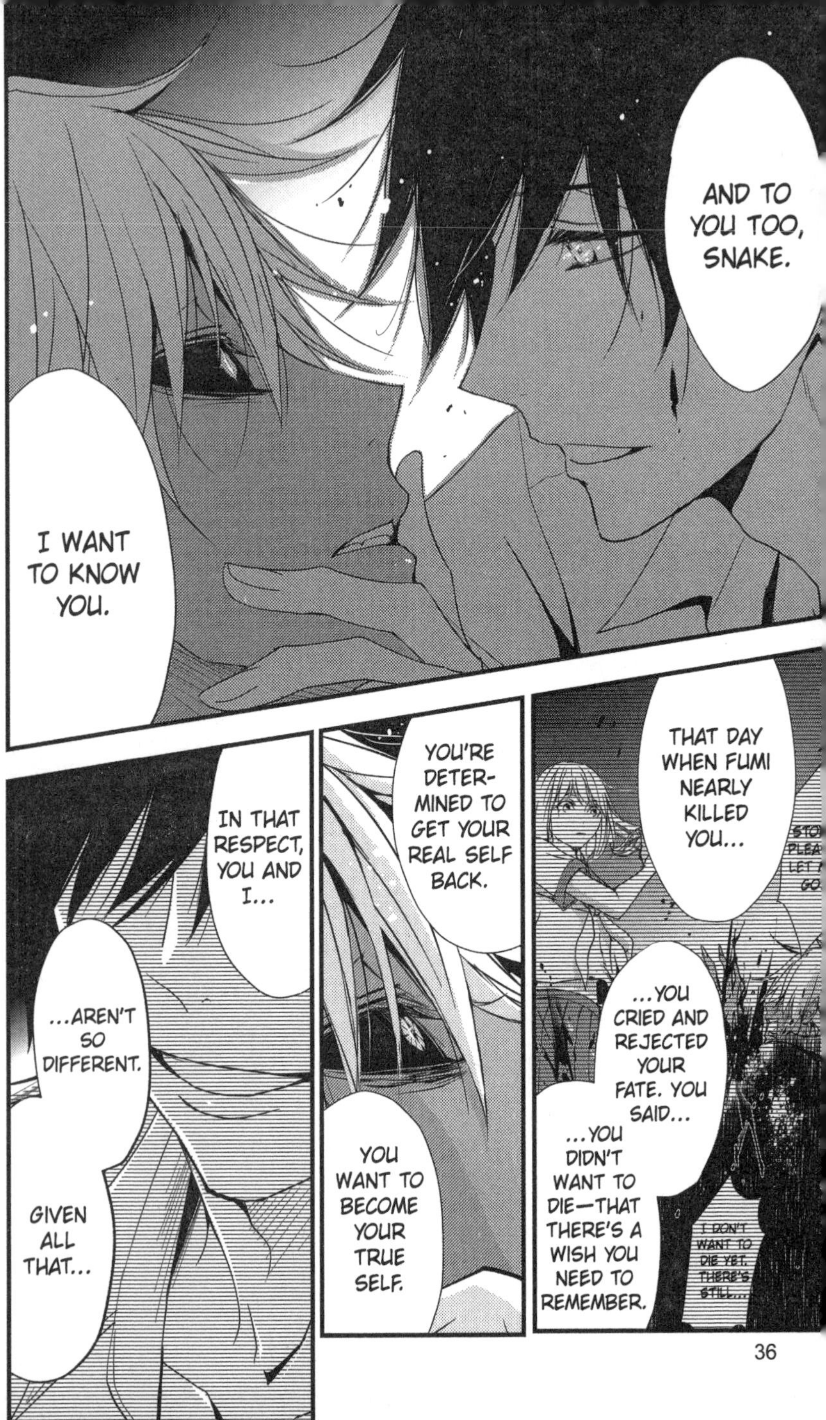
AND TO YOU TOO, SNAKE.
I WANT TO KNOW YOU.
THAT DAY WHEN FUMI NEARLY KILLED YOU...
...YOU CRIED AND REJECTED YOUR FATE. YOU SAID...
...YOU DIDN'T WANT TO DIE—THAT THERE'S A WISH YOU NEED TO REMEMBER.
I DON'T WANT TO DIE YET. THERE'S STILL...
YOU'RE DETER-MINED TO GET YOUR REAL SELF BACK.
YOU WANT TO BECOME YOUR TRUE SELF.
IN THAT RESPECT, YOU AND I...
...AREN'T SO DIFFERENT.
GIVEN ALL THAT...

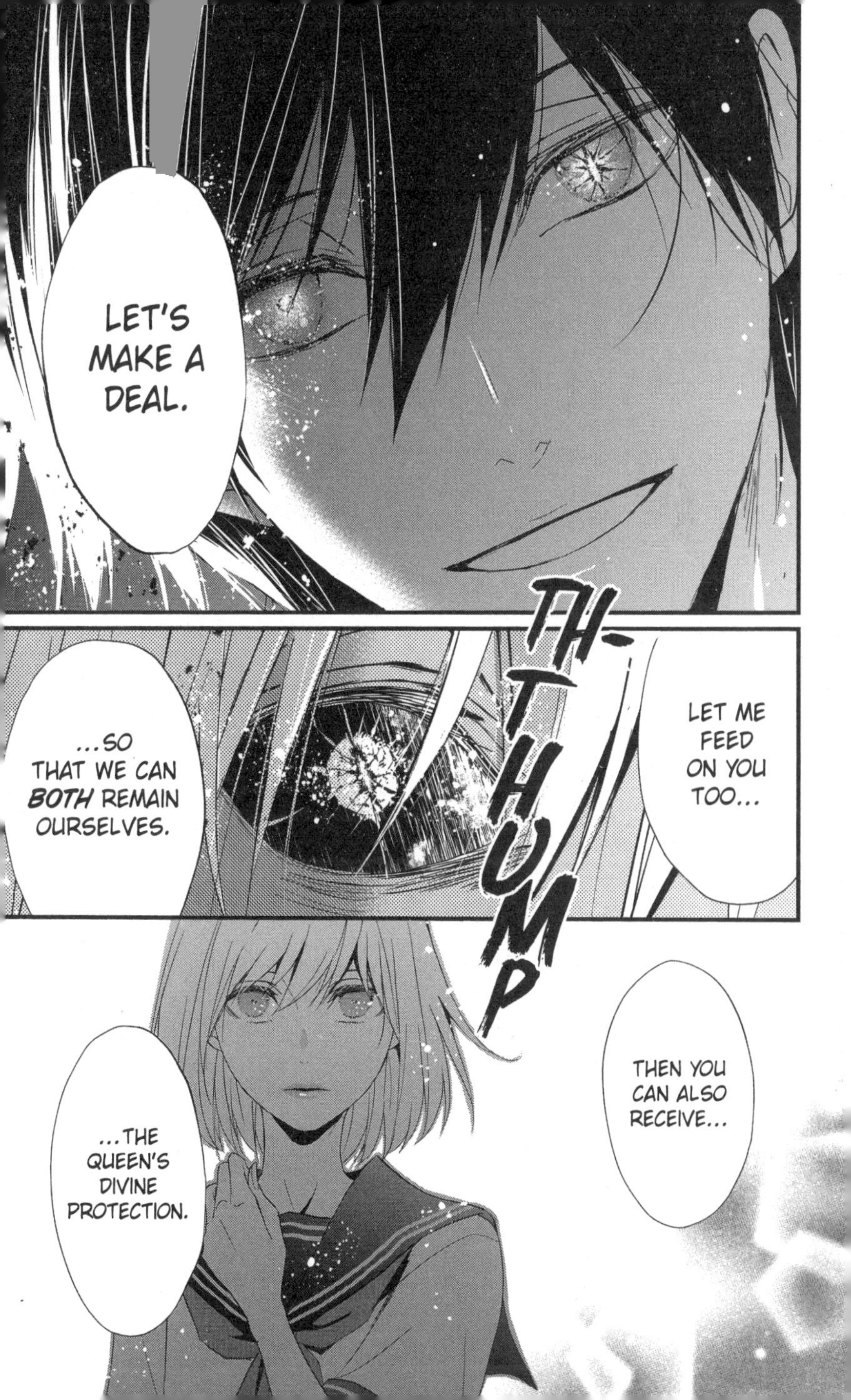
LET'S MAKE A DEAL.
LET ME FEED ON YOU TOO...
TH-THUMP
...SO THAT WE CAN *BOTH* REMAIN OURSELVES.
THEN YOU CAN ALSO RECEIVE...
...THE QUEEN'S DIVINE PROTECTION.

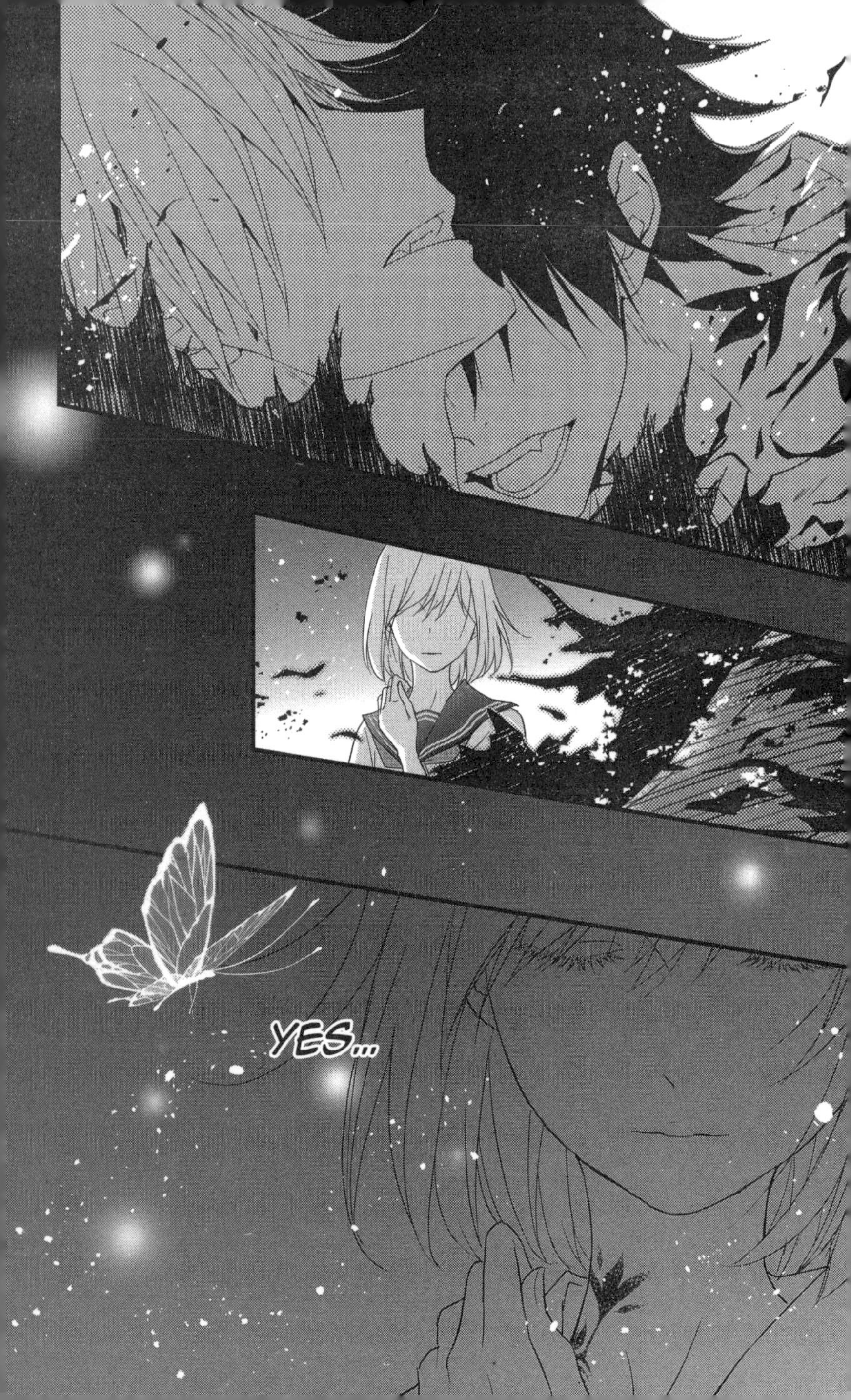
YES...

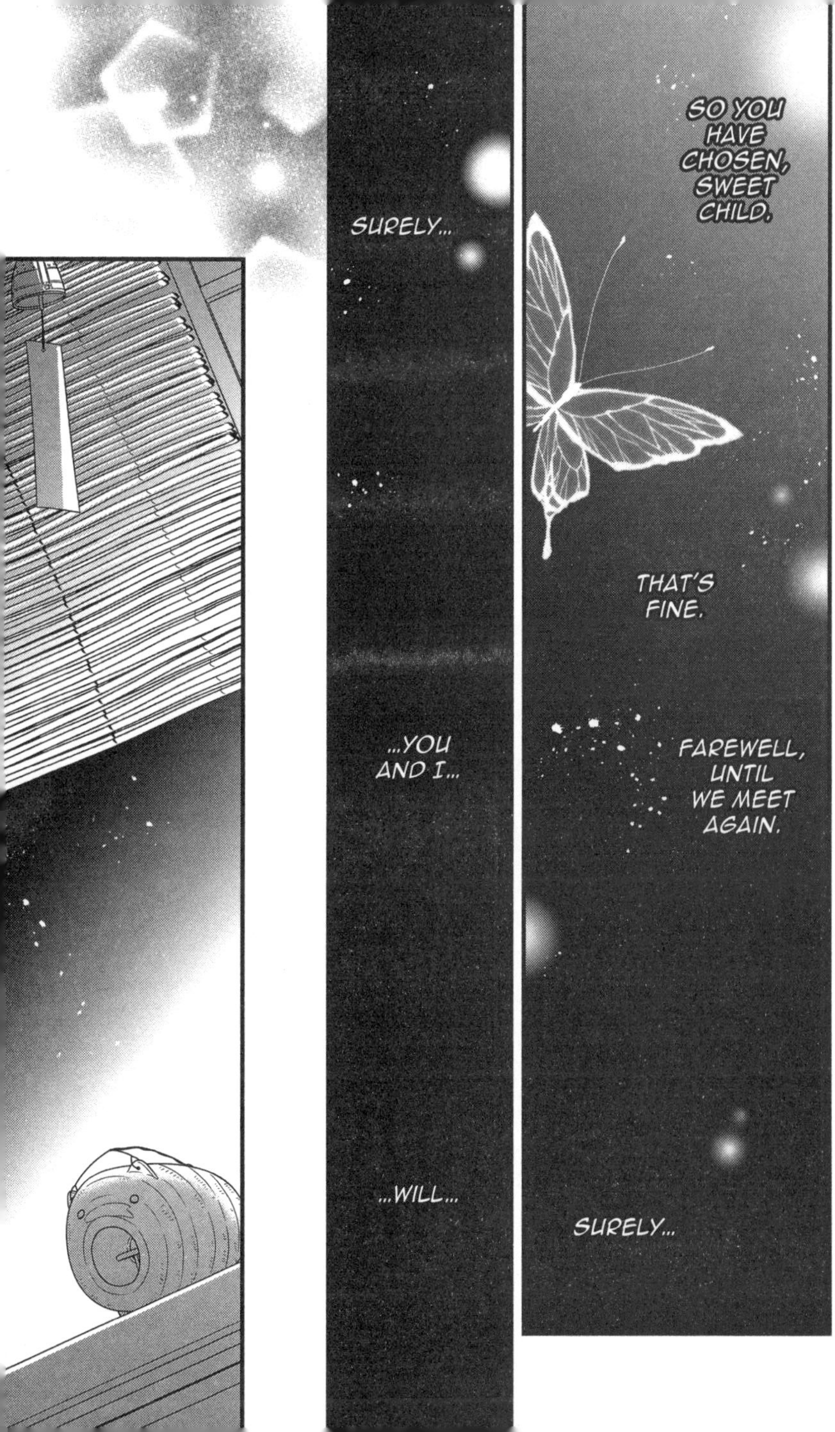
SO YOU HAVE CHOSEN, SWEET CHILD.
THAT'S FINE.
FAREWELL, UNTIL WE MEET AGAIN.
SURELY...
SURELY...
...YOU AND I...
...WILL...

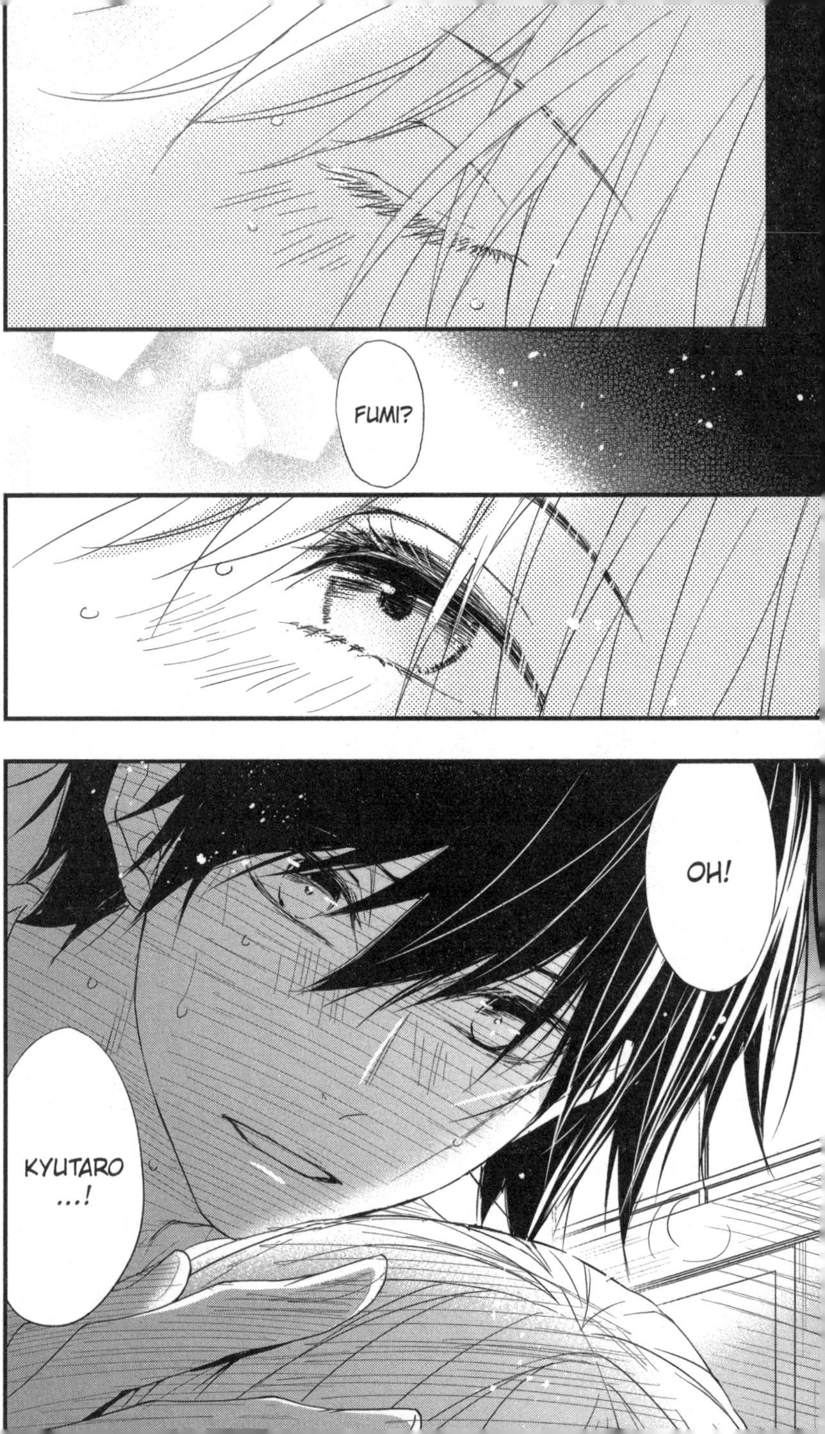
FUMI?
OH!
KYUTARO ...!

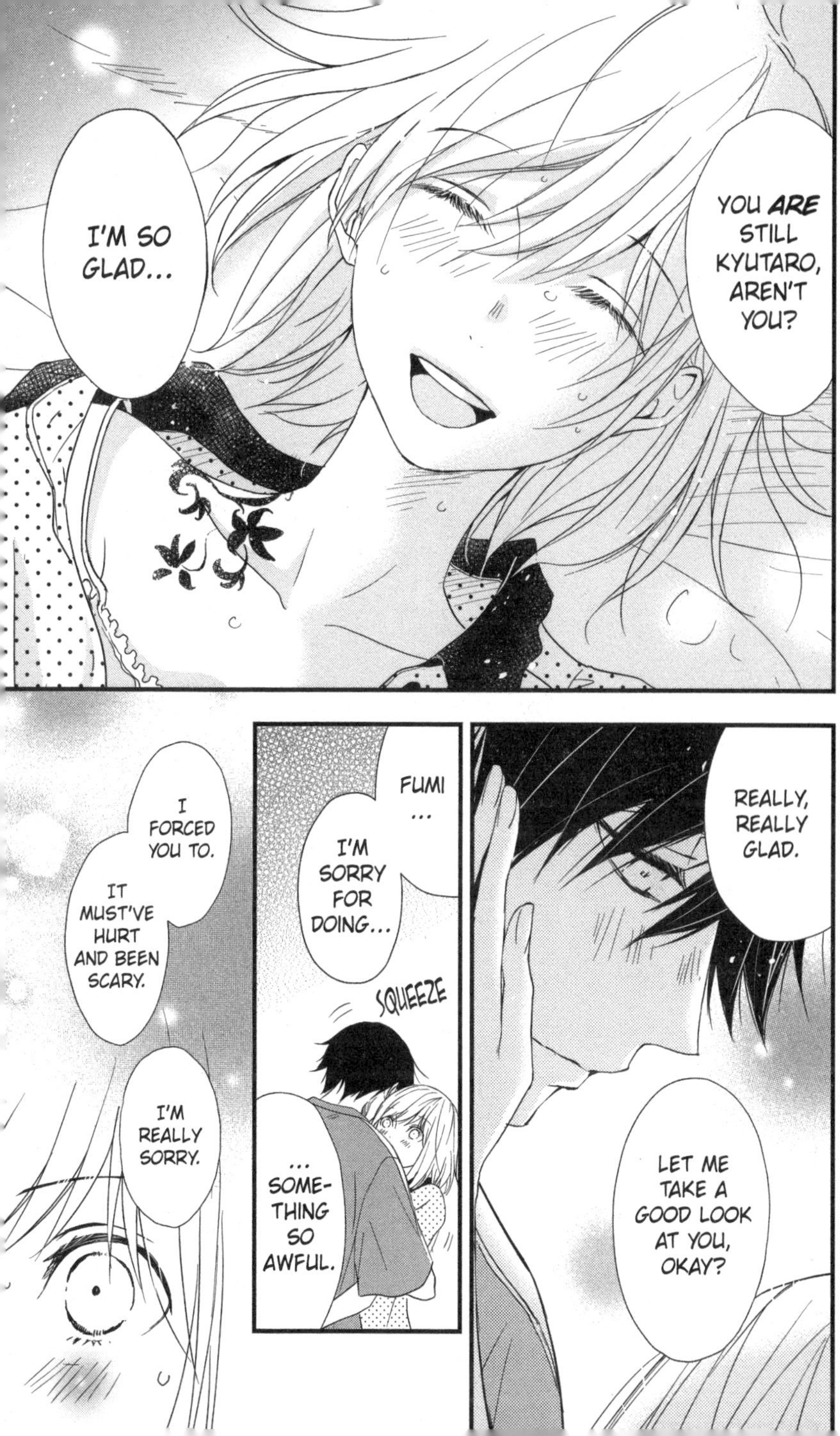
YOU ARE STILL KYUTARO, AREN'T YOU?
I'M SO GLAD...
REALLY, REALLY GLAD.
LET ME TAKE A GOOD LOOK AT YOU, OKAY?
FUMI...
I'M SORRY FOR DOING...
SQUEEZE
...SOME-THING SO AWFUL.
I FORCED YOU TO.
IT MUST'VE HURT AND BEEN SCARY.
I'M REALLY SORRY.

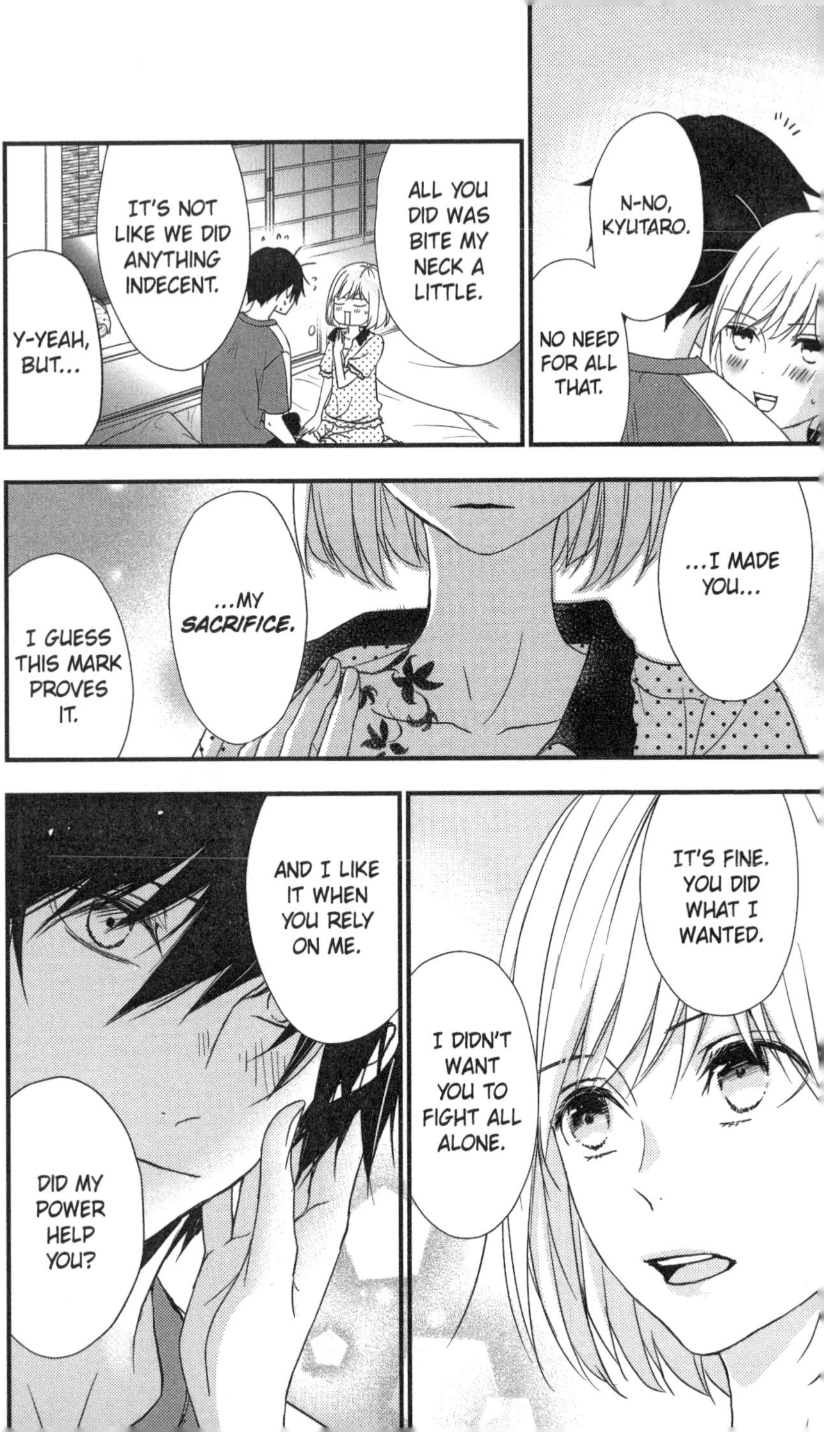
N-NO, KYUTARO.
NO NEED FOR ALL THAT.
ALL YOU DID WAS BITE MY NECK A LITTLE.
IT'S NOT LIKE WE DID ANYTHING INDECENT.
Y-YEAH, BUT...
...I MADE YOU...
...MY *SACRIFICE.*
I GUESS THIS MARK PROVES IT.
IT'S FINE. YOU DID WHAT I WANTED.
I DIDN'T WANT YOU TO FIGHT ALL ALONE.
AND I LIKE IT WHEN YOU RELY ON ME.
DID MY POWER HELP YOU?

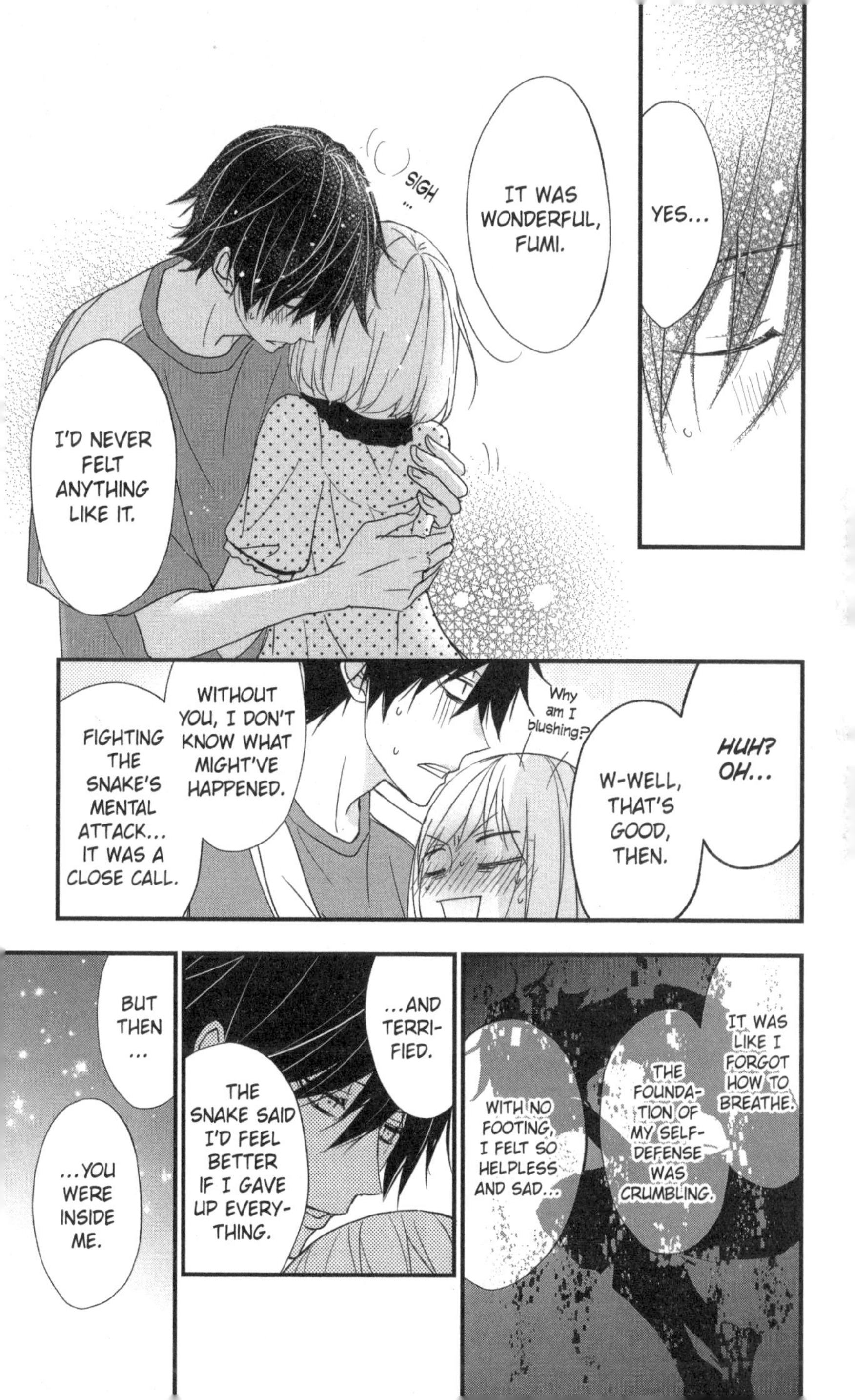
YES...
SIGH...
IT WAS WONDERFUL, FUMI.
I'D NEVER FELT ANYTHING LIKE IT.
HUH? OH...
W-WELL, THAT'S GOOD, THEN.
Why am I blushing?
WITHOUT YOU, I DON'T KNOW WHAT MIGHT'VE HAPPENED.
FIGHTING THE SNAKE'S MENTAL ATTACK... IT WAS A CLOSE CALL.
IT WAS LIKE I FORGOT HOW TO BREATHE.
THE FOUNDATION OF MY SELF-DEFENSE WAS CRUMBLING.
WITH NO FOOTING, I FELT SO HELPLESS AND SAD...
...AND TERRIFIED.
THE SNAKE SAID I'D FEEL BETTER IF I GAVE UP EVERYTHING.
BUT THEN...
...YOU WERE INSIDE ME.

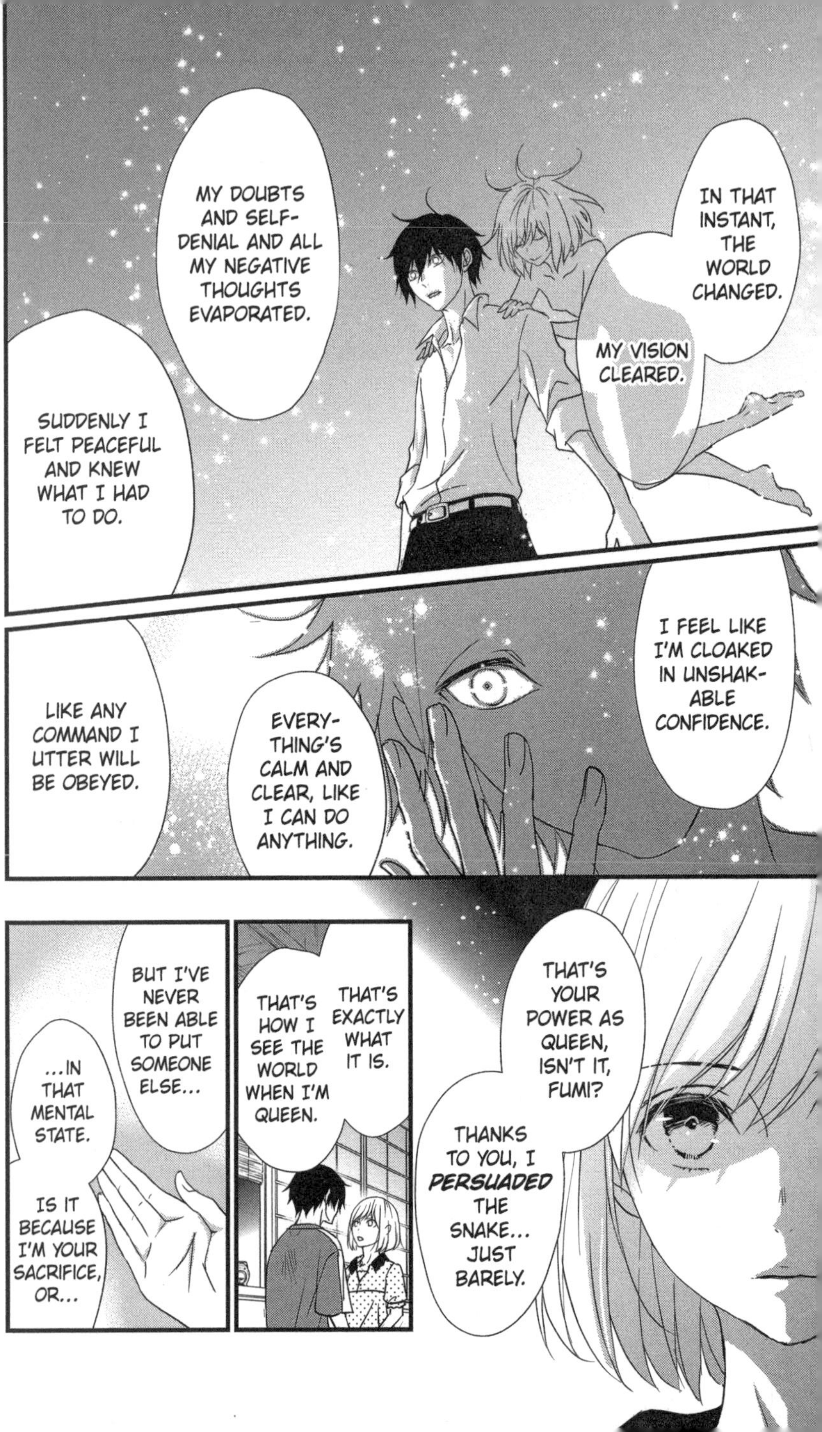
IN THAT INSTANT, THE WORLD CHANGED.
MY VISION CLEARED.
MY DOUBTS AND SELF-DENIAL AND ALL MY NEGATIVE THOUGHTS EVAPORATED.
SUDDENLY I FELT PEACEFUL AND KNEW WHAT I HAD TO DO.
I FEEL LIKE I'M CLOAKED IN UNSHAKABLE CONFIDENCE.
EVERYTHING'S CALM AND CLEAR, LIKE I CAN DO ANYTHING.
LIKE ANY COMMAND I UTTER WILL BE OBEYED.
THAT'S YOUR POWER AS QUEEN, ISN'T IT, FUMI?
THANKS TO YOU, I ***PERSUADED*** THE SNAKE... JUST BARELY.
THAT'S EXACTLY WHAT IT IS.
THAT'S HOW I SEE THE WORLD WHEN I'M QUEEN.
BUT I'VE NEVER BEEN ABLE TO PUT SOMEONE ELSE...
...IN THAT MENTAL STATE.
IS IT BECAUSE I'M YOUR SACRIFICE, OR...

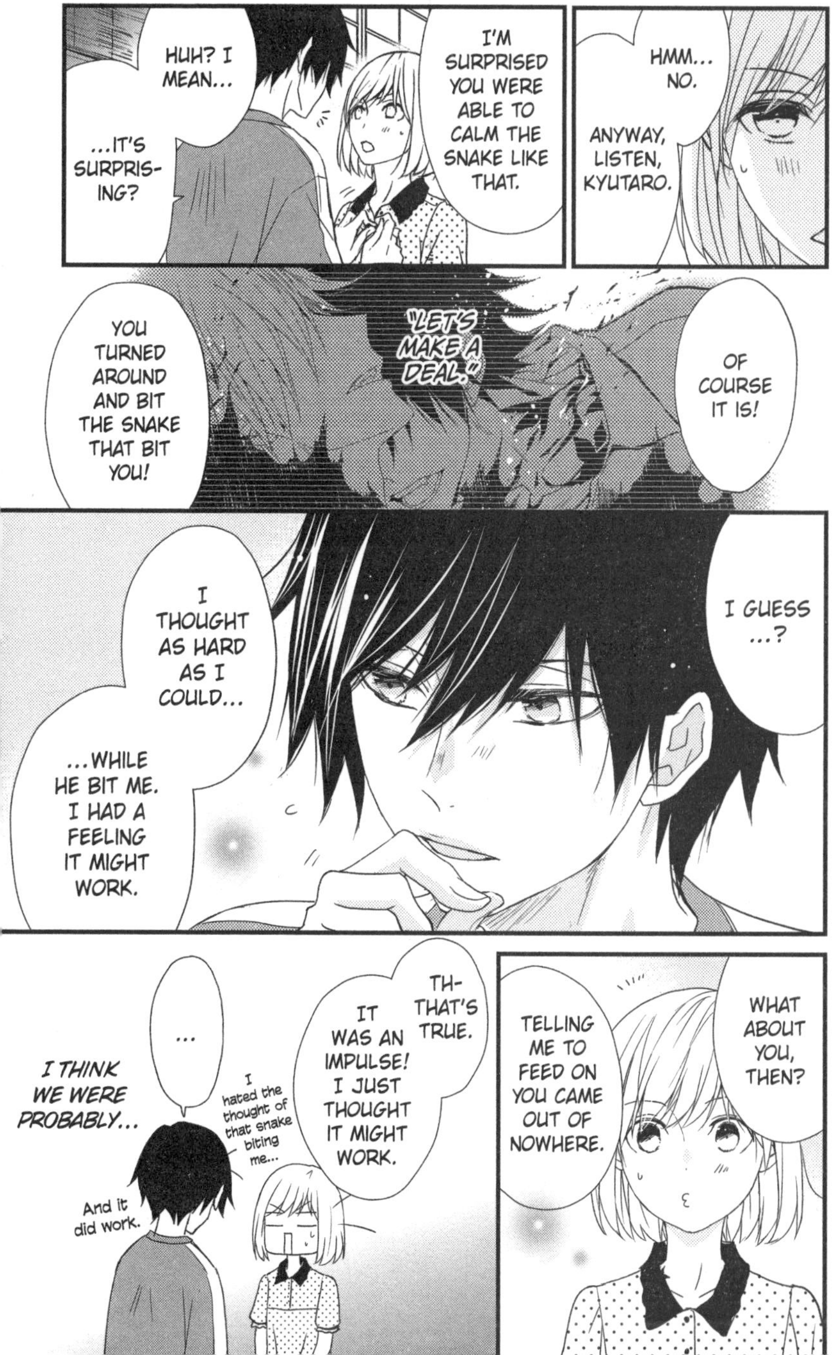
HMM... NO.
ANYWAY, LISTEN, KYUTARO.
I'M SURPRISED YOU WERE ABLE TO CALM THE SNAKE LIKE THAT.
HUH? I MEAN...
...IT'S SURPRISING?
OF COURSE IT IS!
"LET'S MAKE A DEAL."
YOU TURNED AROUND AND BIT THE SNAKE THAT BIT YOU!
I GUESS ...?
I THOUGHT AS HARD AS I COULD...
...WHILE HE BIT ME. I HAD A FEELING IT MIGHT WORK.
WHAT ABOUT YOU, THEN?
TELLING ME TO FEED ON YOU CAME OUT OF NOWHERE.
TH-THAT'S TRUE.
IT WAS AN IMPULSE! I JUST THOUGHT IT MIGHT WORK.
I hated the thought of that snake biting me...
...
And it did work.
I THINK WE WERE PROBABLY...

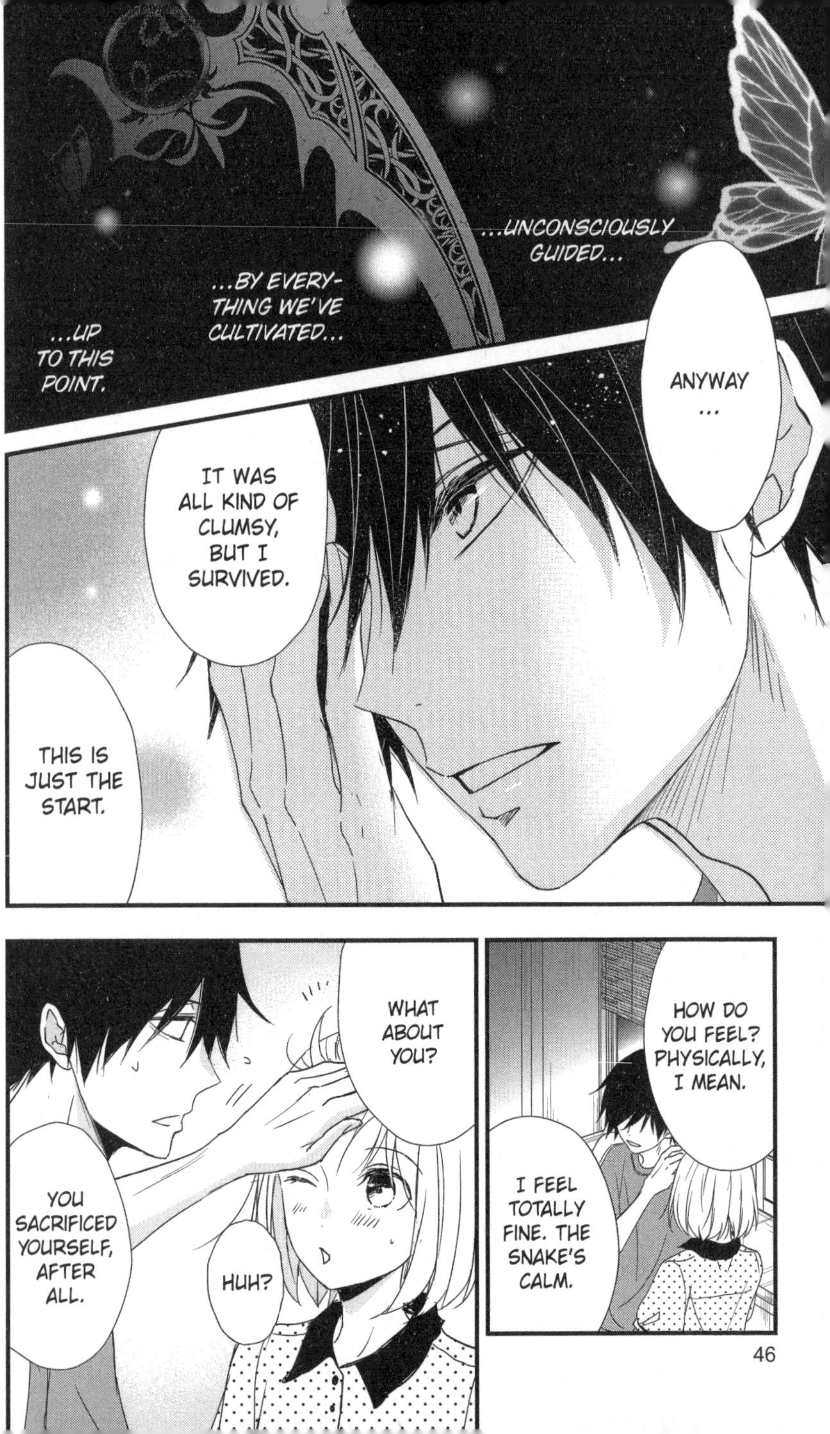
...UNCONSCIOUSLY GUIDED...
...BY EVERYTHING WE'VE CULTIVATED...
...UP TO THIS POINT.
ANYWAY ...
IT WAS ALL KIND OF CLUMSY, BUT I SURVIVED.
THIS IS JUST THE START.
HOW DO YOU FEEL? PHYSICALLY, I MEAN.
I FEEL TOTALLY FINE. THE SNAKE'S CALM.
WHAT ABOUT YOU?
HUH?
YOU SACRIFICED YOURSELF, AFTER ALL.

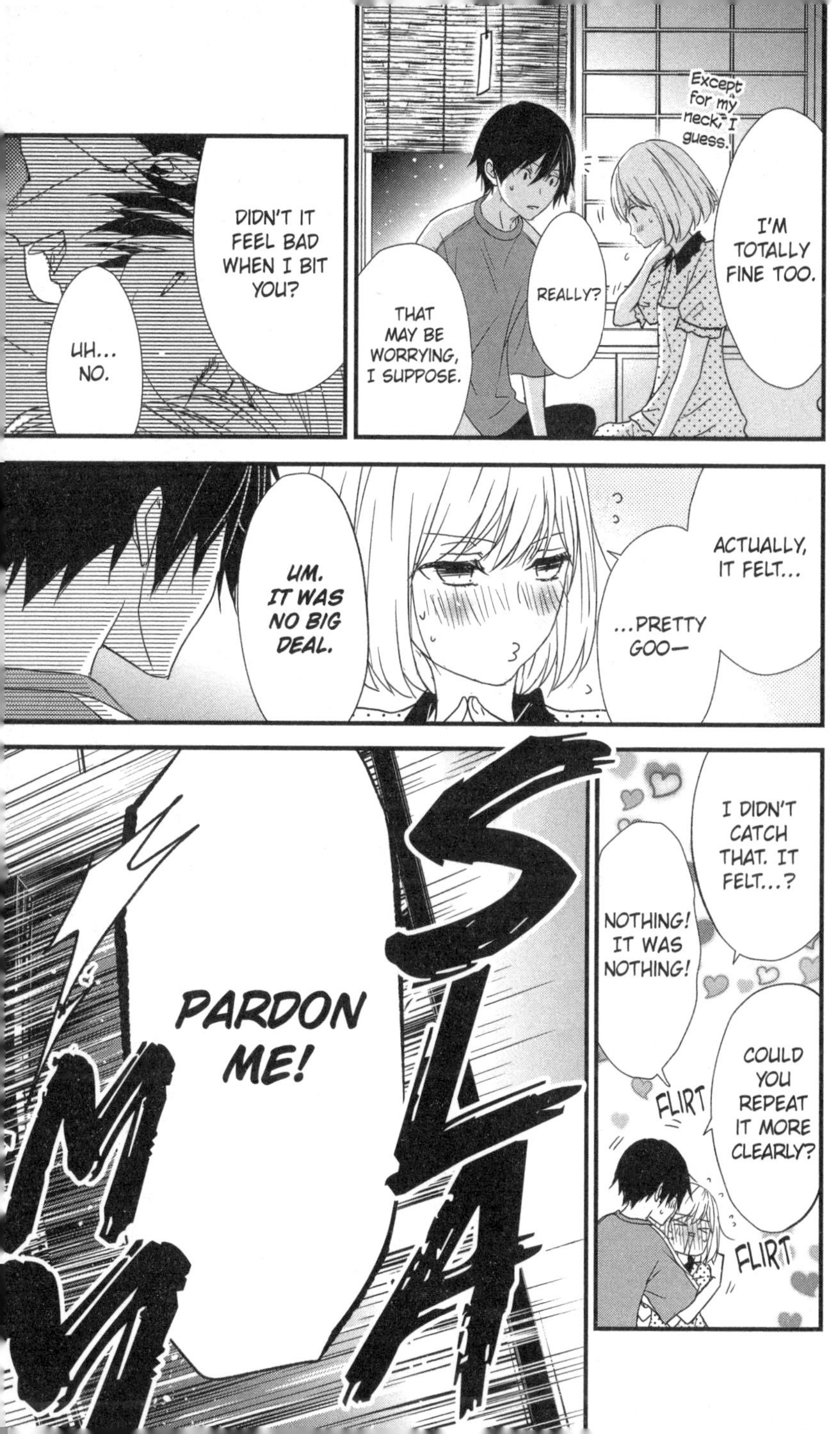
Except for my neck, I guess.
I'M TOTALLY FINE TOO.
REALLY?
THAT MAY BE WORRYING, I SUPPOSE.
DIDN'T IT FEEL BAD WHEN I BIT YOU?
UH... NO.
ACTUALLY, IT FELT...
...PRETTY GOO—
UM. IT WAS NO BIG DEAL.
I DIDN'T CATCH THAT. IT FELT...?
NOTHING! IT WAS NOTHING!
FLIRT
COULD YOU REPEAT IT MORE CLEARLY?
FLIRT
PARDON ME!

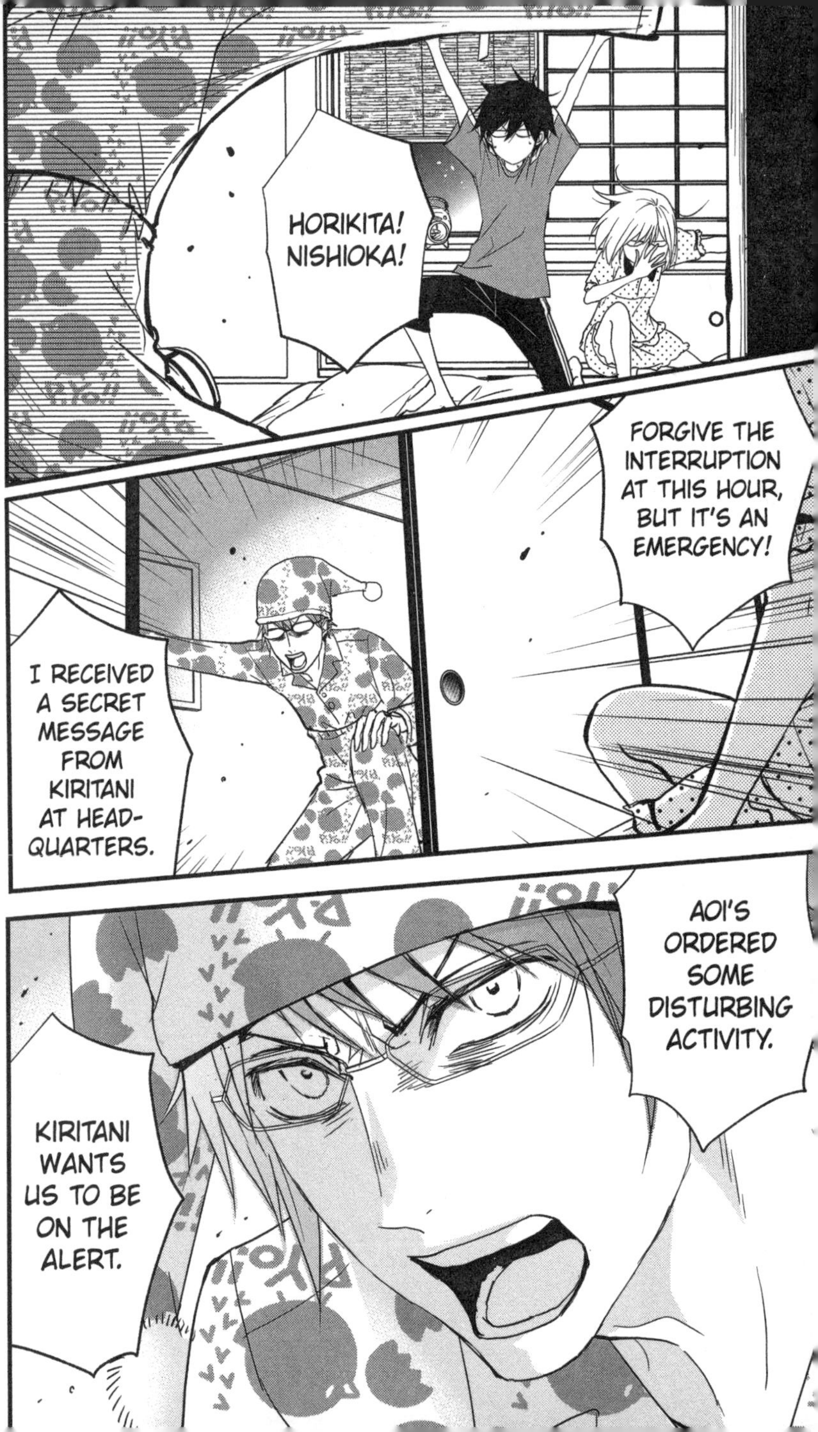
HORIKITA! NISHIOKA!
FORGIVE THE INTERRUPTION AT THIS HOUR, BUT IT'S AN EMERGENCY!
I RECEIVED A SECRET MESSAGE FROM KIRITANI AT HEAD-QUARTERS.
AOI'S ORDERED SOME DISTURBING ACTIVITY.
KIRITANI WANTS US TO BE ON THE ALERT.

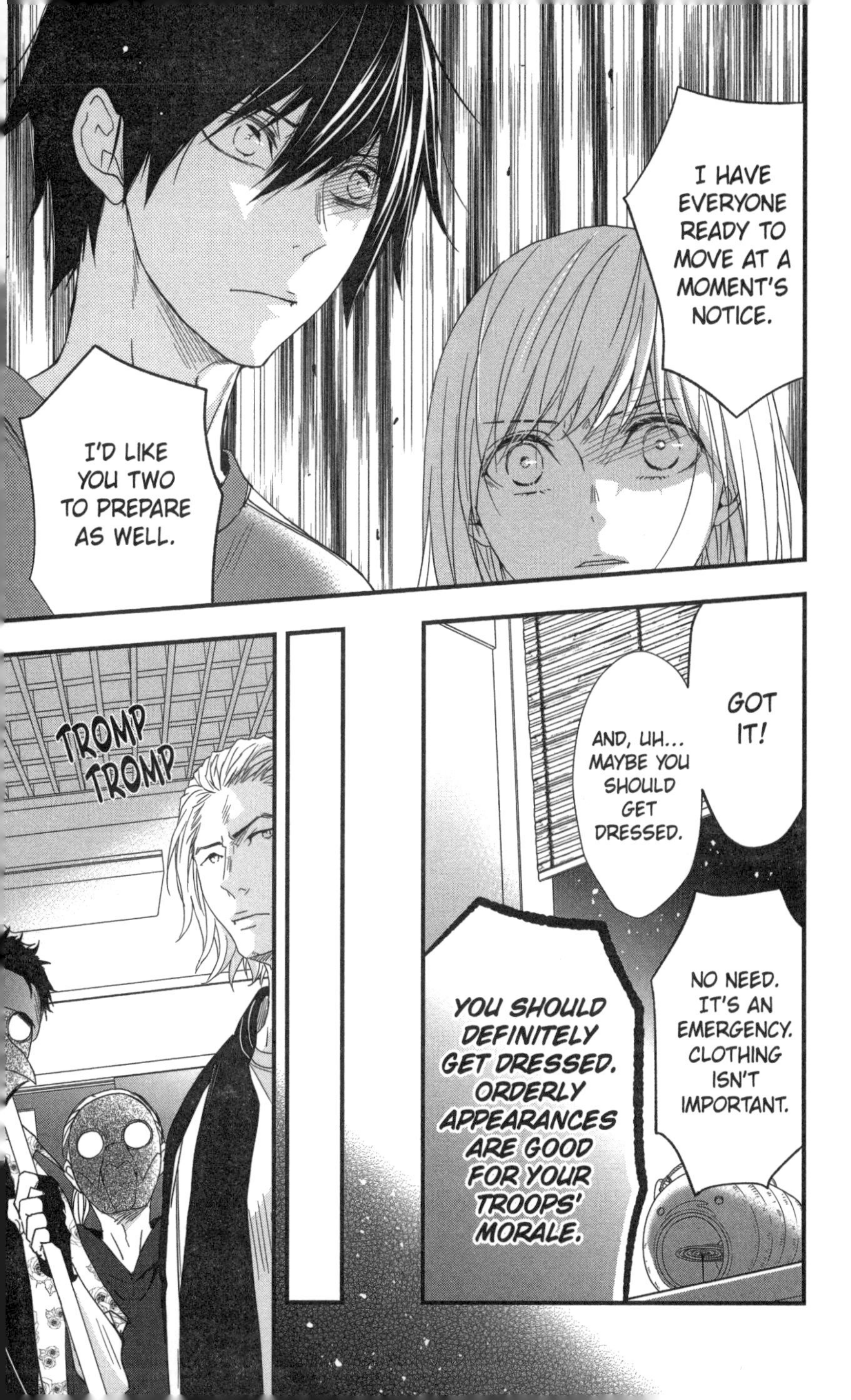
I HAVE EVERYONE READY TO MOVE AT A MOMENT'S NOTICE.
I'D LIKE YOU TWO TO PREPARE AS WELL.
GOT IT!
AND, UH... MAYBE YOU SHOULD GET DRESSED.
NO NEED. IT'S AN EMERGENCY. CLOTHING ISN'T IMPORTANT.
YOU SHOULD DEFINITELY GET DRESSED. ORDERLY APPEARANCES ARE GOOD FOR YOUR TROOPS' MORALE.
TROMP TROMP

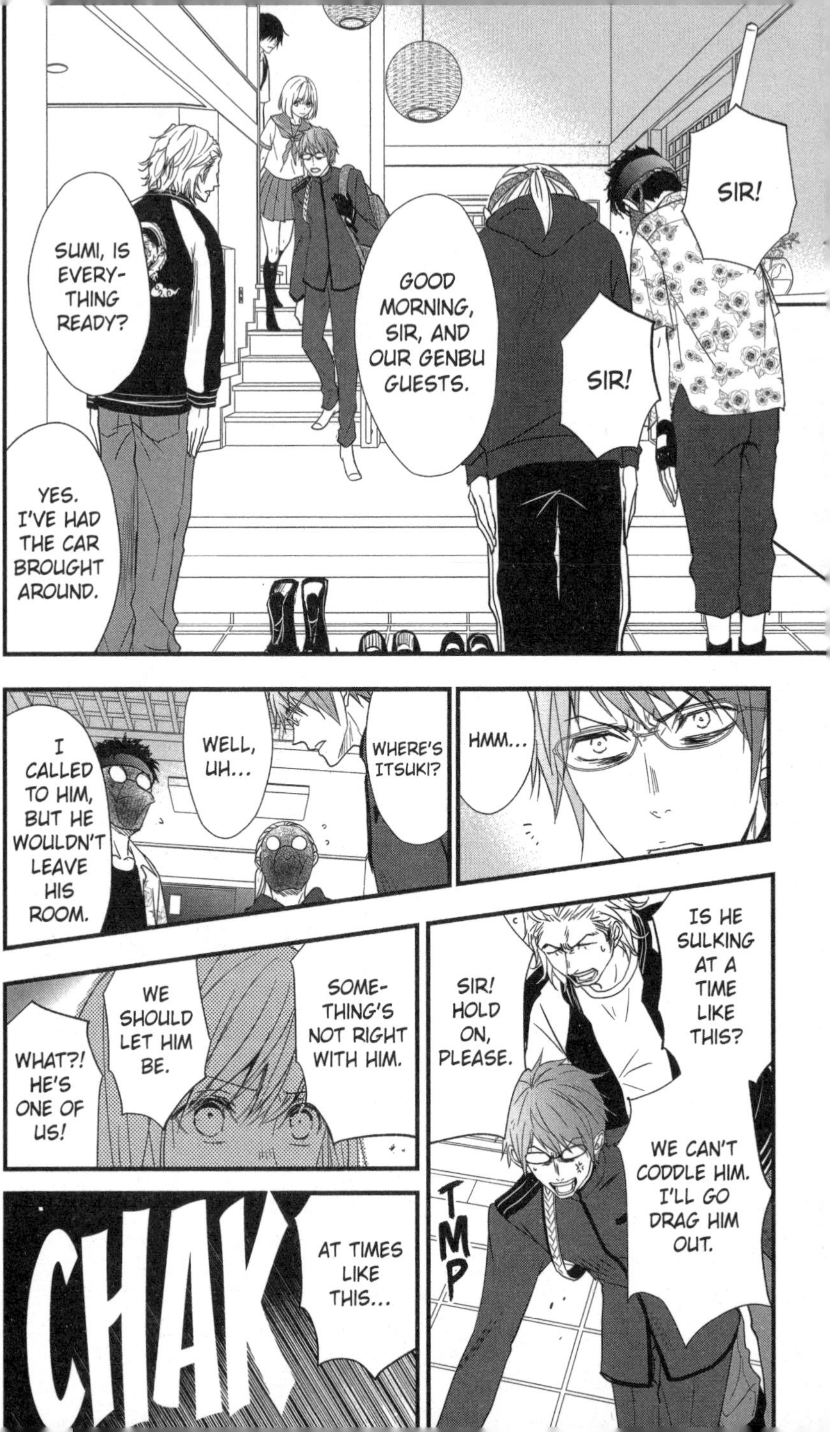
SIR!
SIR!
GOOD MORNING, SIR, AND OUR GENBU GUESTS.
SUMI, IS EVERY-THING READY?
YES. I'VE HAD THE CAR BROUGHT AROUND.
HMM...
WHERE'S ITSUKI?
WELL, UH...
I CALLED TO HIM, BUT HE WOULDN'T LEAVE HIS ROOM.
IS HE SULKING AT A TIME LIKE THIS?
SIR! HOLD ON, PLEASE.
WE CAN'T CODDLE HIM. I'LL GO DRAG HIM OUT.
TMP
SOME-THING'S NOT RIGHT WITH HIM.
WE SHOULD LET HIM BE.
WHAT?! HE'S ONE OF US!
AT TIMES LIKE THIS...
CHAK

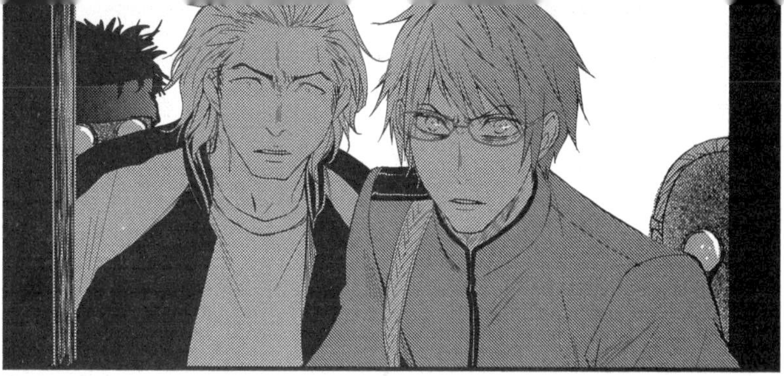
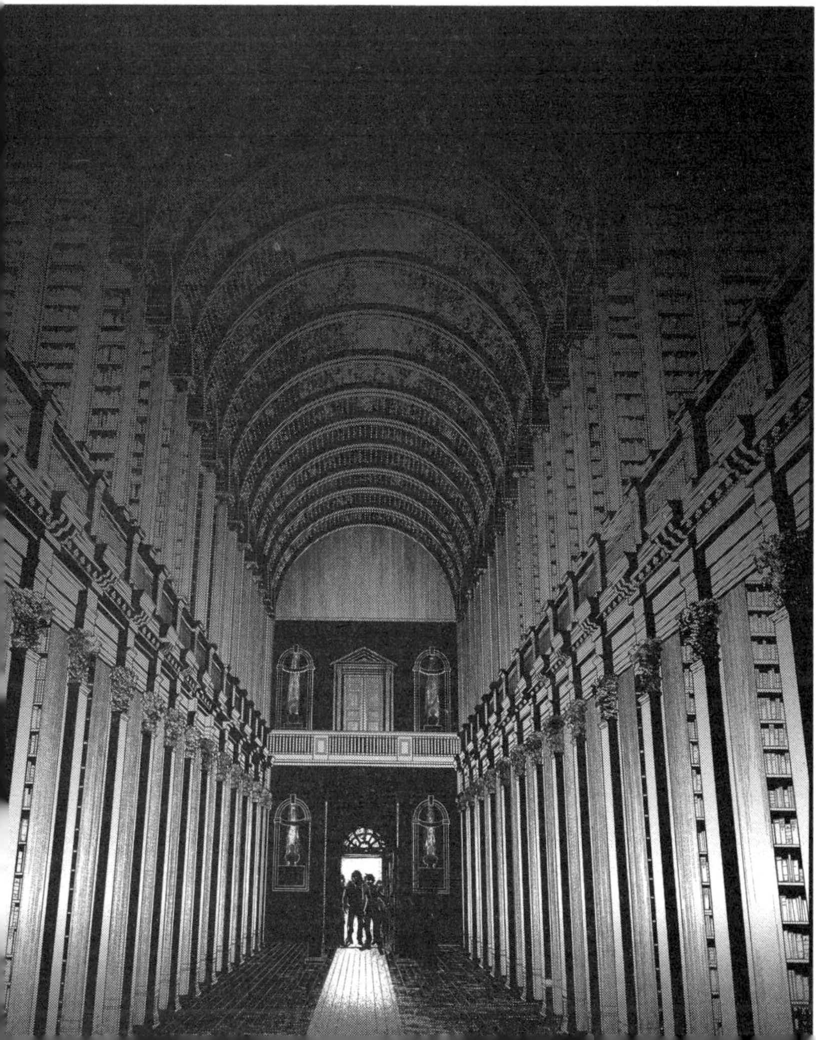

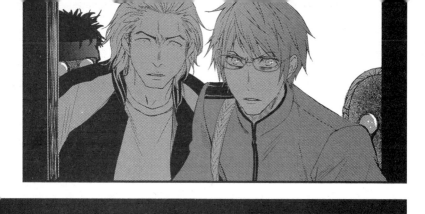

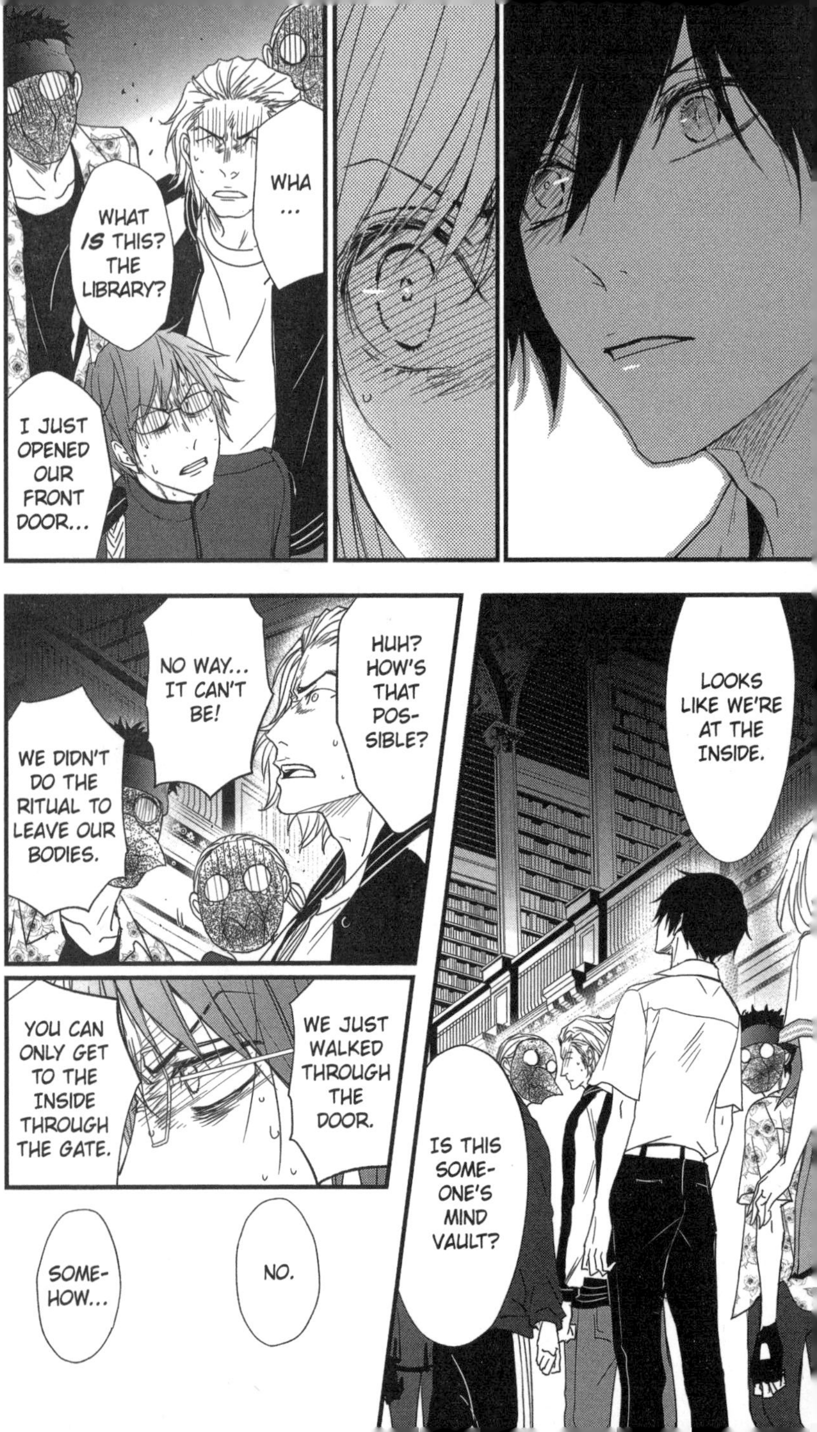
WHA...
WHAT *IS* THIS? THE LIBRARY?
I JUST OPENED OUR FRONT DOOR...
LOOKS LIKE WE'RE AT THE INSIDE.
IS THIS SOMEONE'S MIND VAULT?
HUH? HOW'S THAT POSSIBLE?
NO WAY... IT CAN'T BE!
WE DIDN'T DO THE RITUAL TO LEAVE OUR BODIES.
WE JUST WALKED THROUGH THE DOOR.
YOU CAN ONLY GET TO THE INSIDE THROUGH THE GATE.
NO.
SOMEHOW...

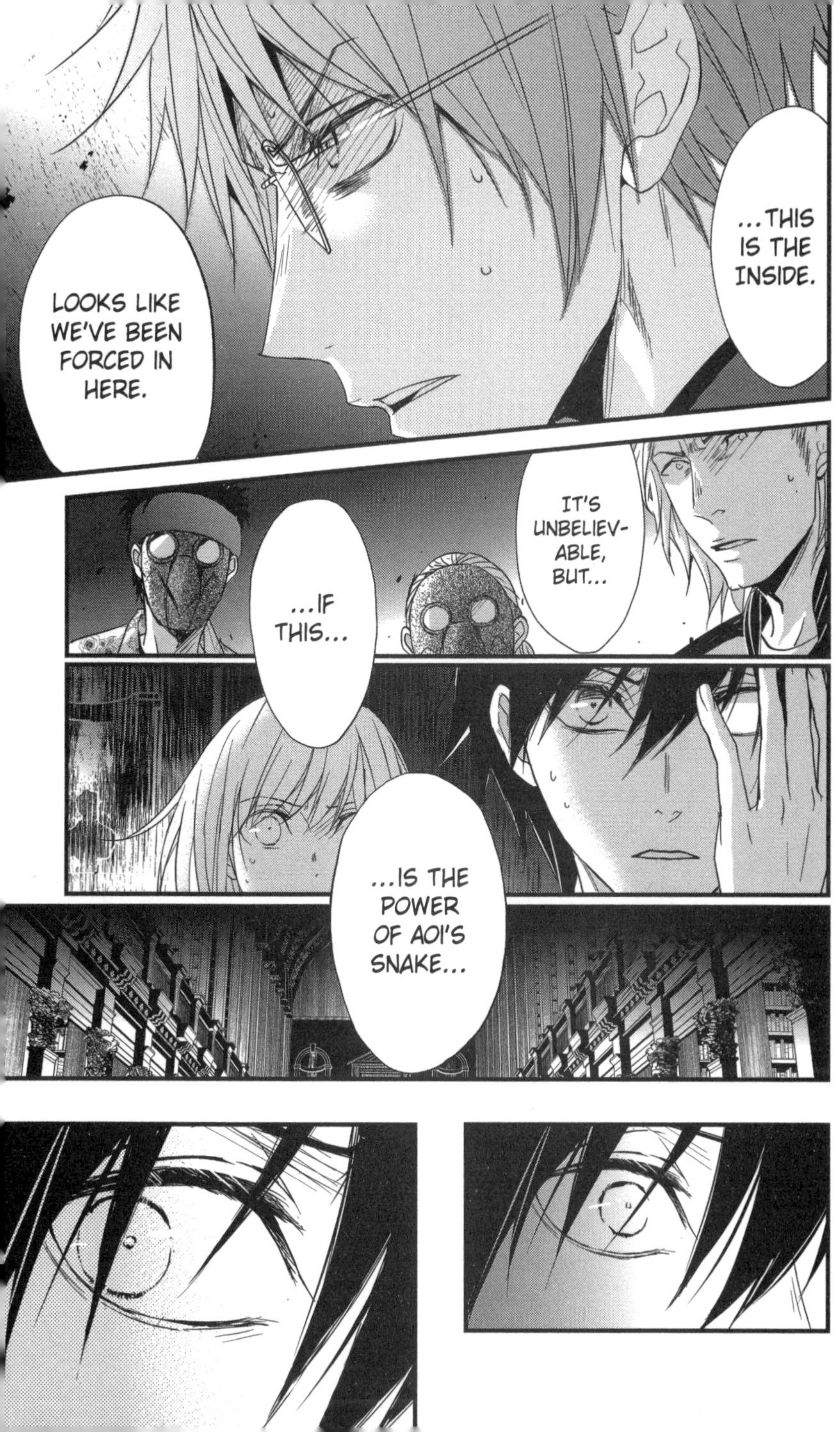
...THIS IS THE INSIDE.
LOOKS LIKE WE'VE BEEN FORCED IN HERE.
IT'S UNBELIEV-ABLE, BUT...
...IF THIS...
...IS THE POWER OF AOI'S SNAKE...

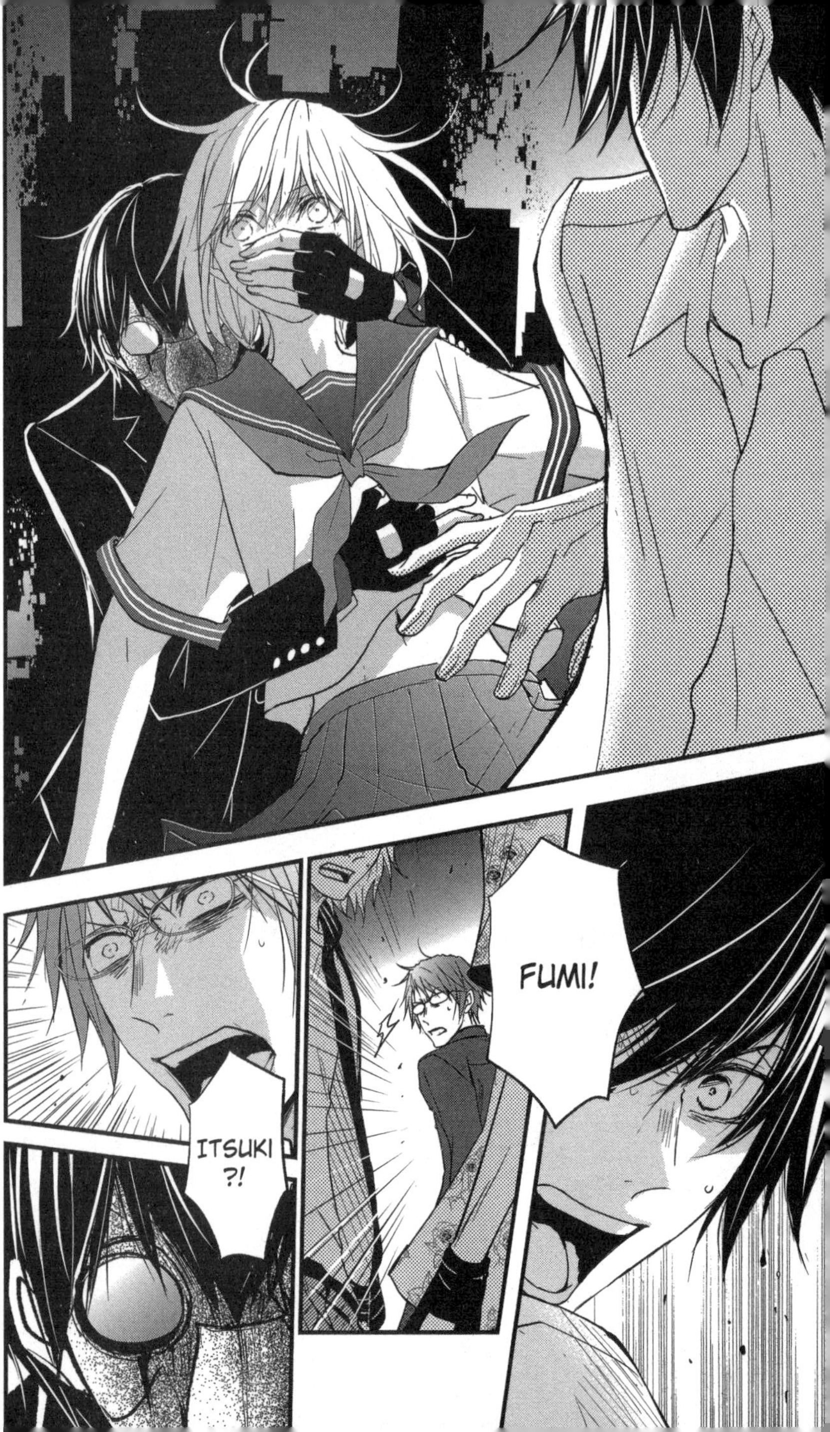
FUMI!
ITSUKI ?!

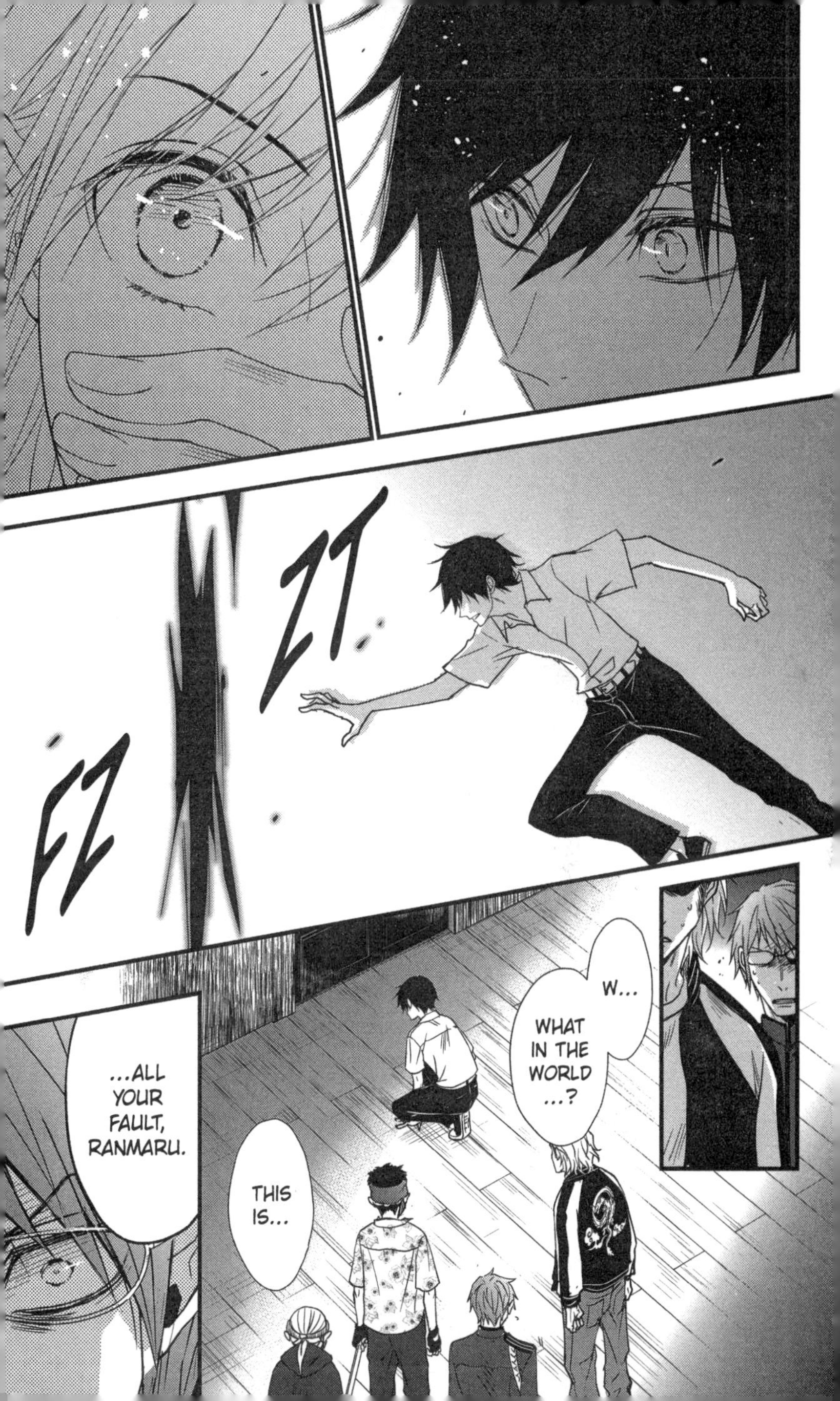
FZZT
W...
WHAT IN THE WORLD ...?
THIS IS...
...ALL YOUR FAULT, RANMARU.

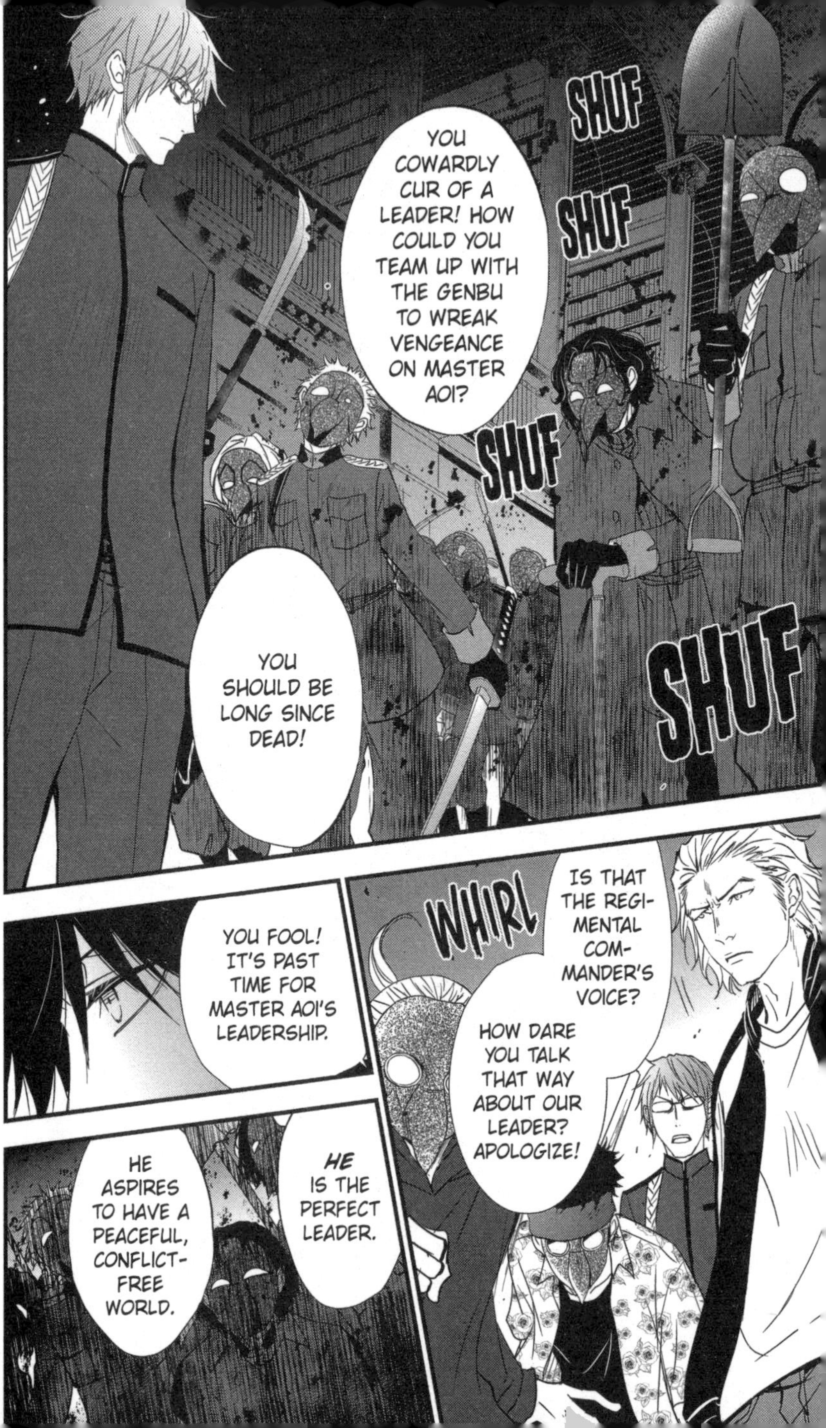
SHUF
SHUF
YOU COWARDLY CUR OF A LEADER! HOW COULD YOU TEAM UP WITH THE GENBU TO WREAK VENGEANCE ON MASTER AOI?
SHUF
SHUF
YOU SHOULD BE LONG SINCE DEAD!
WHIRL
IS THAT THE REGI-MENTAL COM-MANDER'S VOICE?
HOW DARE YOU TALK THAT WAY ABOUT OUR LEADER? APOLOGIZE!
YOU FOOL! IT'S PAST TIME FOR MASTER AOI'S LEADERSHIP.
HE IS THE PERFECT LEADER.
HE ASPIRES TO HAVE A PEACEFUL, CONFLICT-FREE WORLD.

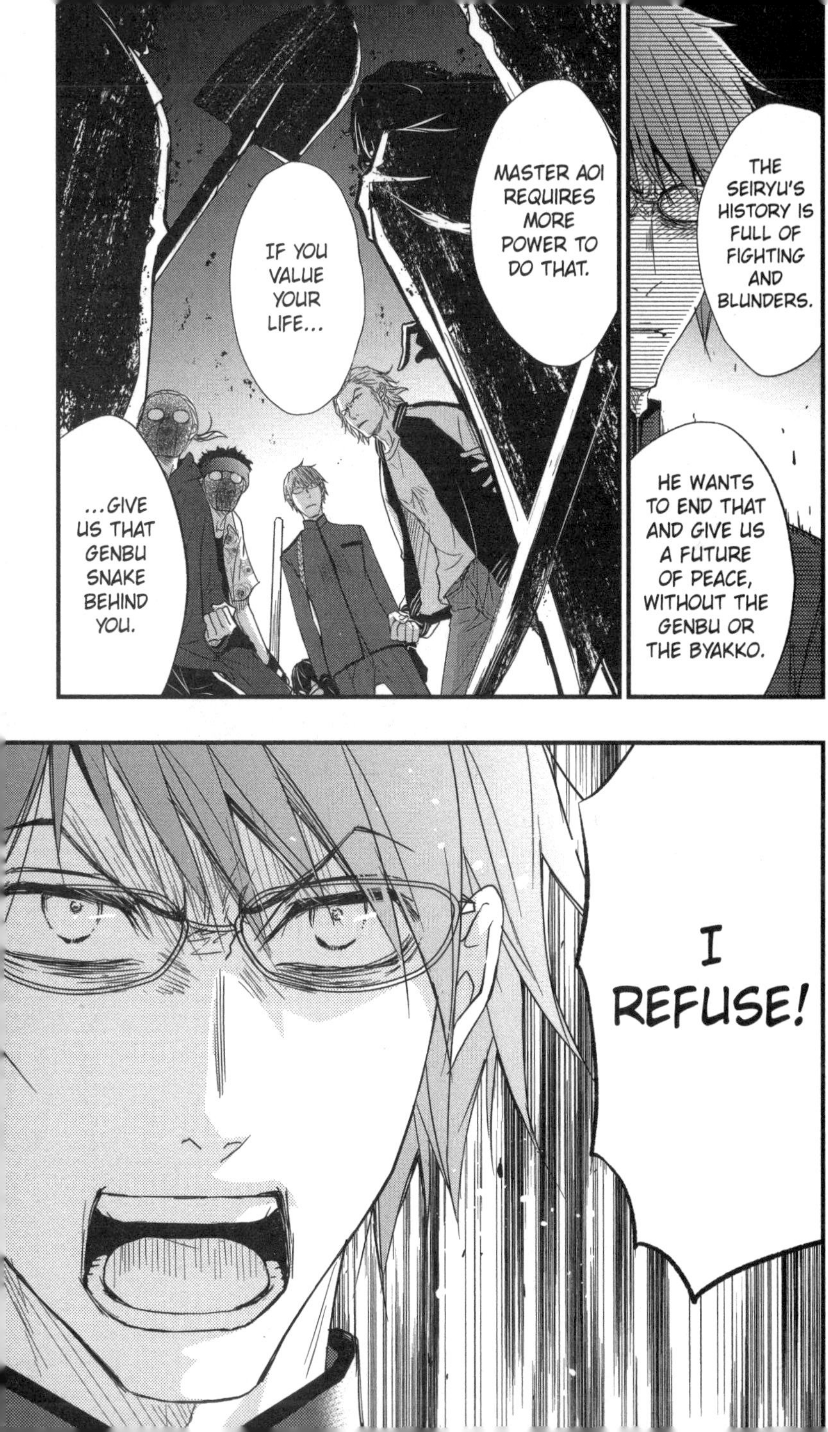
THE SEIRYU'S HISTORY IS FULL OF FIGHTING AND BLUNDERS.
HE WANTS TO END THAT AND GIVE US A FUTURE OF PEACE, WITHOUT THE GENBU OR THE BYAKKO.
MASTER AOI REQUIRES MORE POWER TO DO THAT.
IF YOU VALUE YOUR LIFE...
...GIVE US THAT GENBU SNAKE BEHIND YOU.
I REFUSE!

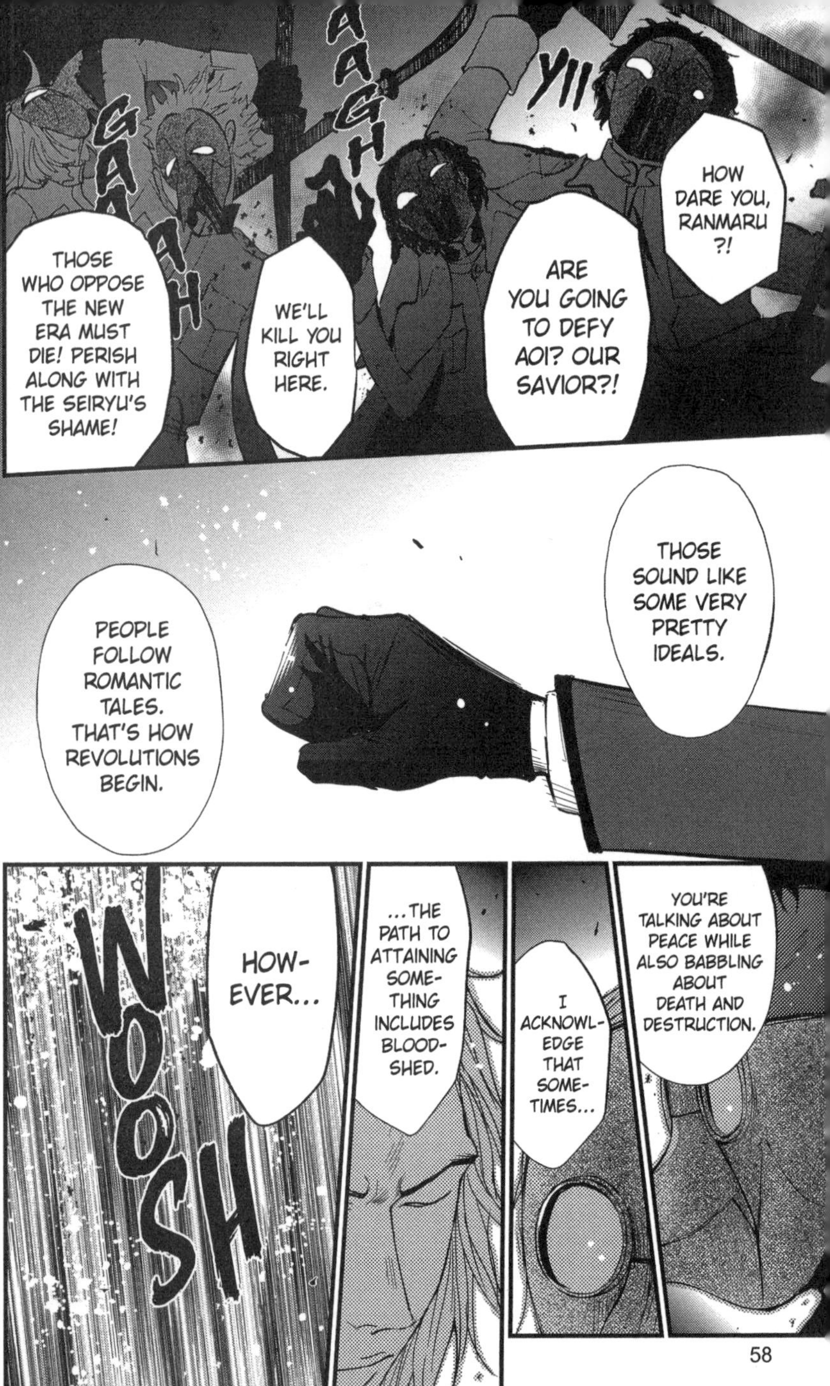
YII
HOW DARE YOU, RANMARU?!
AAAGH
ARE YOU GOING TO DEFY AOI? OUR SAVIOR?!
WE'LL KILL YOU RIGHT HERE.
GAAAH
THOSE WHO OPPOSE THE NEW ERA MUST DIE! PERISH ALONG WITH THE SEIRYU'S SHAME!
THOSE SOUND LIKE SOME VERY PRETTY IDEALS.
PEOPLE FOLLOW ROMANTIC TALES. THAT'S HOW REVOLUTIONS BEGIN.
YOU'RE TALKING ABOUT PEACE WHILE ALSO BABBLING ABOUT DEATH AND DESTRUCTION.
I ACKNOWL-EDGE THAT SOME-TIMES...
...THE PATH TO ATTAINING SOME-THING INCLUDES BLOOD-SHED.
HOW-EVER...
WOOSH

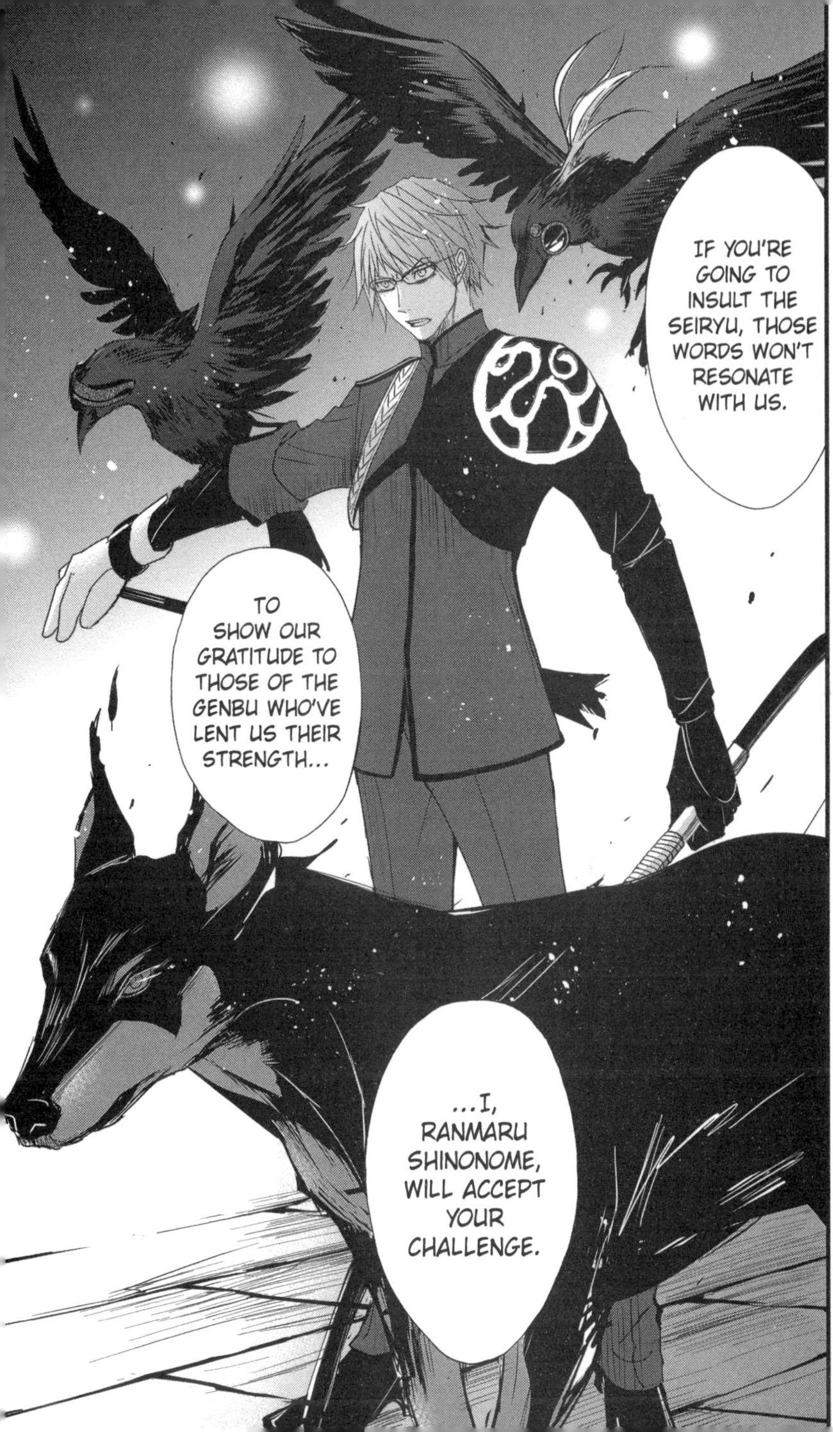
IF YOU'RE GOING TO INSULT THE SEIRYU, THOSE WORDS WON'T RESONATE WITH US.
TO SHOW OUR GRATITUDE TO THOSE OF THE GENBU WHO'VE LENT US THEIR STRENGTH...
...I, RANMARU SHINONOME, WILL ACCEPT YOUR CHALLENGE.

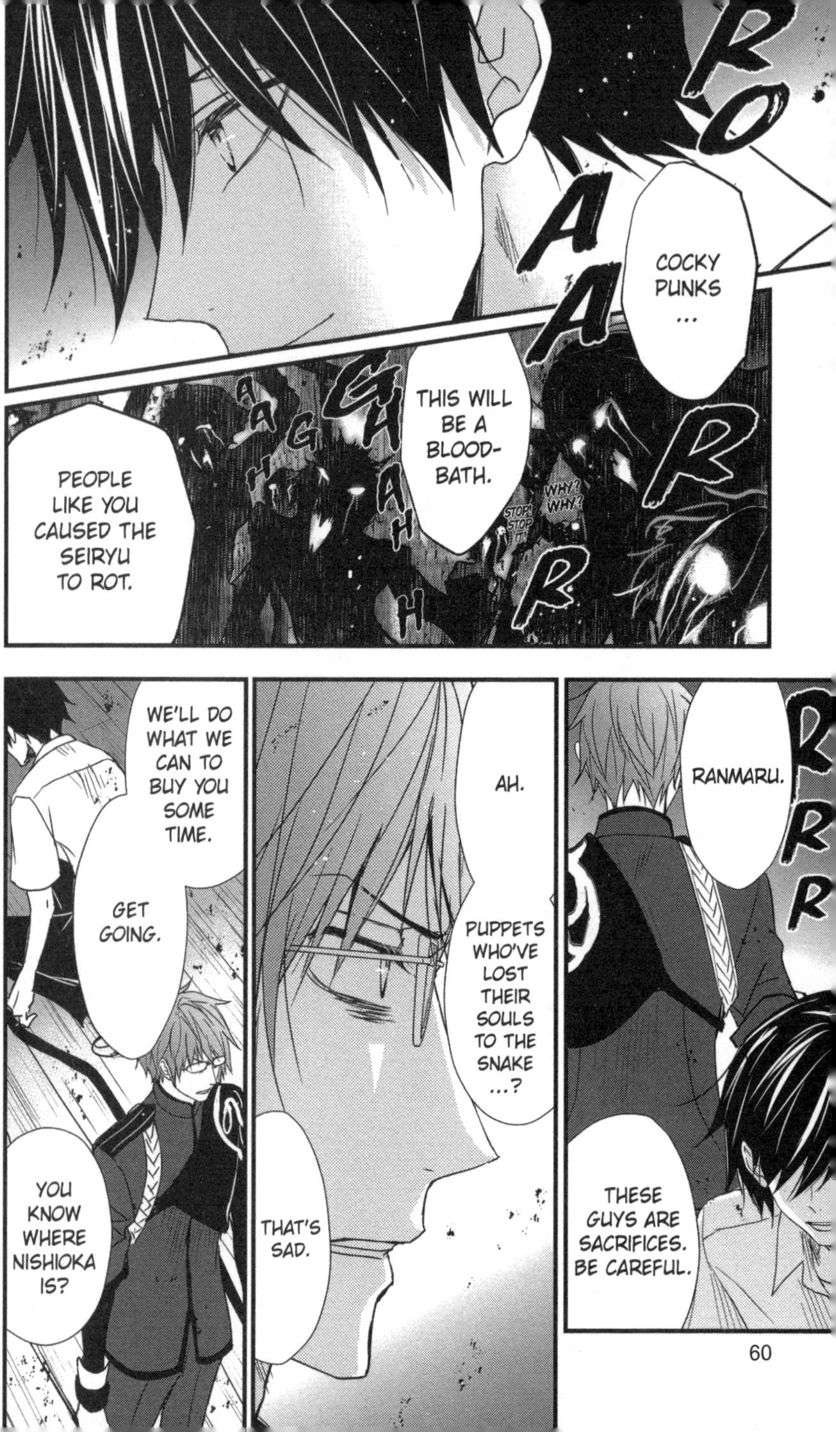
ROAARR
COCKY PUNKS ...
THIS WILL BE A BLOOD-BATH.
WHY? WHY?
STOP! STOP IT!
GHAHH
AAGH
PEOPLE LIKE YOU CAUSED THE SEIRYU TO ROT.
RRRR
RANMARU.
THESE GUYS ARE SACRIFICES. BE CAREFUL.
AH.
PUPPETS WHO'VE LOST THEIR SOULS TO THE SNAKE ...?
THAT'S SAD.
WE'LL DO WHAT WE CAN TO BUY YOU SOME TIME.
GET GOING.
YOU KNOW WHERE NISHIOKA IS?

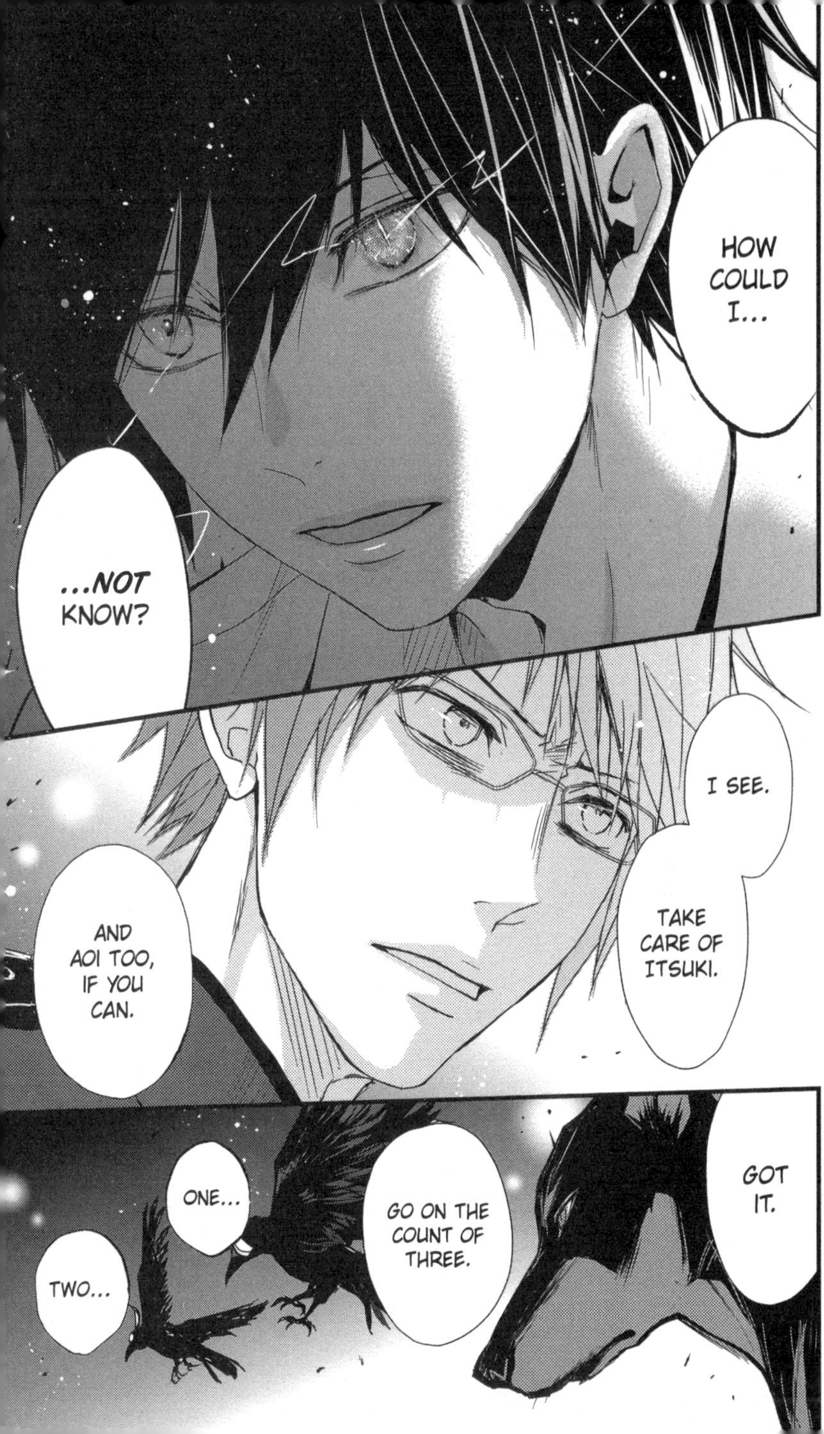
HOW COULD I...
...NOT KNOW?
I SEE.
TAKE CARE OF ITSUKI.
AND AOI TOO, IF YOU CAN.
GOT IT.
GO ON THE COUNT OF THREE.
ONE...
TWO...

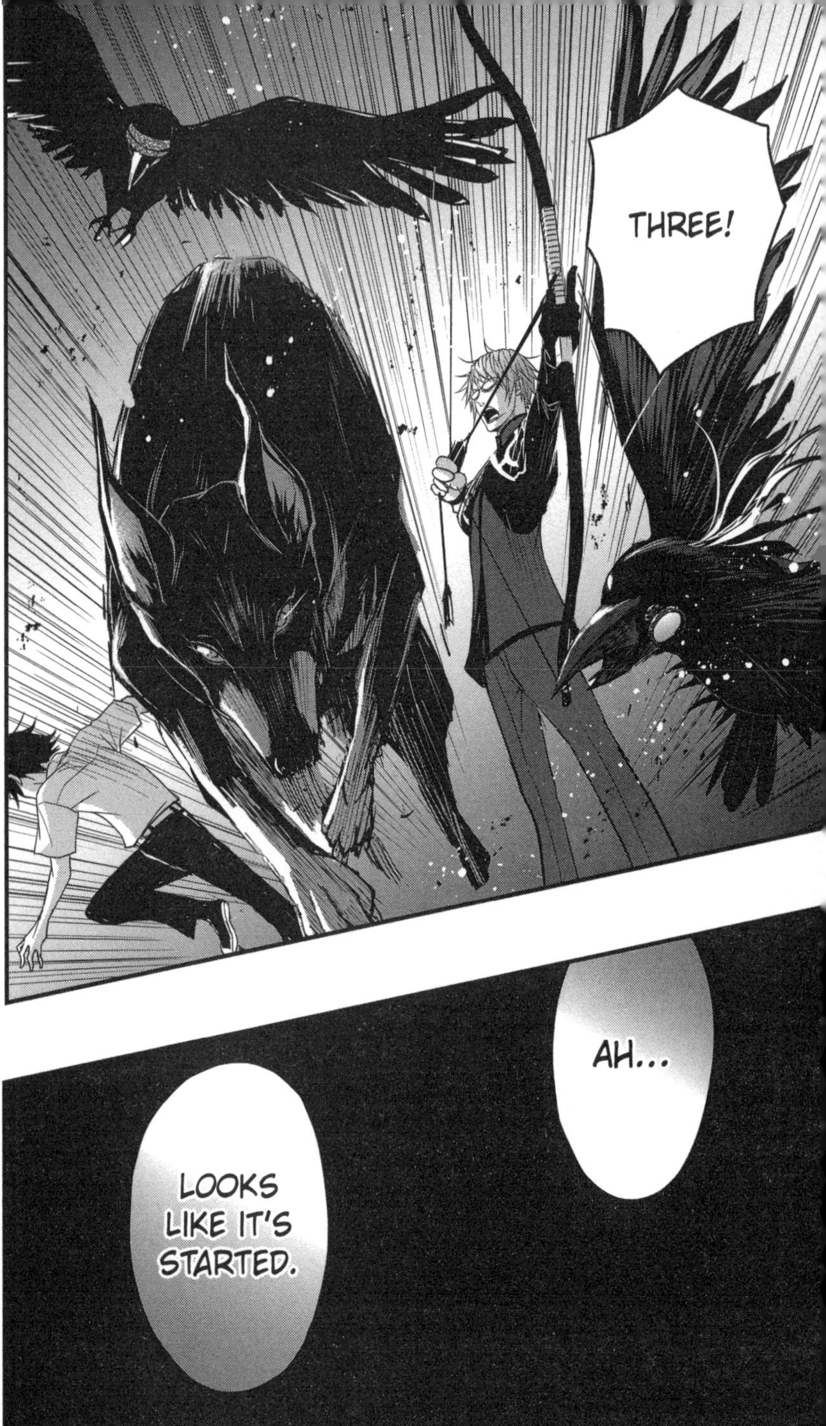
THREE!
AH...
LOOKS LIKE IT'S STARTED.

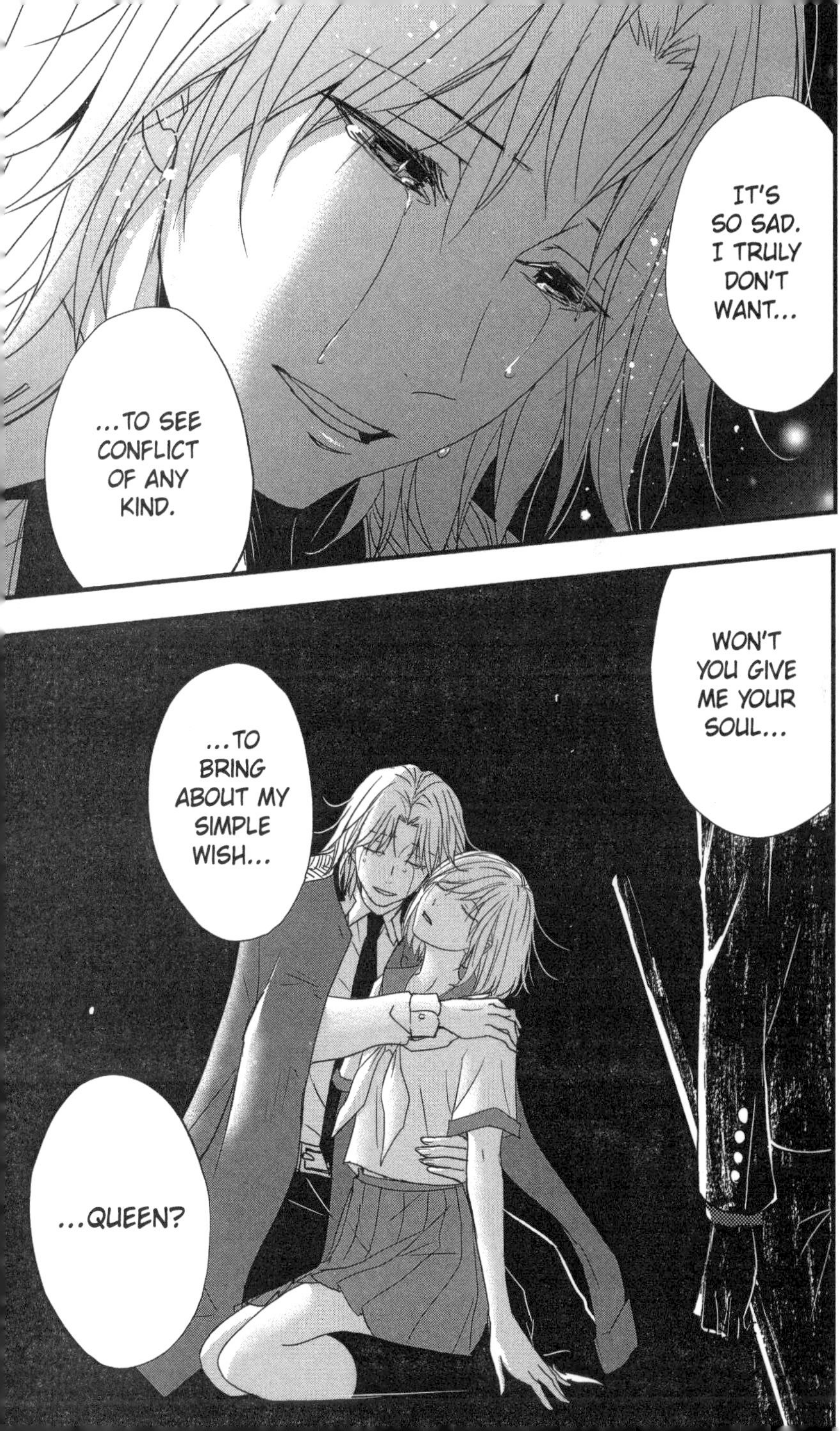
IT'S SO SAD. I TRULY DON'T WANT...
...TO SEE CONFLICT OF ANY KIND.
WON'T YOU GIVE ME YOUR SOUL...
...TO BRING ABOUT MY SIMPLE WISH...
...QUEEN?

KYOUSUKE MOTOMI
C/O QUEEN'S QUALITY EDITOR
VIZ MEDIA
P.O. BOX 77010
SAN FRANCISCO, CA 94107

PLEASE SEND YOUR CORRE-SPONDENCE HERE. ♥
PUFF
PLEASE!
THANKS, AS ALWAYS.
PUFF
MOOF
YES!
MOOF
That looks fun...

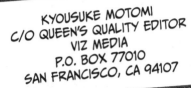

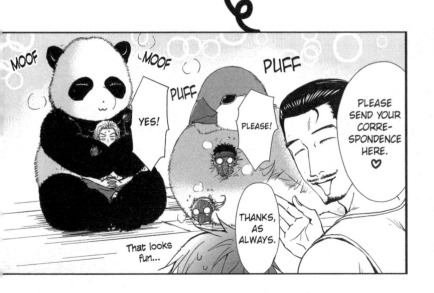

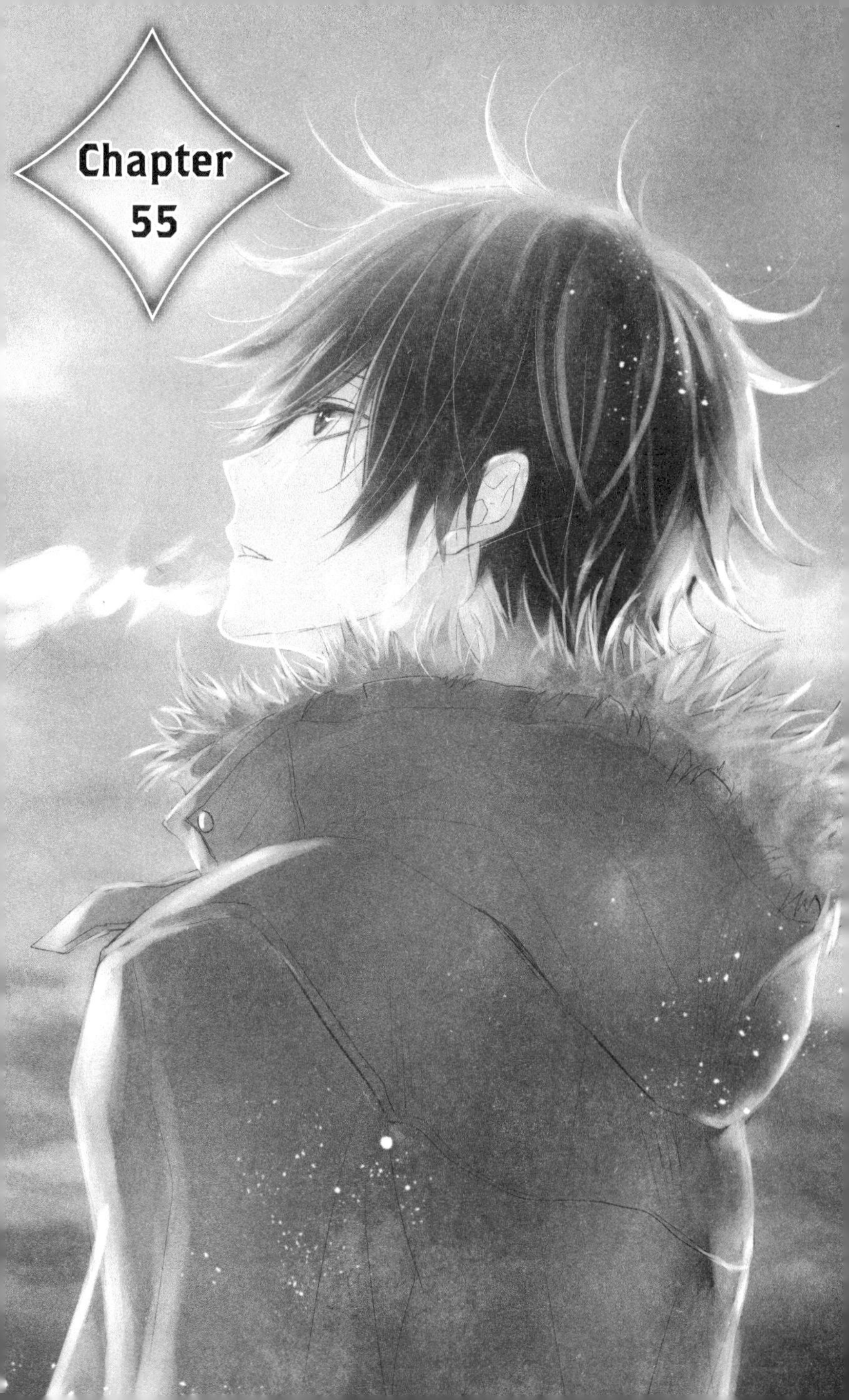
Chapter
55

CHAPTER 55

MONTHLY BETSUCOMI SALE DATE NOTICE ON TWITTER AND INSTAGRAM

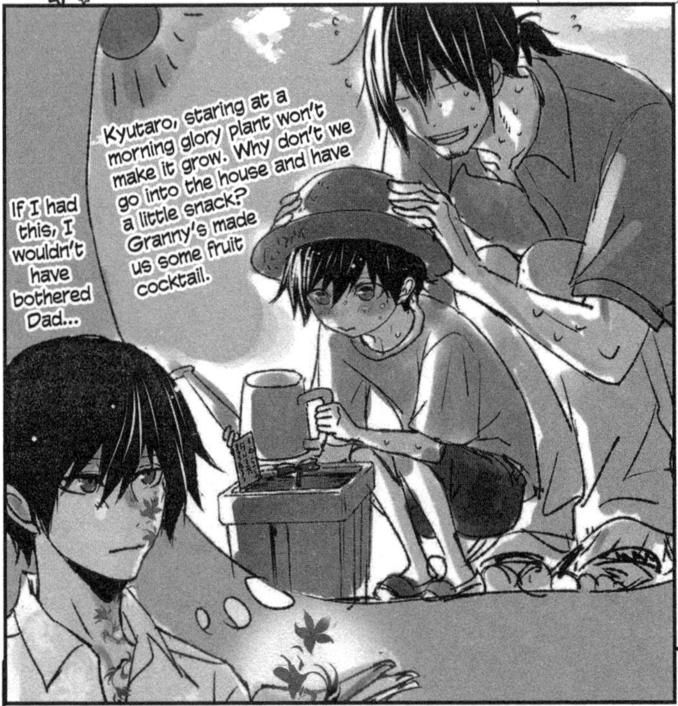
Kyutaro, staring at a morning glory plant won't make it grow. Why don't we go into the house and have a little snack? Granny's made us some fruit cocktail.
If I had this, I wouldn't have bothered Dad...

LET'S SEE... WHAT'S UP IN *QUEEN'S QUALITY* THIS MONTH?
1) A DANCE HALL? IT LOOKS FUN.
2) THAT GRASS SURE GROWS FAST!
3) RANMARU, AFTER BREAKING SO MANY HEADS, YOU CAN'T SAY, "MY HAND SLIPPED."

KYUTARO AND RANMARU DO THEIR BEST, BUT THERE'S A SURPRISE AT THE END OF CHAPTER 55!

I WAS A RATHER DARK CHILD LIKE KYUTARO. I, TOO, WOULD OFTEN SIT AND WAIT FOR THE INSTANT A PLANT WOULD START TO GROW OR FOR A CHRYSALIS OR INSECT EGG TO HATCH. THAT WOULD ALWAYS HAPPEN IN THE DARK OF THE NIGHT...

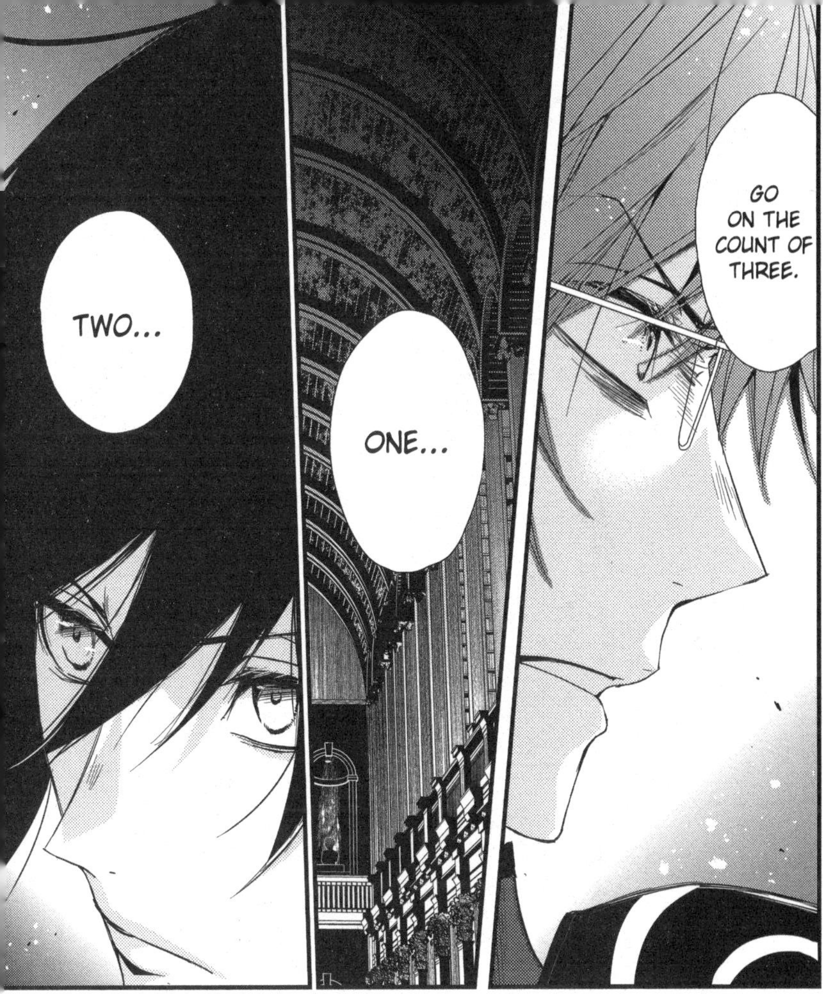
GO ON THE COUNT OF THREE.
ONE...
TWO...

What's Been Going On ②

I've been doing something called "morning pages" every day for over three months now. I just spend 10-15 minutes writing whatever comes to mind in a notebook. Since I started doing it, I seem to have gotten better at storyboarding. I strongly recommend it to anyone who tends to overthink things and has trouble moving forward (and that includes me).

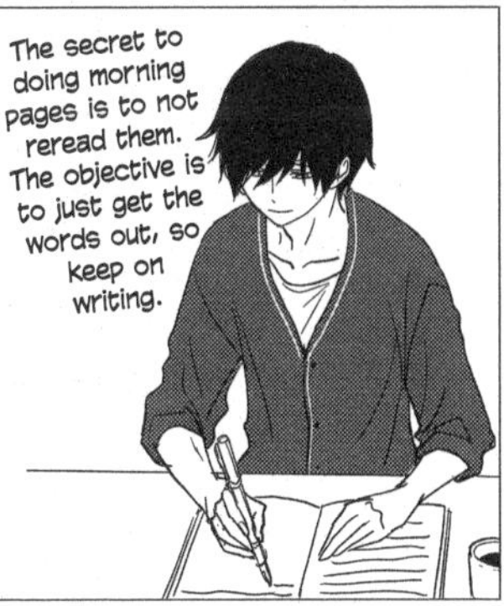
The secret to doing morning pages is to not reread them. The objective is to just get the words out, so keep on writing.

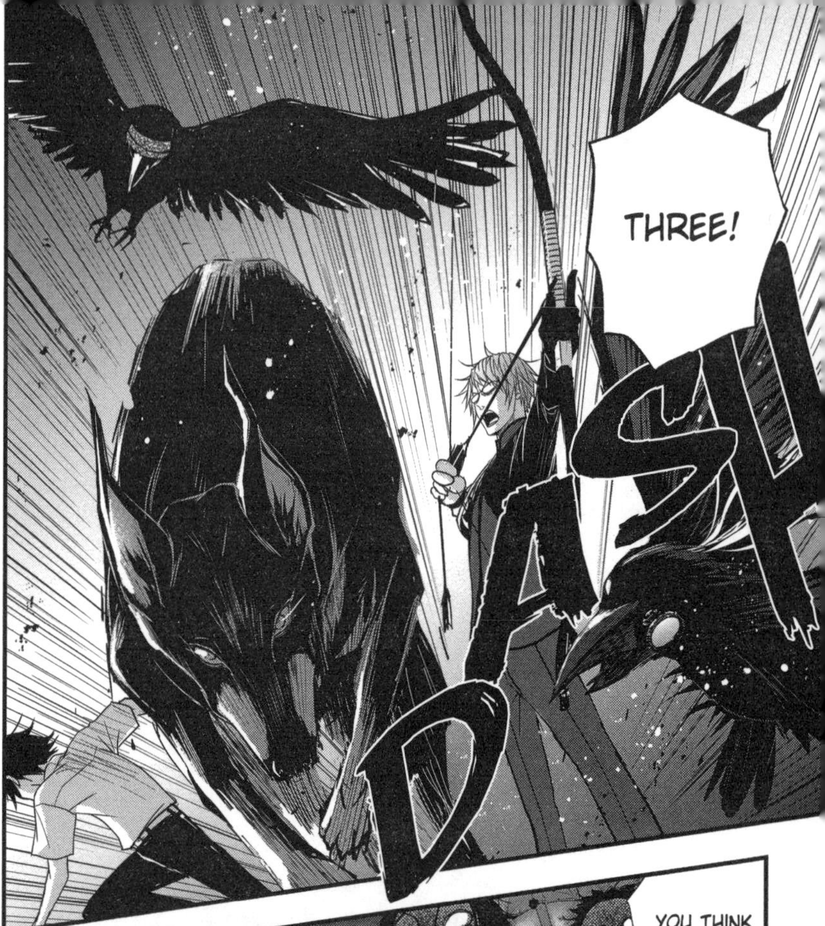
THREE!
DASH
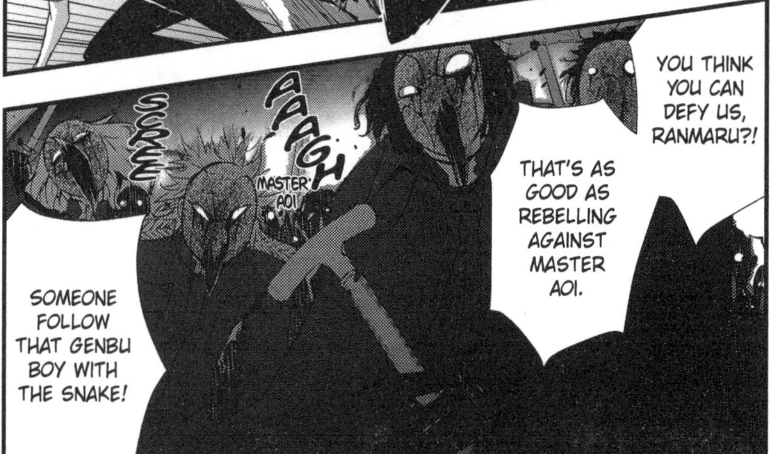
YOU THINK YOU CAN DEFY US, RANMARU?!
THAT'S AS GOOD AS REBELLING AGAINST MASTER AOI.
AAAGH
MASTER AOI
SCRAW
SOMEONE FOLLOW THAT GENBU BOY WITH THE SNAKE!

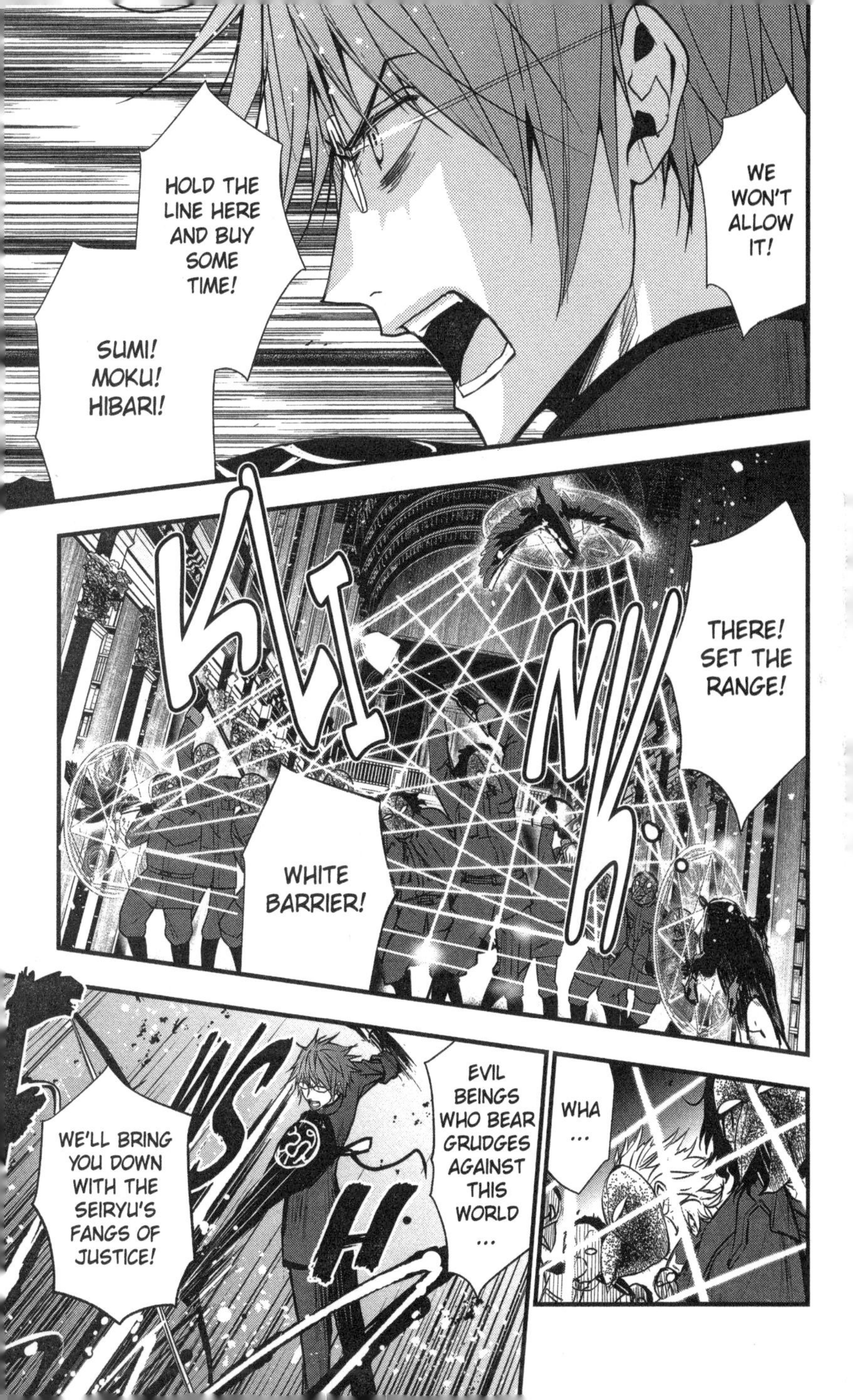
WE WON'T ALLOW IT!
HOLD THE LINE HERE AND BUY SOME TIME!
SUMI! MOKU! HIBARI!
THERE! SET THE RANGE!
KLINK
WHITE BARRIER!
WHA ...
EVIL BEINGS WHO BEAR GRUDGES AGAINST THIS WORLD ...
WSH
WE'LL BRING YOU DOWN WITH THE SEIRYU'S FANGS OF JUSTICE!

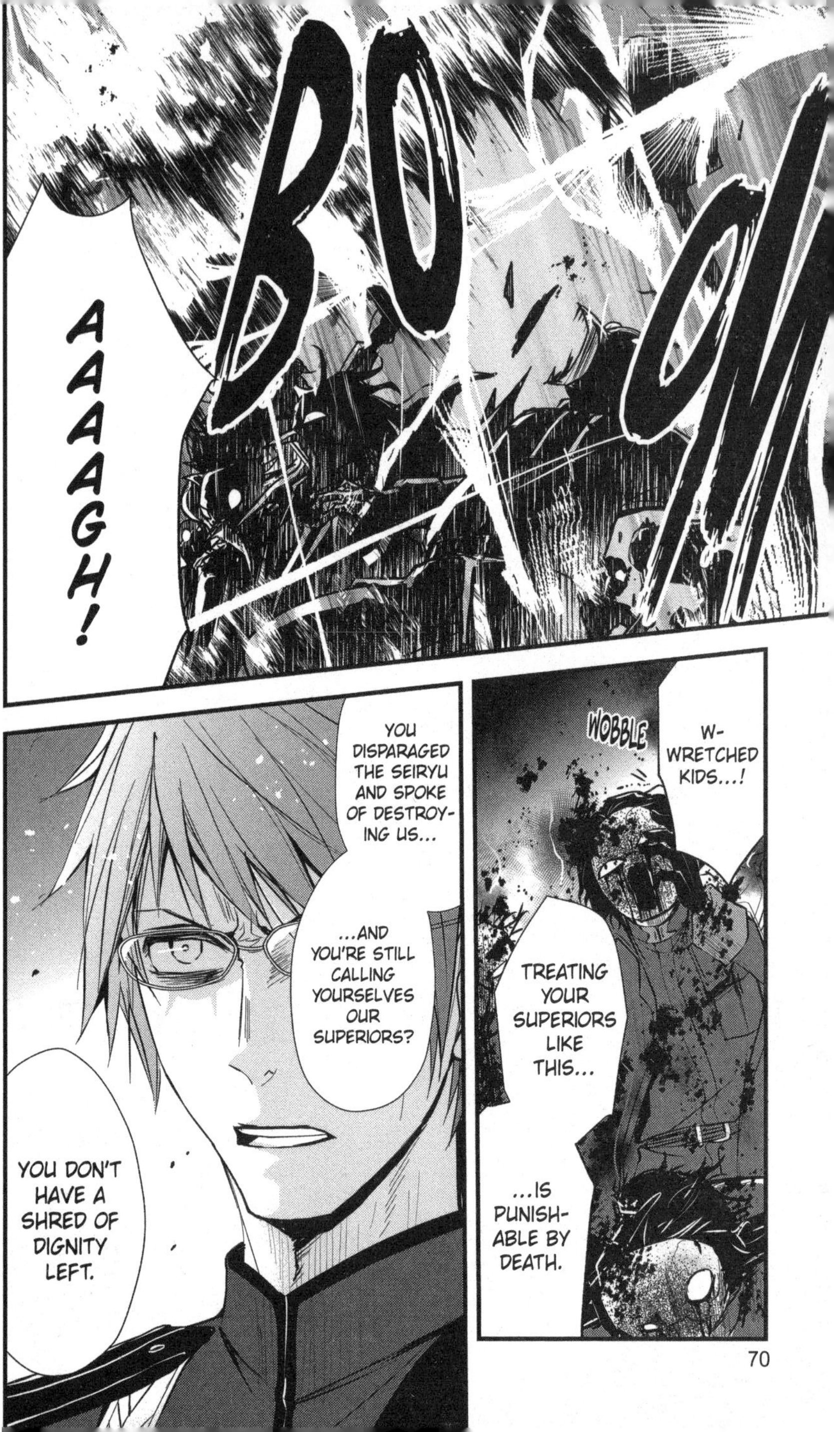
BOOM
AAAAAGH!
WOBBLE
W-WRETCHED KIDS...!
TREATING YOUR SUPERIORS LIKE THIS...
...IS PUNISHABLE BY DEATH.
YOU DISPARAGED THE SEIRYU AND SPOKE OF DESTROYING US...
...AND YOU'RE STILL CALLING YOURSELVES OUR SUPERIORS?
YOU DON'T HAVE A SHRED OF DIGNITY LEFT.

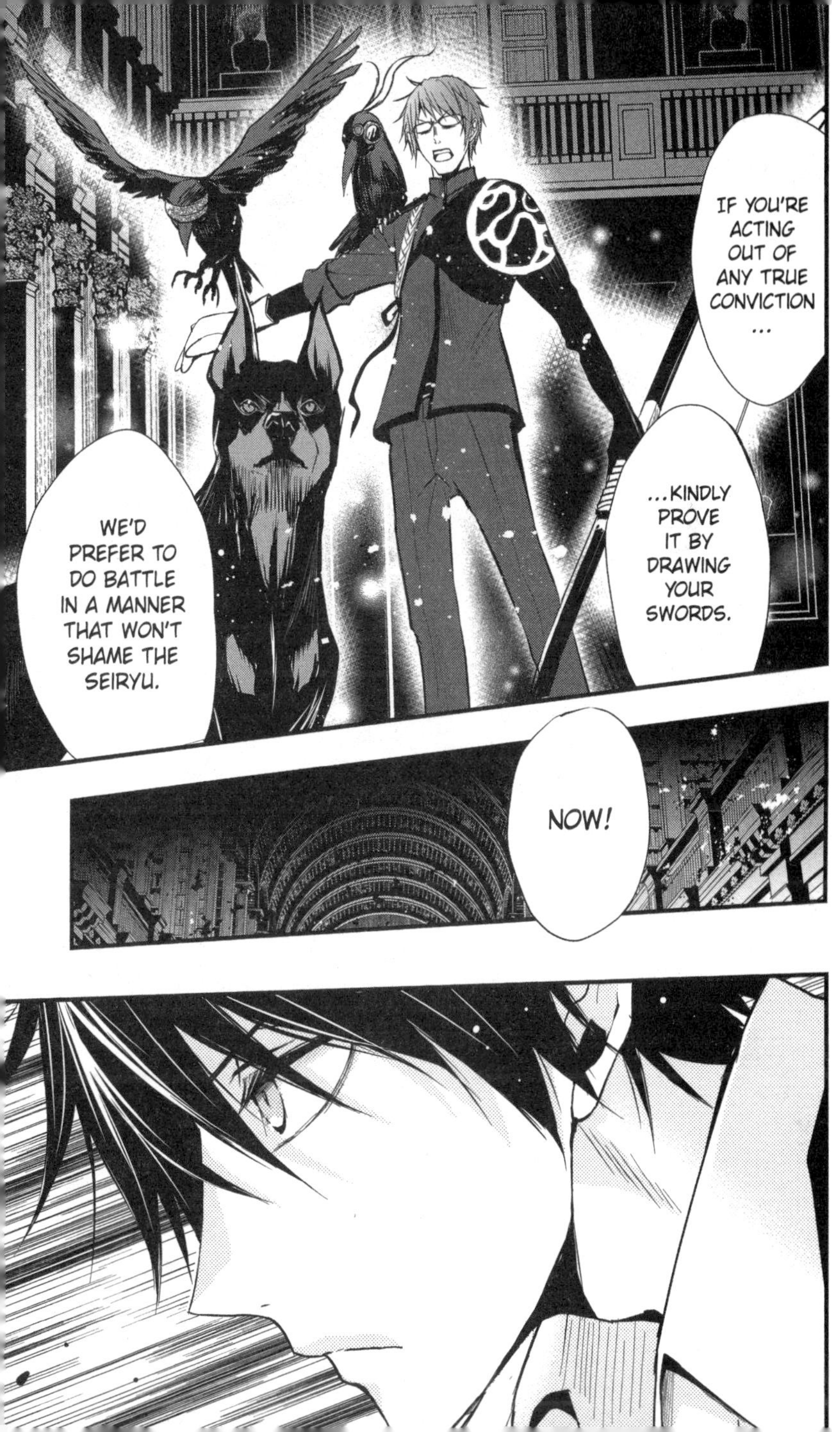
IF YOU'RE ACTING OUT OF ANY TRUE CONVICTION ...
...KINDLY PROVE IT BY DRAWING YOUR SWORDS.
WE'D PREFER TO DO BATTLE IN A MANNER THAT WON'T SHAME THE SEIRYU.
NOW!

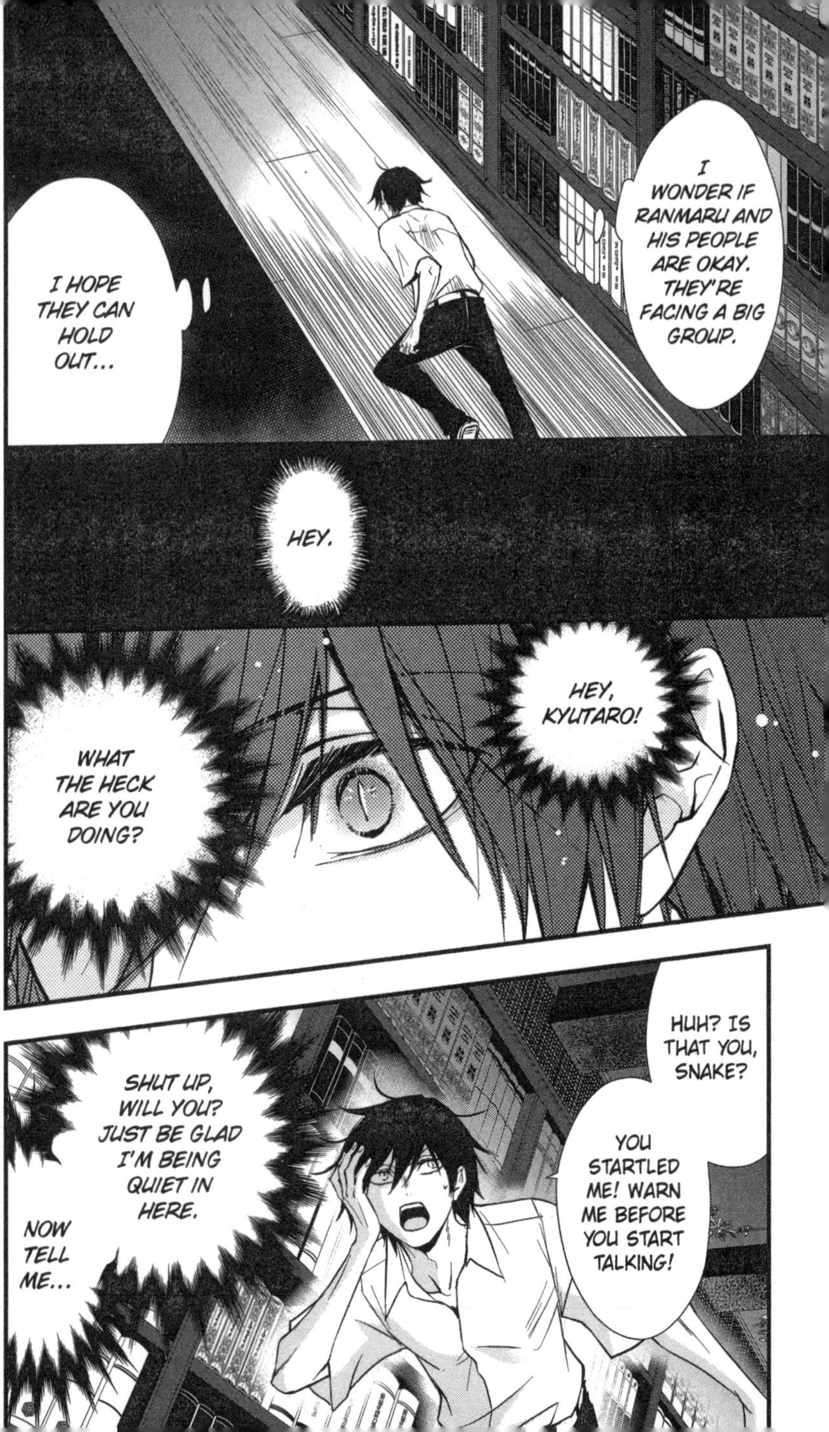
I WONDER IF RANMARU AND HIS PEOPLE ARE OKAY. THEY'RE FACING A BIG GROUP.
I HOPE THEY CAN HOLD OUT...
HEY.
HEY, KYUTARO!
WHAT THE HECK ARE YOU DOING?
HUH? IS THAT YOU, SNAKE?
YOU STARTLED ME! WARN ME BEFORE YOU START TALKING!
SHUT UP, WILL YOU? JUST BE GLAD I'M BEING QUIET IN HERE.
NOW TELL ME...

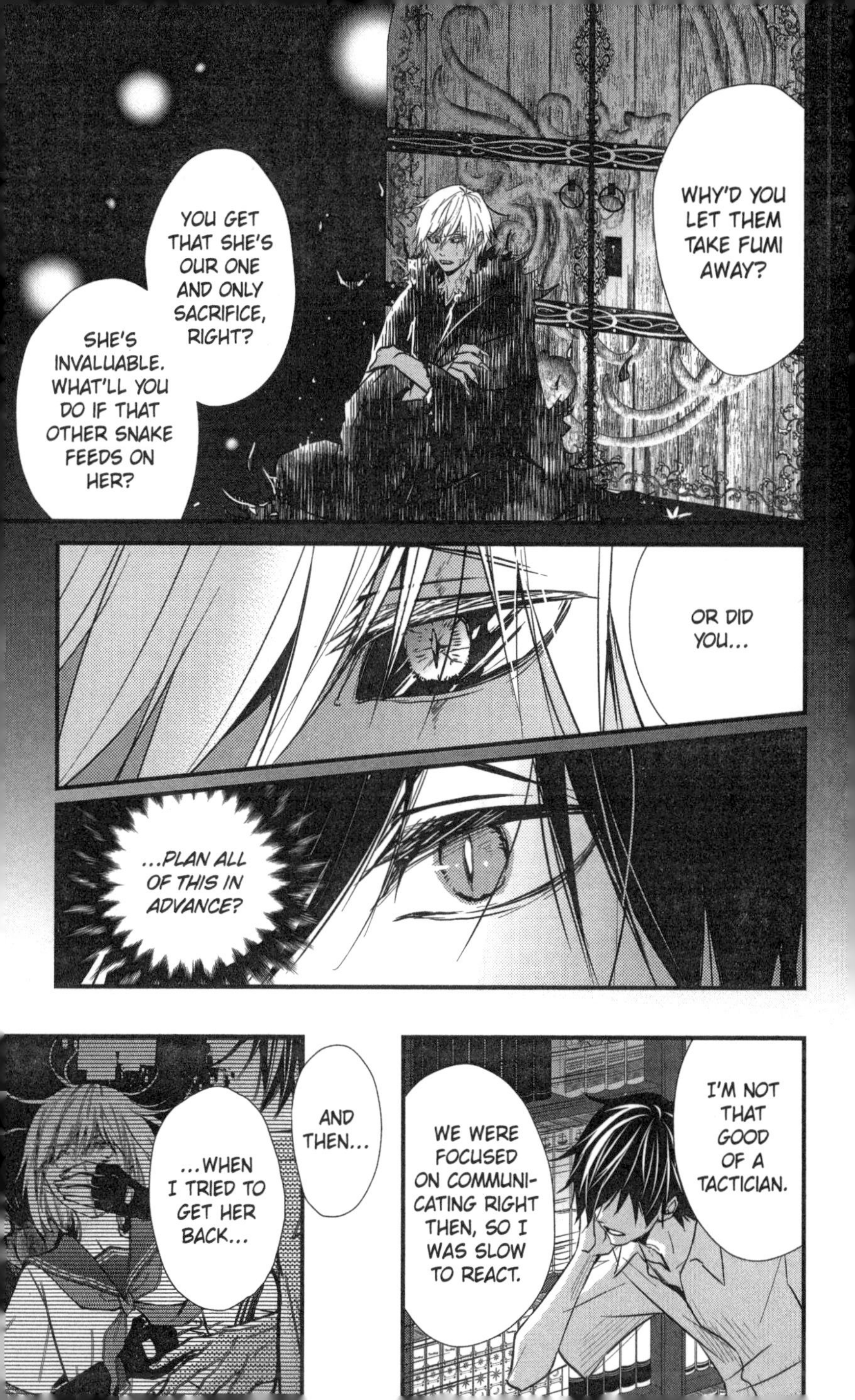
WHY'D YOU LET THEM TAKE FUMI AWAY?
YOU GET THAT SHE'S OUR ONE AND ONLY SACRIFICE, RIGHT?
SHE'S INVALUABLE. WHAT'LL YOU DO IF THAT OTHER SNAKE FEEDS ON HER?
OR DID YOU...
...PLAN ALL OF THIS IN ADVANCE?
I'M NOT THAT GOOD OF A TACTICIAN.
WE WERE FOCUSED ON COMMUNI-CATING RIGHT THEN, SO I WAS SLOW TO REACT.
AND THEN...
...WHEN I TRIED TO GET HER BACK...

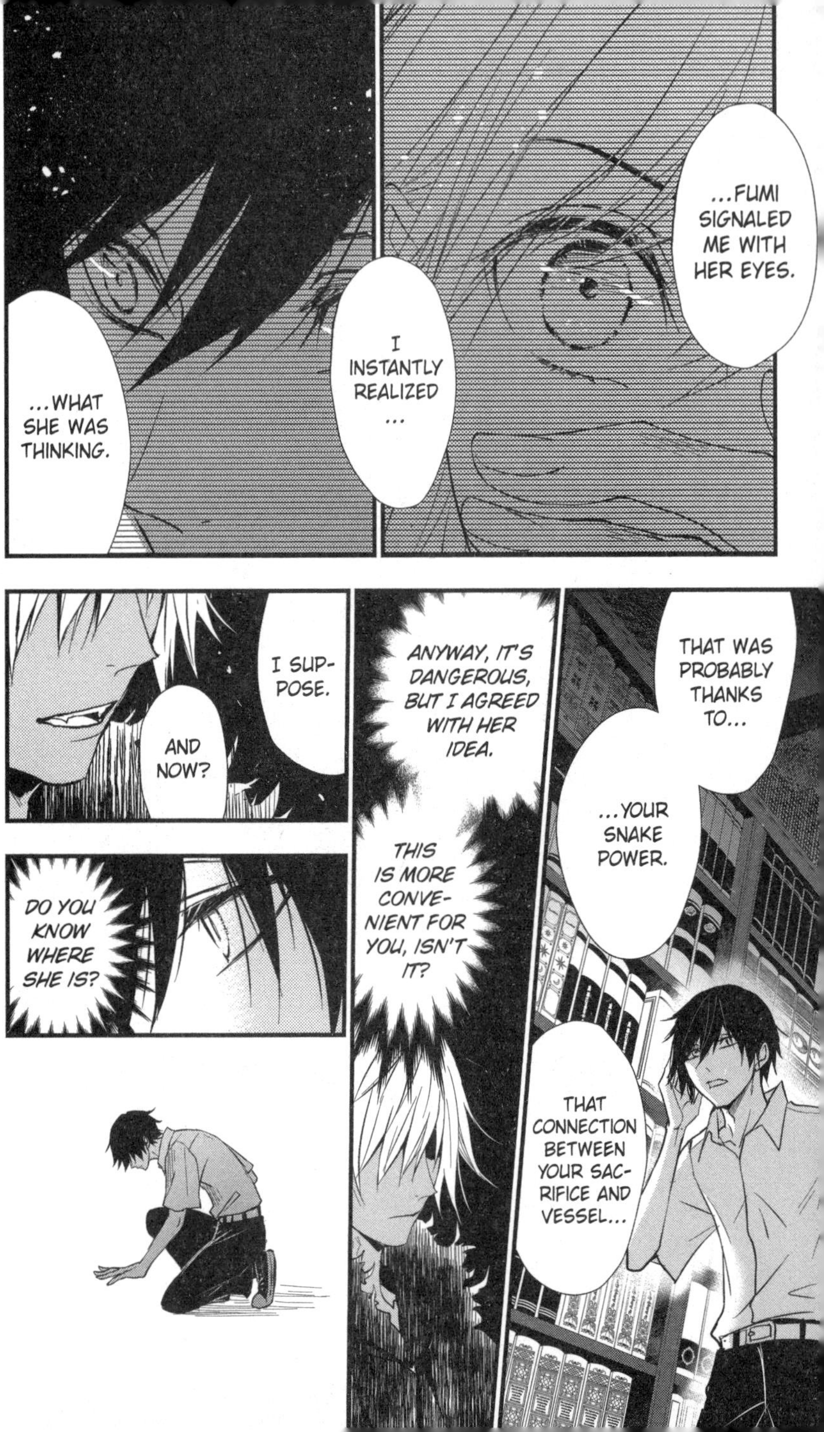
...FUMI SIGNALED ME WITH HER EYES.
I INSTANTLY REALIZED...
...WHAT SHE WAS THINKING.
THAT WAS PROBABLY THANKS TO...
...YOUR SNAKE POWER.
THAT CONNECTION BETWEEN YOUR SACRIFICE AND VESSEL...
ANYWAY, IT'S DANGEROUS, BUT I AGREED WITH HER IDEA.
THIS IS MORE CONVENIENT FOR YOU, ISN'T IT?
I SUPPOSE.
AND NOW?
DO YOU KNOW WHERE SHE IS?

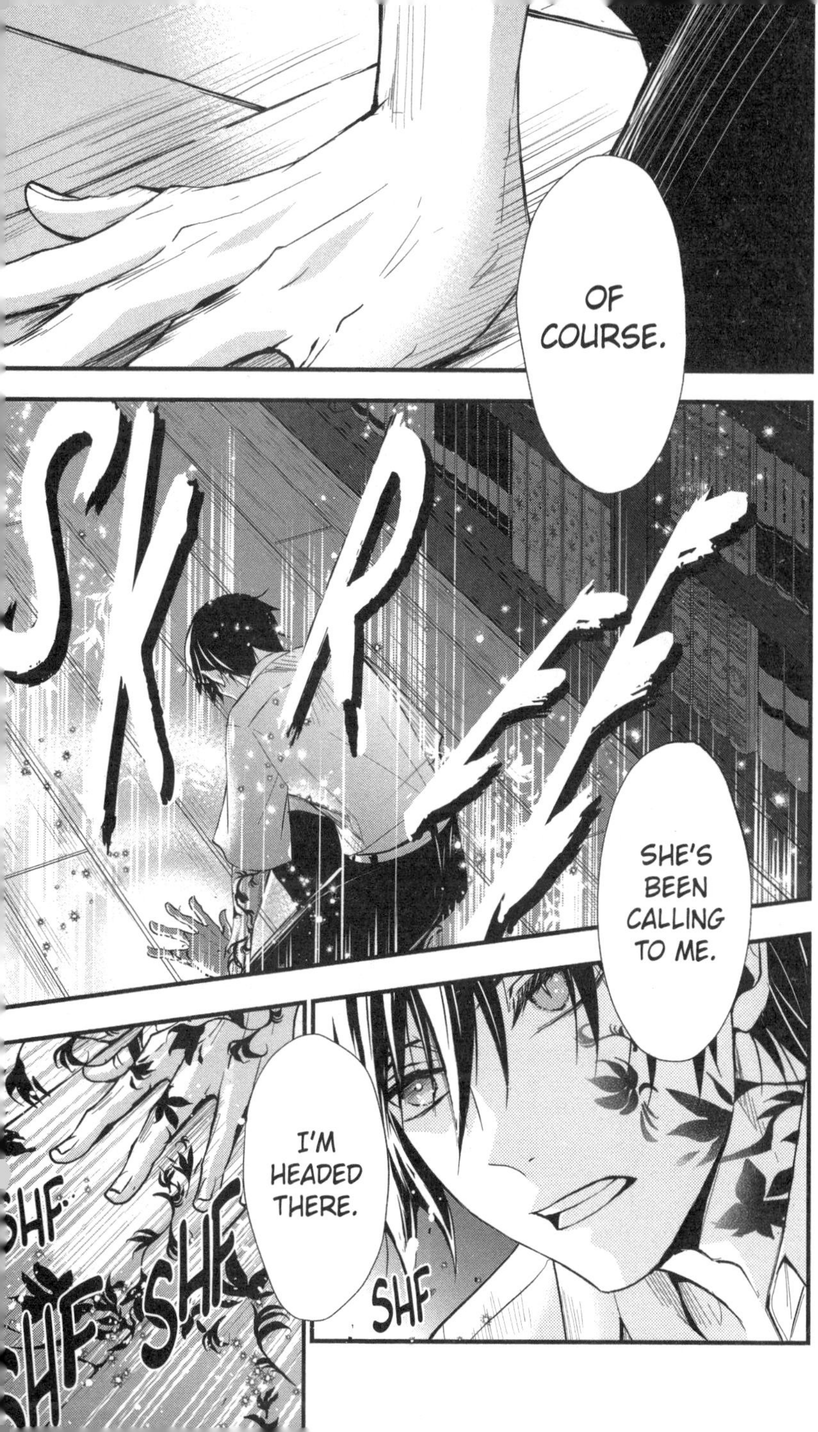
OF COURSE.
SHE'S BEEN CALLING TO ME.
I'M HEADED THERE.
SHF
SHF...
SHF
SHF
SHF

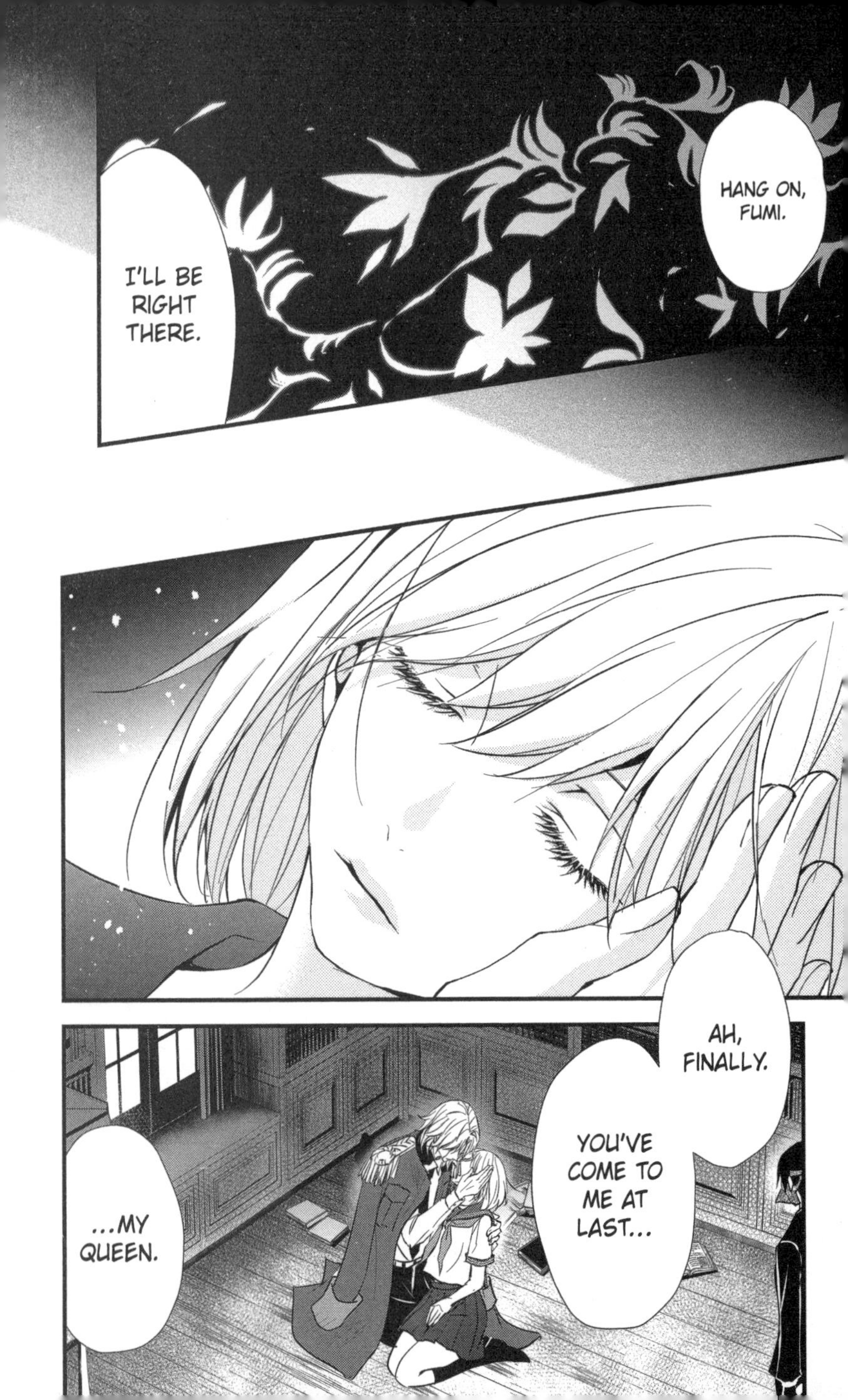
HANG ON, FUMI.
I'LL BE RIGHT THERE.
AH, FINALLY.
YOU'VE COME TO ME AT LAST...
...MY QUEEN.

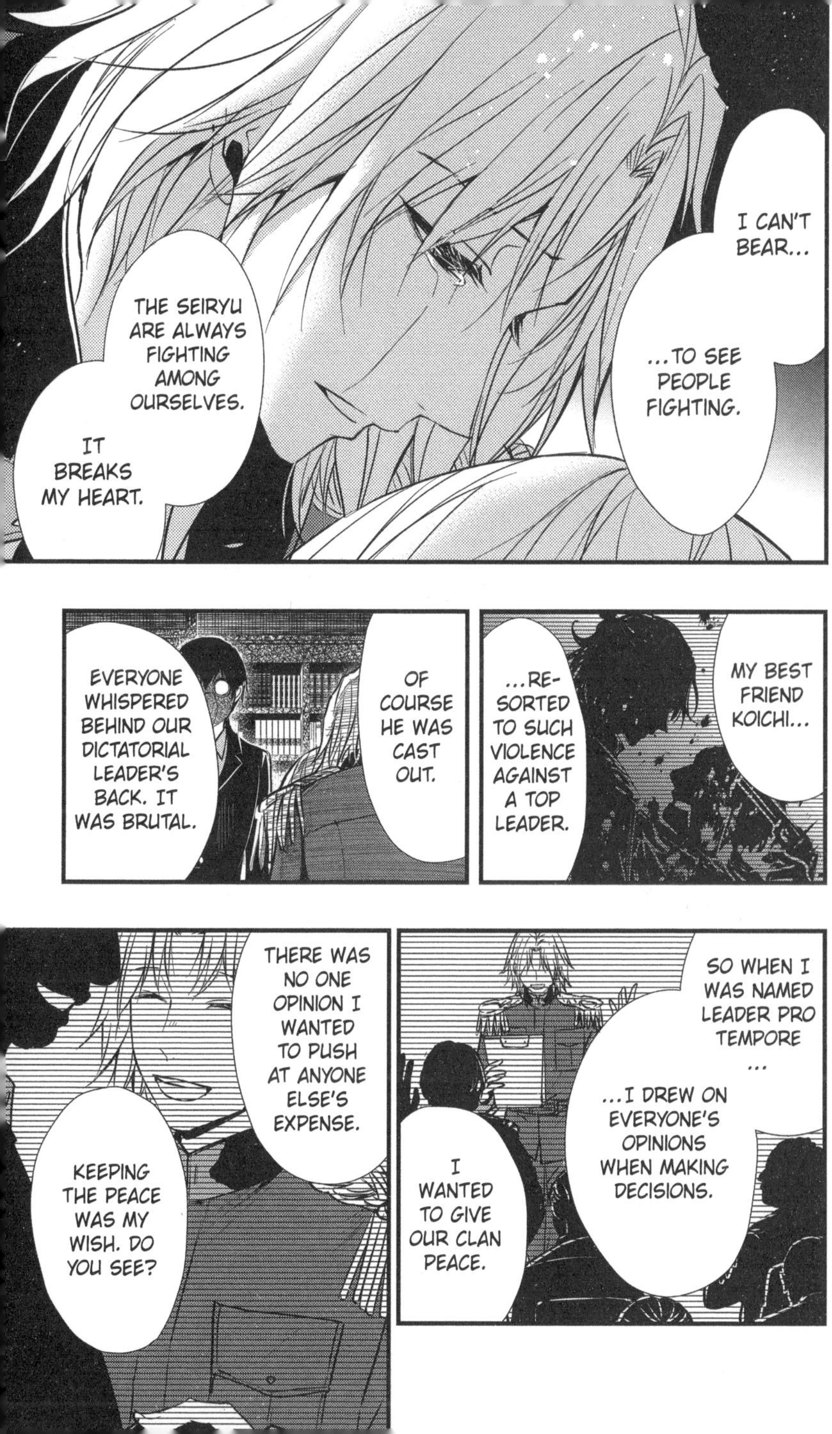
I CAN'T BEAR...
...TO SEE PEOPLE FIGHTING.
THE SEIRYU ARE ALWAYS FIGHTING AMONG OURSELVES.
IT BREAKS MY HEART.
MY BEST FRIEND KOICHI...
...RE-SORTED TO SUCH VIOLENCE AGAINST A TOP LEADER.
OF COURSE HE WAS CAST OUT.
EVERYONE WHISPERED BEHIND OUR DICTATORIAL LEADER'S BACK. IT WAS BRUTAL.
SO WHEN I WAS NAMED LEADER PRO TEMPORE...
...I DREW ON EVERYONE'S OPINIONS WHEN MAKING DECISIONS.
I WANTED TO GIVE OUR CLAN PEACE.
THERE WAS NO ONE OPINION I WANTED TO PUSH AT ANYONE ELSE'S EXPENSE.
KEEPING THE PEACE WAS MY WISH. DO YOU SEE?

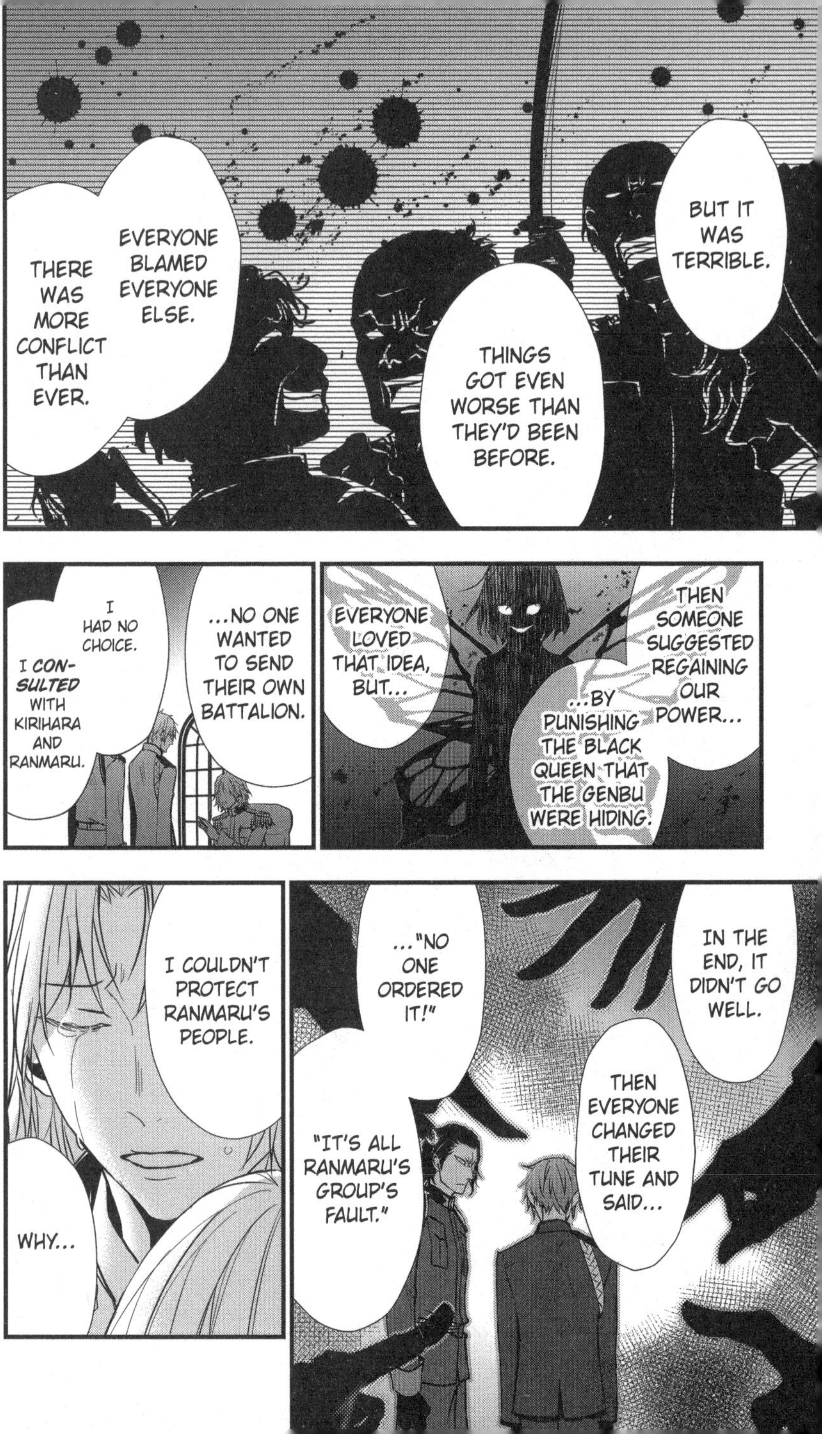
BUT IT WAS TERRIBLE.
THINGS GOT EVEN WORSE THAN THEY'D BEEN BEFORE.
EVERYONE BLAMED EVERYONE ELSE.
THERE WAS MORE CONFLICT THAN EVER.
THEN SOMEONE SUGGESTED REGAINING OUR POWER...
...BY PUNISHING THE BLACK QUEEN THAT THE GENBU WERE HIDING.
EVERYONE LOVED THAT IDEA, BUT...
...NO ONE WANTED TO SEND THEIR OWN BATTALION.
I HAD NO CHOICE.
I ***CONSULTED*** WITH KIRIHARA AND RANMARU.
IN THE END, IT DIDN'T GO WELL.
THEN EVERYONE CHANGED THEIR TUNE AND SAID...
..."NO ONE ORDERED IT!"
"IT'S ALL RANMARU'S GROUP'S FAULT."
I COULDN'T PROTECT RANMARU'S PEOPLE.
WHY...

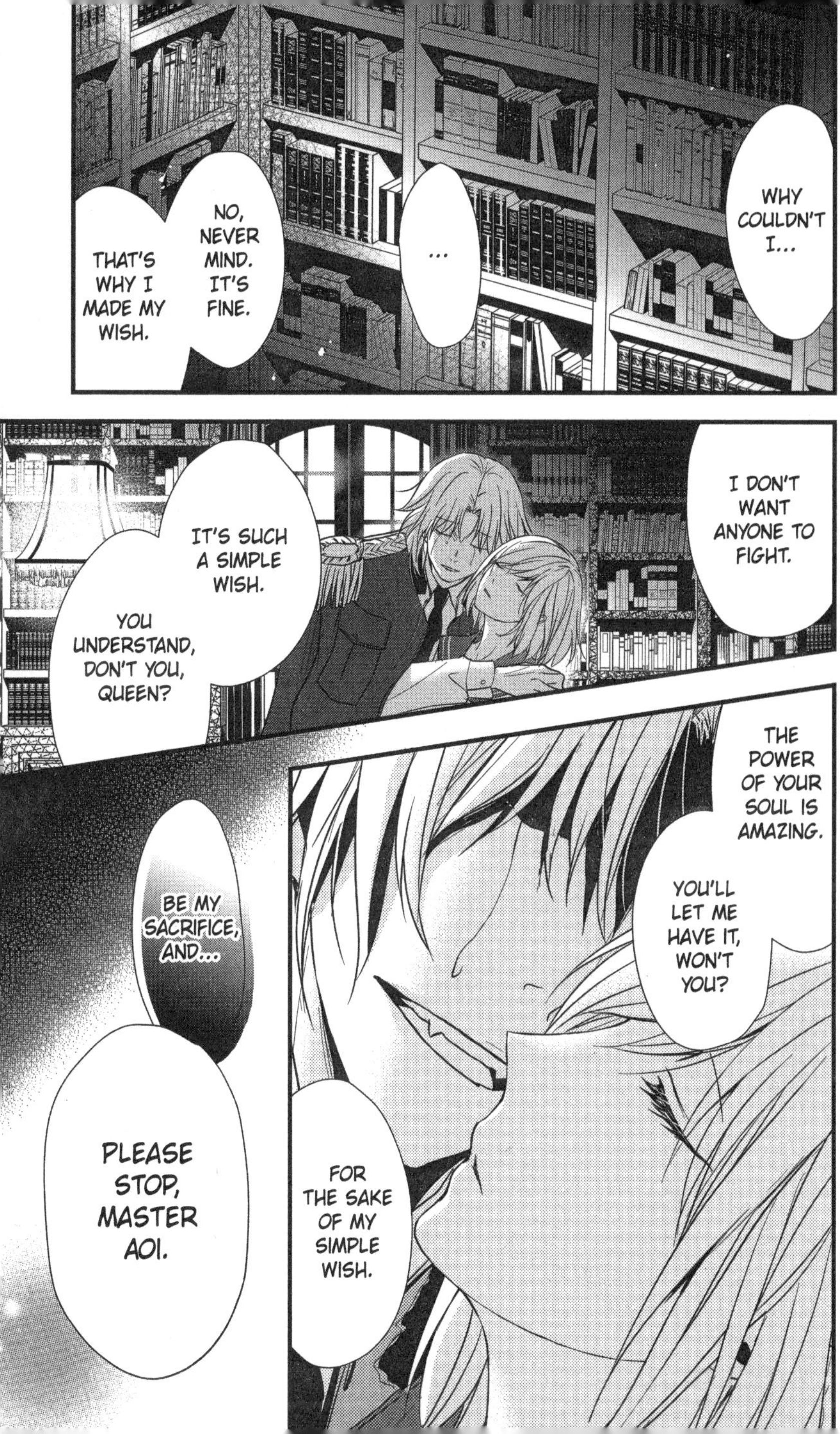
WHY COULDN'T I...
...
NO, NEVER MIND. IT'S FINE.
THAT'S WHY I MADE MY WISH.
I DON'T WANT ANYONE TO FIGHT.
IT'S SUCH A SIMPLE WISH.
YOU UNDERSTAND, DON'T YOU, QUEEN?
THE POWER OF YOUR SOUL IS AMAZING.
YOU'LL LET ME HAVE IT, WON'T YOU?
BE MY SACRIFICE, AND...
FOR THE SAKE OF MY SIMPLE WISH.
PLEASE STOP, MASTER AOI.

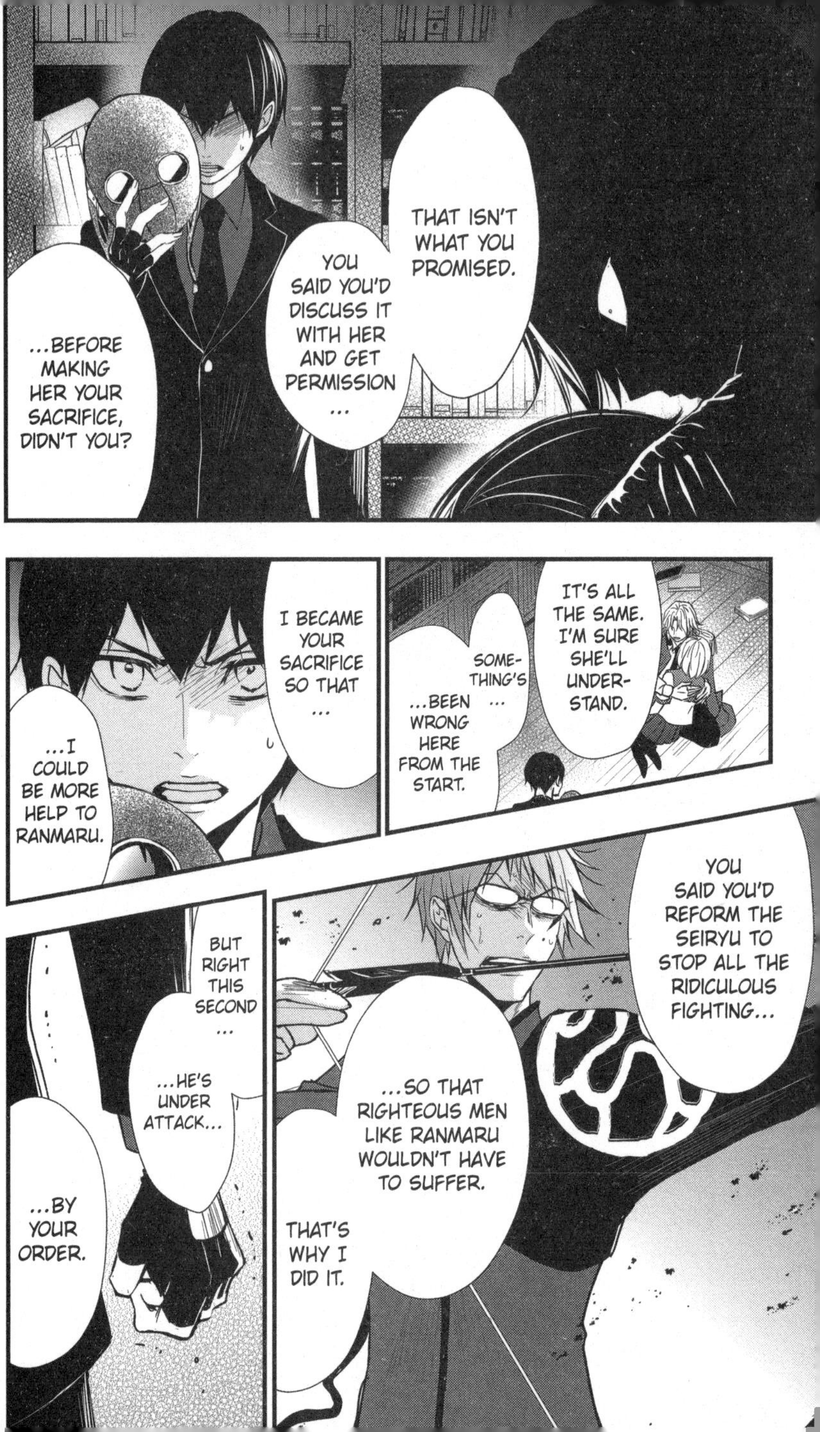
THAT ISN'T WHAT YOU PROMISED.
YOU SAID YOU'D DISCUSS IT WITH HER AND GET PERMISSION ...
...BEFORE MAKING HER YOUR SACRIFICE, DIDN'T YOU?
IT'S ALL THE SAME. I'M SURE SHE'LL UNDER-STAND.
SOME-THING'S ...
...BEEN WRONG HERE FROM THE START.
I BECAME YOUR SACRIFICE SO THAT ...
...I COULD BE MORE HELP TO RANMARU.
YOU SAID YOU'D REFORM THE SEIRYU TO STOP ALL THE RIDICULOUS FIGHTING...
...SO THAT RIGHTEOUS MEN LIKE RANMARU WOULDN'T HAVE TO SUFFER.
THAT'S WHY I DID IT.
BUT RIGHT THIS SECOND ...
...HE'S UNDER ATTACK...
...BY YOUR ORDER.

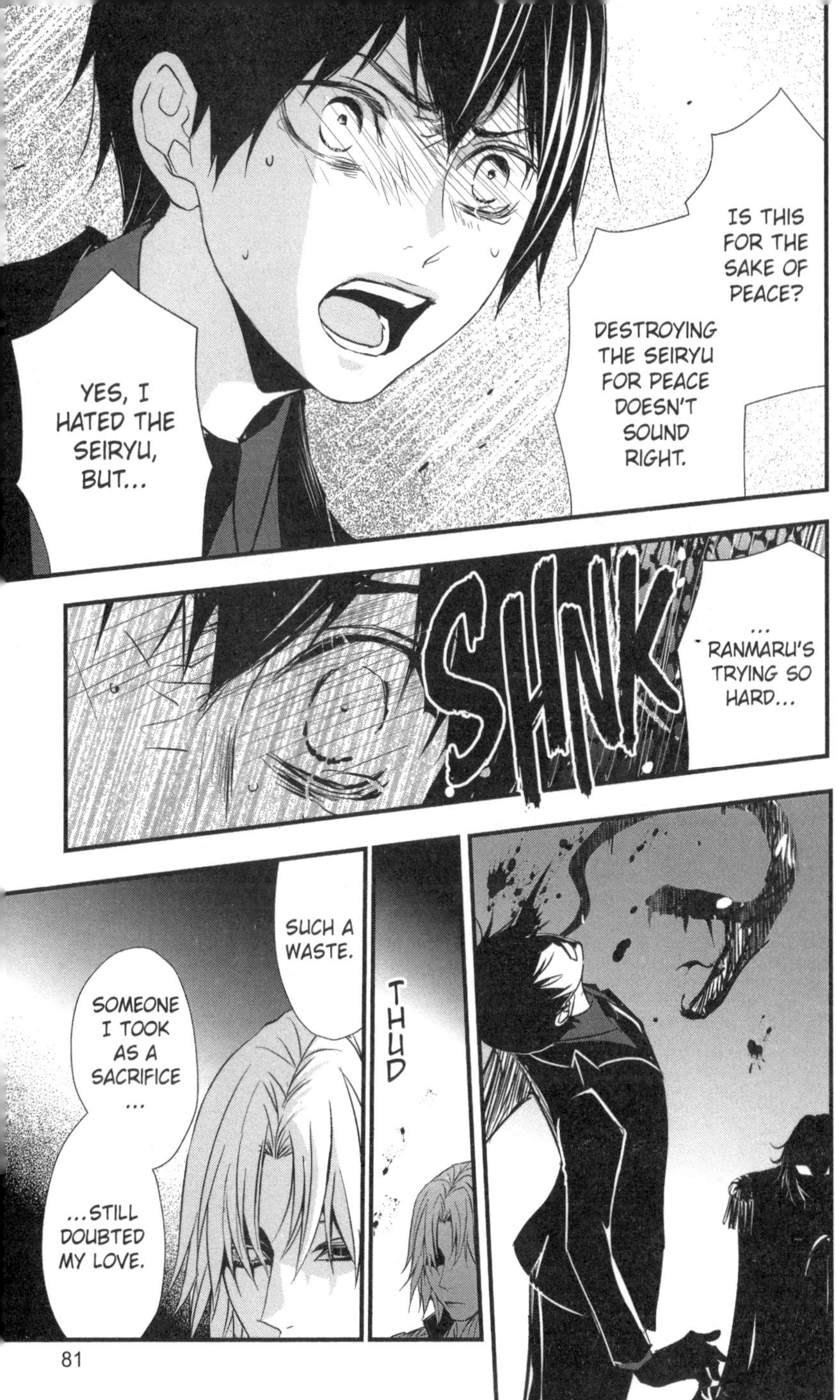
IS THIS FOR THE SAKE OF PEACE?
DESTROYING THE SEIRYU FOR PEACE DOESN'T SOUND RIGHT.
YES, I HATED THE SEIRYU, BUT...
... RANMARU'S TRYING SO HARD...
SHNK
THUD
SUCH A WASTE.
SOMEONE I TOOK AS A SACRIFICE ...
...STILL DOUBTED MY LOVE.

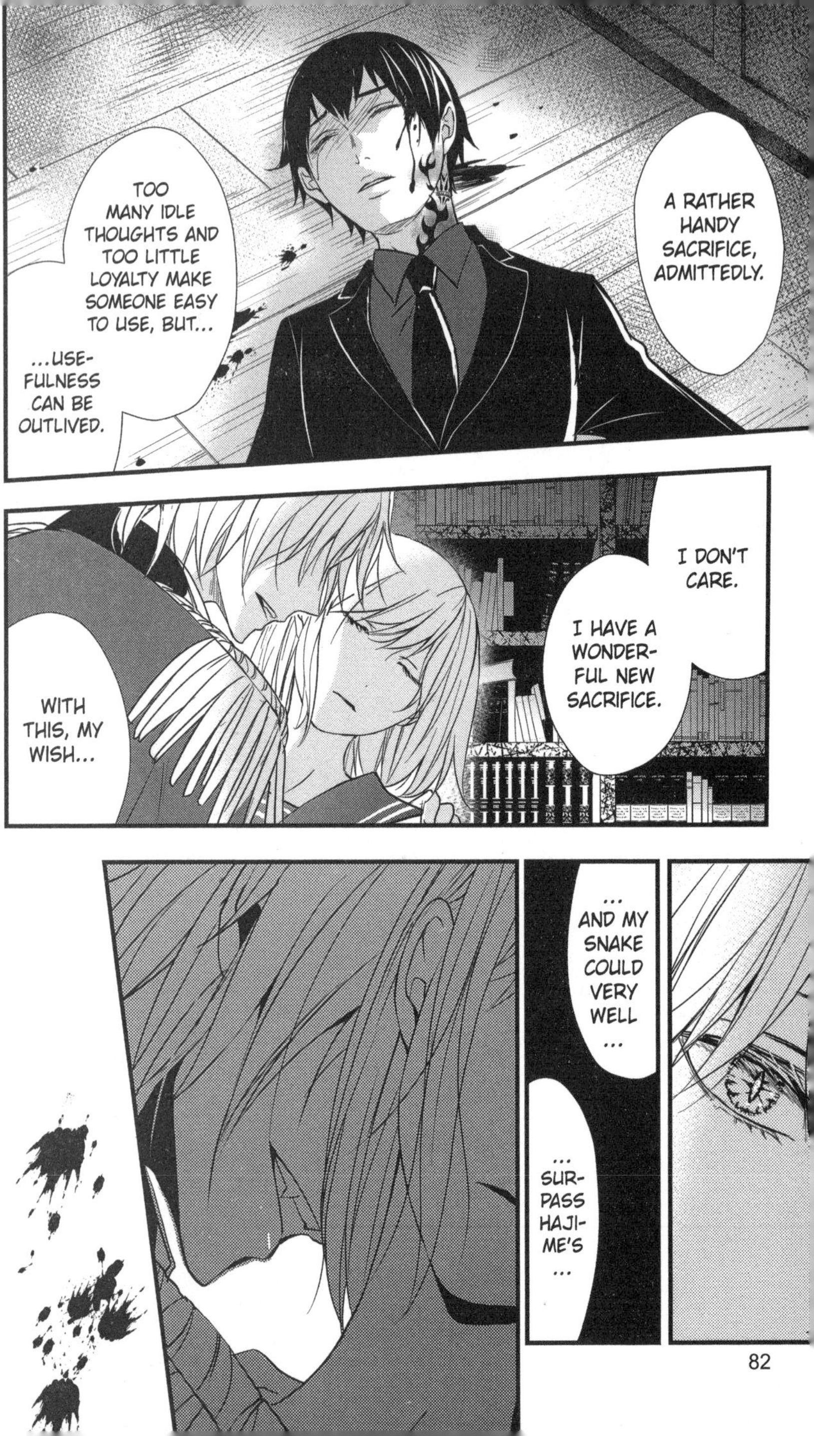
A RATHER HANDY SACRIFICE, ADMITTEDLY.
TOO MANY IDLE THOUGHTS AND TOO LITTLE LOYALTY MAKE SOMEONE EASY TO USE, BUT...
...USE-FULNESS CAN BE OUTLIVED.
I DON'T CARE.
I HAVE A WONDER-FUL NEW SACRIFICE.
WITH THIS, MY WISH...
... AND MY SNAKE COULD VERY WELL ...
... SUR-PASS HAJI-ME'S ...

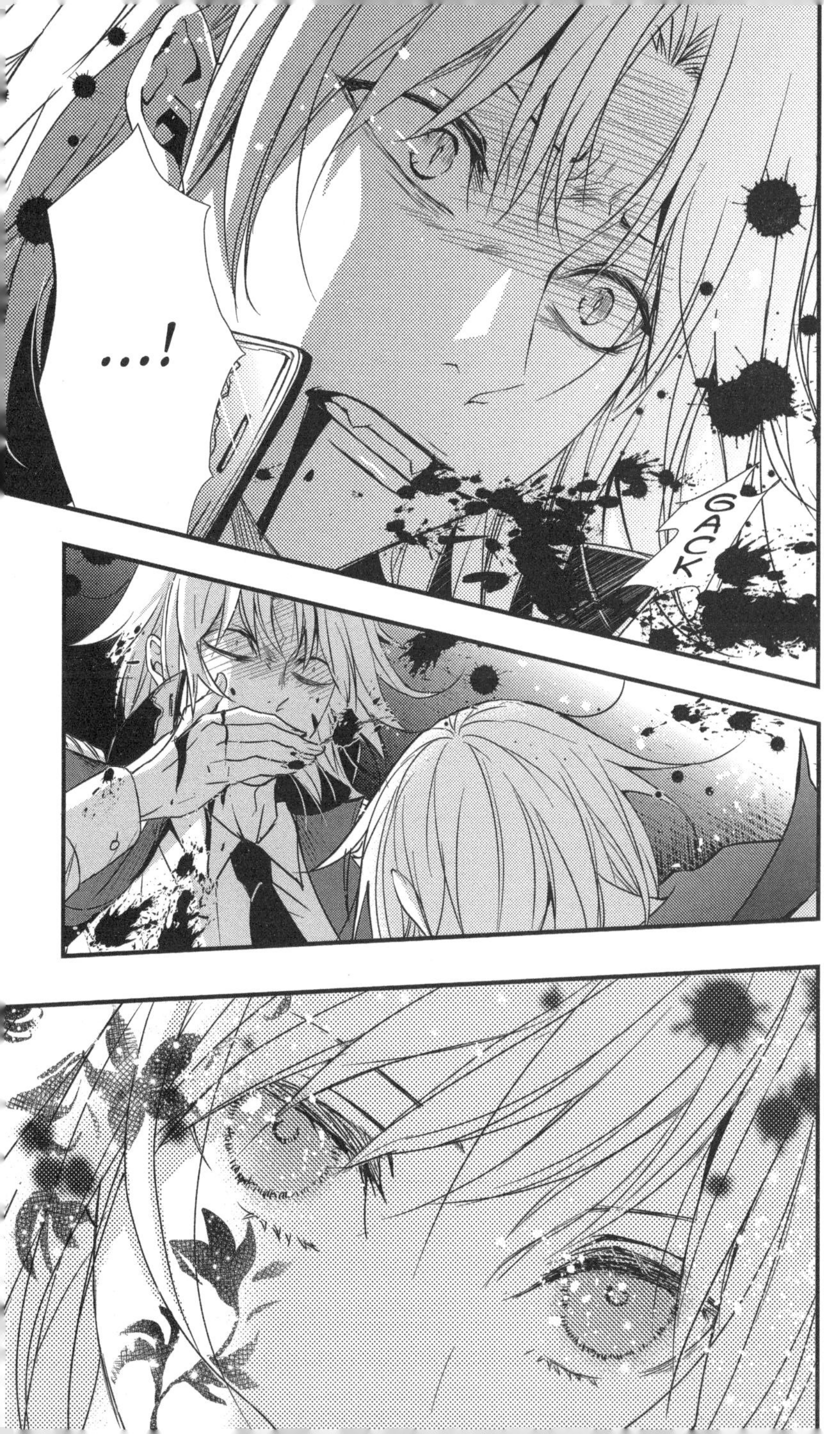
...!
GACK

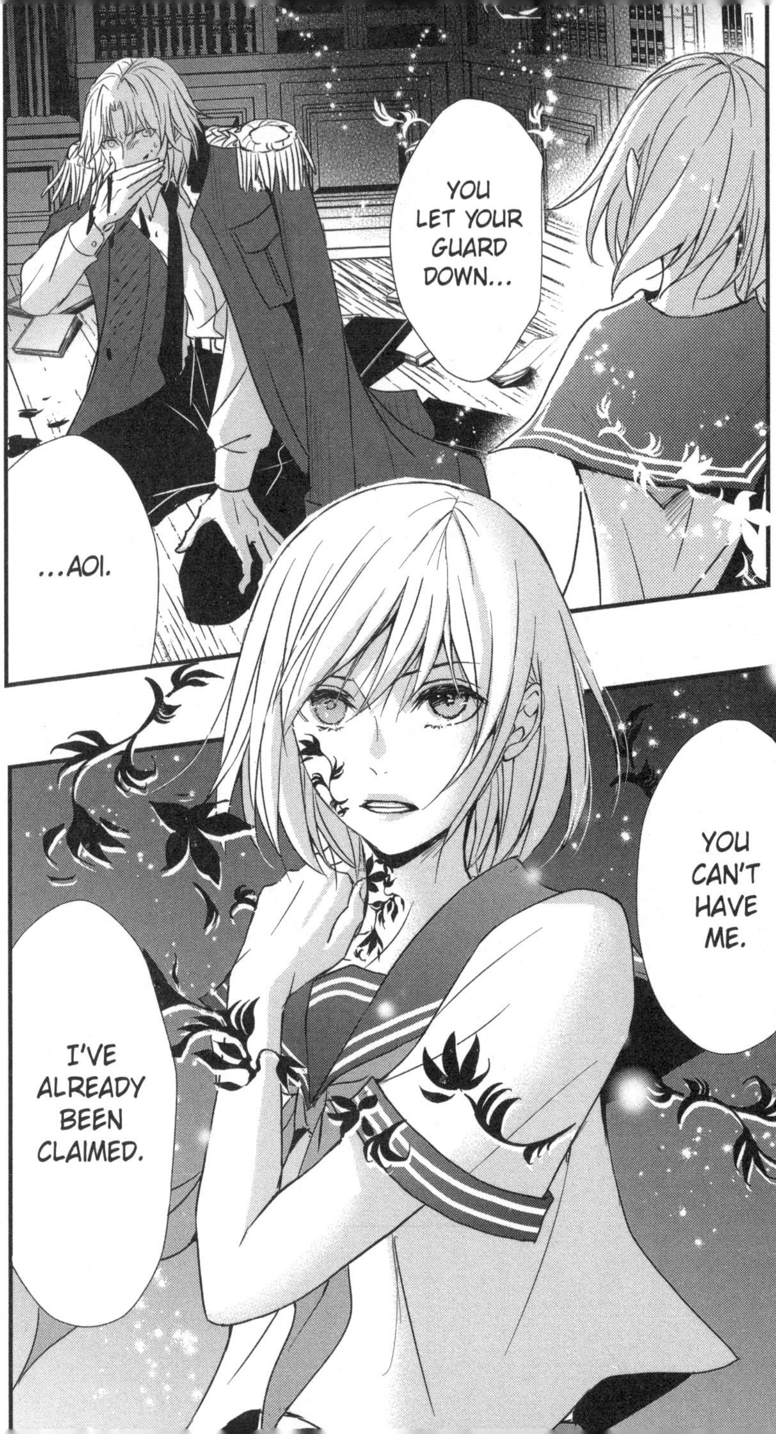
YOU LET YOUR GUARD DOWN...
...AOI.
YOU CAN'T HAVE ME.
I'VE ALREADY BEEN CLAIMED.

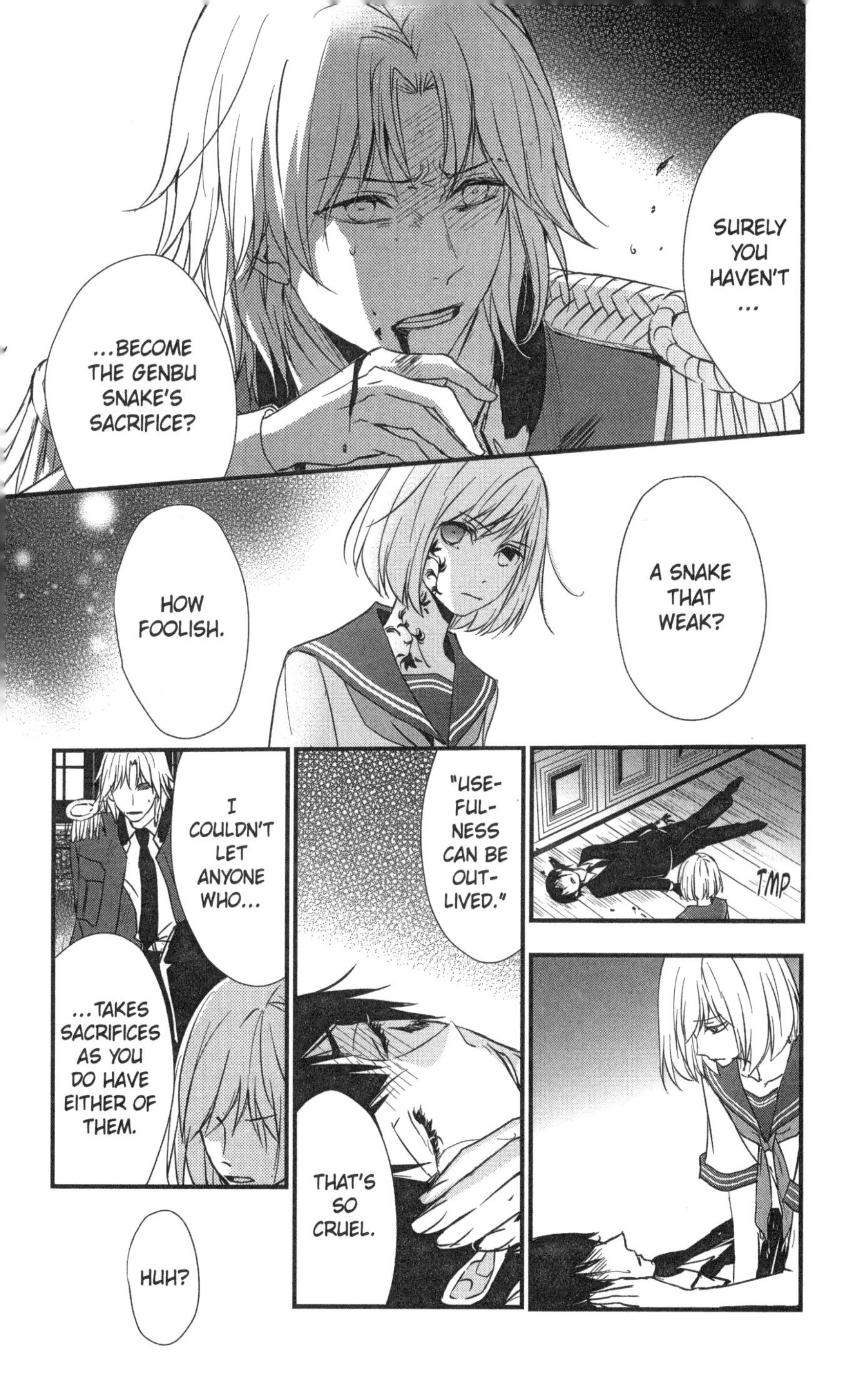
SURELY YOU HAVEN'T ...
...BECOME THE GENBU SNAKE'S SACRIFICE?
A SNAKE THAT WEAK?
HOW FOOLISH.
TMP
"USE-FUL-NESS CAN BE OUT-LIVED."
THAT'S SO CRUEL.
I COULDN'T LET ANYONE WHO...
...TAKES SACRIFICES AS YOU DO HAVE EITHER OF THEM.
HUH?

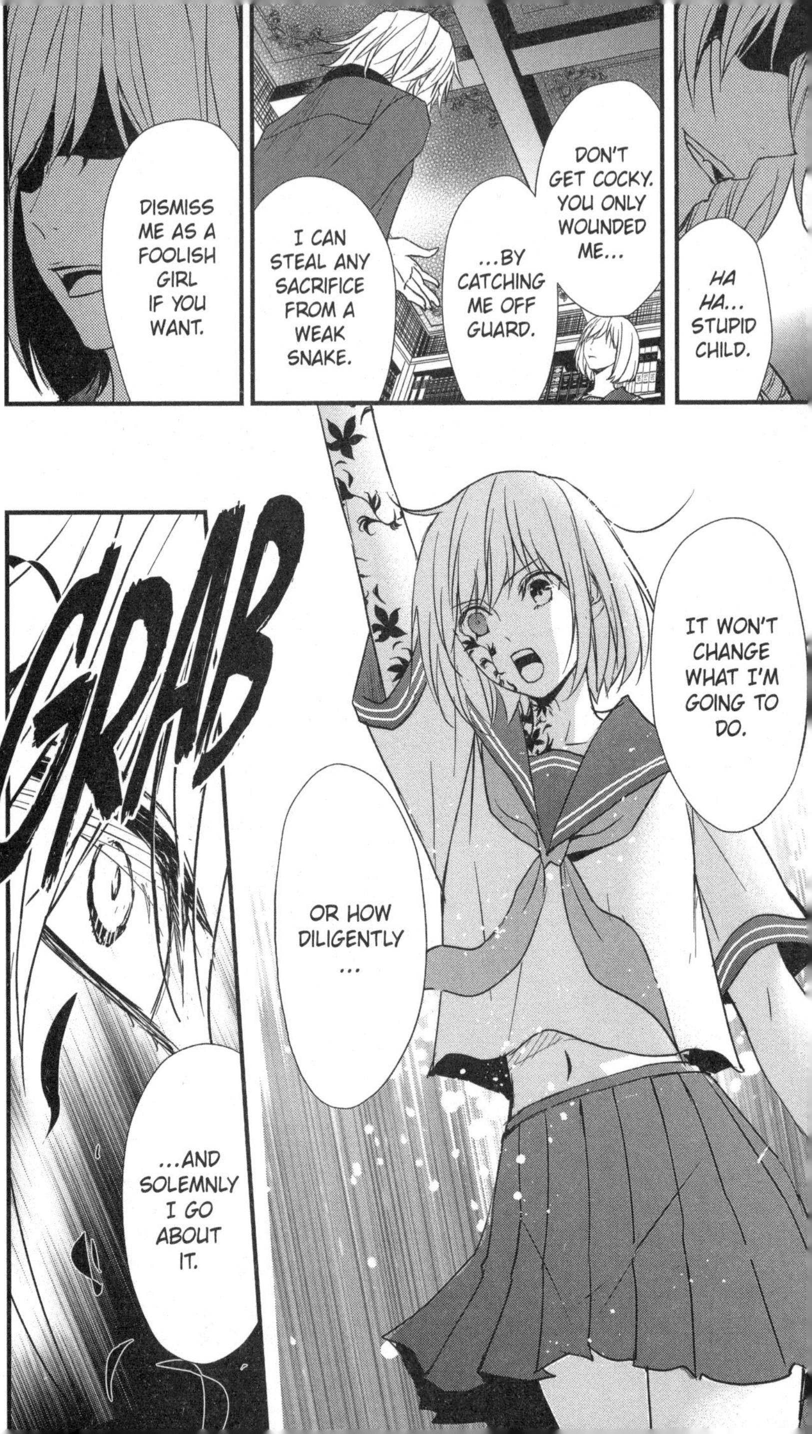
HA HA... STUPID CHILD.
DON'T GET COCKY. YOU ONLY WOUNDED ME...
...BY CATCHING ME OFF GUARD.
I CAN STEAL ANY SACRIFICE FROM A WEAK SNAKE.
DISMISS ME AS A FOOLISH GIRL IF YOU WANT.
IT WON'T CHANGE WHAT I'M GOING TO DO.
OR HOW DILIGENTLY ...
...AND SOLEMNLY I GO ABOUT IT.
GRAB

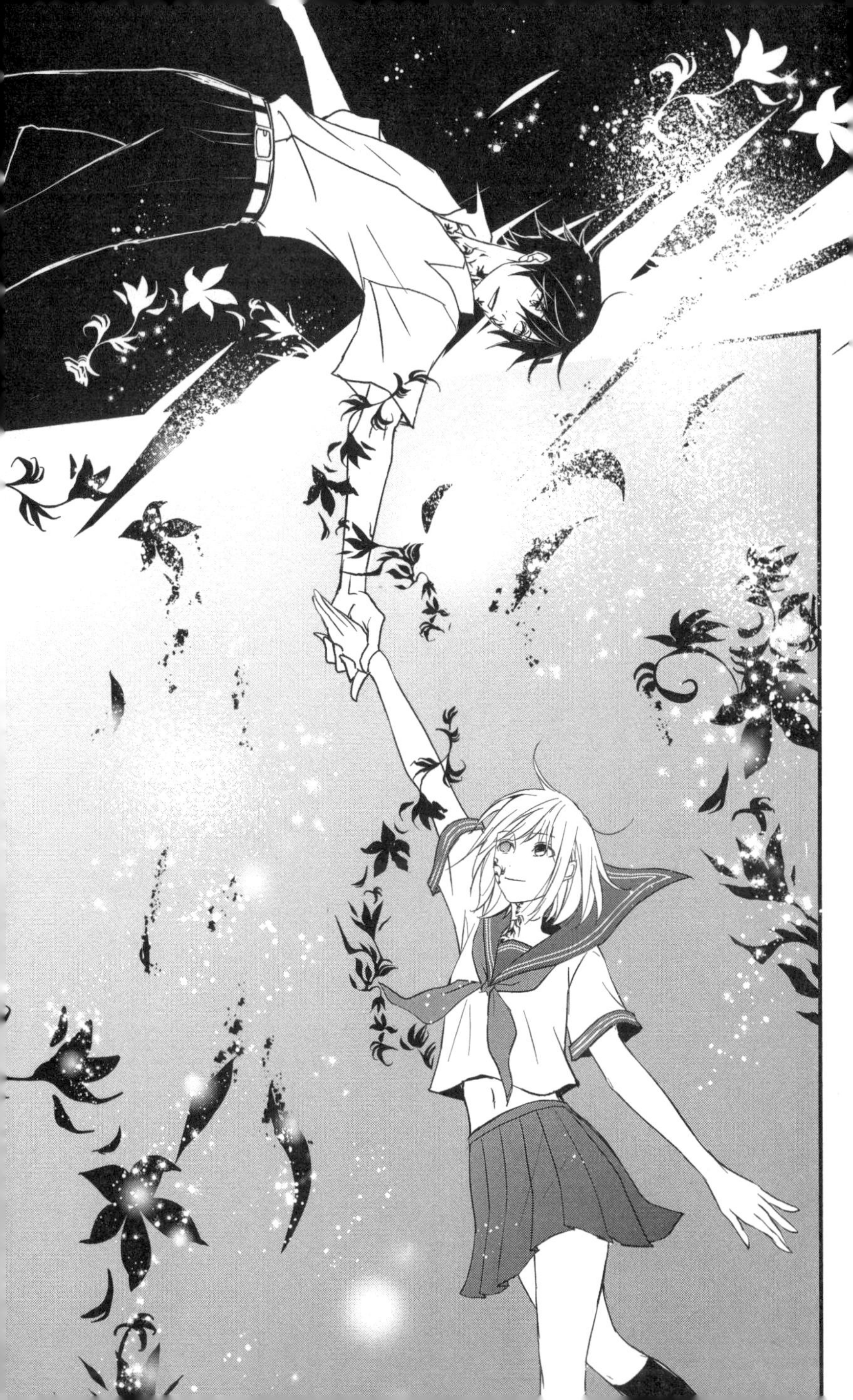

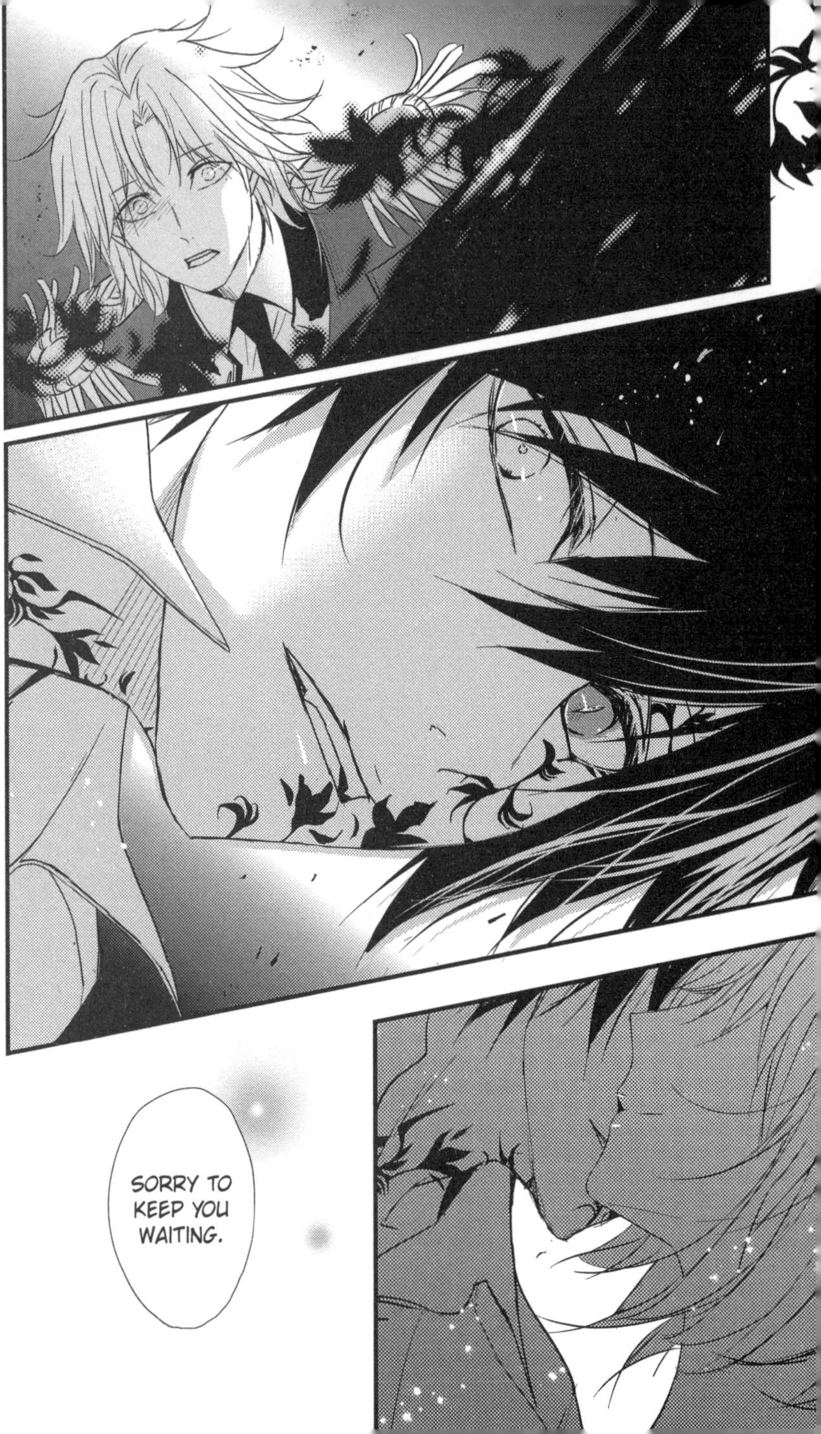
SORRY TO KEEP YOU WAITING.

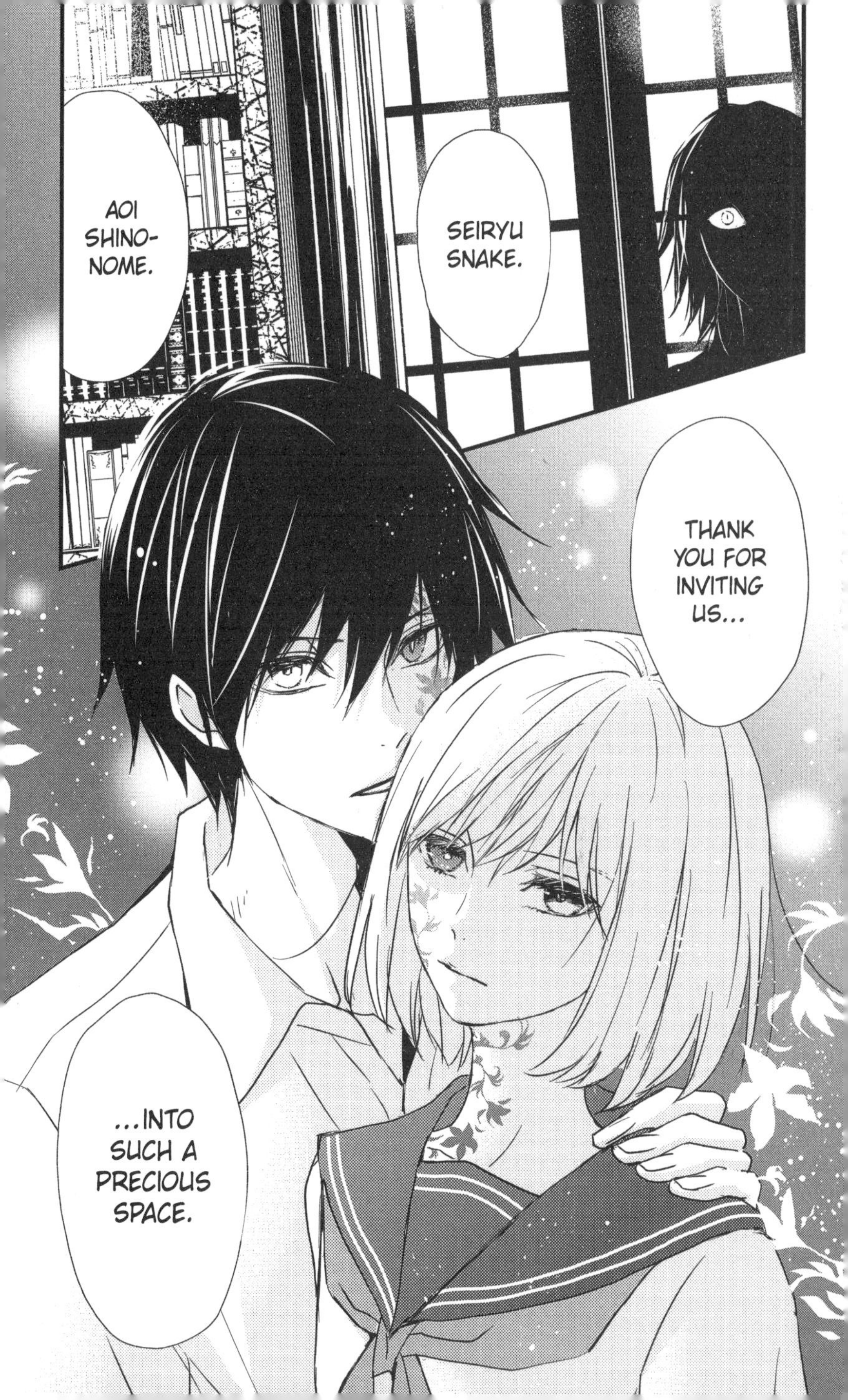
SEIRYU SNAKE.
AOI SHINONOME.
THANK YOU FOR INVITING US...
...INTO SUCH A PRECIOUS SPACE.

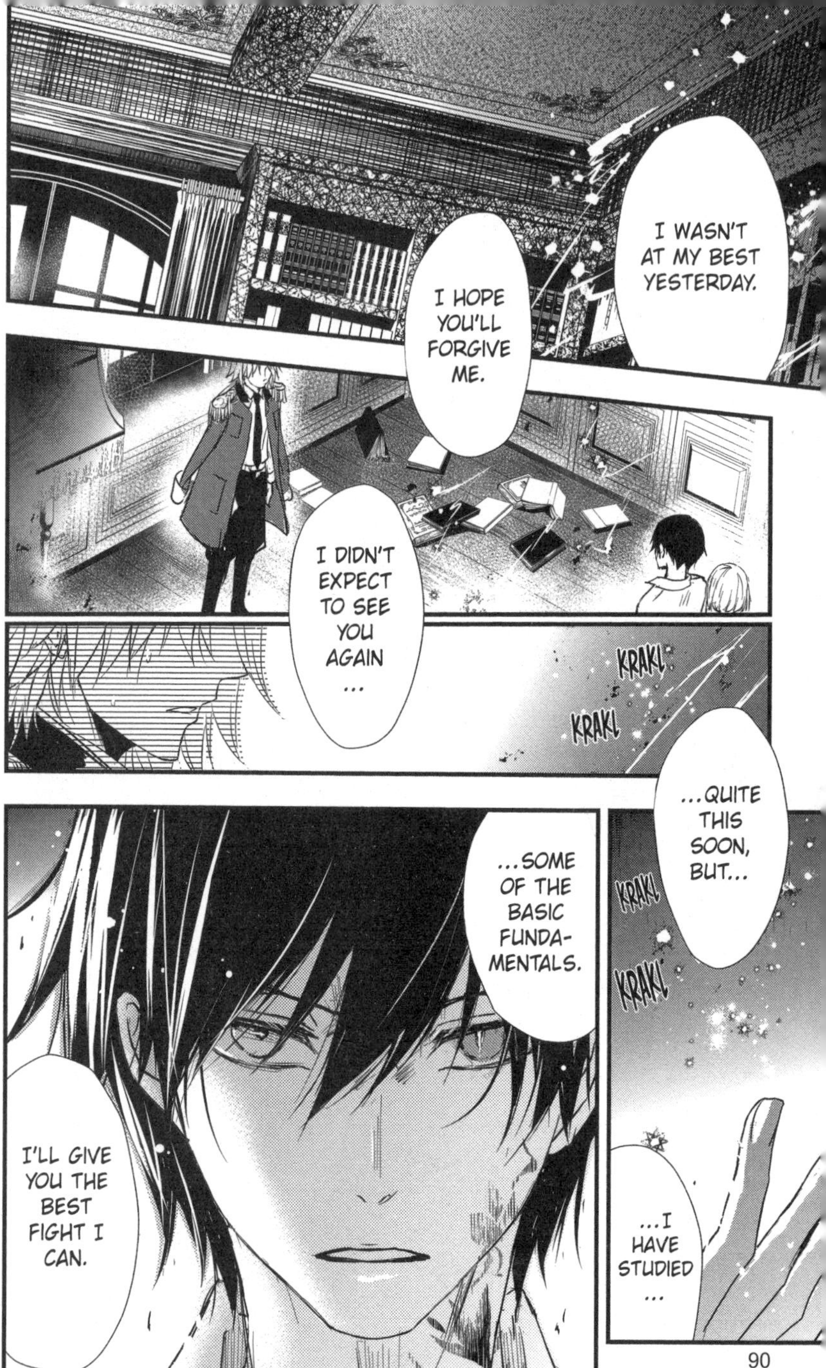
I WASN'T AT MY BEST YESTERDAY.
I HOPE YOU'LL FORGIVE ME.
I DIDN'T EXPECT TO SEE YOU AGAIN ...
KRAK!
KRAK!
...QUITE THIS SOON, BUT...
KRAK!
KRAK!
...I HAVE STUDIED ...
...SOME OF THE BASIC FUNDA-MENTALS.
I'LL GIVE YOU THE BEST FIGHT I CAN.

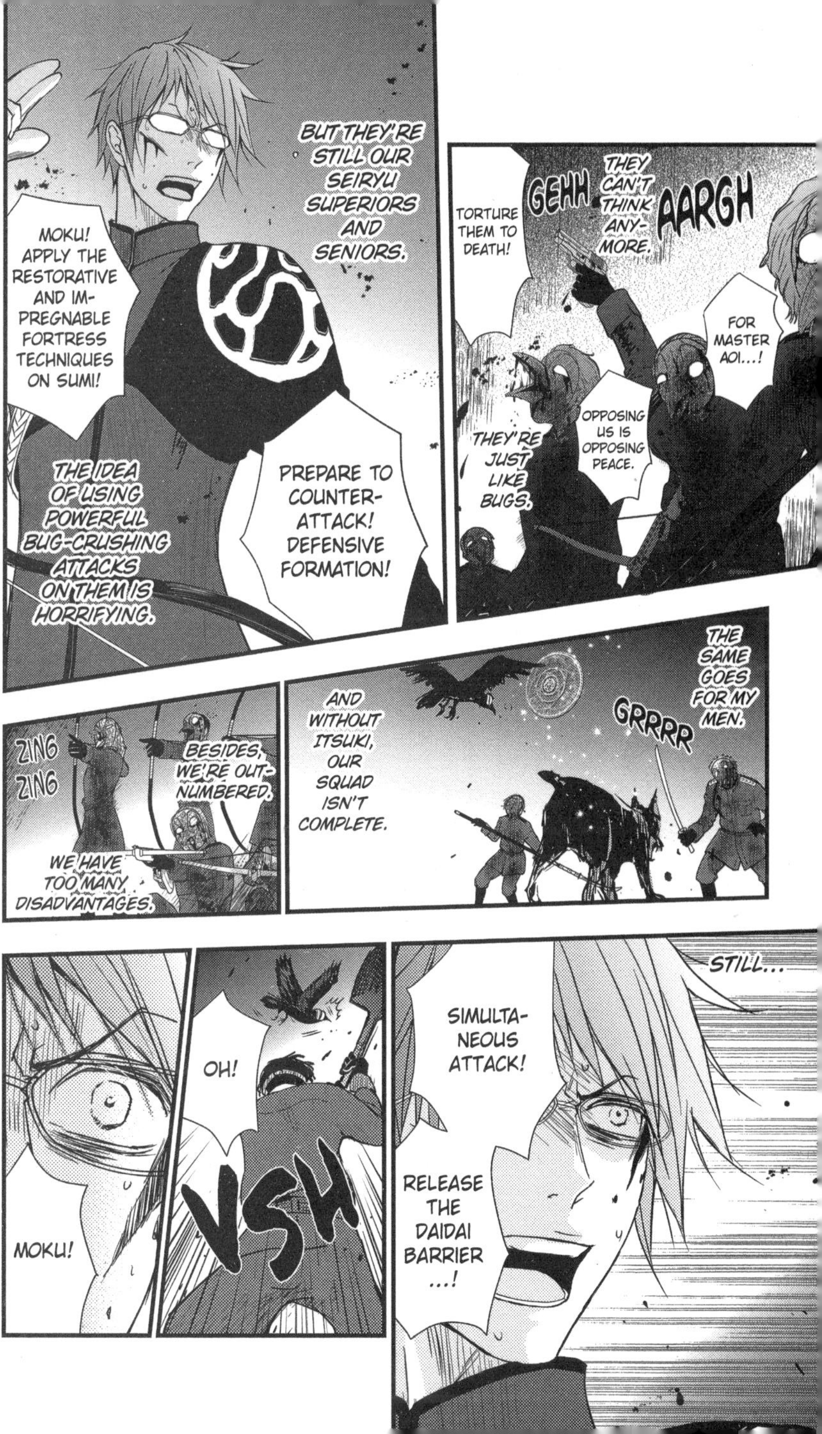
AARGH
FOR MASTER AOI...!
THEY CAN'T THINK ANY-MORE.
GEHH
TORTURE THEM TO DEATH!
OPPOSING US IS OPPOSING PEACE.
THEY'RE JUST LIKE BUGS.
BUT THEY'RE STILL OUR SEIRYU SUPERIORS AND SENIORS.
MOKU! APPLY THE RESTORATIVE AND IM-PREGNABLE FORTRESS TECHNIQUES ON SUMI!
PREPARE TO COUNTER-ATTACK! DEFENSIVE FORMATION!
THE IDEA OF USING POWERFUL BUG-CRUSHING ATTACKS ON THEM IS HORRIFYING.
THE SAME GOES FOR MY MEN.
GRRRR
AND WITHOUT ITSUKI, OUR SQUAD ISN'T COMPLETE.
BESIDES, WE'RE OUT-NUMBERED.
ZING
ZING
WE HAVE TOO MANY DISADVANTAGES.
STILL...
SIMULTA-NEOUS ATTACK!
RELEASE THE DAIDAI BARRIER ...!
OH!
VSH
MOKU!

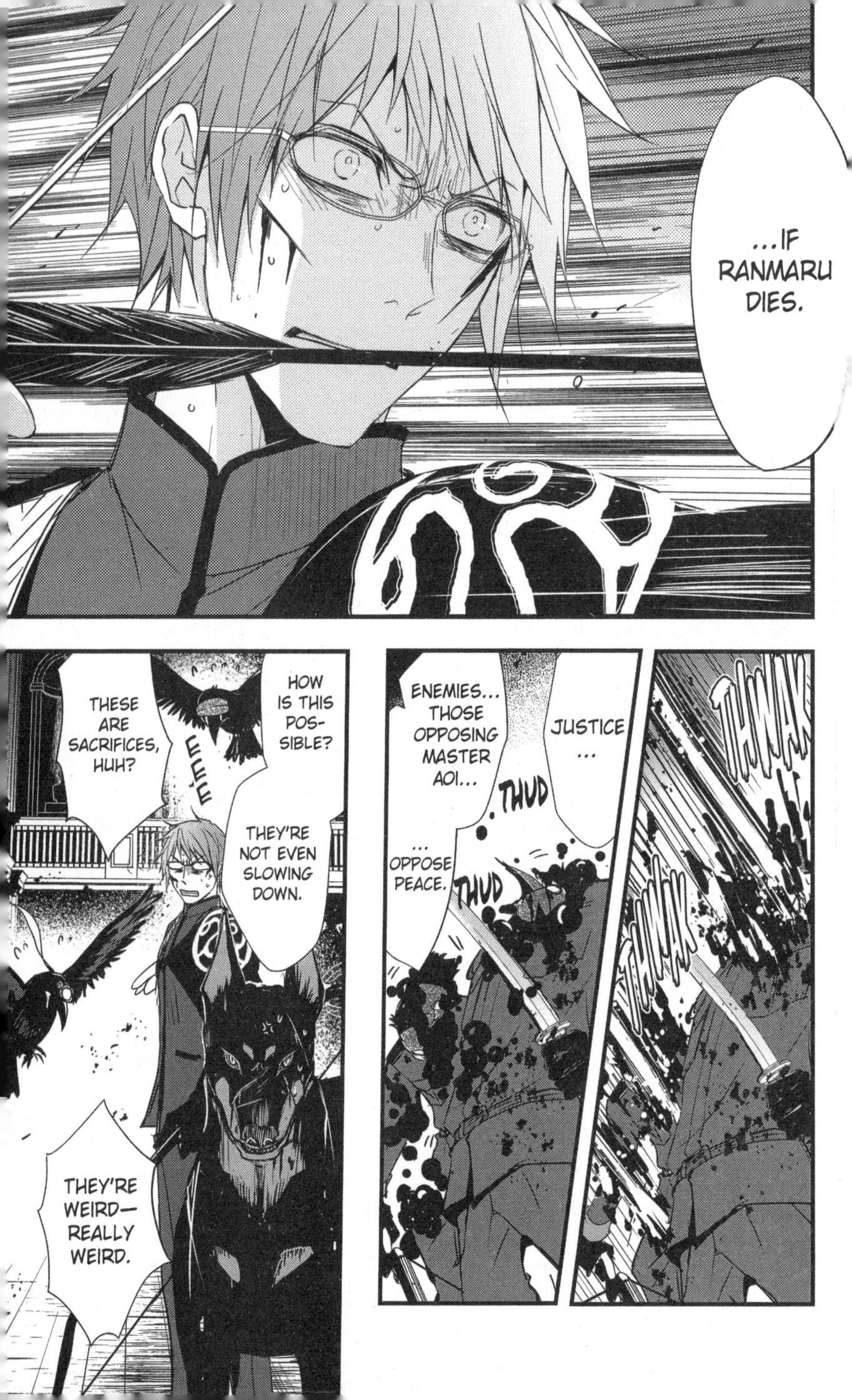
...IF RANMARU DIES.
THWAK
THWAK
JUSTICE...
ENEMIES... THOSE OPPOSING MASTER AOI...
THUD
...OPPOSE PEACE.
THUD
HOW IS THIS POS-SIBLE?
THESE ARE SACRIFICES, HUH?
EEEE
THEY'RE NOT EVEN SLOWING DOWN.
THEY'RE WEIRD—REALLY WEIRD.

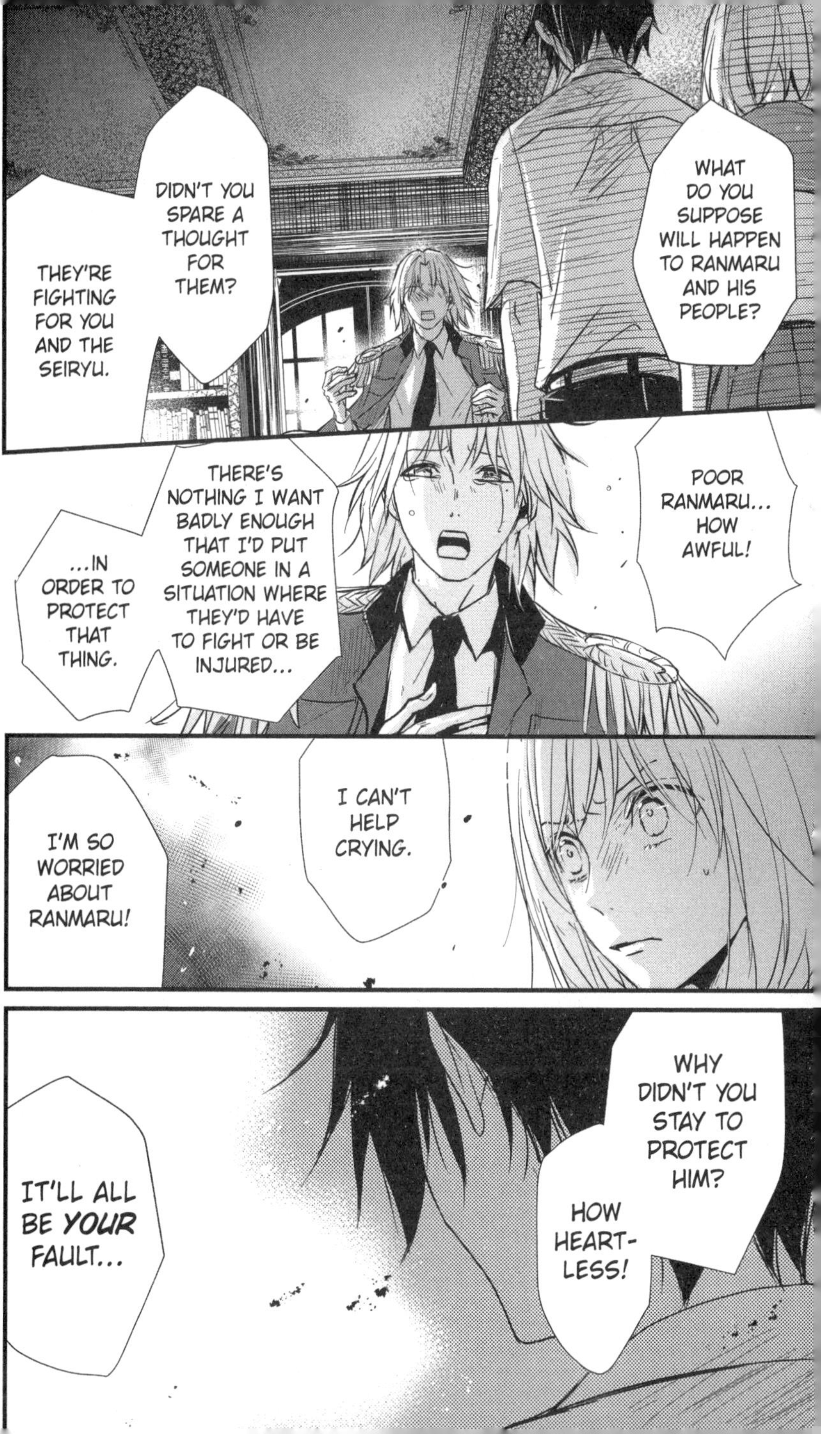
WHAT DO YOU SUPPOSE WILL HAPPEN TO RANMARU AND HIS PEOPLE?
DIDN'T YOU SPARE A THOUGHT FOR THEM?
THEY'RE FIGHTING FOR YOU AND THE SEIRYU.
POOR RANMARU... HOW AWFUL!
THERE'S NOTHING I WANT BADLY ENOUGH THAT I'D PUT SOMEONE IN A SITUATION WHERE THEY'D HAVE TO FIGHT OR BE INJURED...
...IN ORDER TO PROTECT THAT THING.
I CAN'T HELP CRYING.
I'M SO WORRIED ABOUT RANMARU!
WHY DIDN'T YOU STAY TO PROTECT HIM?
HOW HEART-LESS!
IT'LL ALL BE ***YOUR*** FAULT...

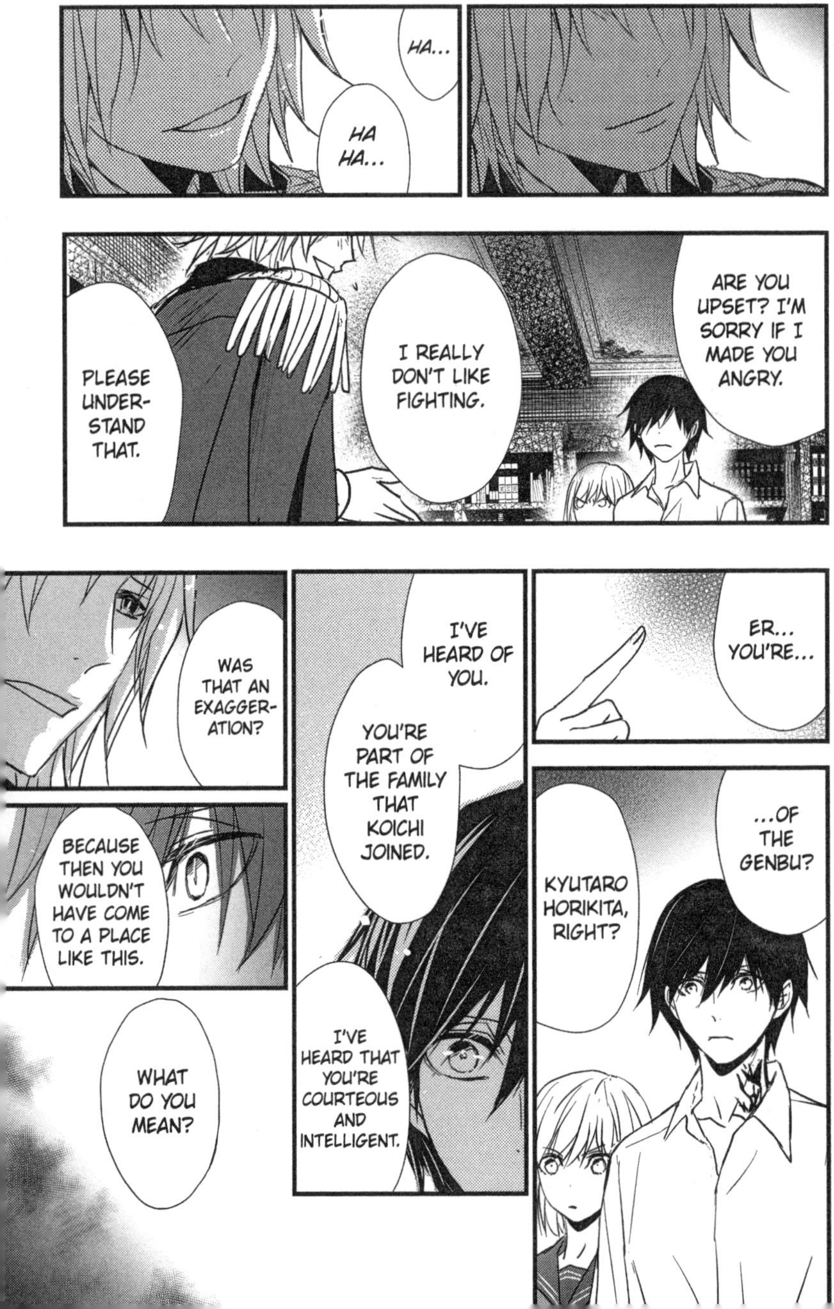
HA...
HA HA...
ARE YOU UPSET? I'M SORRY IF I MADE YOU ANGRY.
I REALLY DON'T LIKE FIGHTING.
PLEASE UNDER-STAND THAT.
ER... YOU'RE...
...OF THE GENBU?
KYUTARO HORIKITA, RIGHT?
I'VE HEARD OF YOU.
YOU'RE PART OF THE FAMILY THAT KOICHI JOINED.
I'VE HEARD THAT YOU'RE COURTEOUS AND INTELLIGENT.
WAS THAT AN EXAGGER-ATION?
BECAUSE THEN YOU WOULDN'T HAVE COME TO A PLACE LIKE THIS.
WHAT DO YOU MEAN?

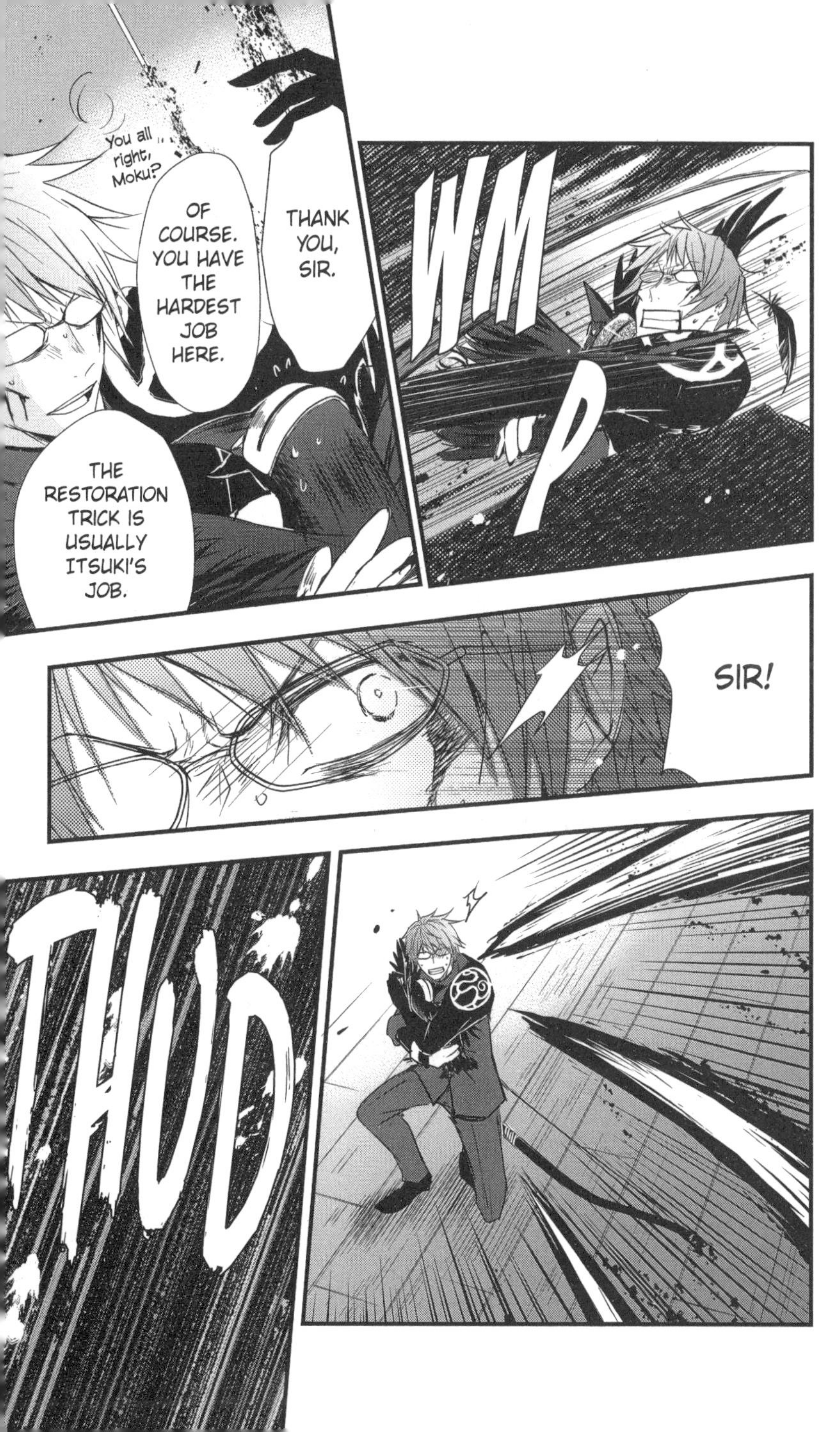
You all right, Moku?
OF COURSE. YOU HAVE THE HARDEST JOB HERE.
THANK YOU, SIR.
THE RESTORATION TRICK IS USUALLY ITSUKI'S JOB.
WHMP
SIR!
THUD

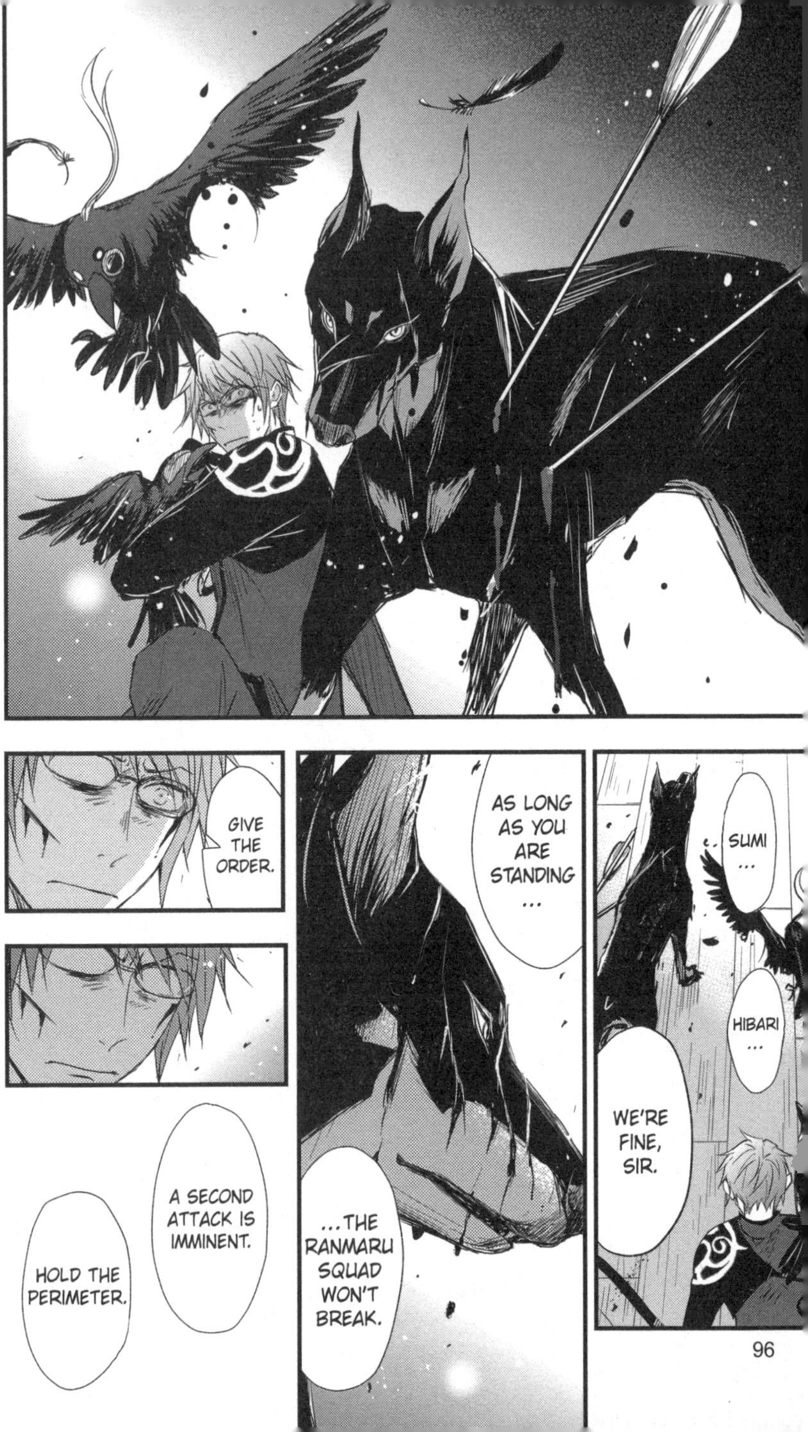
SUMI ...
HIBARI ...
WE'RE FINE, SIR.
AS LONG AS YOU ARE STANDING ...
...THE RANMARU SQUAD WON'T BREAK.
GIVE THE ORDER.
A SECOND ATTACK IS IMMINENT.
HOLD THE PERIMETER.

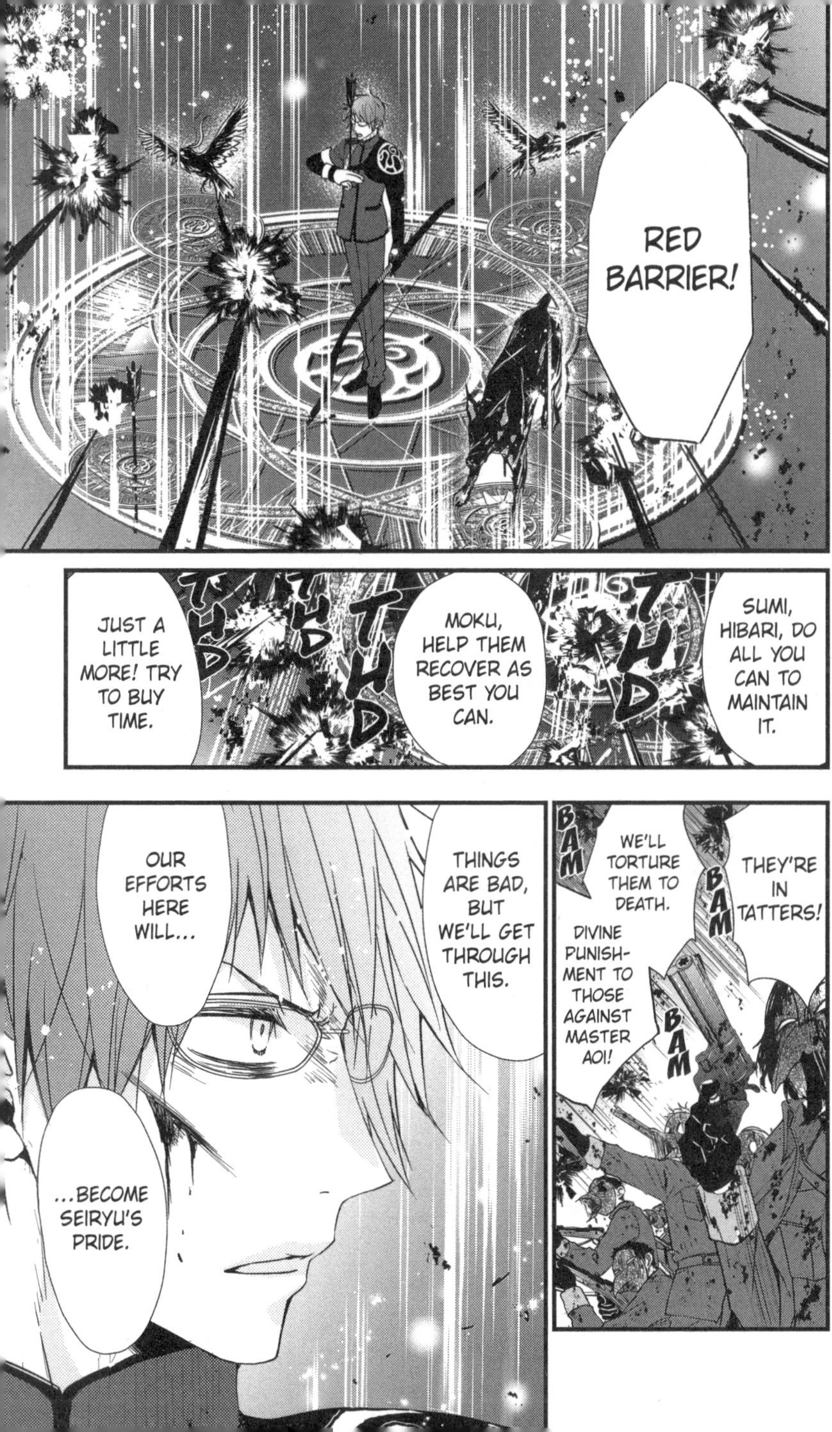
RED BARRIER!
SUMI, HIBARI, DO ALL YOU CAN TO MAINTAIN IT.
THUD
THUD
MOKU, HELP THEM RECOVER AS BEST YOU CAN.
THUD
THUD
JUST A LITTLE MORE! TRY TO BUY TIME.
THEY'RE IN TATTERS!
BAM
WE'LL TORTURE THEM TO DEATH.
BAM
DIVINE PUNISHMENT TO THOSE AGAINST MASTER AOI!
BAM
THINGS ARE BAD, BUT WE'LL GET THROUGH THIS.
OUR EFFORTS HERE WILL...
...BECOME SEIRYU'S PRIDE.

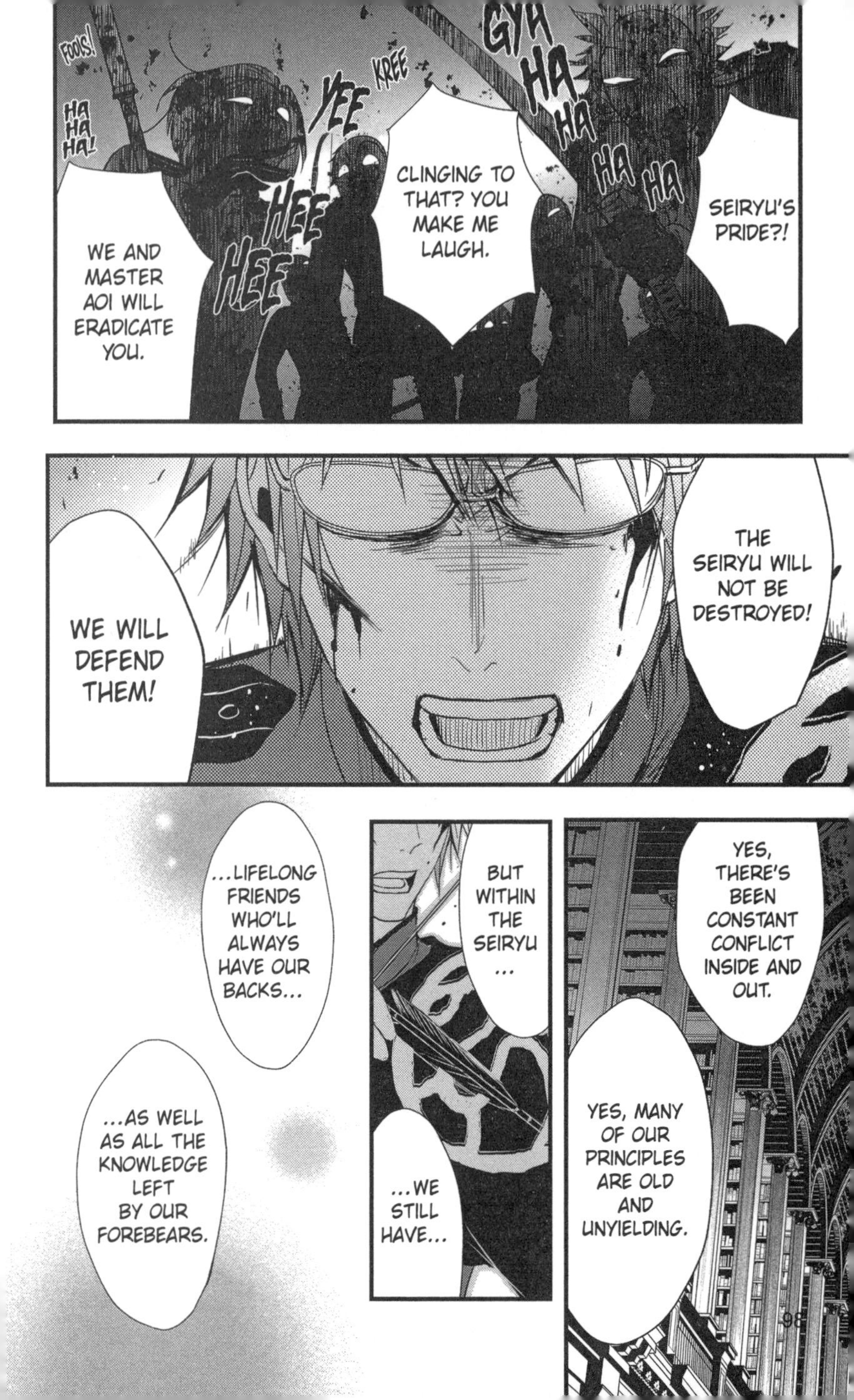
GYAHAHAHAHA
SEIRYU'S PRIDE?!
KREE
CLINGING TO THAT? YOU MAKE ME LAUGH.
YEE HEE HEE
FOOLS! HA HA HA!
WE AND MASTER AOI WILL ERADICATE YOU.
THE SEIRYU WILL NOT BE DESTROYED!
WE WILL DEFEND THEM!
YES, THERE'S BEEN CONSTANT CONFLICT INSIDE AND OUT.
YES, MANY OF OUR PRINCIPLES ARE OLD AND UNYIELDING.
BUT WITHIN THE SEIRYU...
...WE STILL HAVE...
...LIFELONG FRIENDS WHO'LL ALWAYS HAVE OUR BACKS...
...AS WELL AS ALL THE KNOWLEDGE LEFT BY OUR FOREBEARS.

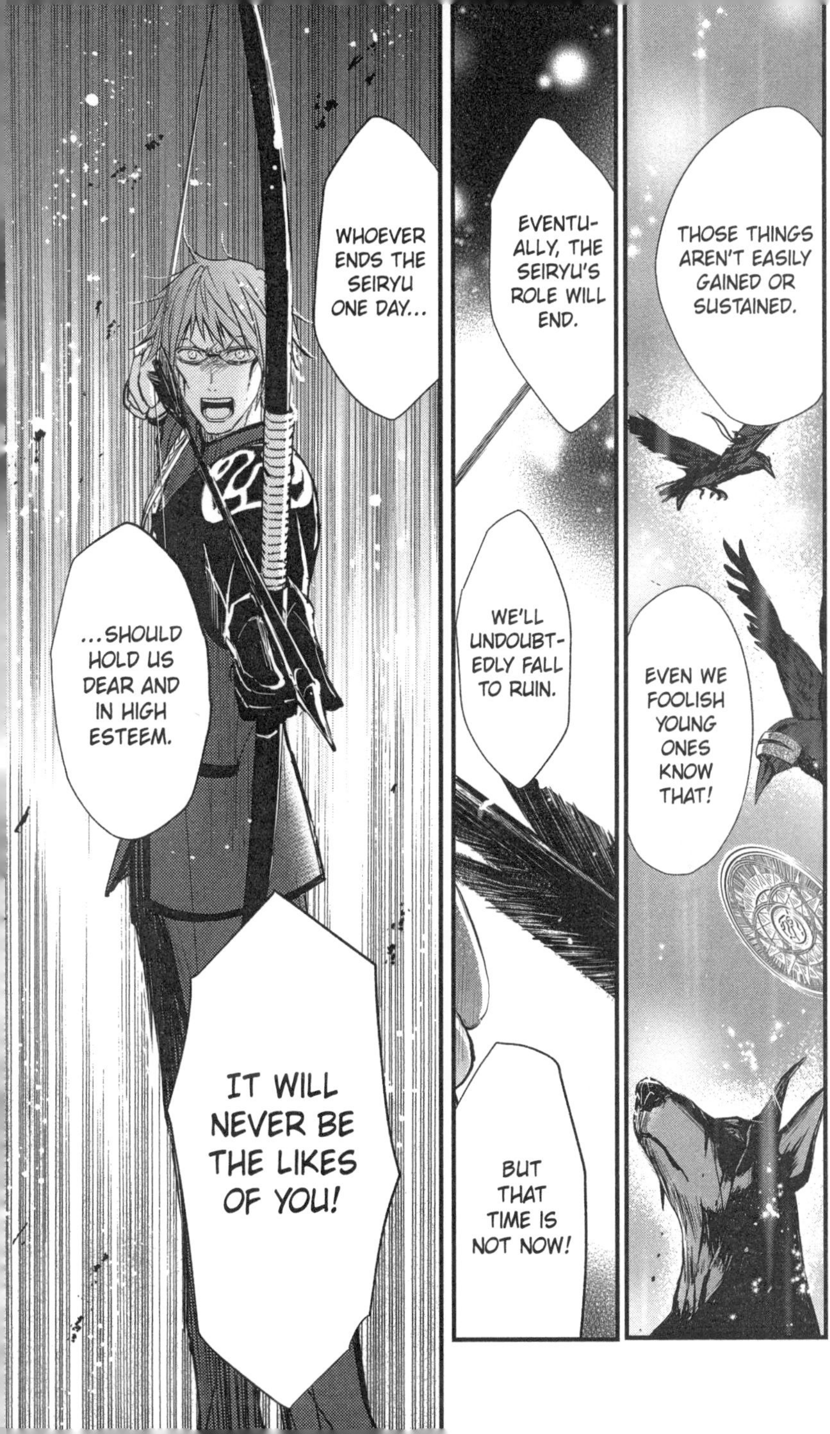
THOSE THINGS AREN'T EASILY GAINED OR SUSTAINED.
EVEN WE FOOLISH YOUNG ONES KNOW THAT!
EVENTU-ALLY, THE SEIRYU'S ROLE WILL END.
WE'LL UNDOUBT-EDLY FALL TO RUIN.
BUT THAT TIME IS NOT NOW!
WHOEVER ENDS THE SEIRYU ONE DAY...
...SHOULD HOLD US DEAR AND IN HIGH ESTEEM.
IT WILL NEVER BE THE LIKES OF YOU!

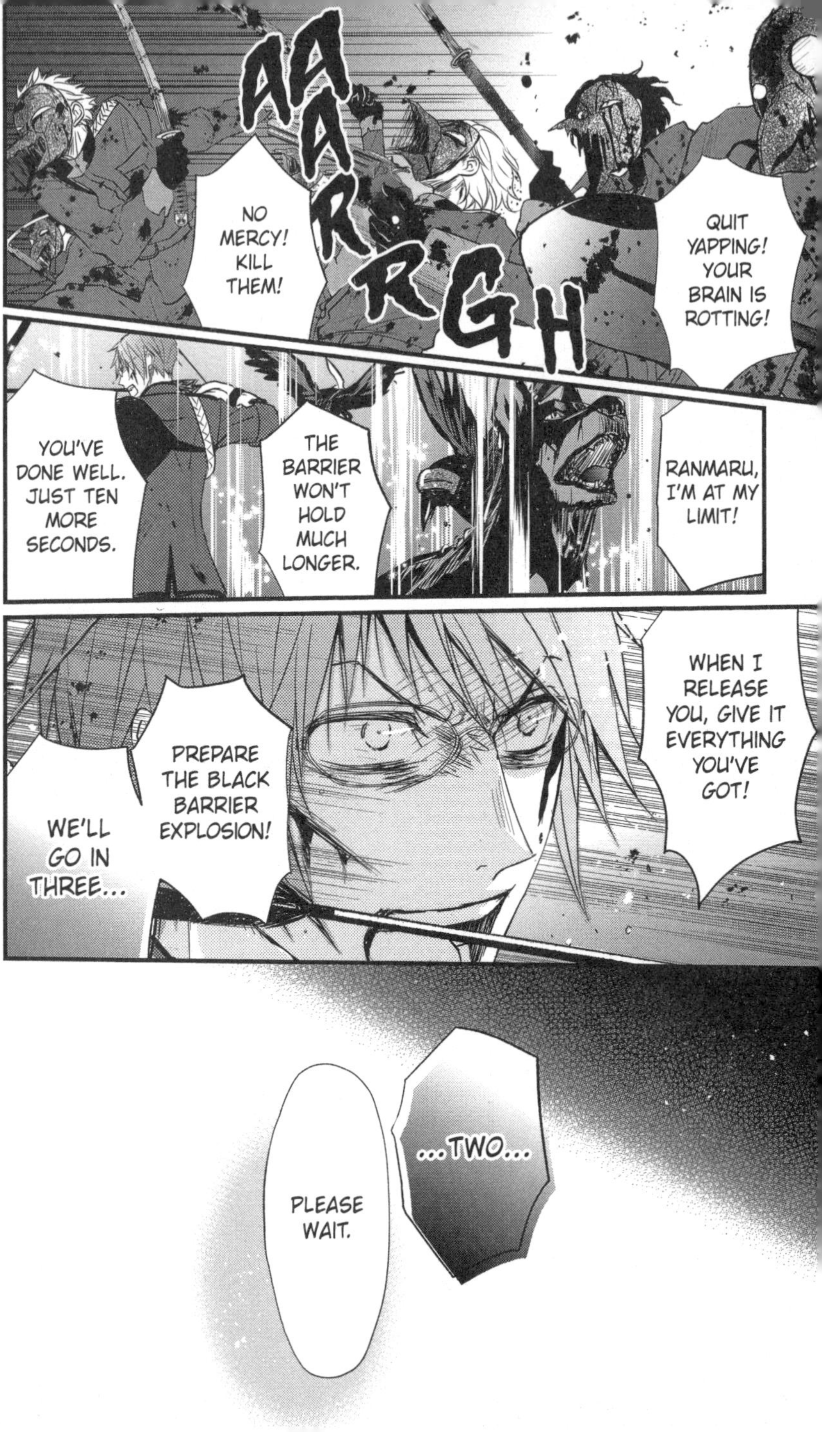
QUIT YAPPING! YOUR BRAIN IS ROTTING!
AAARRGH
NO MERCY! KILL THEM!
RANMARU, I'M AT MY LIMIT!
THE BARRIER WON'T HOLD MUCH LONGER.
YOU'VE DONE WELL. JUST TEN MORE SECONDS.
WHEN I RELEASE YOU, GIVE IT EVERYTHING YOU'VE GOT!
PREPARE THE BLACK BARRIER EXPLOSION!
WE'LL GO IN THREE...
...TWO...
PLEASE WAIT.

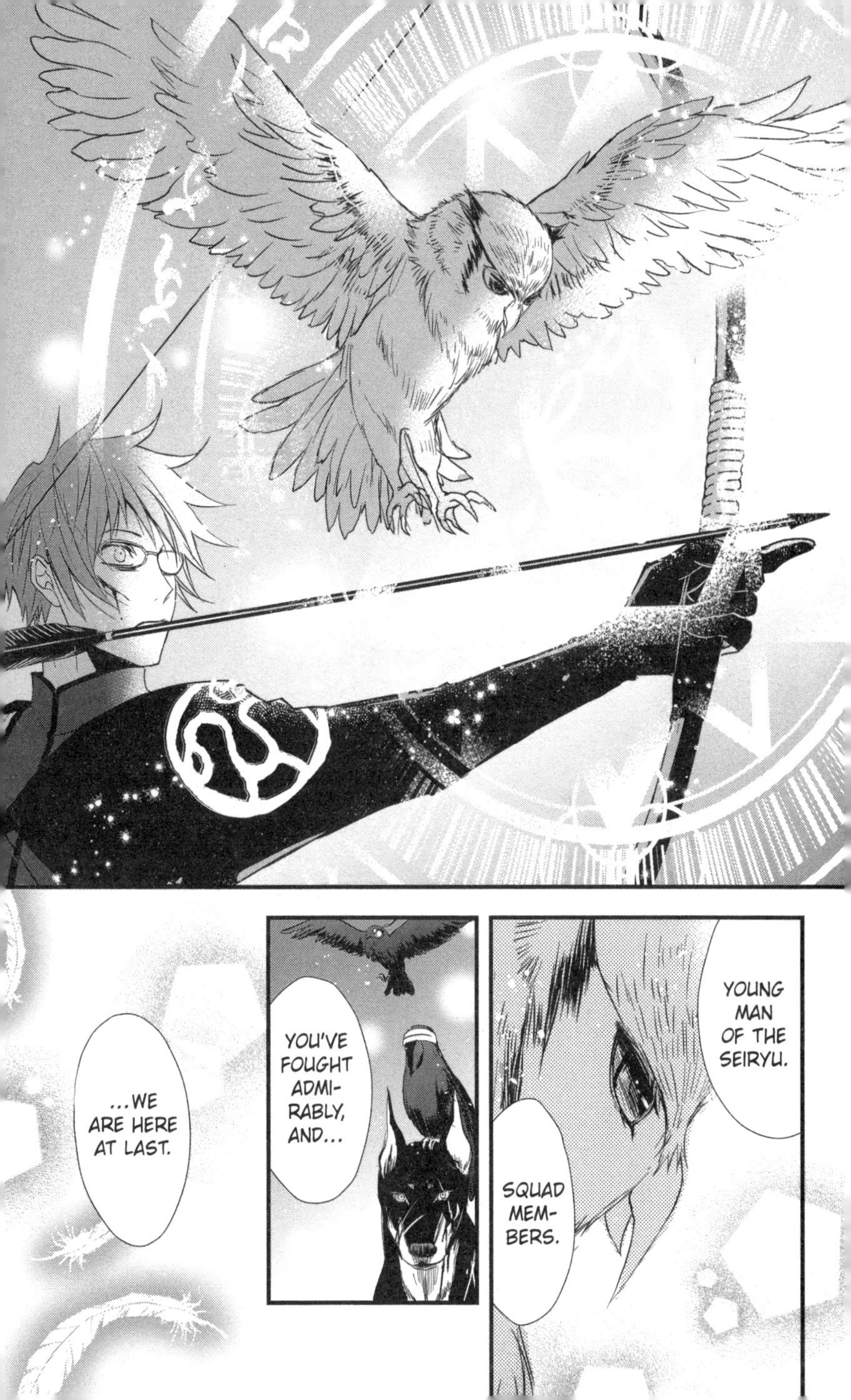
YOUNG MAN OF THE SEIRYU.
SQUAD MEM-BERS.
YOU'VE FOUGHT ADMI-RABLY, AND...
...WE ARE HERE AT LAST.

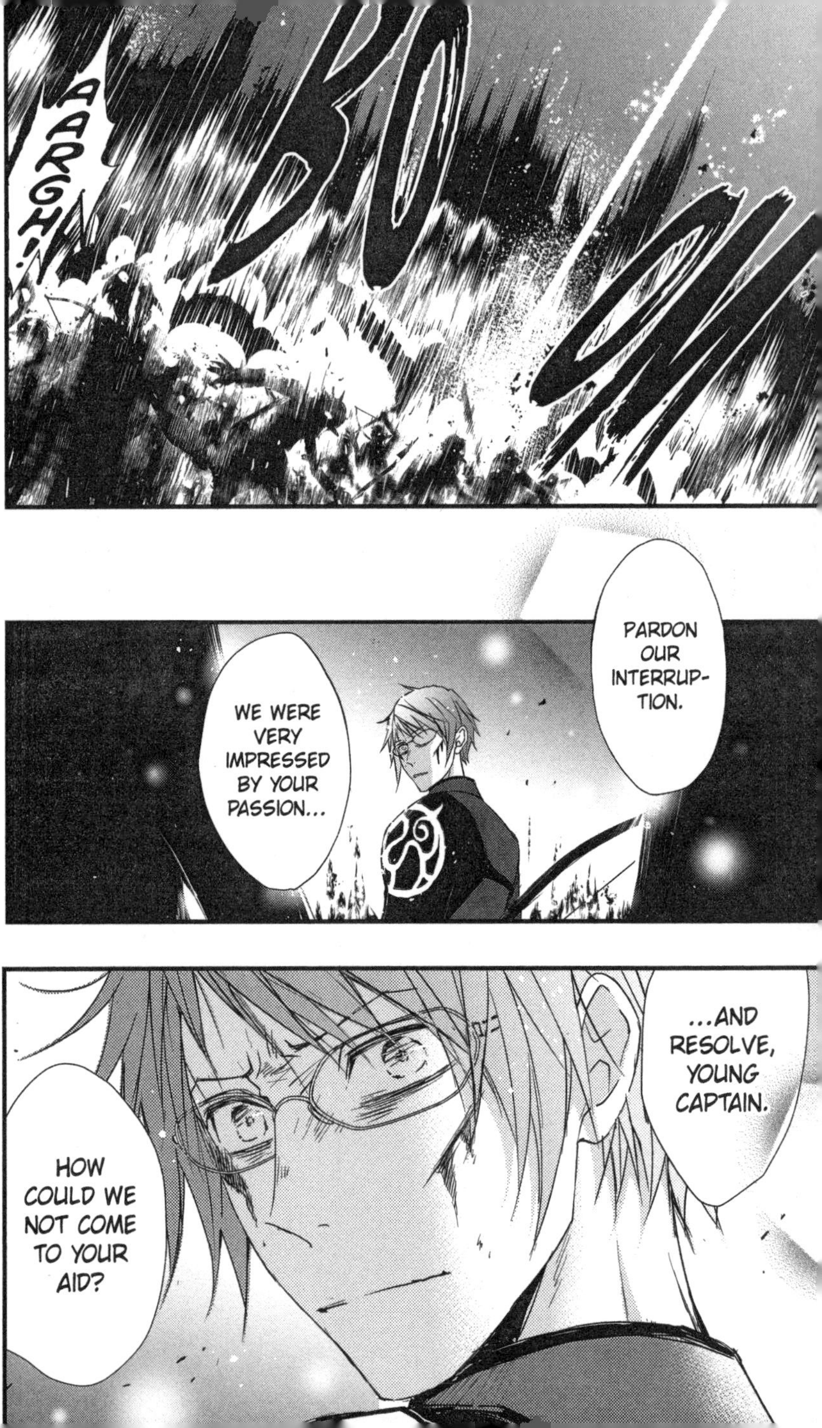
BOOM
AARGH!!
PARDON OUR INTERRUP-TION.
WE WERE VERY IMPRESSED BY YOUR PASSION...
...AND RESOLVE, YOUNG CAPTAIN.
HOW COULD WE NOT COME TO YOUR AID?

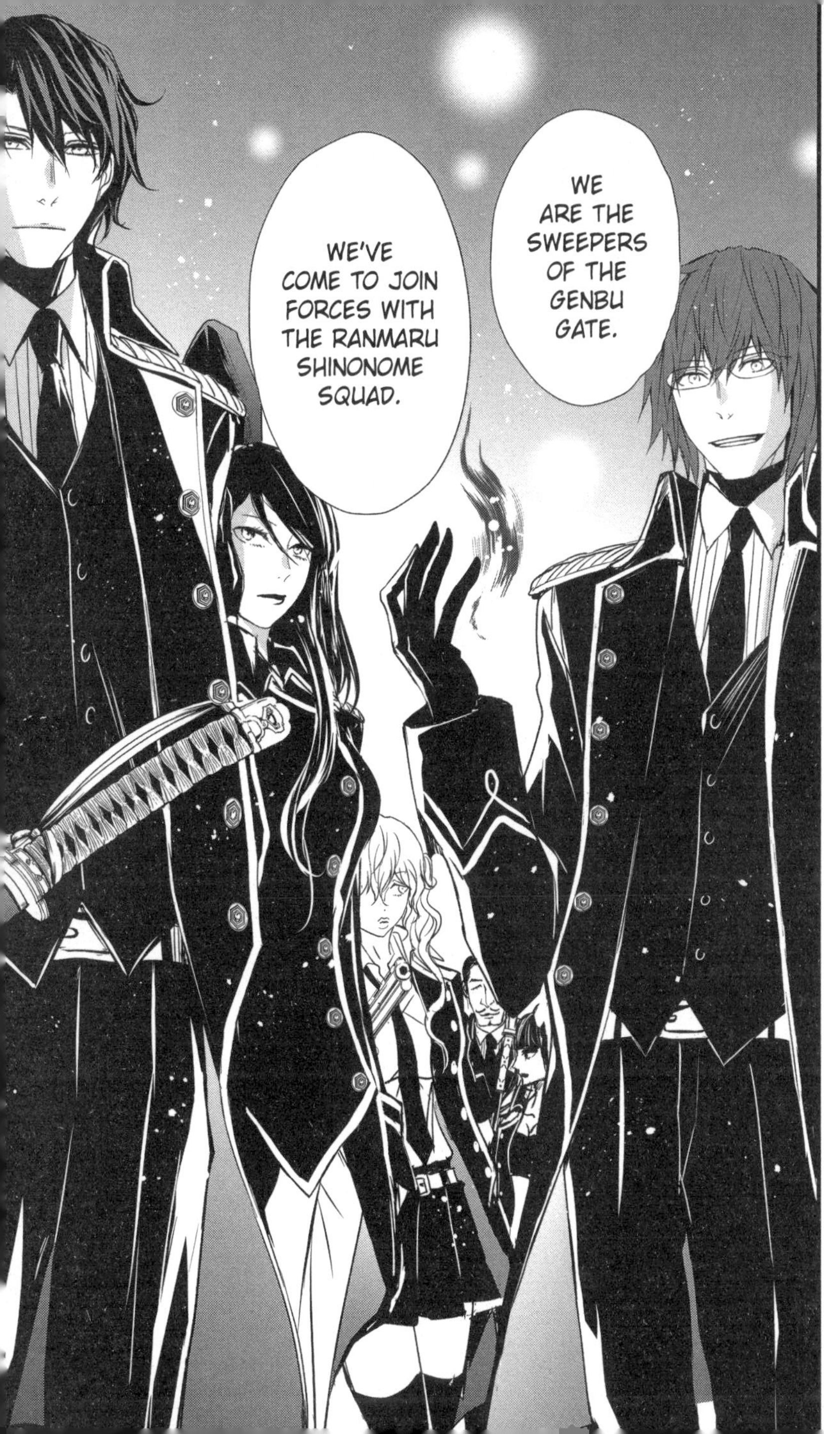
WE ARE THE SWEEPERS OF THE GENBU GATE.
WE'VE COME TO JOIN FORCES WITH THE RANMARU SHINONOME SQUAD.

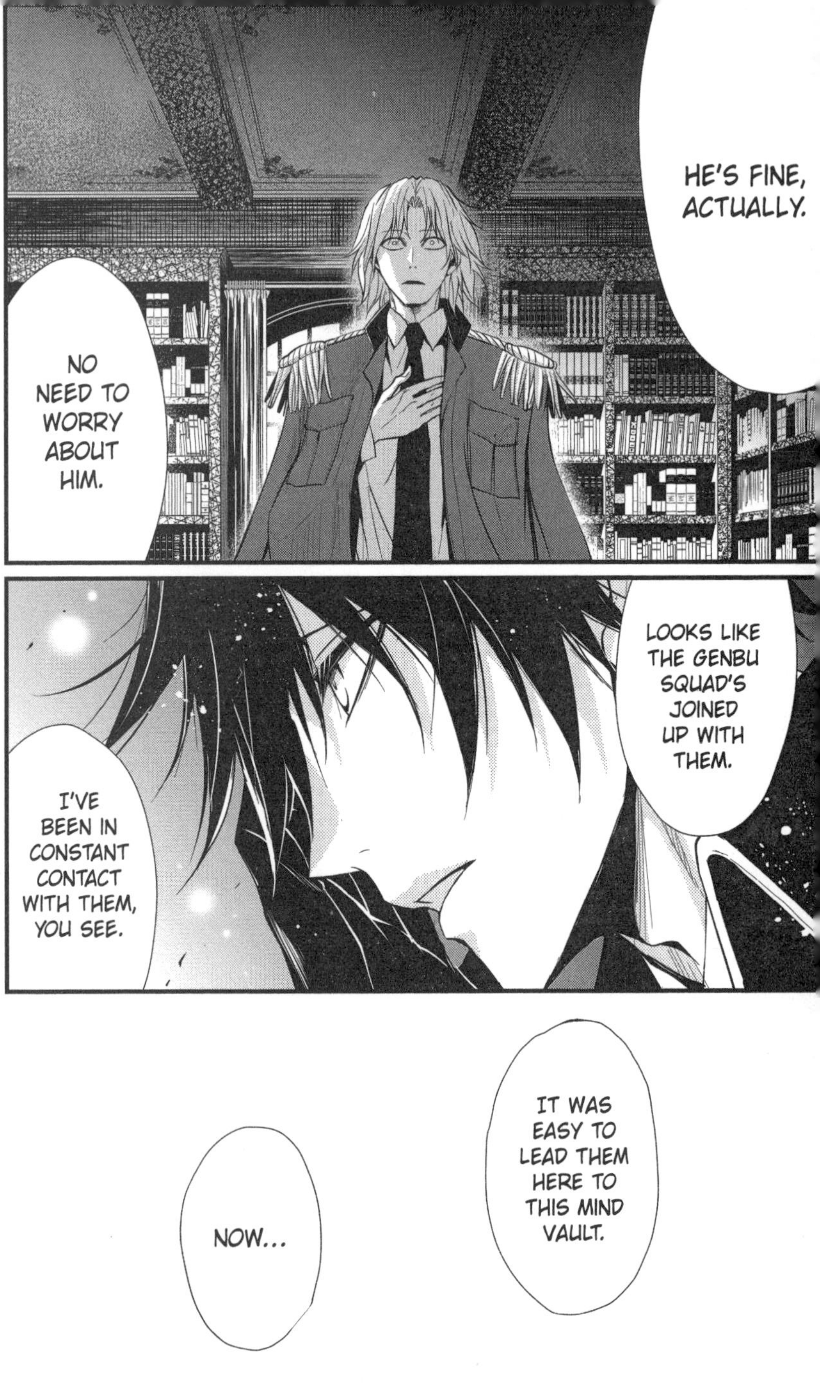
HE'S FINE, ACTUALLY.
NO NEED TO WORRY ABOUT HIM.
LOOKS LIKE THE GENBU SQUAD'S JOINED UP WITH THEM.
I'VE BEEN IN CONSTANT CONTACT WITH THEM, YOU SEE.
IT WAS EASY TO LEAD THEM HERE TO THIS MIND VAULT.
NOW...

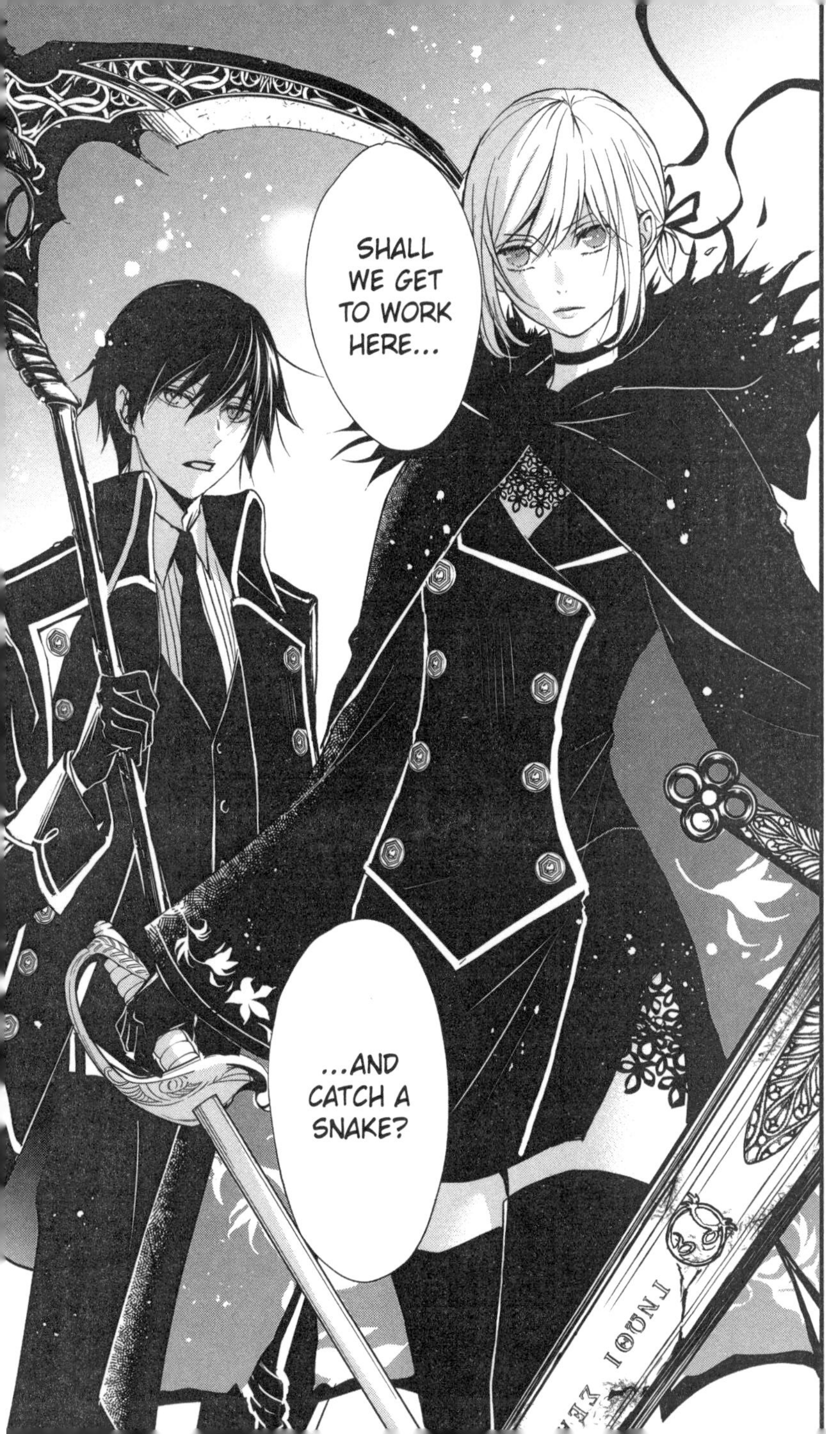
SHALL WE GET TO WORK HERE...
...AND CATCH A SNAKE?

MONTHLY BETSUCOMI SALE DATE NOTICE ON TWITTER AND INSTAGRAM

CHAPTER 56

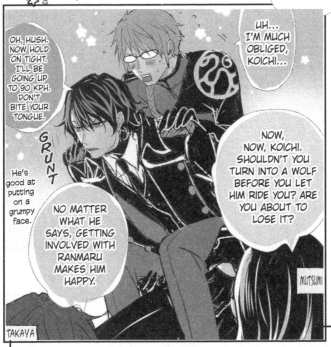

UH... I'M MUCH OBLIGED, KOICHI...
OH, HUSH. NOW HOLD ON TIGHT. I'LL BE GOING UP TO 90 KPH. DON'T BITE YOUR TONGUE.
NOW, NOW, KOICHI. SHOULDN'T YOU TURN INTO A WOLF BEFORE YOU LET HIM RIDE YOU? ARE YOU ABOUT TO LOSE IT?
GRUNT
He's good at putting on a grumpy face.
NO MATTER WHAT HE SAYS, GETTING INVOLVED WITH RANMARU MAKES HIM HAPPY.
MUTSUMI
TAKAYA

LET'S SEE... WHAT'S UP IN *QUEEN'S QUALITY* THIS MONTH?
1) MIZUHO AND HIS FRIENDS BRING ON THE WHOLE SHOJO MANGA VIBE.
2) KYUTARO HAS TAKEN ON A VILLAIN LOOK THIS MONTH.
3) KOICHI AND RANMARU MUST FEEL UNCOMFORTABLE APPEARING TOGETHER.
THIS CHAPTER SEEMS TO BE ABOUT KOICHI. FEWER PAGES, BUT LOOK, THERE'S A DOG!

I FINALLY HAVE A JAVA SPARROW IN THIS CHAPTER! IT'S SUPPOSED TO BE A CINNAMON JAVA, BUT I COLORED IT SILVER THE OTHER DAY. JAVA SPARROWS ARE CUTE NO MATTER WHAT COLOR THEY ARE.

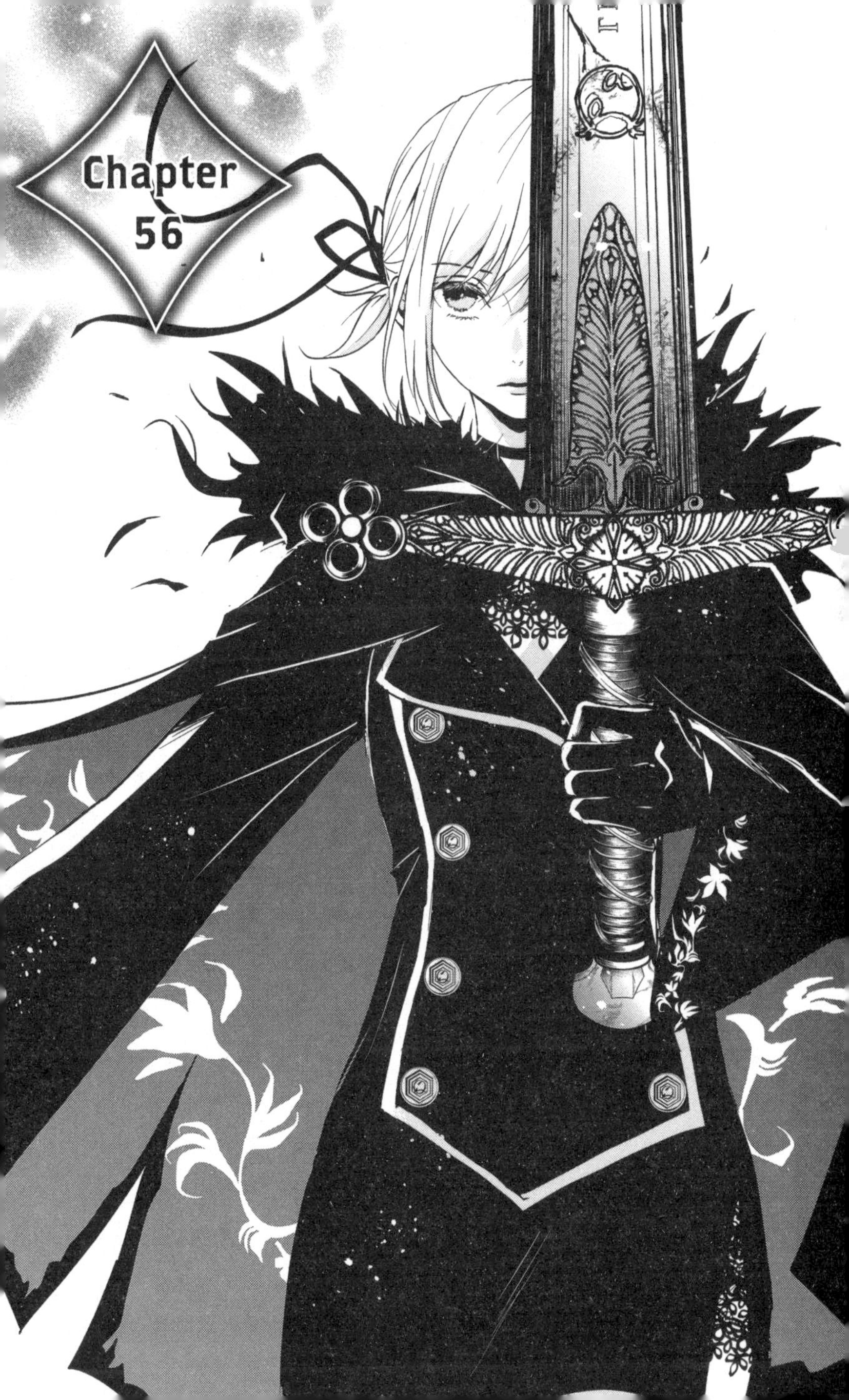
Chapter 56

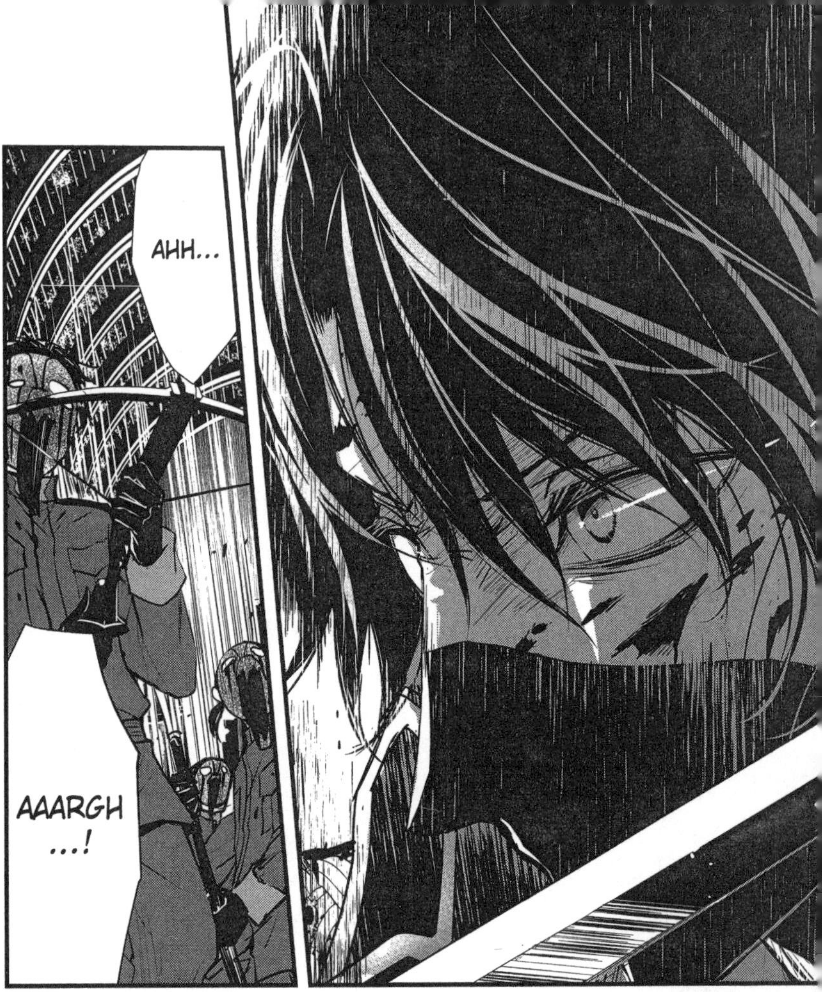
AHH...
AAARGH ...!

What's Been Going On ③
I've been doing a lot of cooking lately. Perhaps it's because working virtually has given variety to my work life. I've gotten in the habit of trying out any interesting recipes I see on Twitter. Recently I tried Tottori soul food using ginger, ground beef and chopped natto stir-fried together and seasoned with dashi stock, sugar and Tabasco. It was delicious! Went well with beer.

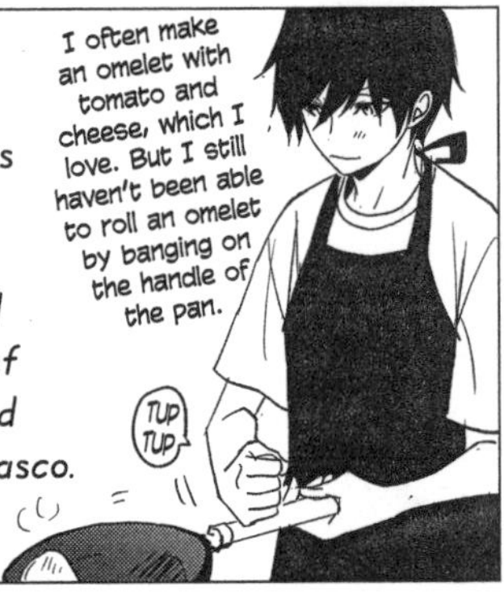
I often make an omelet with tomato and cheese, which I love. But I still haven't been able to roll an omelet by banging on the handle of the pan.
TUP TUP

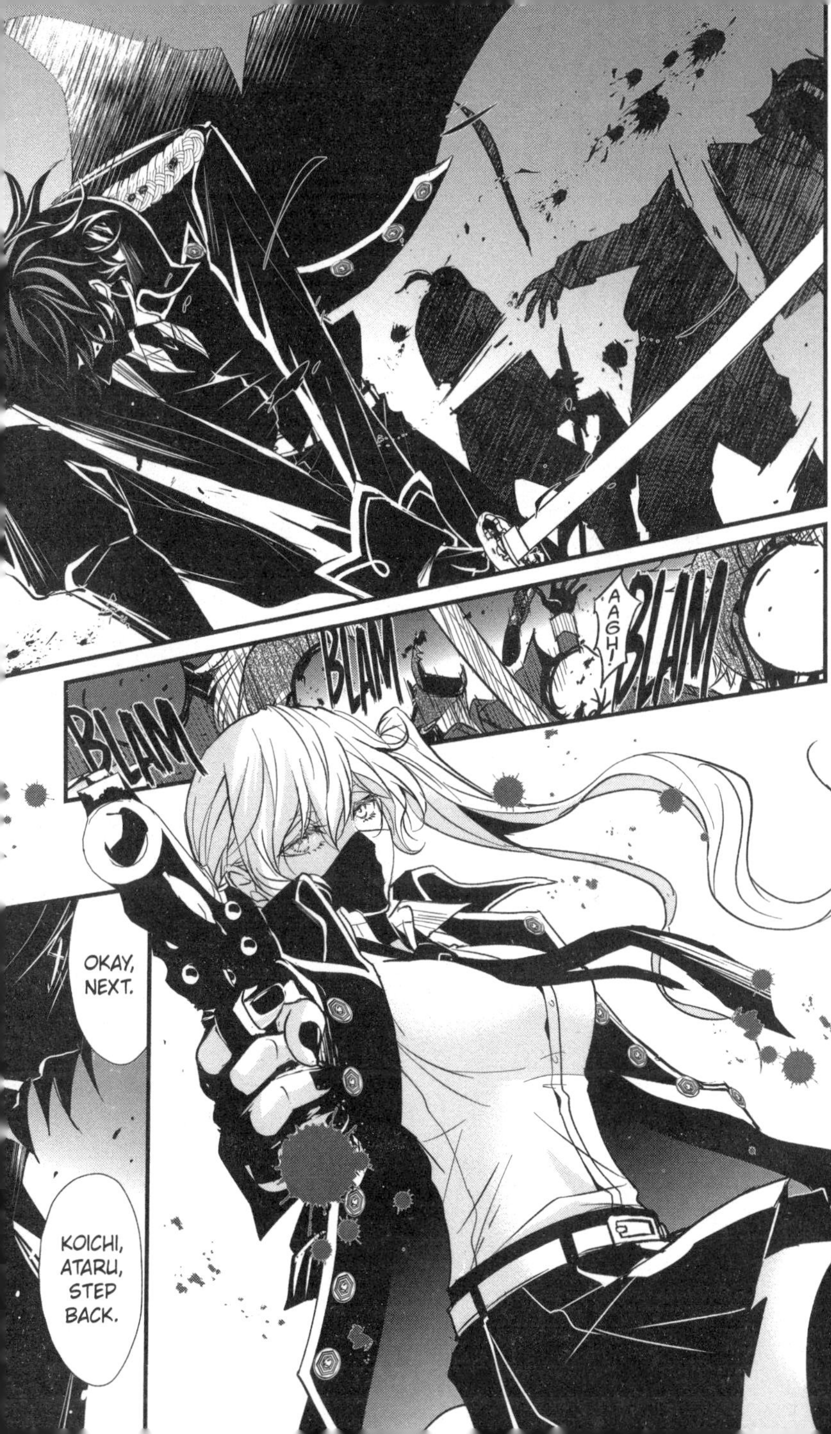
BLAM
AAGH!
BLAM
BLAM
OKAY, NEXT.
KOICHI, ATARU, STEP BACK.

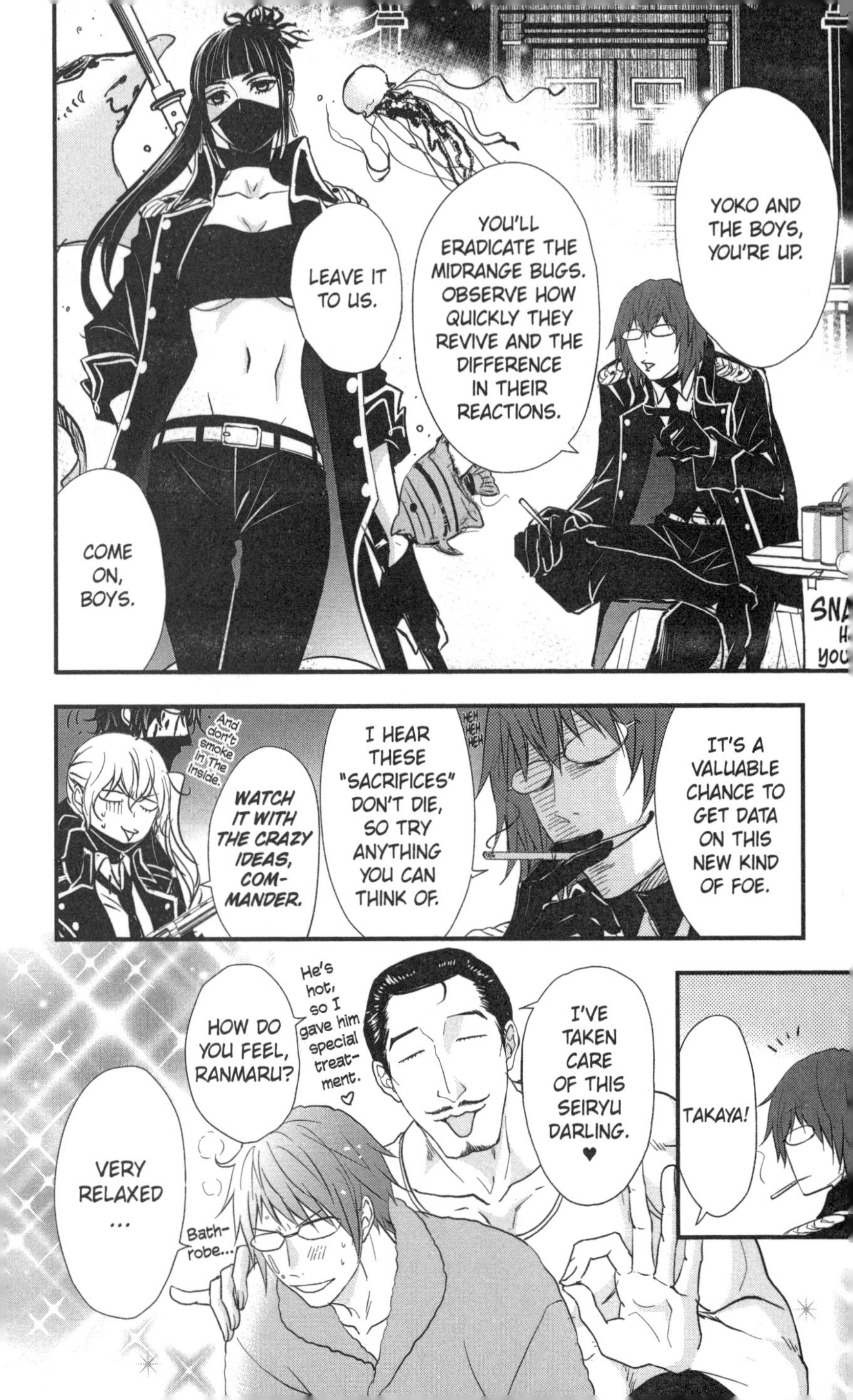
YOKO AND THE BOYS, YOU'RE UP.
YOU'LL ERADICATE THE MIDRANGE BUGS. OBSERVE HOW QUICKLY THEY REVIVE AND THE DIFFERENCE IN THEIR REACTIONS.
LEAVE IT TO US.
COME ON, BOYS.
IT'S A VALUABLE CHANCE TO GET DATA ON THIS NEW KIND OF FOE.
HEH HEH HEH
I HEAR THESE "SACRIFICES" DON'T DIE, SO TRY ANYTHING YOU CAN THINK OF.
WATCH IT WITH THE CRAZY IDEAS, COM-MANDER.
And don't smoke in The Inside.
TAKAYA!
I'VE TAKEN CARE OF THIS SEIRYU DARLING. ♥
He's hot, so I gave him special treat-ment. ♡
HOW DO YOU FEEL, RANMARU?
VERY RELAXED ...
Bath-robe...

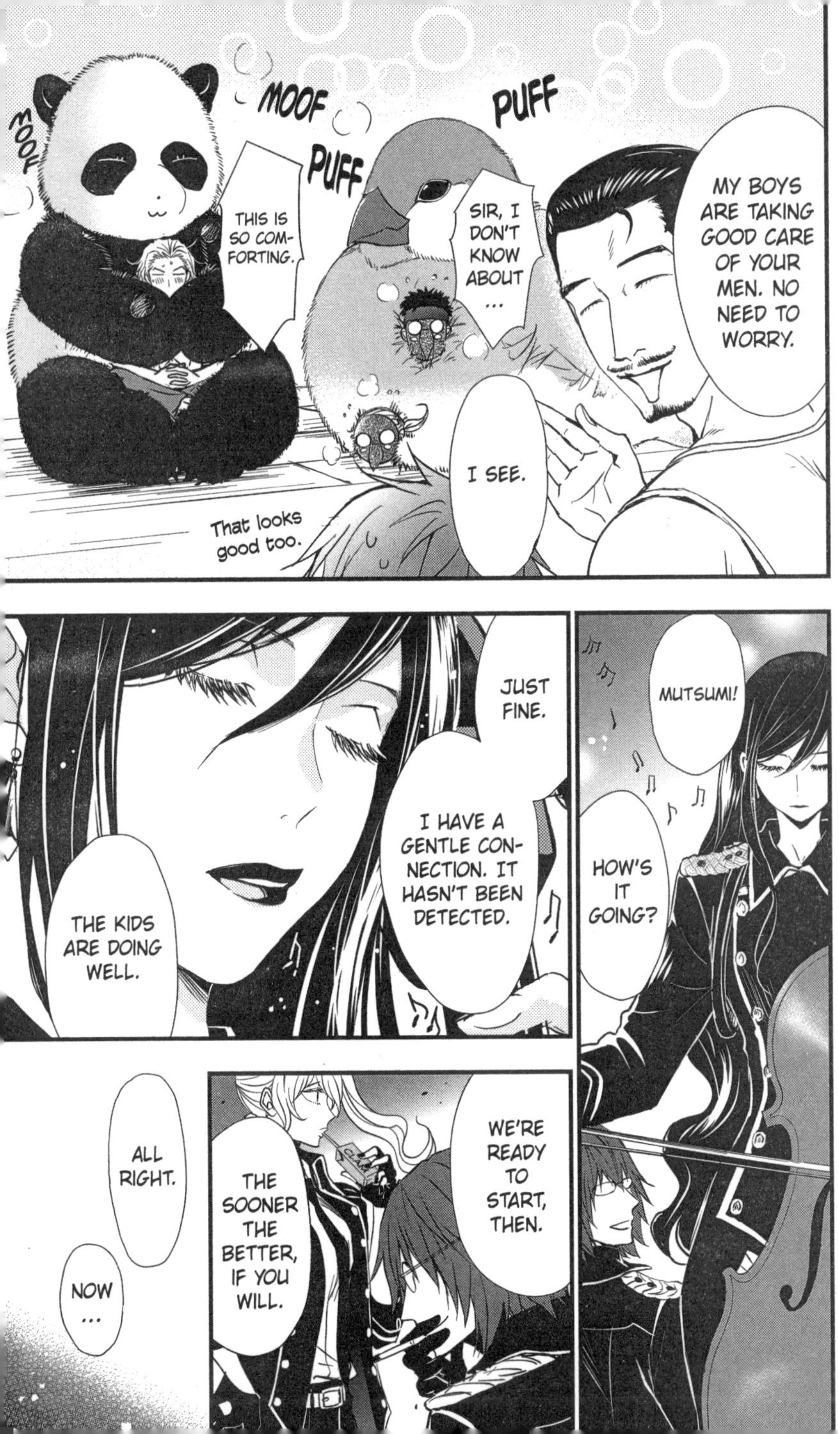
MY BOYS ARE TAKING GOOD CARE OF YOUR MEN. NO NEED TO WORRY.
PUFF
SIR, I DON'T KNOW ABOUT ...
I SEE.
PUFF
MOOF
THIS IS SO COM-FORTING.
MOOF
That looks good too.
MUTSUMI!
HOW'S IT GOING?
JUST FINE.
I HAVE A GENTLE CON-NECTION. IT HASN'T BEEN DETECTED.
THE KIDS ARE DOING WELL.
WE'RE READY TO START, THEN.
THE SOONER THE BETTER, IF YOU WILL.
ALL RIGHT.
NOW ...

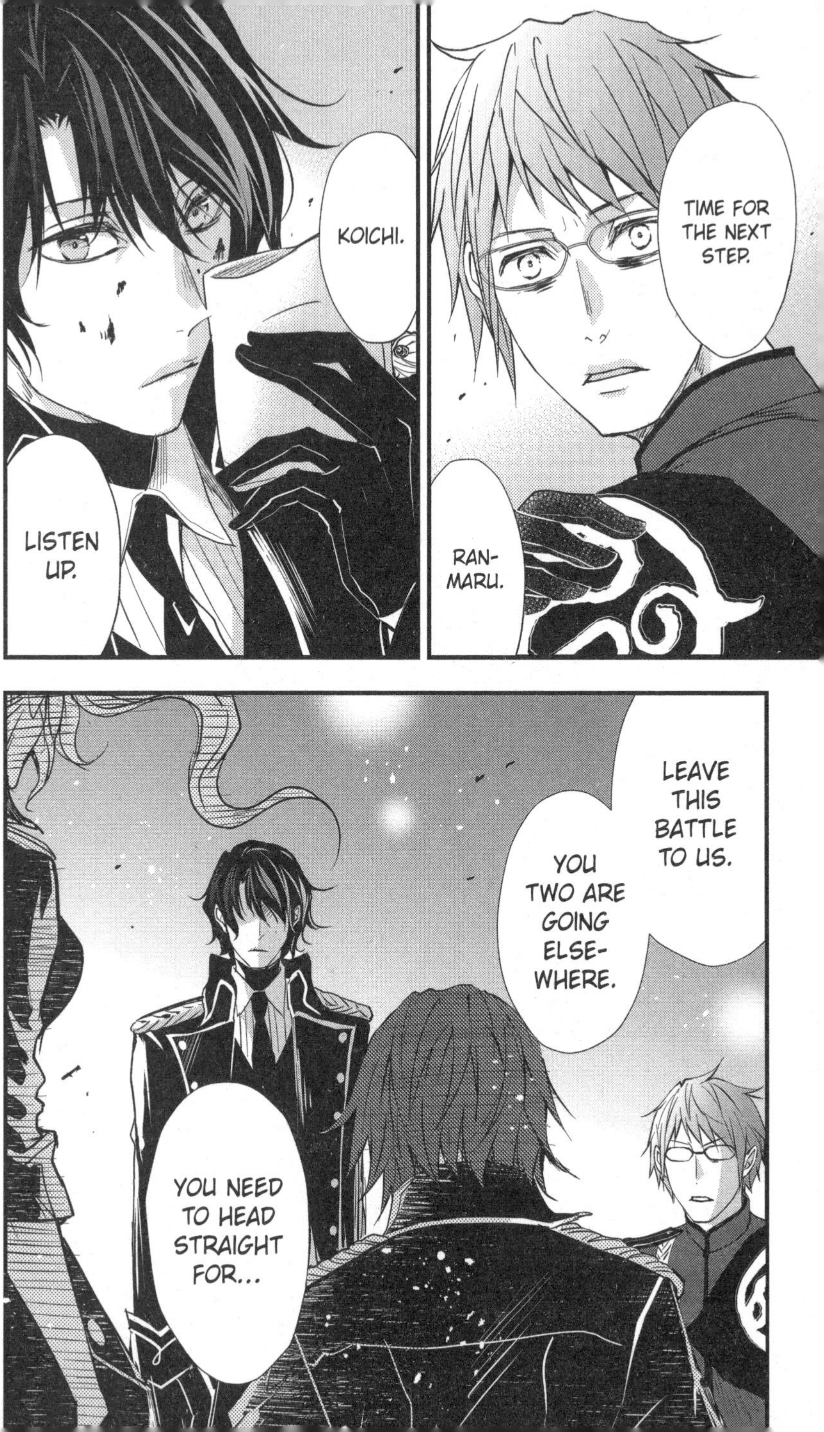
TIME FOR THE NEXT STEP.
RAN-MARU.
KOICHI.
LISTEN UP.
LEAVE THIS BATTLE TO US.
YOU TWO ARE GOING ELSE-WHERE.
YOU NEED TO HEAD STRAIGHT FOR...

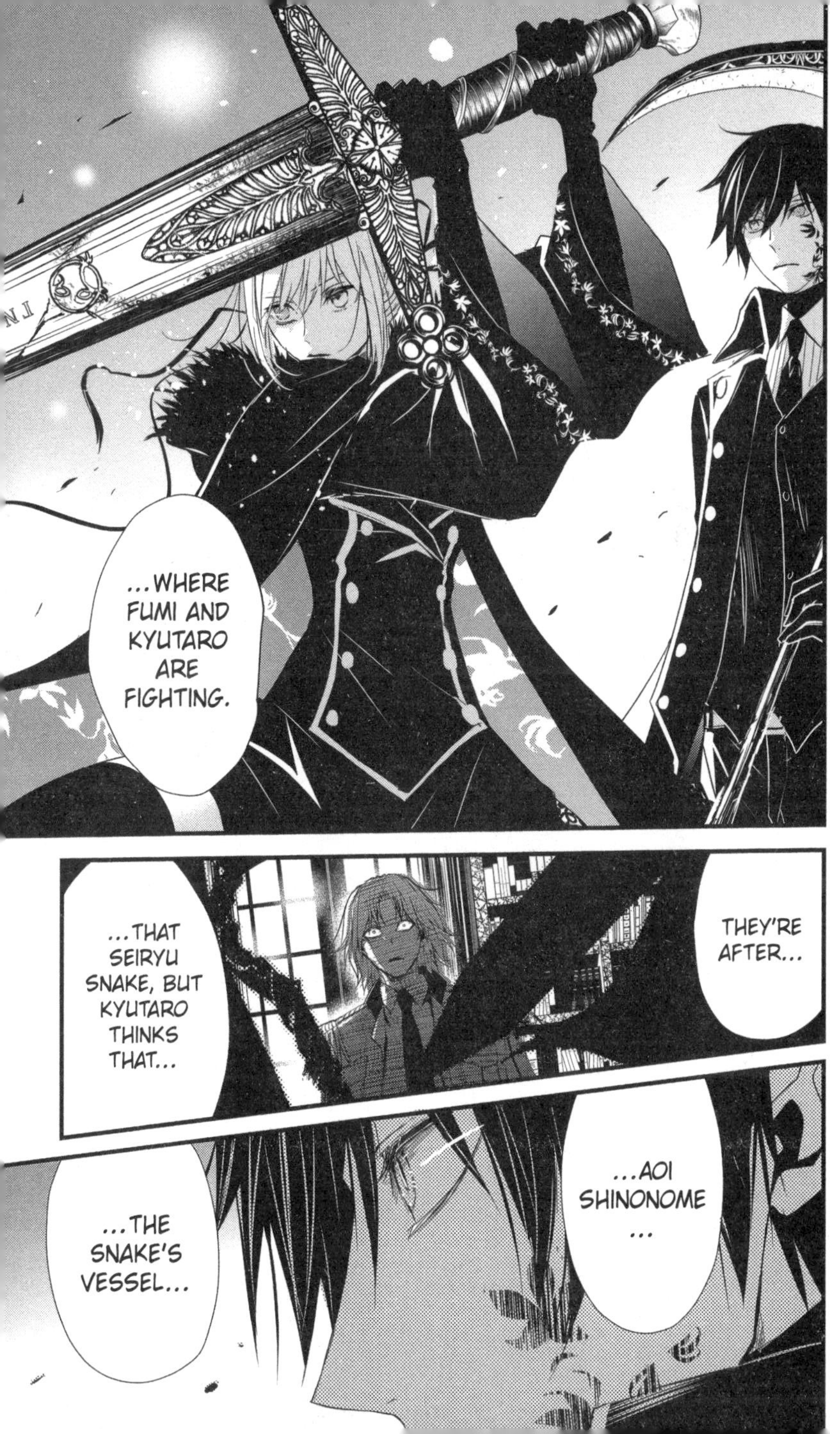
...WHERE FUMI AND KYUTARO ARE FIGHTING.
THEY'RE AFTER...
...THAT SEIRYU SNAKE, BUT KYUTARO THINKS THAT...
...AOI SHINONOME ...
...THE SNAKE'S VESSEL...

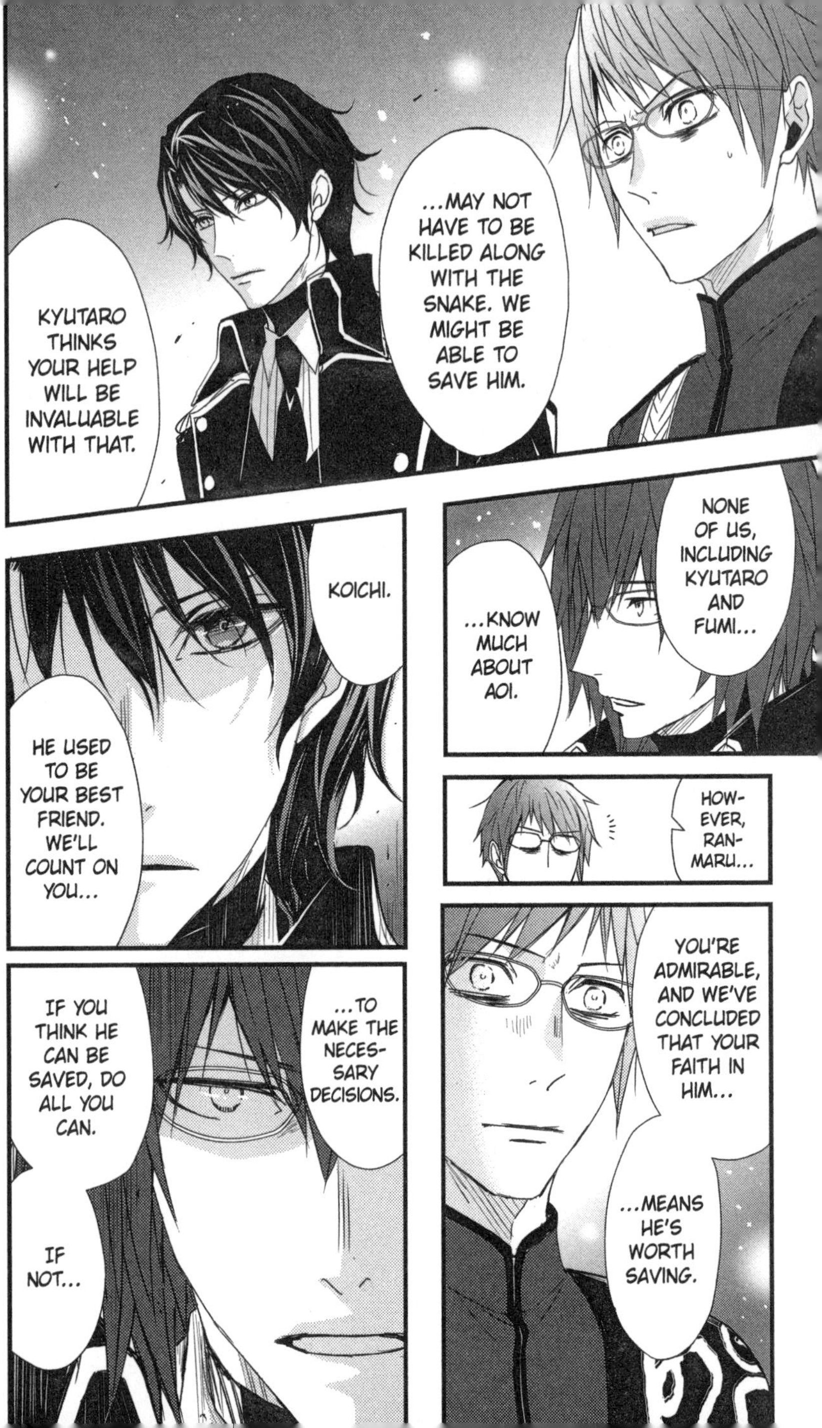
...MAY NOT HAVE TO BE KILLED ALONG WITH THE SNAKE. WE MIGHT BE ABLE TO SAVE HIM.
KYUTARO THINKS YOUR HELP WILL BE INVALUABLE WITH THAT.
NONE OF US, INCLUDING KYUTARO AND FUMI...
...KNOW MUCH ABOUT AOI.
HOW-EVER, RAN-MARU...
YOU'RE ADMIRABLE, AND WE'VE CONCLUDED THAT YOUR FAITH IN HIM...
...MEANS HE'S WORTH SAVING.
KOICHI.
HE USED TO BE YOUR BEST FRIEND. WE'LL COUNT ON YOU...
...TO MAKE THE NECES-SARY DECISIONS.
IF YOU THINK HE CAN BE SAVED, DO ALL YOU CAN.
IF NOT...

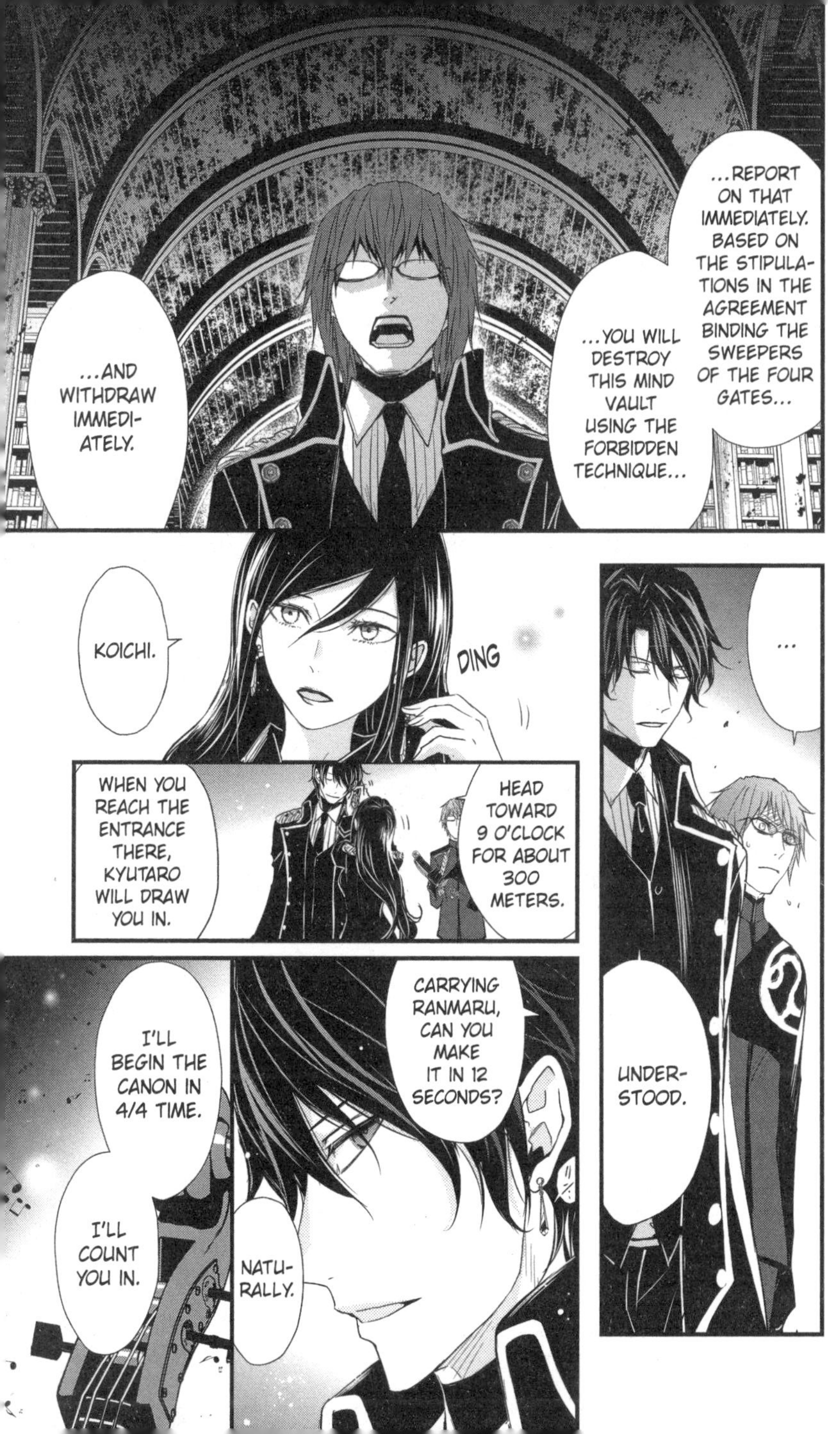
...REPORT ON THAT IMMEDIATELY. BASED ON THE STIPULATIONS IN THE AGREEMENT BINDING THE SWEEPERS OF THE FOUR GATES...
...YOU WILL DESTROY THIS MIND VAULT USING THE FORBIDDEN TECHNIQUE...
...AND WITHDRAW IMMEDIATELY.
...
UNDERSTOOD.
DING
KOICHI.
HEAD TOWARD 9 O'CLOCK FOR ABOUT 300 METERS.
WHEN YOU REACH THE ENTRANCE THERE, KYUTARO WILL DRAW YOU IN.
CARRYING RANMARU, CAN YOU MAKE IT IN 12 SECONDS?
NATURALLY.
I'LL BEGIN THE CANON IN 4/4 TIME.
I'LL COUNT YOU IN.

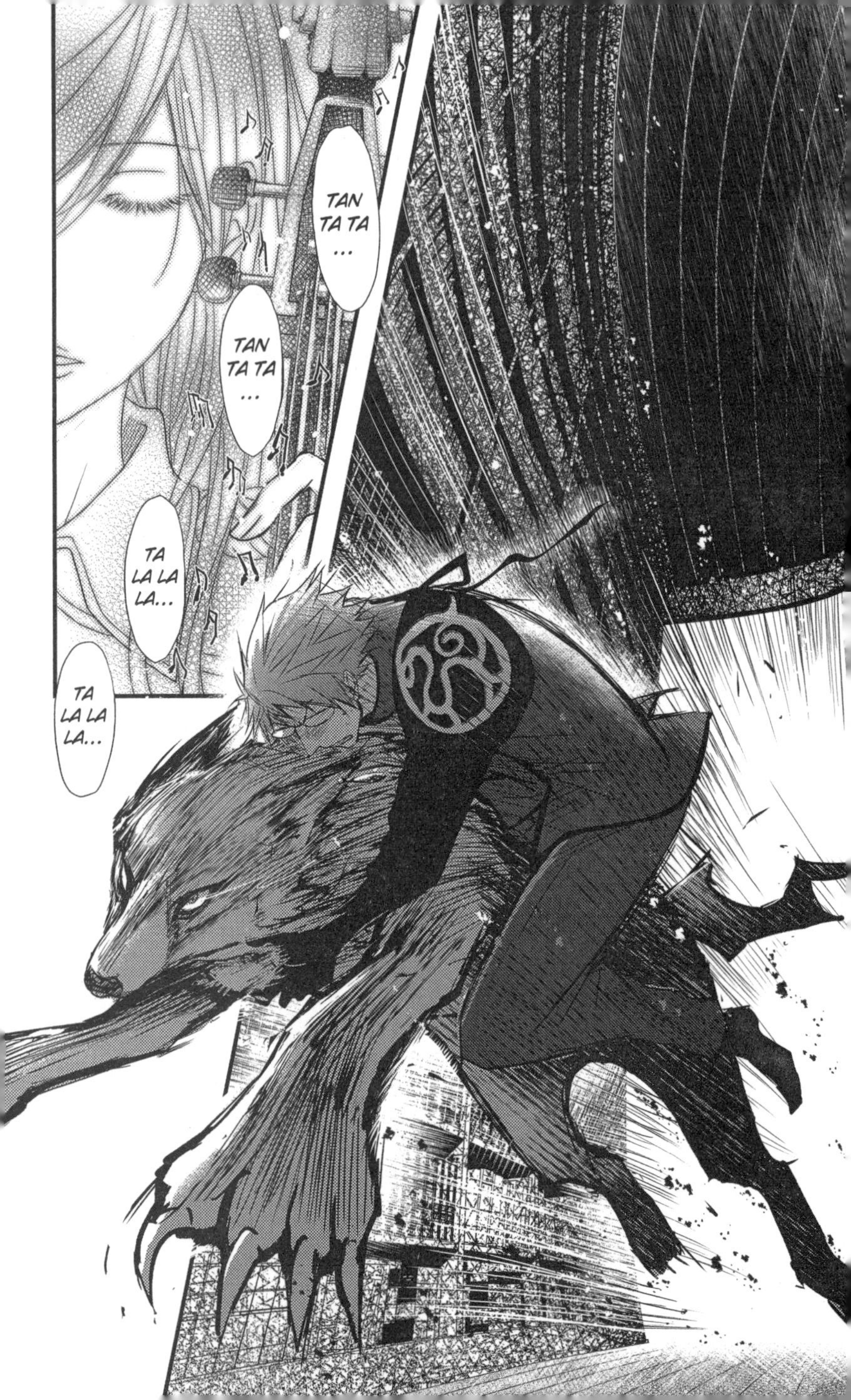
TAN TA TA ...
TAN TA TA ...
TA LA LA LA...
TA LA LA LA...

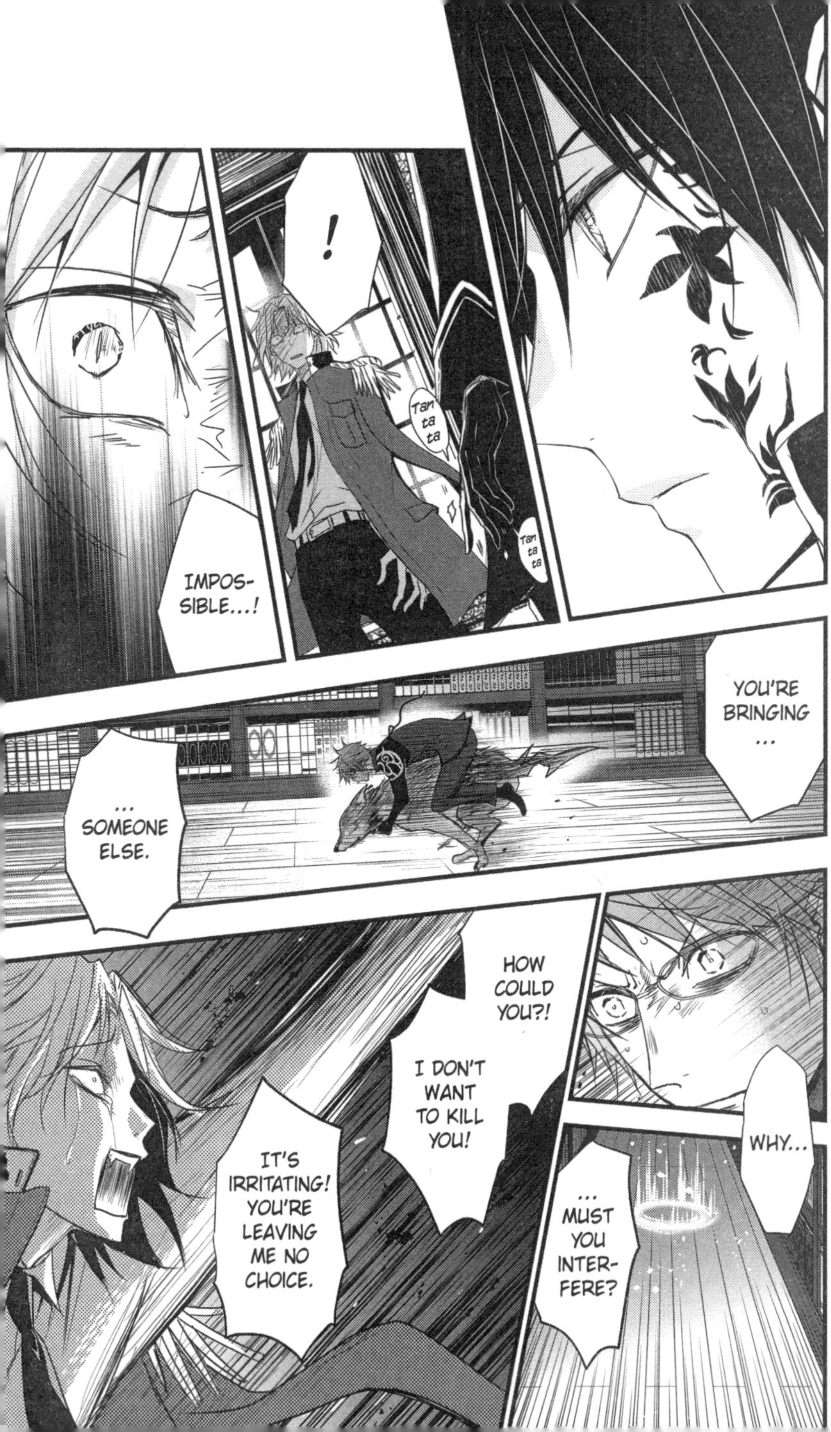
!
Tan ta ta
Tan ta ta
IMPOSSIBLE...!
YOU'RE BRINGING ...
... SOMEONE ELSE.
WHY...
... MUST YOU INTERFERE?
HOW COULD YOU?!
I DON'T WANT TO KILL YOU!
IT'S IRRITATING! YOU'RE LEAVING ME NO CHOICE.

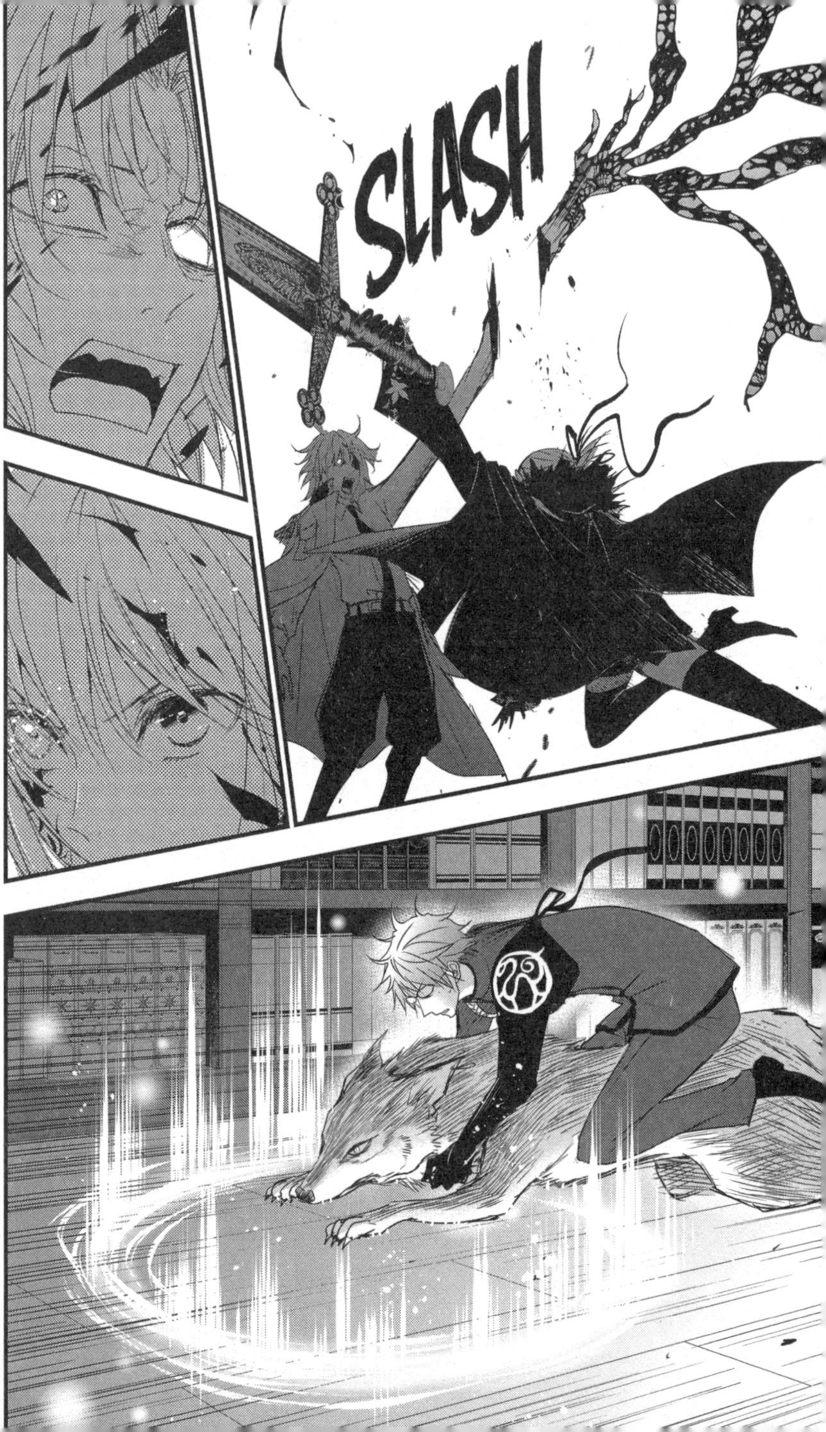
SLASH

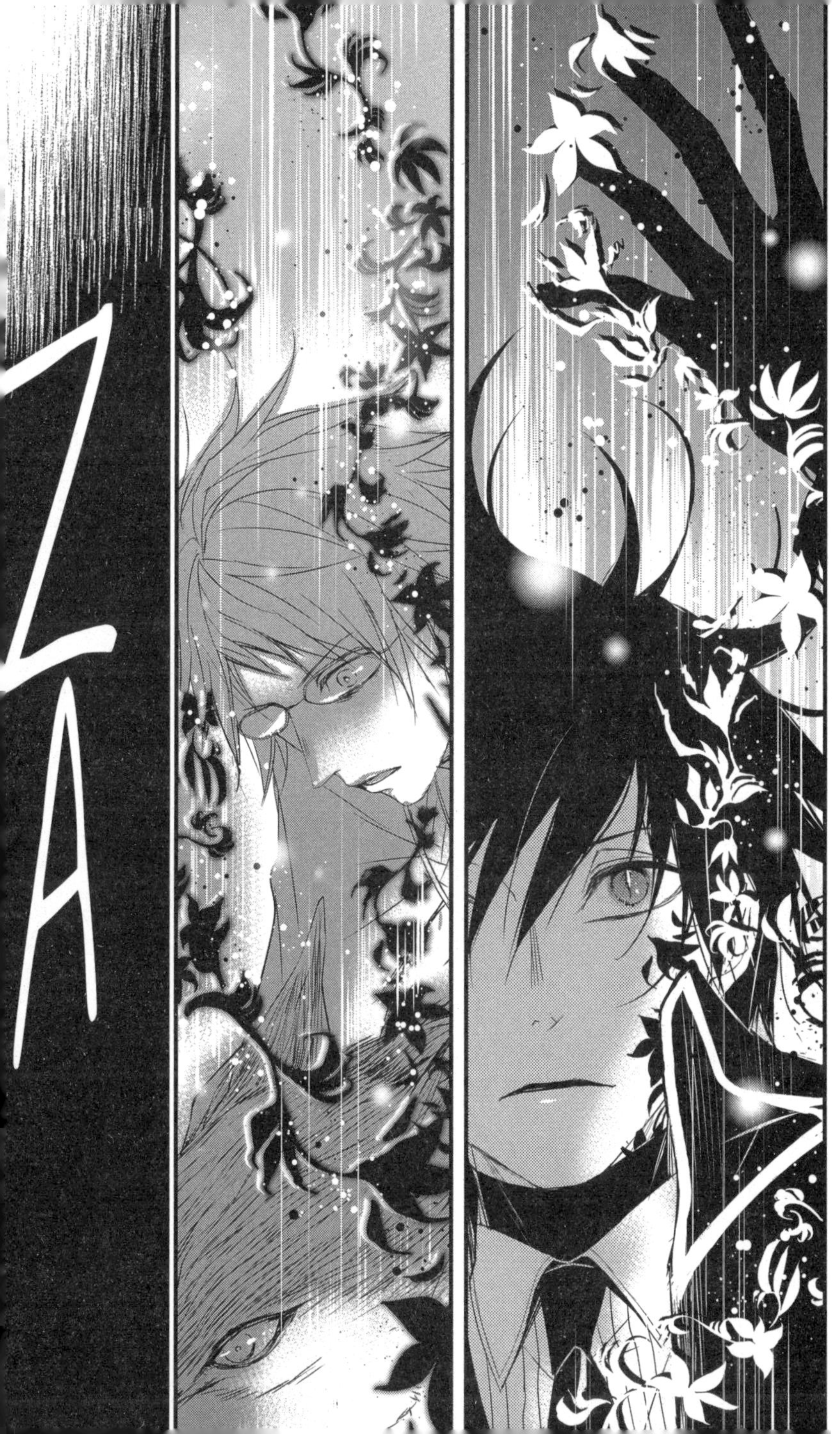
ZA

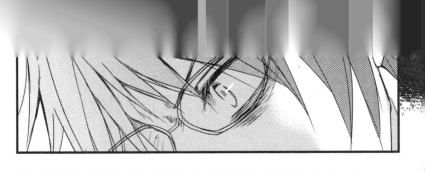

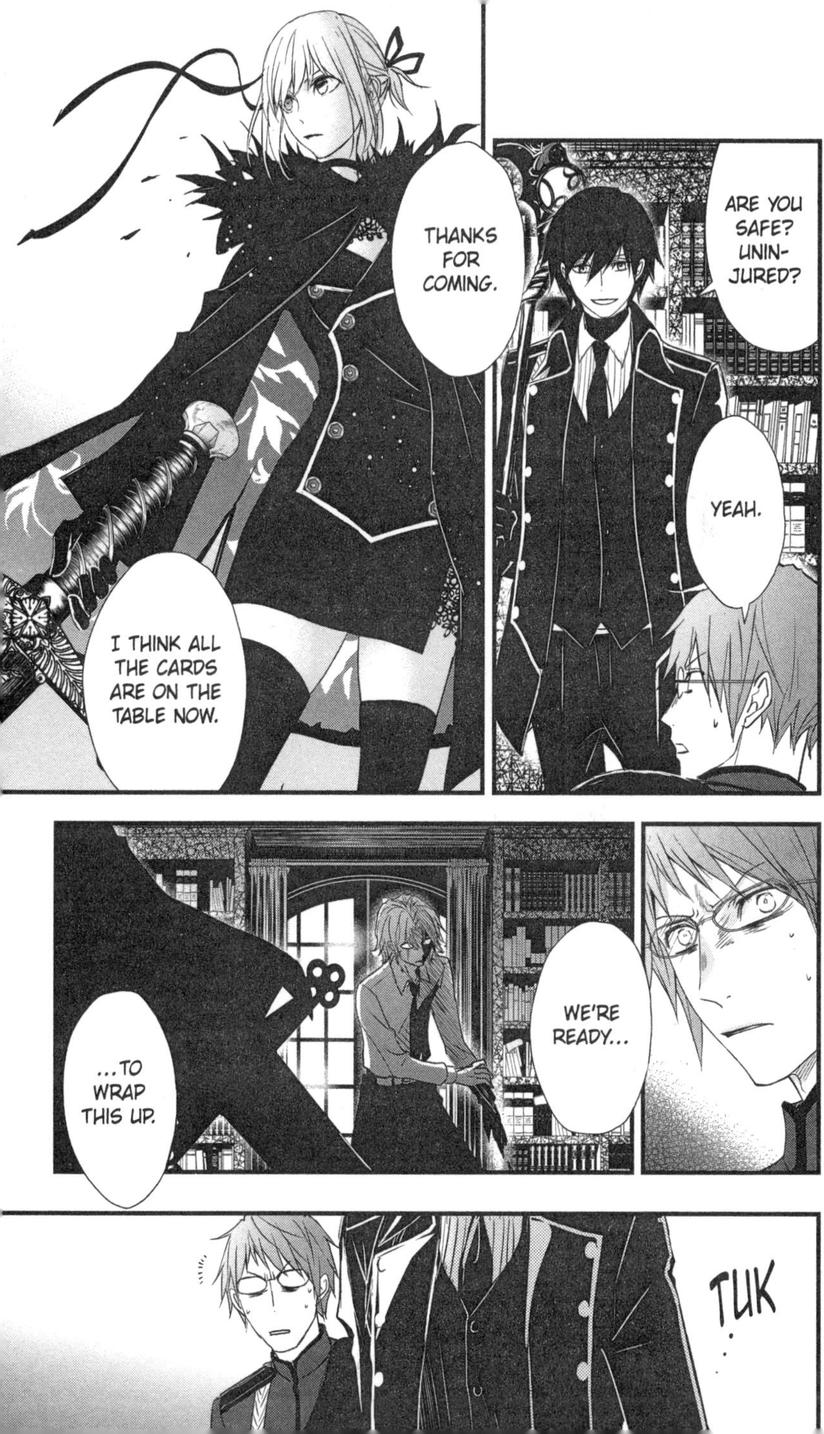
ARE YOU SAFE? UNIN-JURED?
YEAH.
THANKS FOR COMING.
I THINK ALL THE CARDS ARE ON THE TABLE NOW.
WE'RE READY...
...TO WRAP THIS UP.
TUK

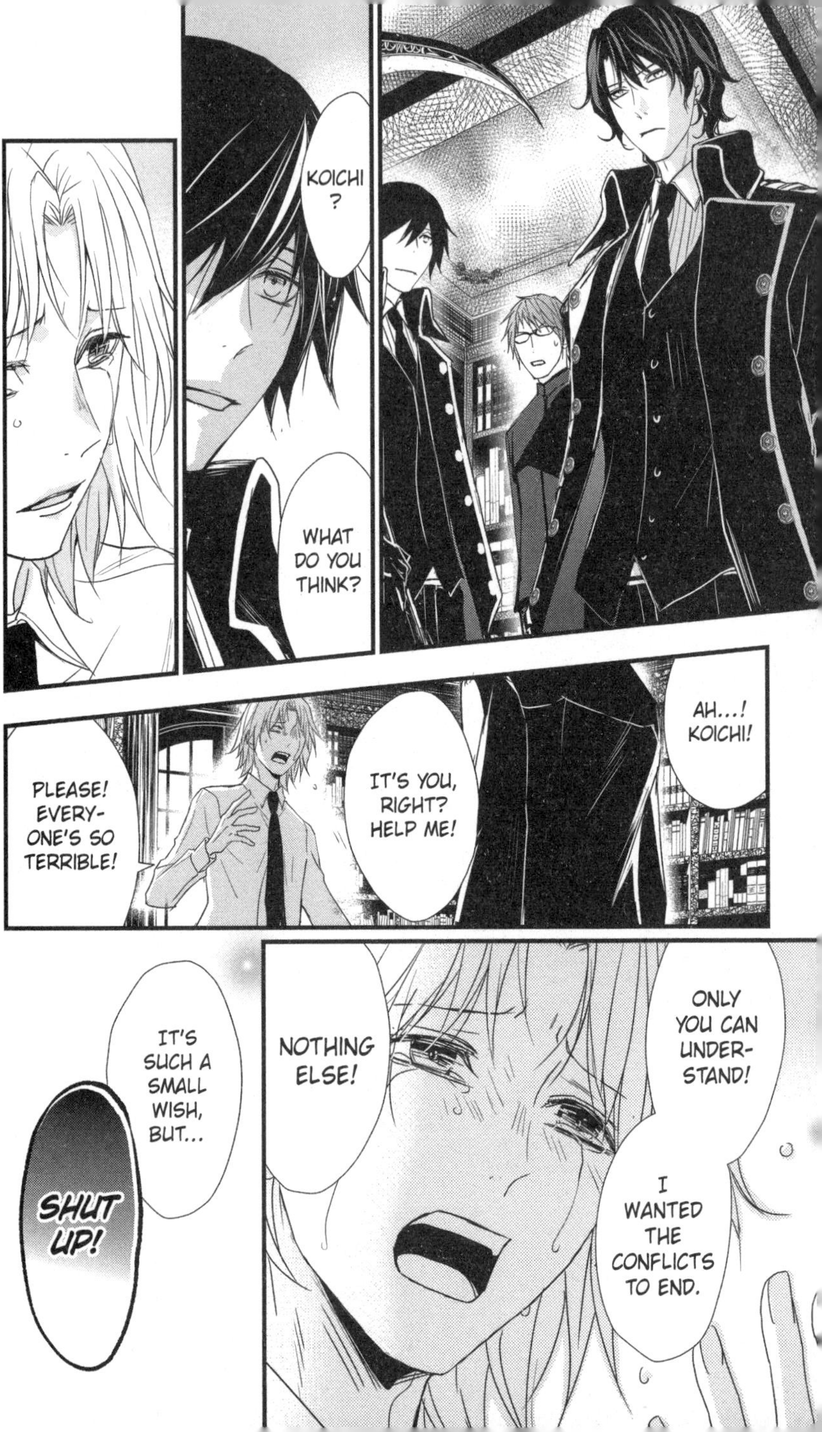
KOICHI?
WHAT DO YOU THINK?
AH...! KOICHI!
IT'S YOU, RIGHT? HELP ME!
PLEASE! EVERY-ONE'S SO TERRIBLE!
ONLY YOU CAN UNDER-STAND!
I WANTED THE CONFLICTS TO END.
NOTHING ELSE!
IT'S SUCH A SMALL WISH, BUT...
SHUT UP!

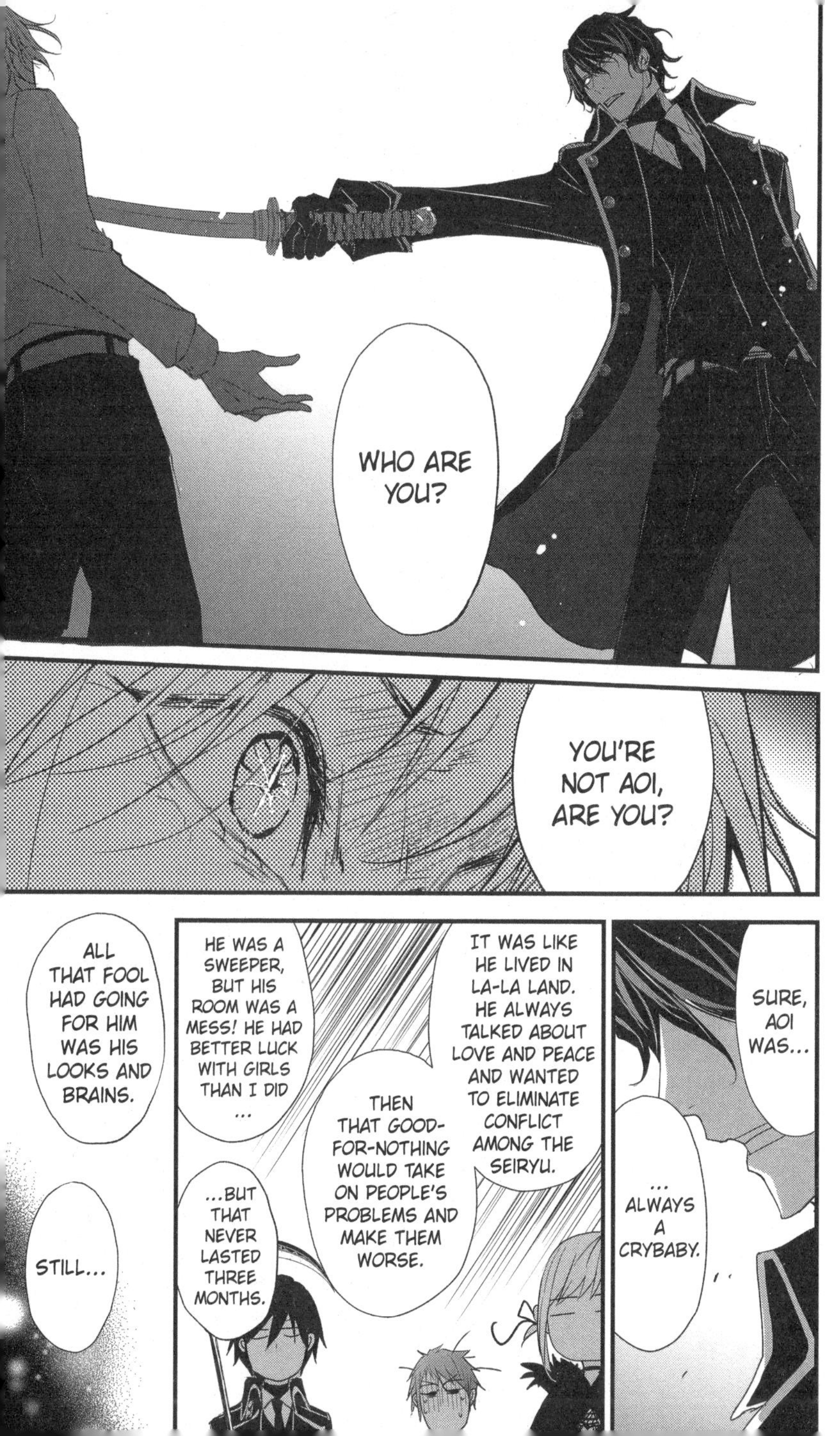
WHO ARE YOU?
YOU'RE NOT AOI, ARE YOU?
SURE, AOI WAS...
...ALWAYS A CRYBABY.
IT WAS LIKE HE LIVED IN LA-LA LAND. HE ALWAYS TALKED ABOUT LOVE AND PEACE AND WANTED TO ELIMINATE CONFLICT AMONG THE SEIRYU.
HE WAS A SWEEPER, BUT HIS ROOM WAS A MESS! HE HAD BETTER LUCK WITH GIRLS THAN I DID...
THEN THAT GOOD-FOR-NOTHING WOULD TAKE ON PEOPLE'S PROBLEMS AND MAKE THEM WORSE.
...BUT THAT NEVER LASTED THREE MONTHS.
ALL THAT FOOL HAD GOING FOR HIM WAS HIS LOOKS AND BRAINS.
STILL...

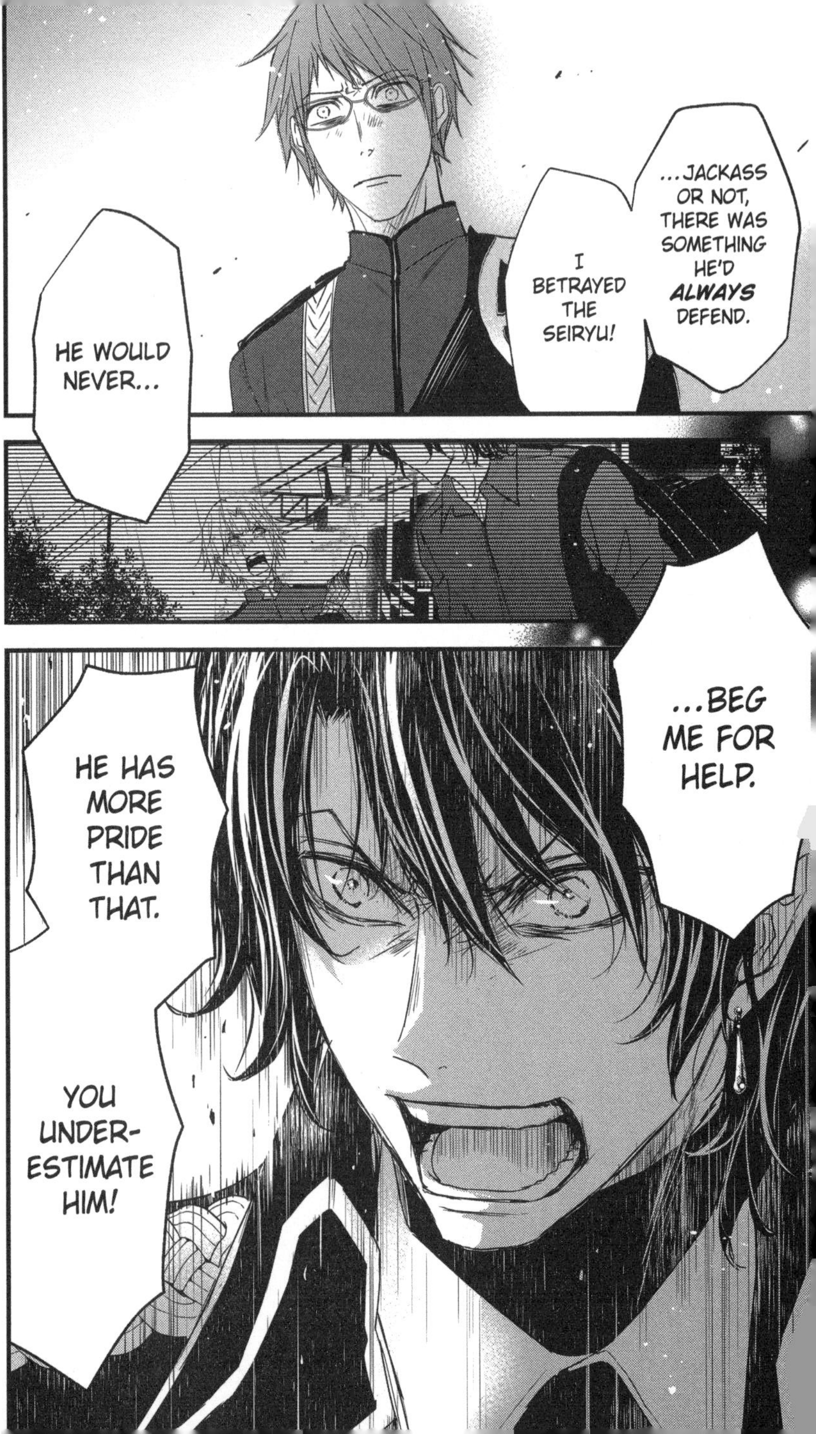
...JACKASS OR NOT, THERE WAS SOMETHING HE'D **ALWAYS** DEFEND.
I BETRAYED THE SEIRYU!
HE WOULD NEVER...
...BEG ME FOR HELP.
HE HAS MORE PRIDE THAN THAT.
YOU UNDER-ESTIMATE HIM!

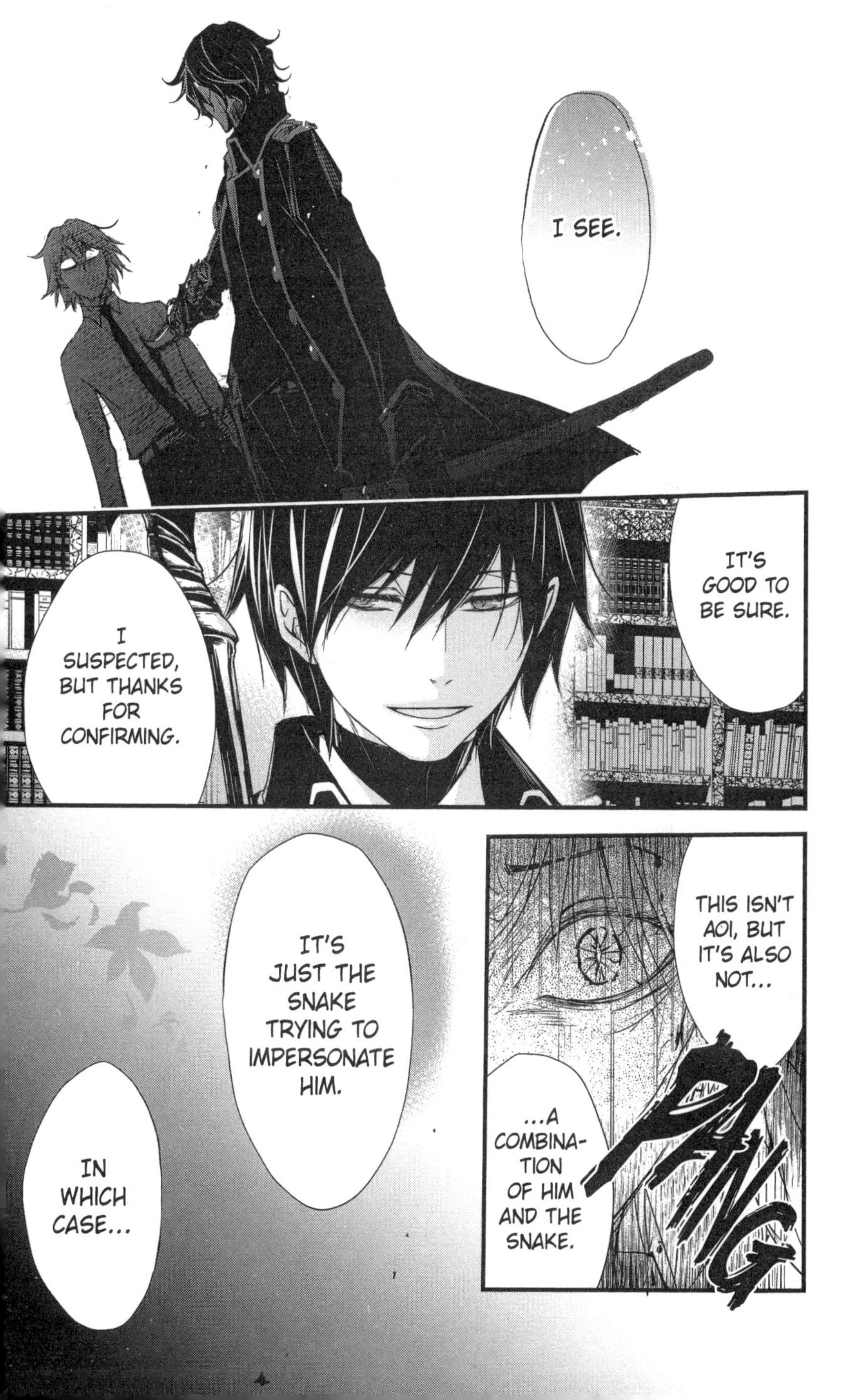
I SEE.
IT'S GOOD TO BE SURE.
I SUSPECTED, BUT THANKS FOR CONFIRMING.
THIS ISN'T AOI, BUT IT'S ALSO NOT...
...A COMBINA-TION OF HIM AND THE SNAKE.
PANG
IT'S JUST THE SNAKE TRYING TO IMPERSONATE HIM.
IN WHICH CASE...

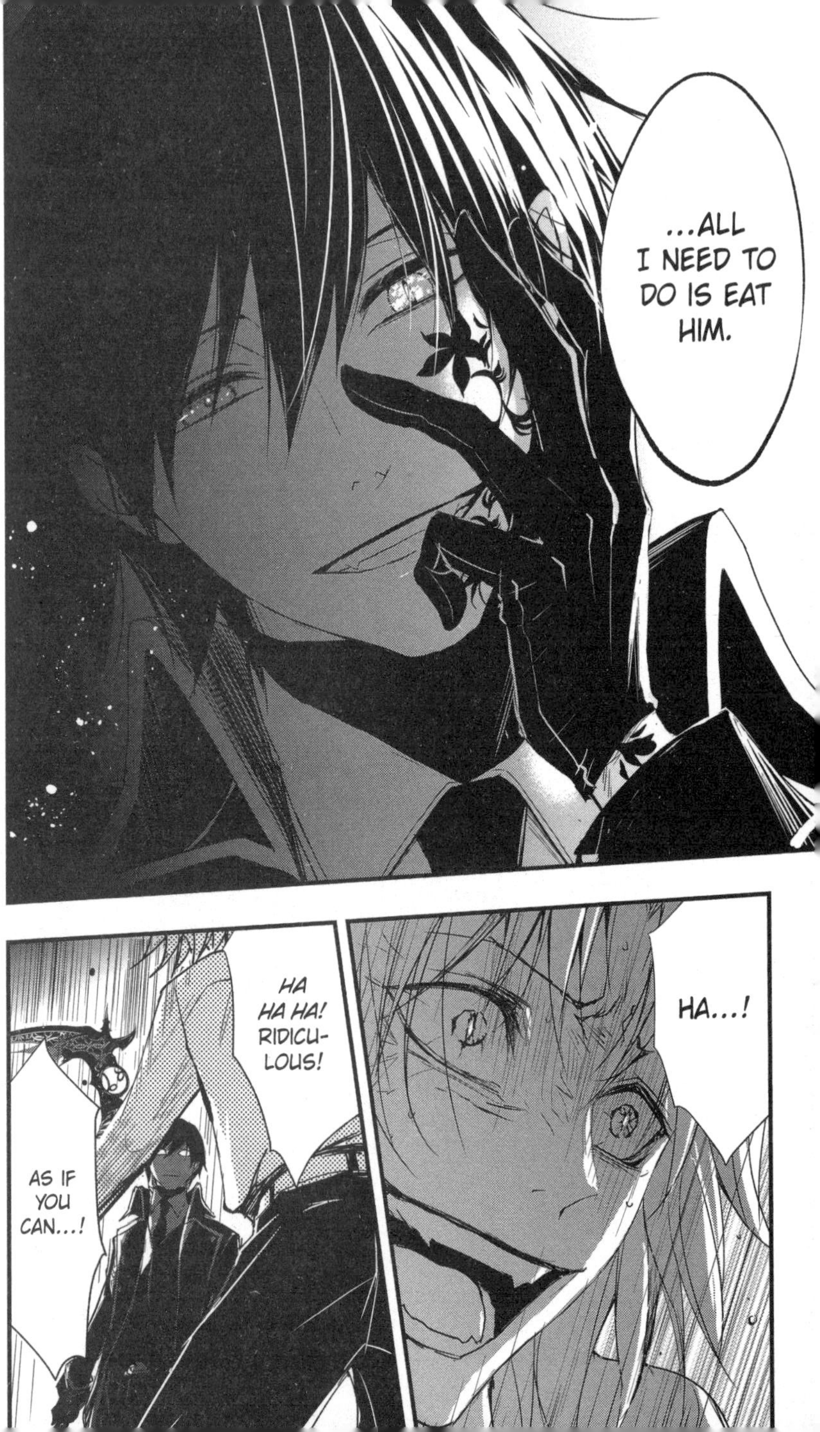
...ALL I NEED TO DO IS EAT HIM.
HA...!
HA HA HA! RIDICULOUS!
AS IF YOU CAN...!

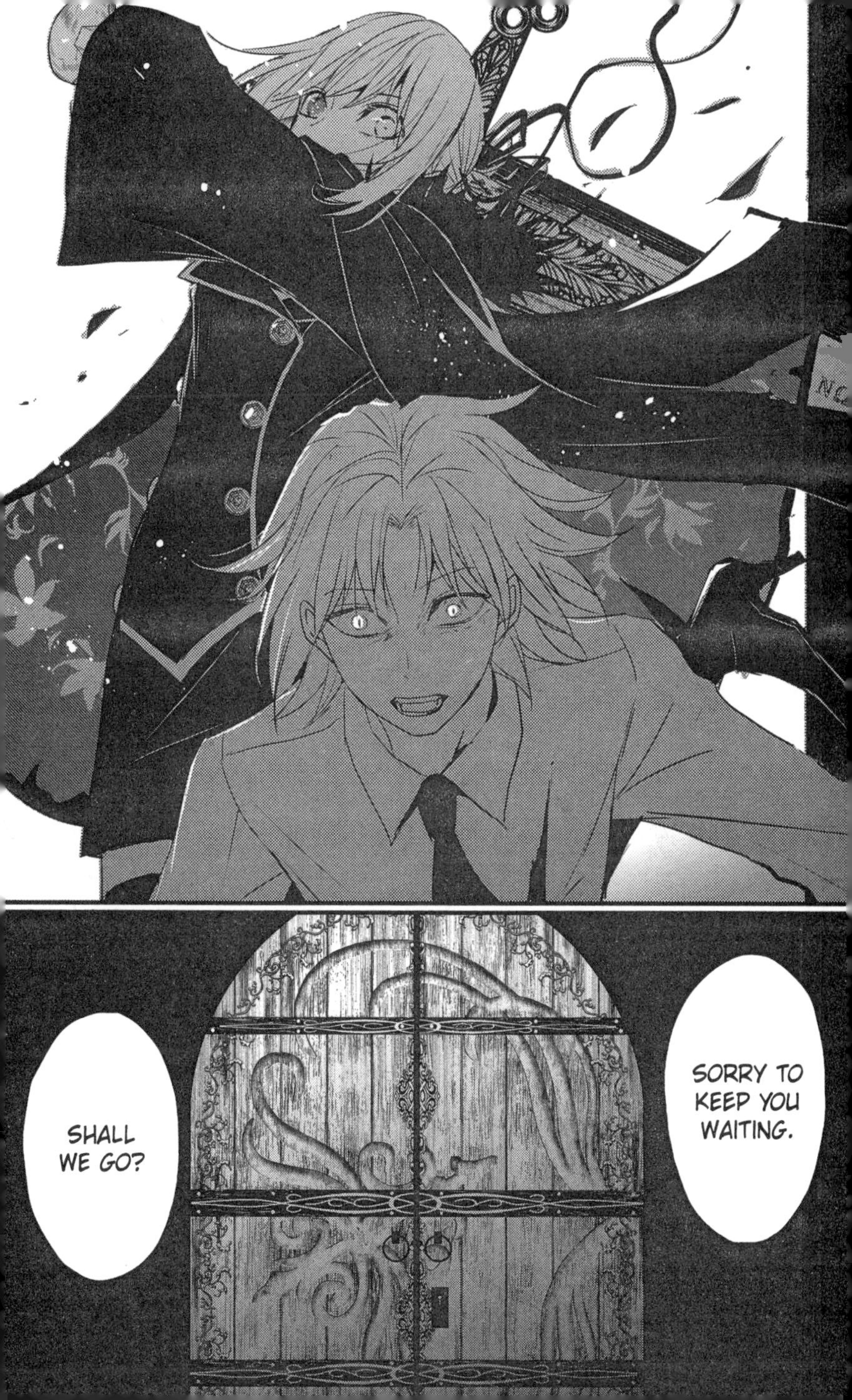
SORRY TO KEEP YOU WAITING.
SHALL WE GO?

MONTHLY BETSUCOMI SALE DATE NOTICE ON TWITTER AND INSTAGRAM

CHAPTER 57

Important Genbu Meeting
Re: The True Queen's (Fumi) New Costume
* Based on the Genbu uniform
* Inspired by former Queen Toko's costume
* Miniskirt, since she's young
+A longer cape would be cute. (Mutsumi)
* Add fur to make it look more luxurious. (Koichi)
* A flower design would look elegant. (Miyako)
* The neckline shouldn't be too low, should it? (Takaya)
TO BE BLUNT, WHAT'S THE POINT IF THERE'S NOTHING TO SHOW?
I JUST DON'T THINK IT ADDS ANY-THING.
OF COURSE IT MATTERS! EVERYONE'S ENTITLED TO FLAUNT WHATEVER THEY HAVE!
?
SHOWING A BIT OF SKIN IS MORE FASHIONABLE THAN SHOWING NOTHING BUT BLACK. BESIDES, IT'S CUTE! MORE IMPORTANTLY, IT'LL GIVE ME MORE ENERGY!
Kyutaro's just an ordinary boy, isn't he?

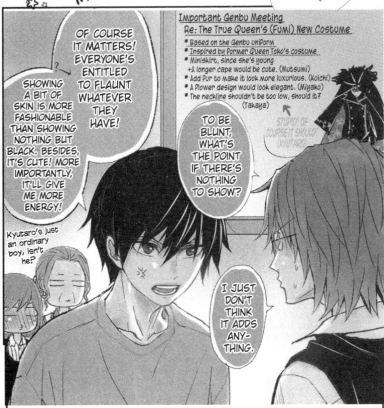

LET'S SEE... WHAT'S UP IN *QUEEN'S QUALITY* THIS MONTH?
1) MEAN KYUTARO POKES THE SAME SPOT KOICHI DID THE LAST TIME.
2) SHIRTS USED TO BE NORMAL BEFORE.
3) FUMI'S OPEN NECKLINE LOOKS A LITTLE FORCED.

KYUTARO AND RANMARU DO THEIR BEST TO SHOW OFF, BUT IT LOOKS LIKE CHAPTER 57 BELONGS TO KOICHI AND AOI.

THERE ARE A LOT OF WORDS IN THIS PICTURE, SO I TRIED TO BLOW IT UP AS MUCH AS POSSIBLE. IT'S PROBABLY STILL HARD TO READ, SO PLEASE TAKE A LOOK AT IT ON TWITTER OR INSTAGRAM.

Chapter 57

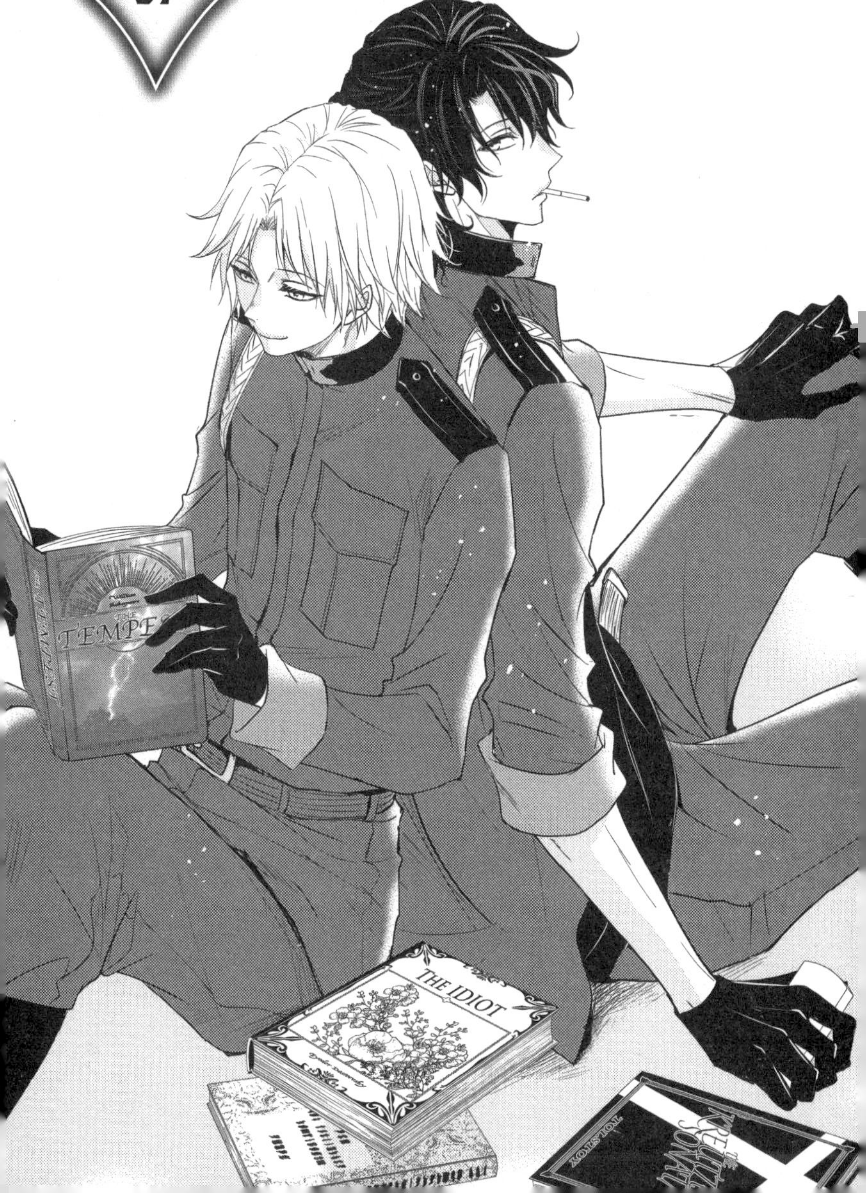
THE IDIOT
TOLSTOY

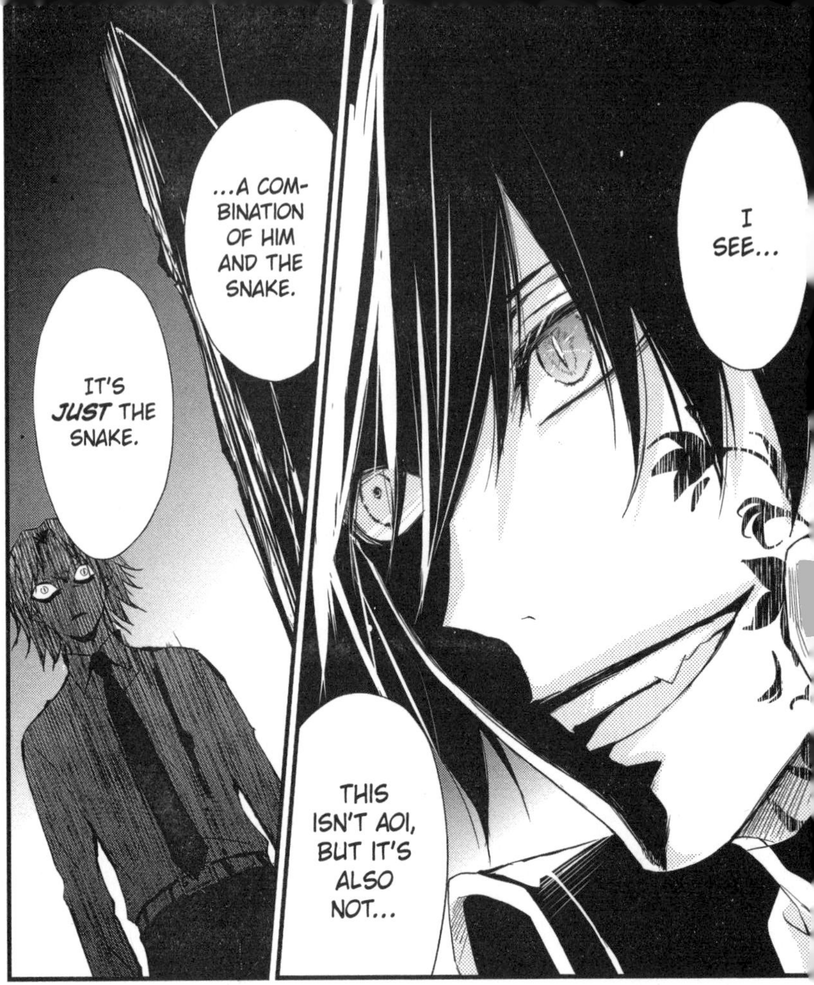
I SEE...
THIS ISN'T AOI, BUT IT'S ALSO NOT...
...A COMBINATION OF HIM AND THE SNAKE.
IT'S *JUST* THE SNAKE.

Volume 12 has gone on sale much later than was announced in volume 11. I have to apologize to all my readers who were eagerly looking forward to this. The delay was not due to health problems (I've been quite well), but because the editorial department asked me to do an extra and a new one-shot story. I had quite a number of extras prepared, so they were published as a volume before I could get to volume 12. I hope you will be able to read that as well.

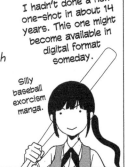

I hadn't done a new one-shot in about 14 years. This one might become available in digital format someday.

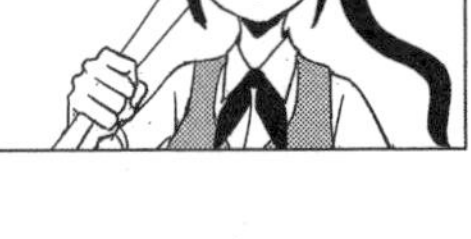
Silly baseball exorcism manga.

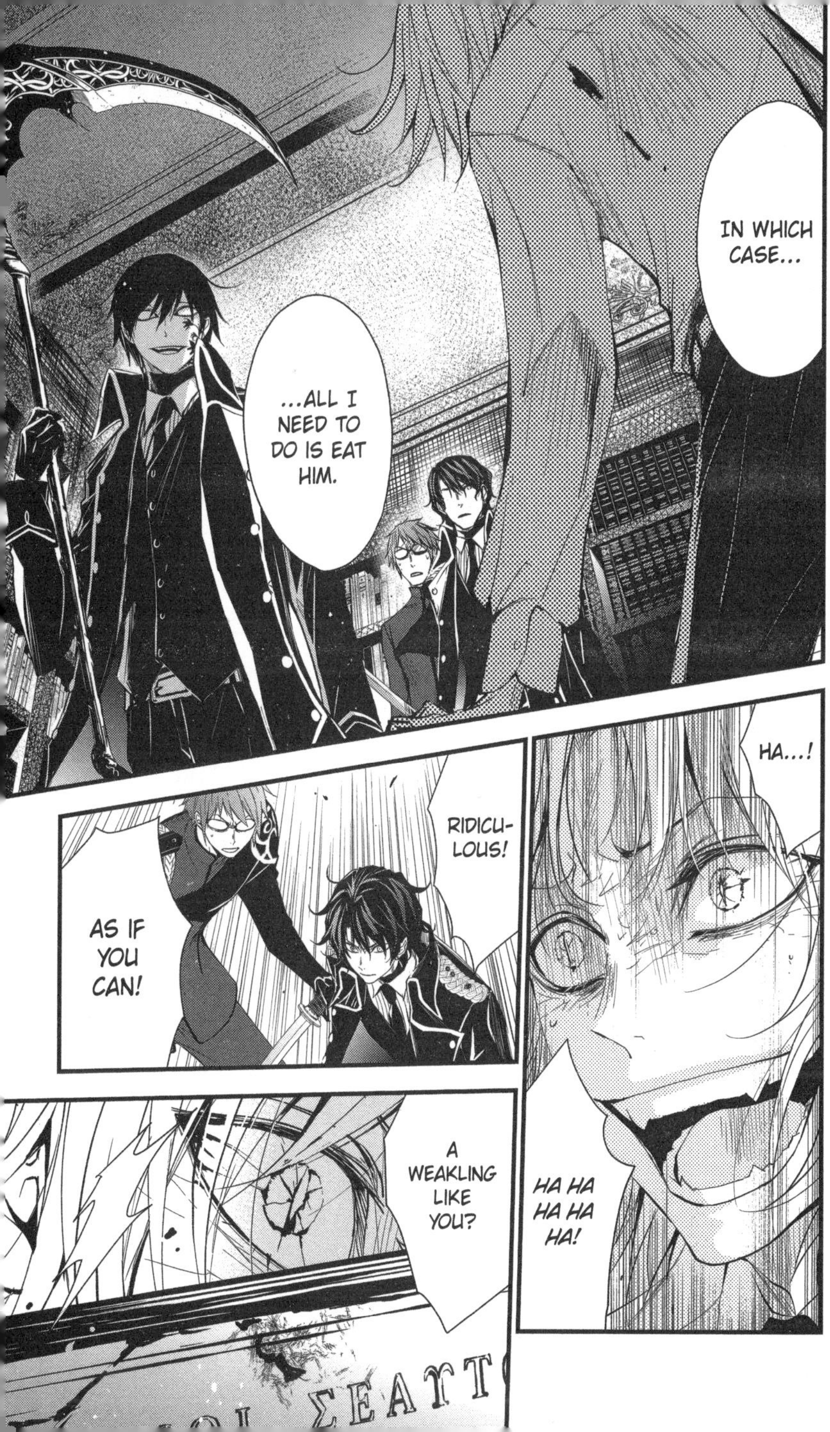
IN WHICH CASE...
...ALL I NEED TO DO IS EAT HIM.
HA...!
HA HA HA HA HA!
RIDICU-LOUS!
AS IF YOU CAN!
A WEAKLING LIKE YOU?

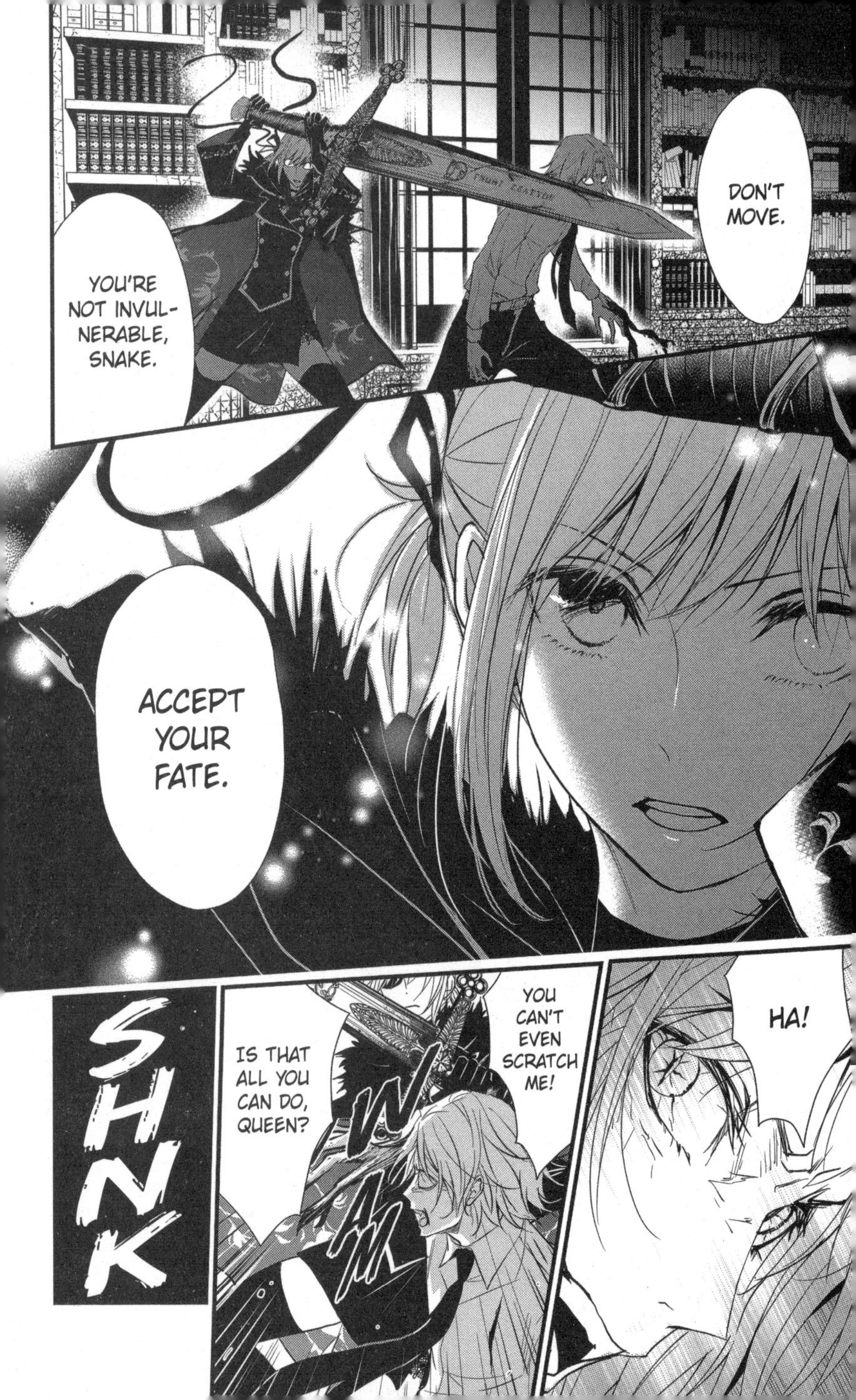
DON'T MOVE.
YOU'RE NOT INVUL-NERABLE, SNAKE.
ACCEPT YOUR FATE.
HA!
YOU CAN'T EVEN SCRATCH ME!
IS THAT ALL YOU CAN DO, QUEEN?
SHNK

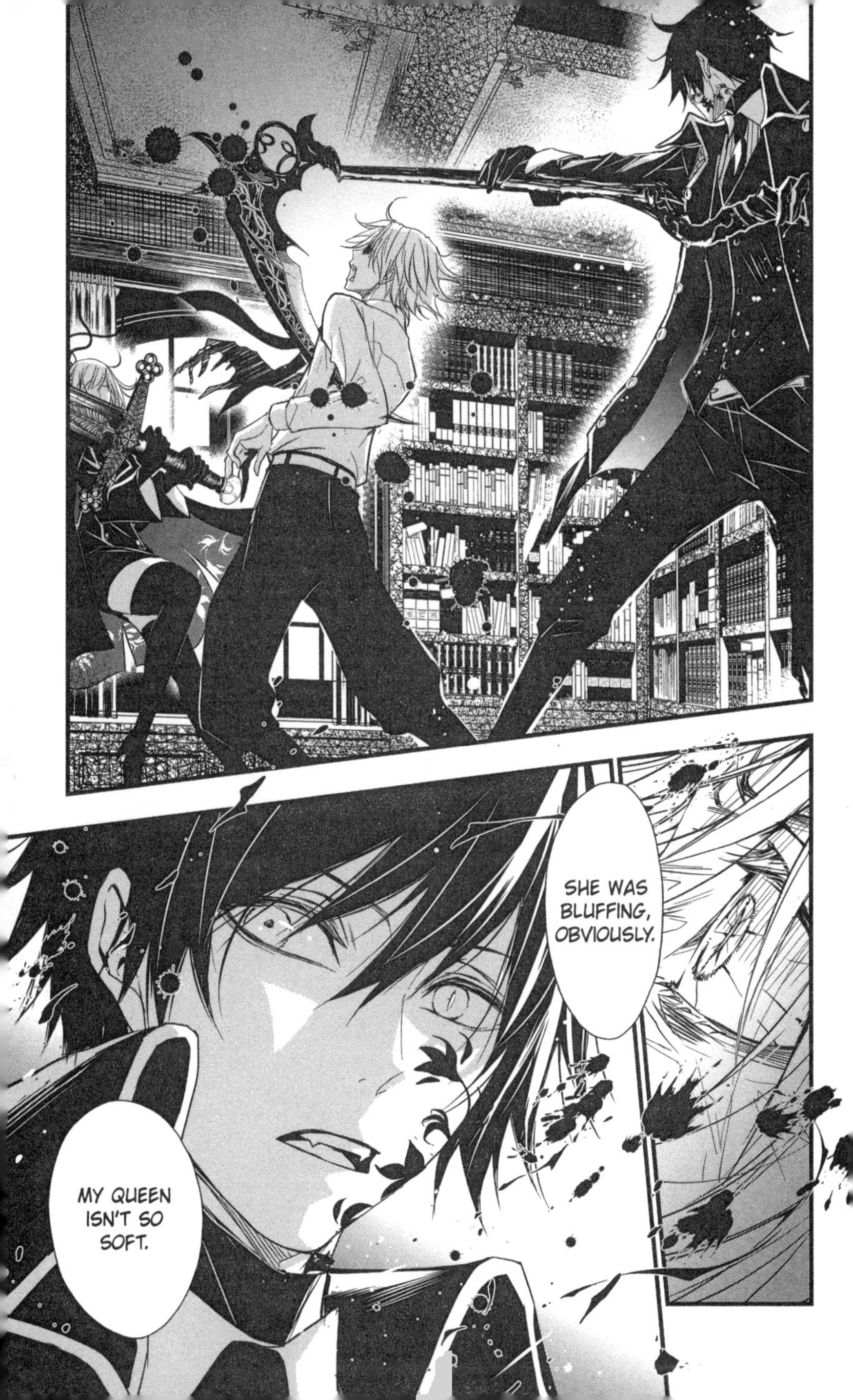
SHE WAS BLUFFING, OBVIOUSLY.
MY QUEEN ISN'T SO SOFT.

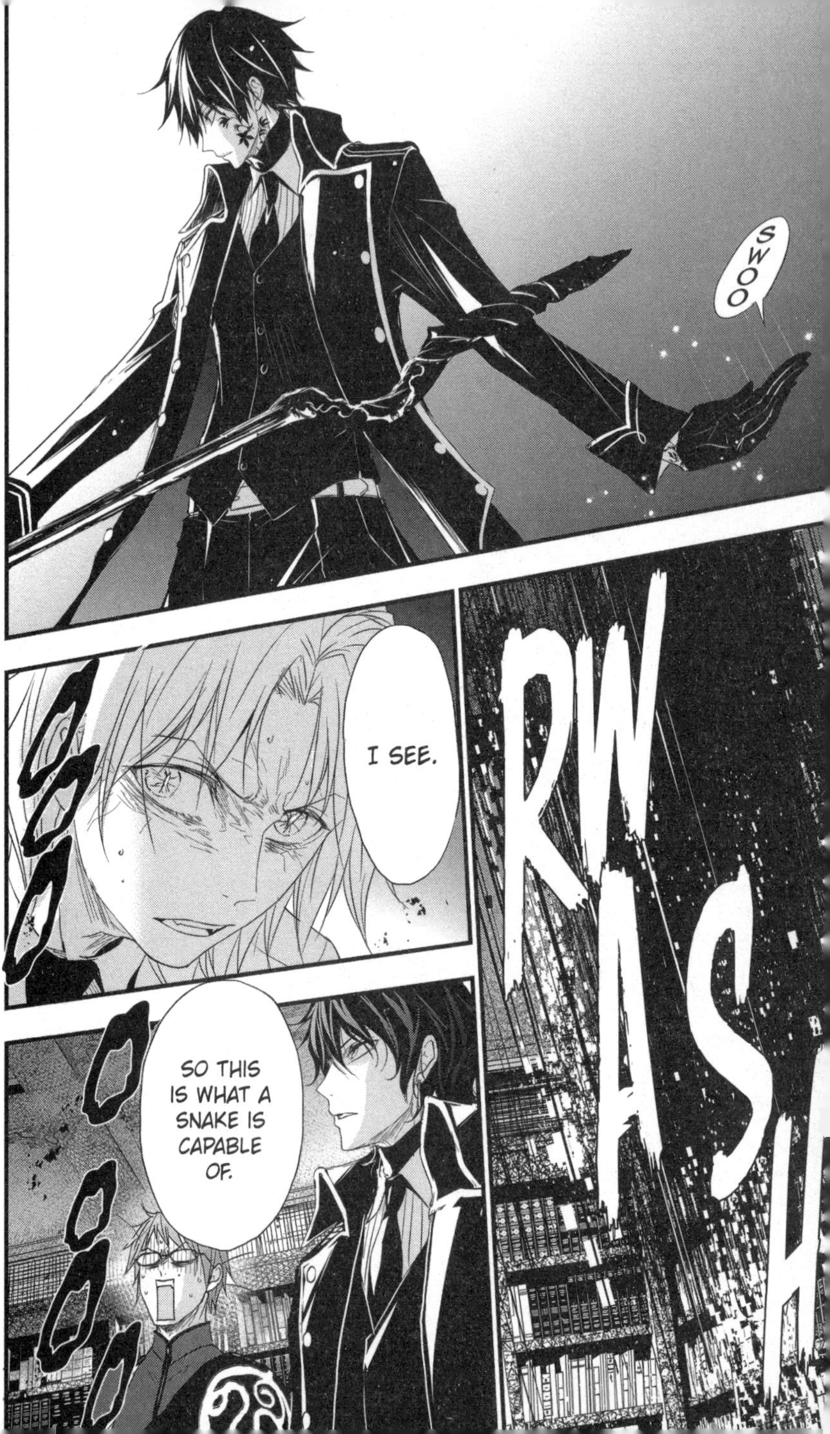
SWOO
RWASH
I SEE.
SO THIS IS WHAT A SNAKE IS CAPABLE OF.

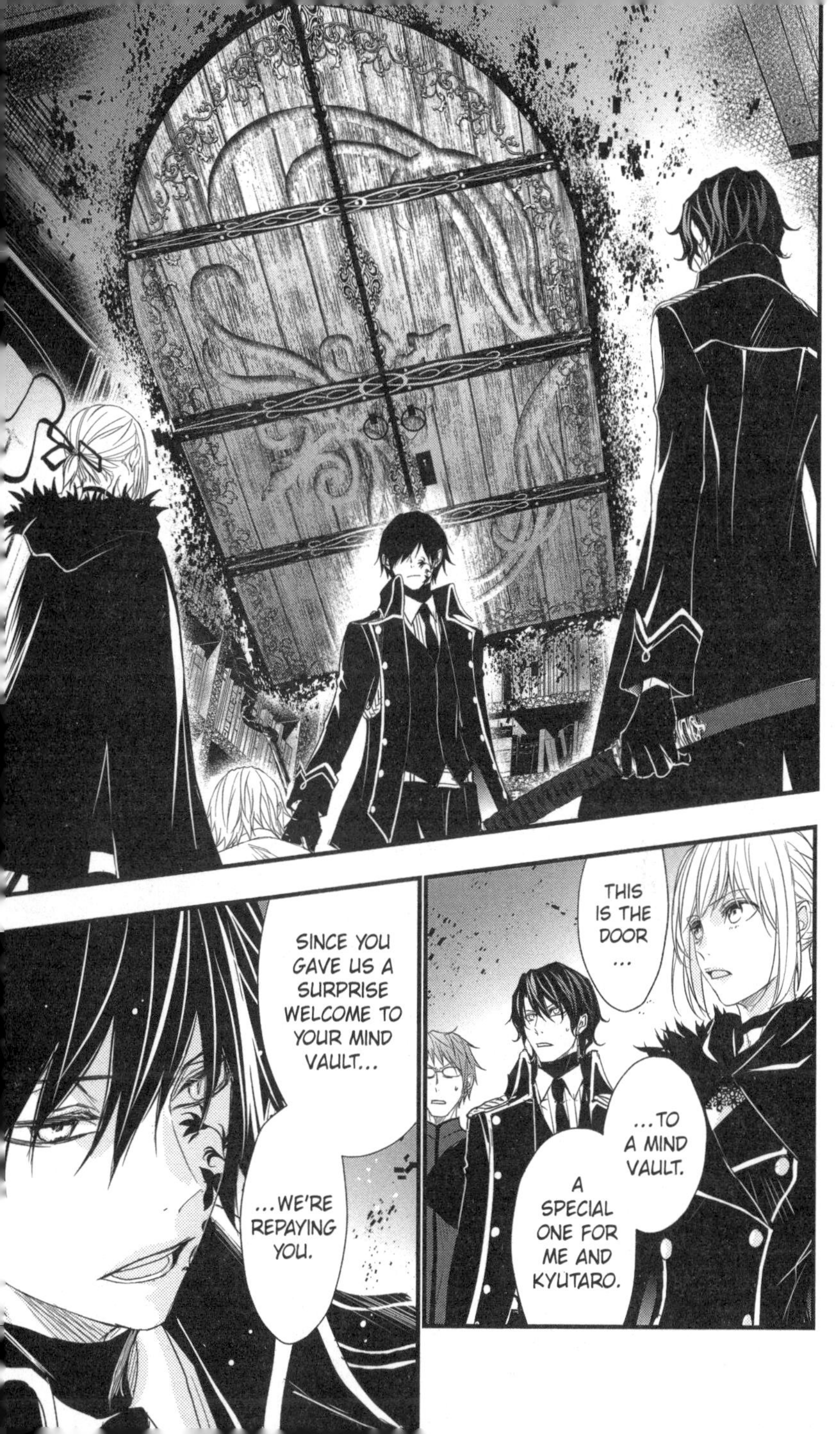
THIS IS THE DOOR...
...TO A MIND VAULT.
A SPECIAL ONE FOR ME AND KYUTARO.
SINCE YOU GAVE US A SURPRISE WELCOME TO YOUR MIND VAULT...
...WE'RE REPAYING YOU.

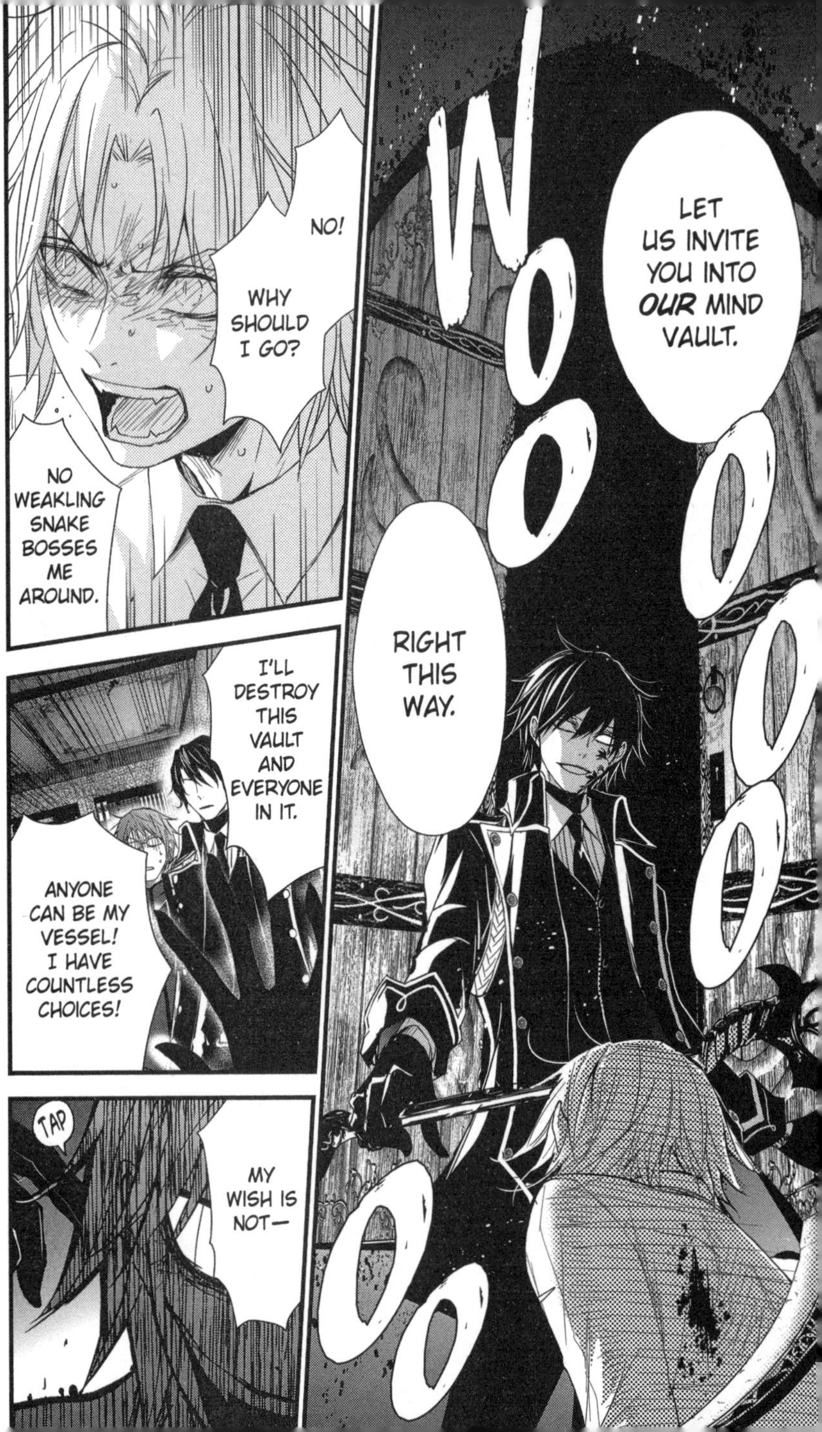
LET US INVITE YOU INTO *OUR* MIND VAULT.
WOOOOOOO
RIGHT THIS WAY.
NO!
WHY SHOULD I GO?
NO WEAKLING SNAKE BOSSES ME AROUND.
I'LL DESTROY THIS VAULT AND EVERYONE IN IT.
ANYONE CAN BE MY VESSEL! I HAVE COUNTLESS CHOICES!
TAP
MY WISH IS NOT—

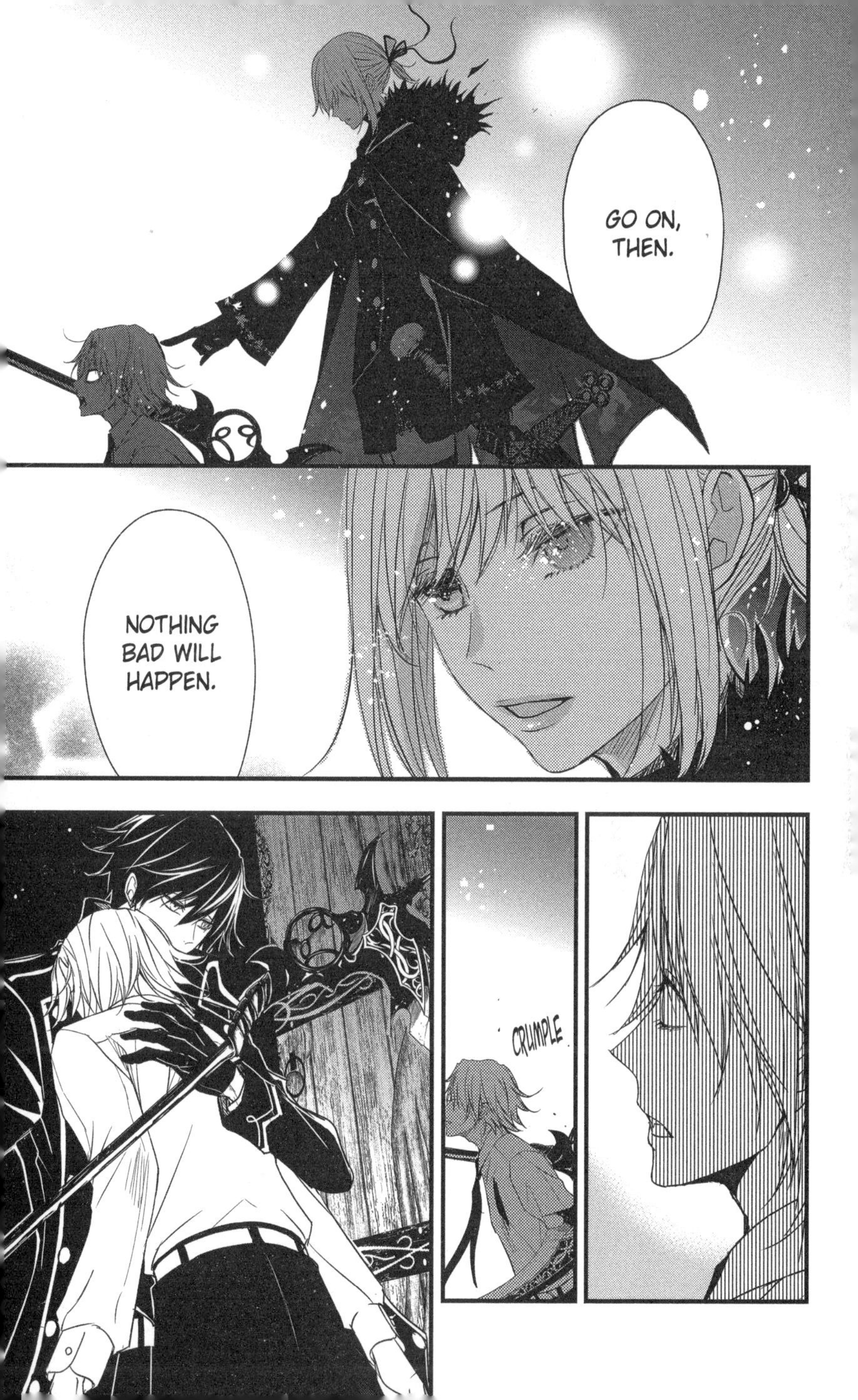
GO ON, THEN.
NOTHING BAD WILL HAPPEN.
CRUMPLE

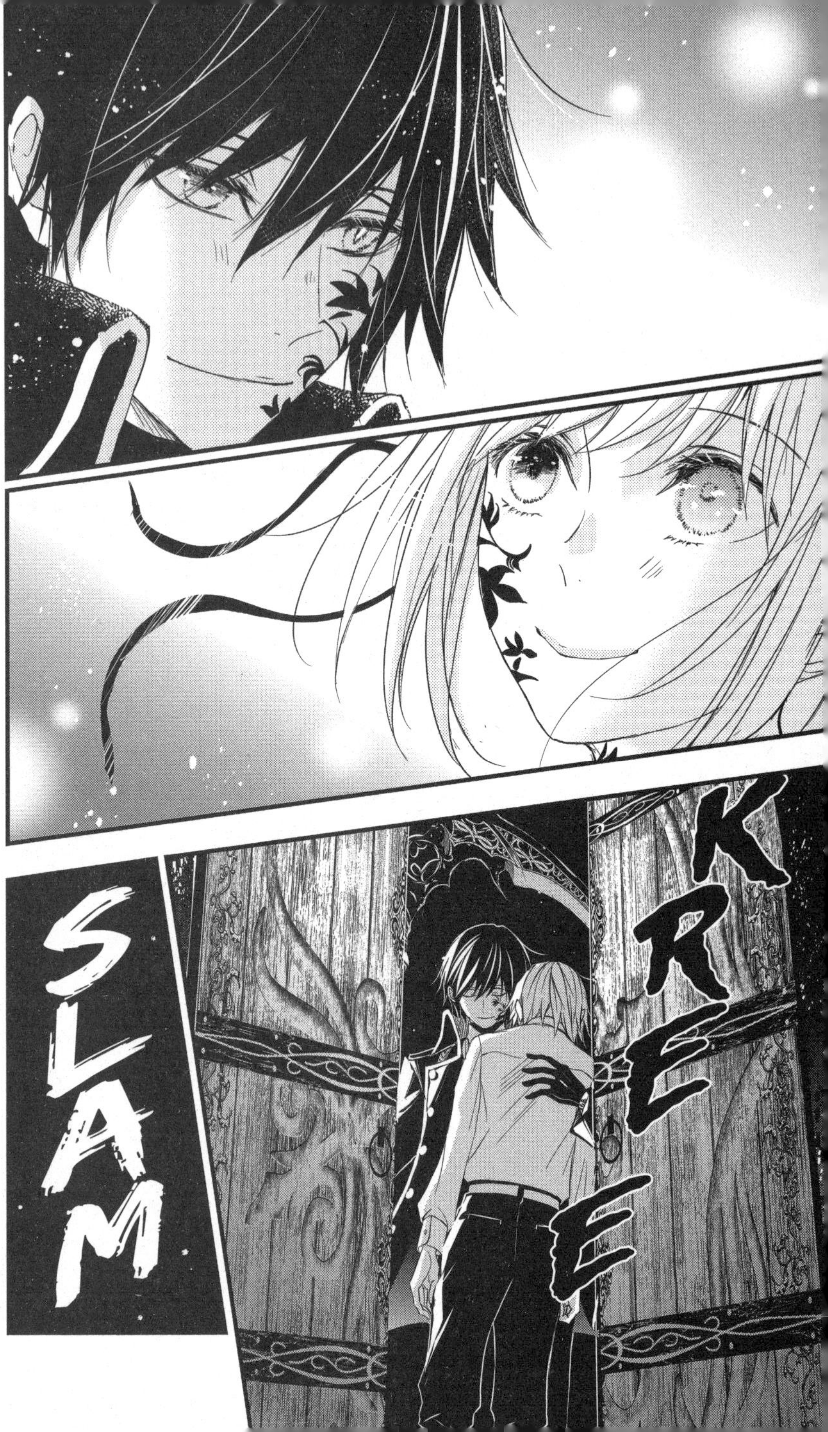
KREEE
SLAM

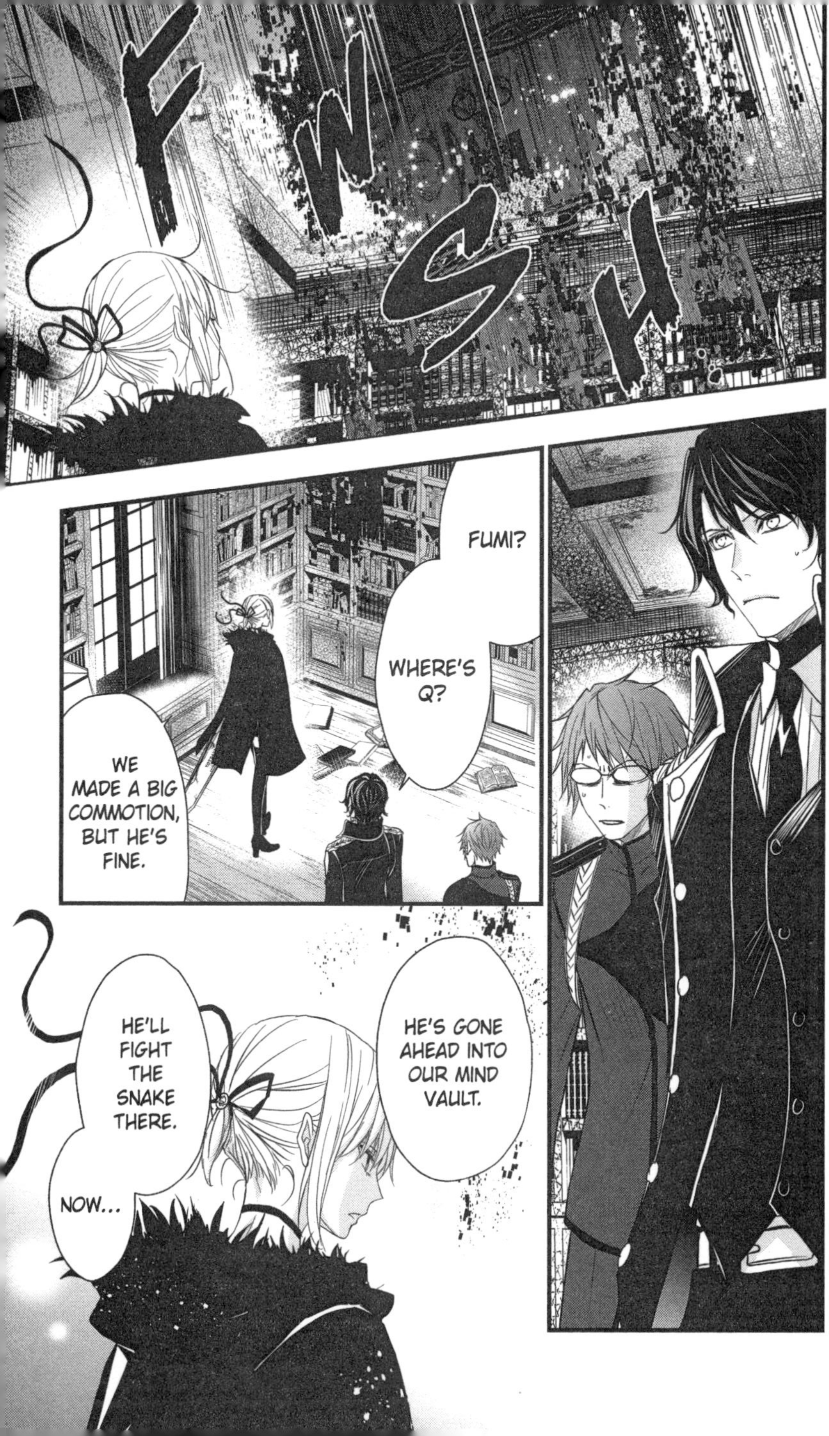
FWSH
FUMI?
WHERE'S Q?
WE MADE A BIG COMMOTION, BUT HE'S FINE.
HE'S GONE AHEAD INTO OUR MIND VAULT.
HE'LL FIGHT THE SNAKE THERE.
NOW...

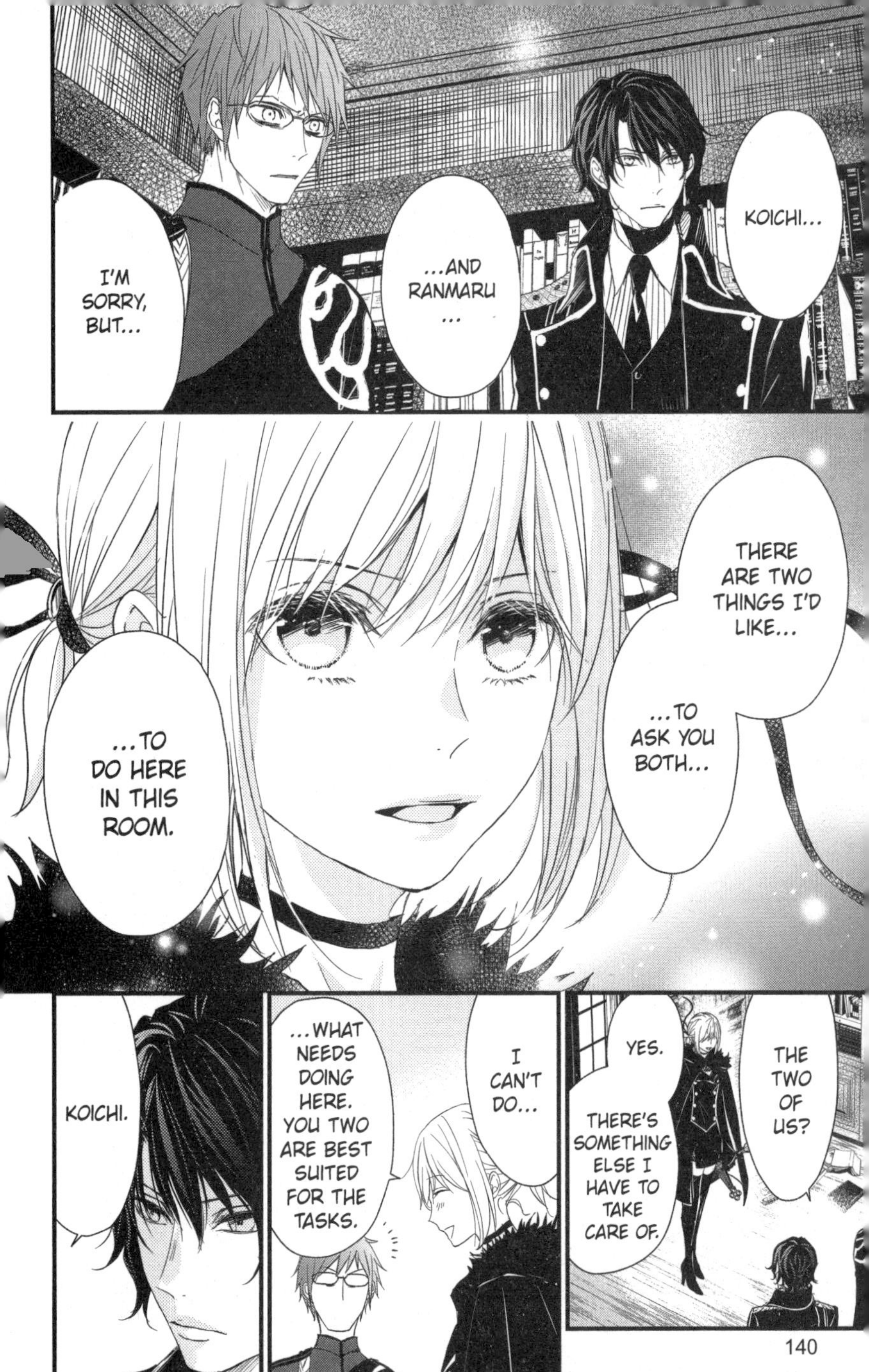
KOICHI...
...AND RANMARU ...
I'M SORRY, BUT...
THERE ARE TWO THINGS I'D LIKE...
...TO ASK YOU BOTH...
...TO DO HERE IN THIS ROOM.
THE TWO OF US?
YES.
THERE'S SOMETHING ELSE I HAVE TO TAKE CARE OF.
I CAN'T DO...
...WHAT NEEDS DOING HERE. YOU TWO ARE BEST SUITED FOR THE TASKS.
KOICHI.

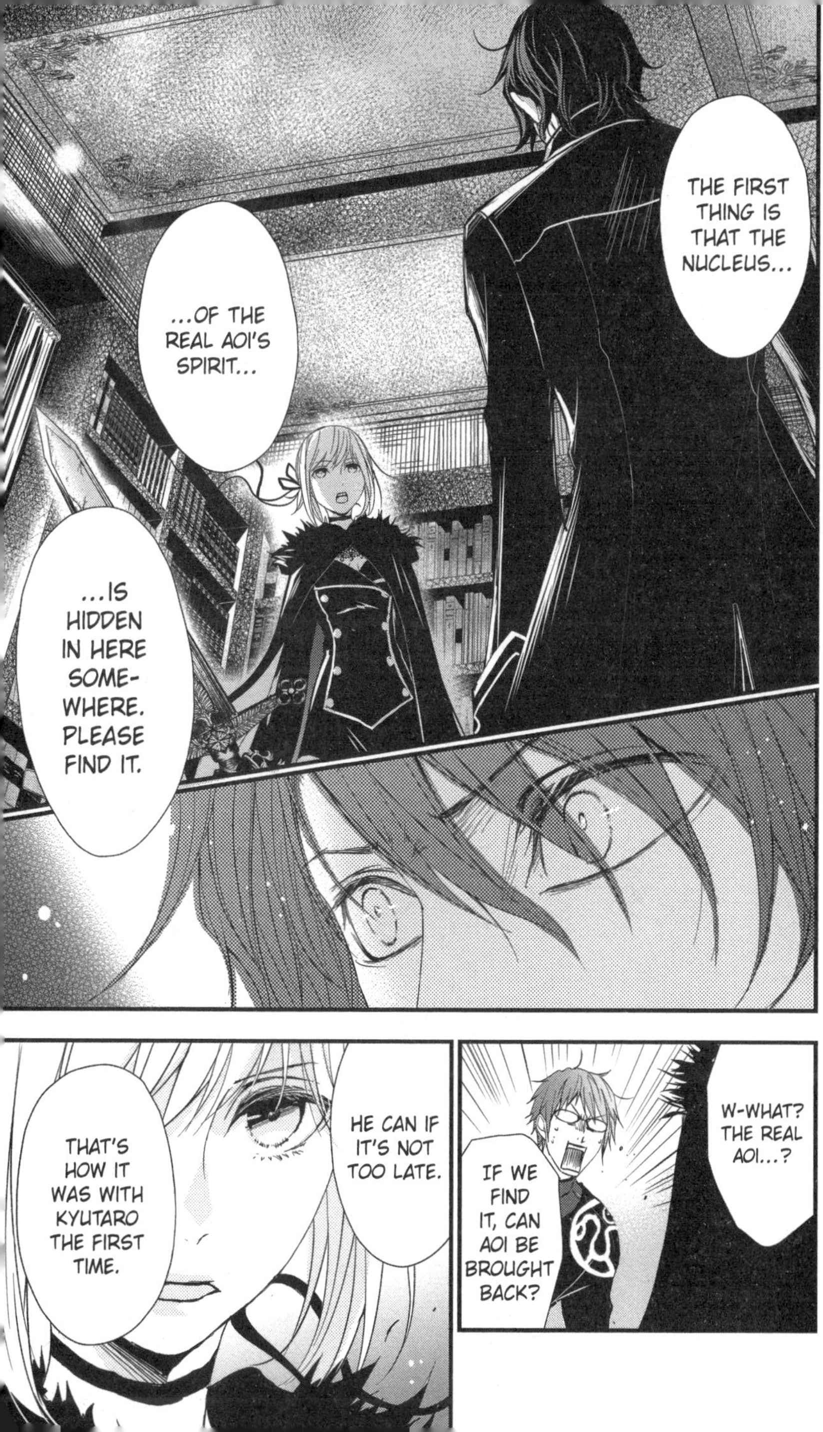
THE FIRST THING IS THAT THE NUCLEUS...
...OF THE REAL AOI'S SPIRIT...
...IS HIDDEN IN HERE SOME-WHERE. PLEASE FIND IT.
W-WHAT? THE REAL AOI...?
IF WE FIND IT, CAN AOI BE BROUGHT BACK?
HE CAN IF IT'S NOT TOO LATE.
THAT'S HOW IT WAS WITH KYUTARO THE FIRST TIME.

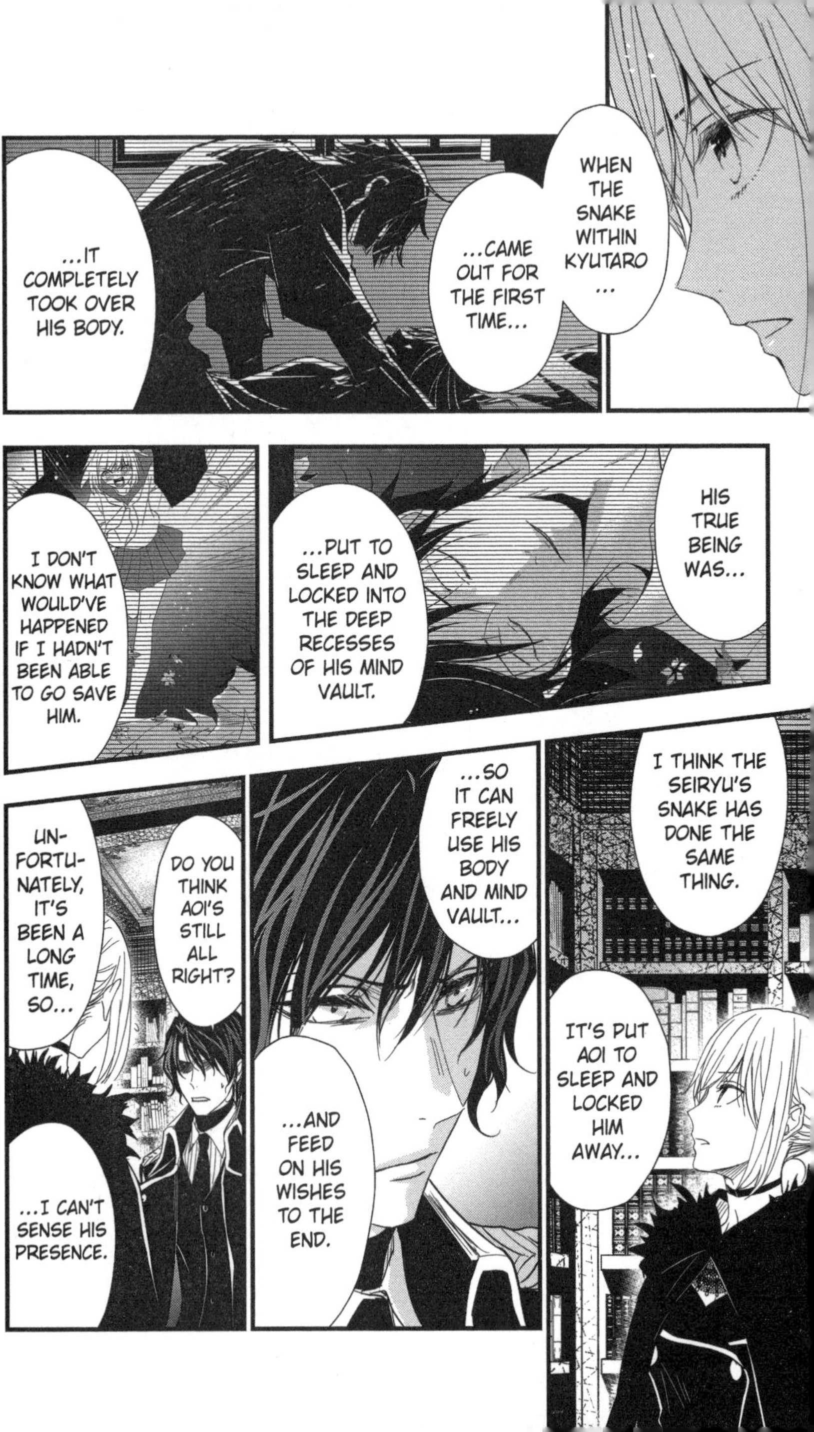
WHEN THE SNAKE WITHIN KYUTARO...
...CAME OUT FOR THE FIRST TIME...
...IT COMPLETELY TOOK OVER HIS BODY.
HIS TRUE BEING WAS...
...PUT TO SLEEP AND LOCKED INTO THE DEEP RECESSES OF HIS MIND VAULT.
I DON'T KNOW WHAT WOULD'VE HAPPENED IF I HADN'T BEEN ABLE TO GO SAVE HIM.
I THINK THE SEIRYU'S SNAKE HAS DONE THE SAME THING.
IT'S PUT AOI TO SLEEP AND LOCKED HIM AWAY...
...SO IT CAN FREELY USE HIS BODY AND MIND VAULT...
...AND FEED ON HIS WISHES TO THE END.
DO YOU THINK AOI'S STILL ALL RIGHT?
UN-FORTU-NATELY, IT'S BEEN A LONG TIME, SO...
...I CAN'T SENSE HIS PRESENCE.

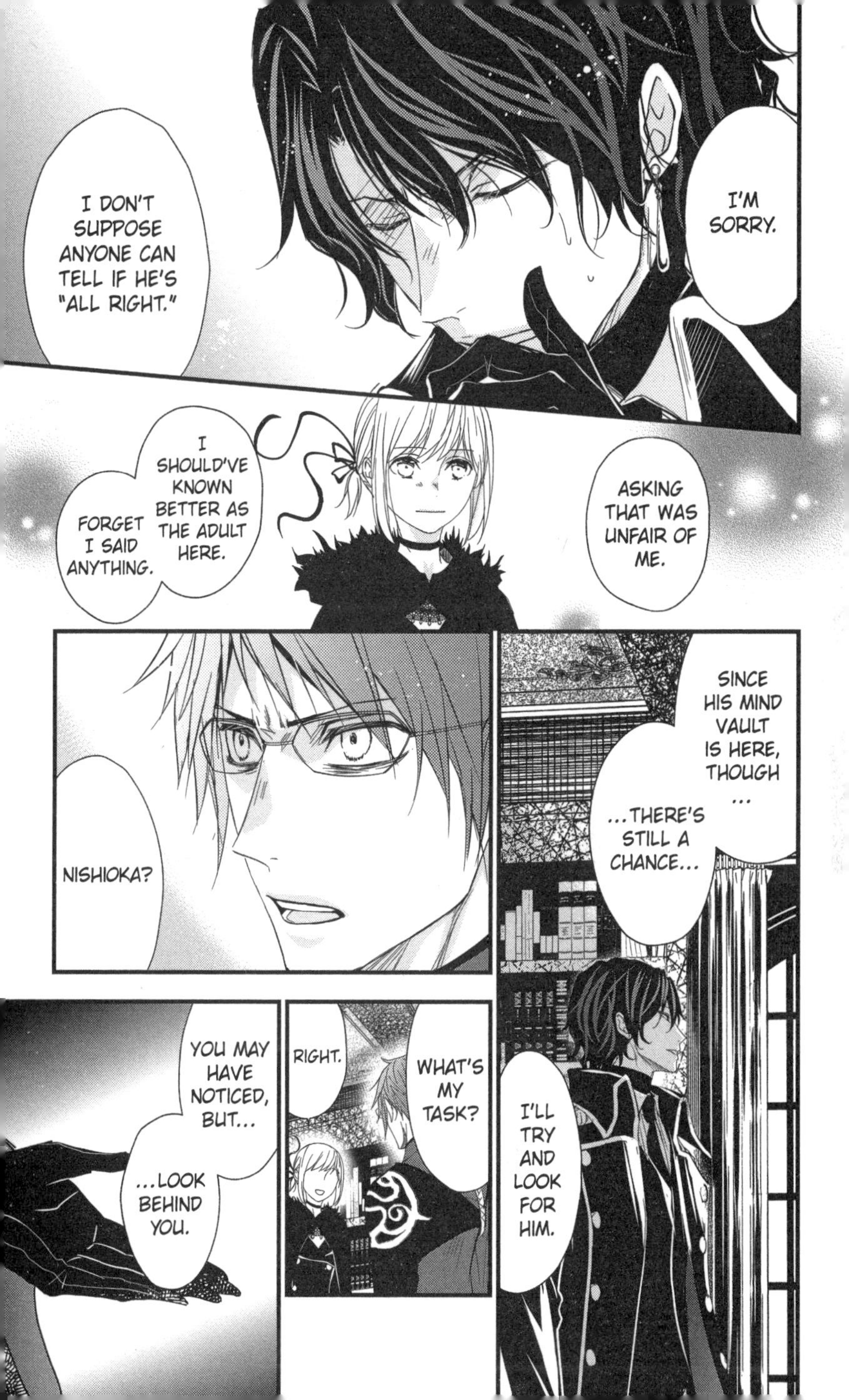
I'M SORRY.
I DON'T SUPPOSE ANYONE CAN TELL IF HE'S "ALL RIGHT."
ASKING THAT WAS UNFAIR OF ME.
I SHOULD'VE KNOWN BETTER AS THE ADULT HERE.
FORGET I SAID ANYTHING.
SINCE HIS MIND VAULT IS HERE, THOUGH…
…THERE'S STILL A CHANCE…
I'LL TRY AND LOOK FOR HIM.
NISHIOKA?
WHAT'S MY TASK?
RIGHT.
YOU MAY HAVE NOTICED, BUT…
…LOOK BEHIND YOU.

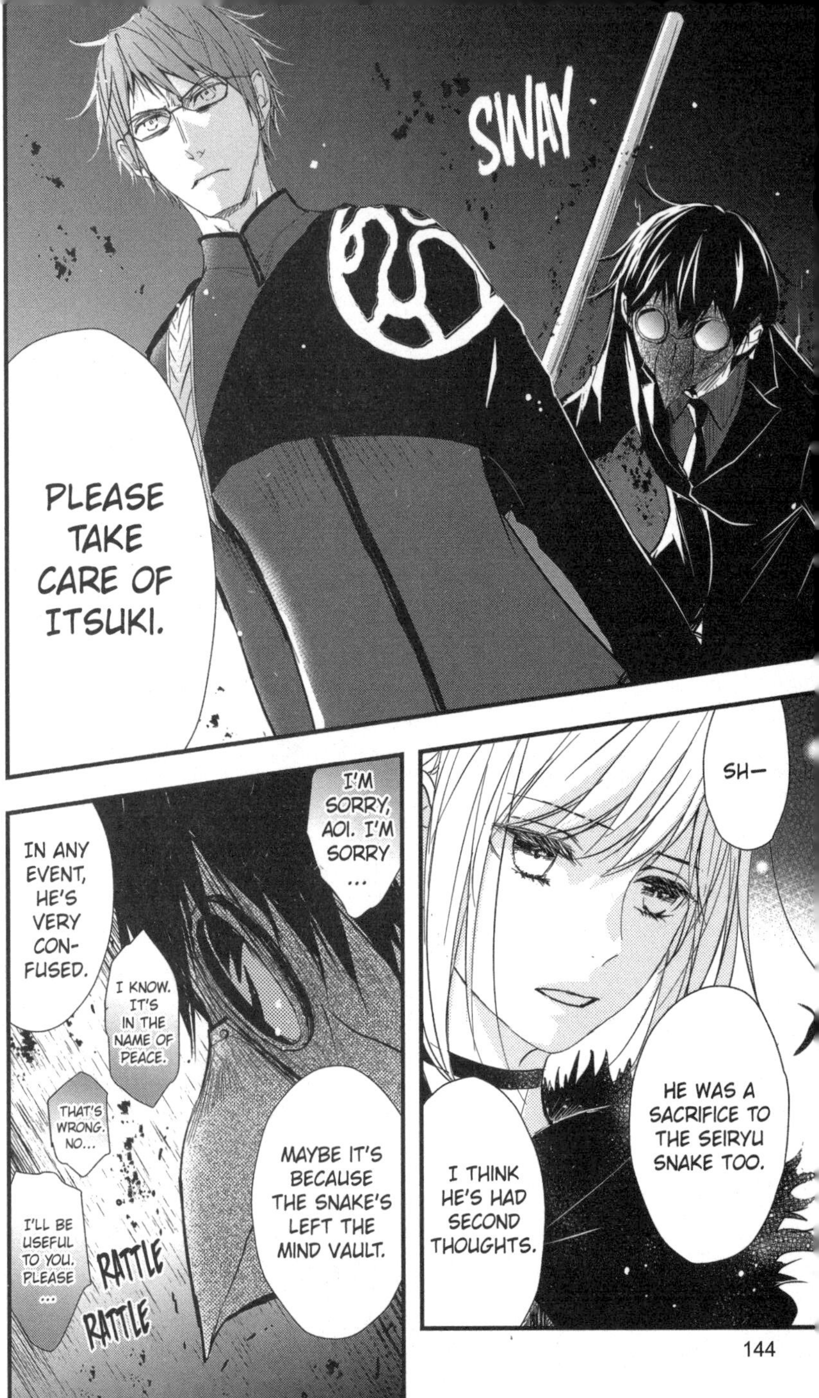
SWAY
PLEASE TAKE CARE OF ITSUKI.
SH—
HE WAS A SACRIFICE TO THE SEIRYU SNAKE TOO.
I THINK HE'S HAD SECOND THOUGHTS.
I'M SORRY, AOI. I'M SORRY...
MAYBE IT'S BECAUSE THE SNAKE'S LEFT THE MIND VAULT.
IN ANY EVENT, HE'S VERY CONFUSED.
I KNOW. IT'S IN THE NAME OF PEACE.
THAT'S WRONG. NO...
I'LL BE USEFUL TO YOU. PLEASE...
RATTLE
RATTLE

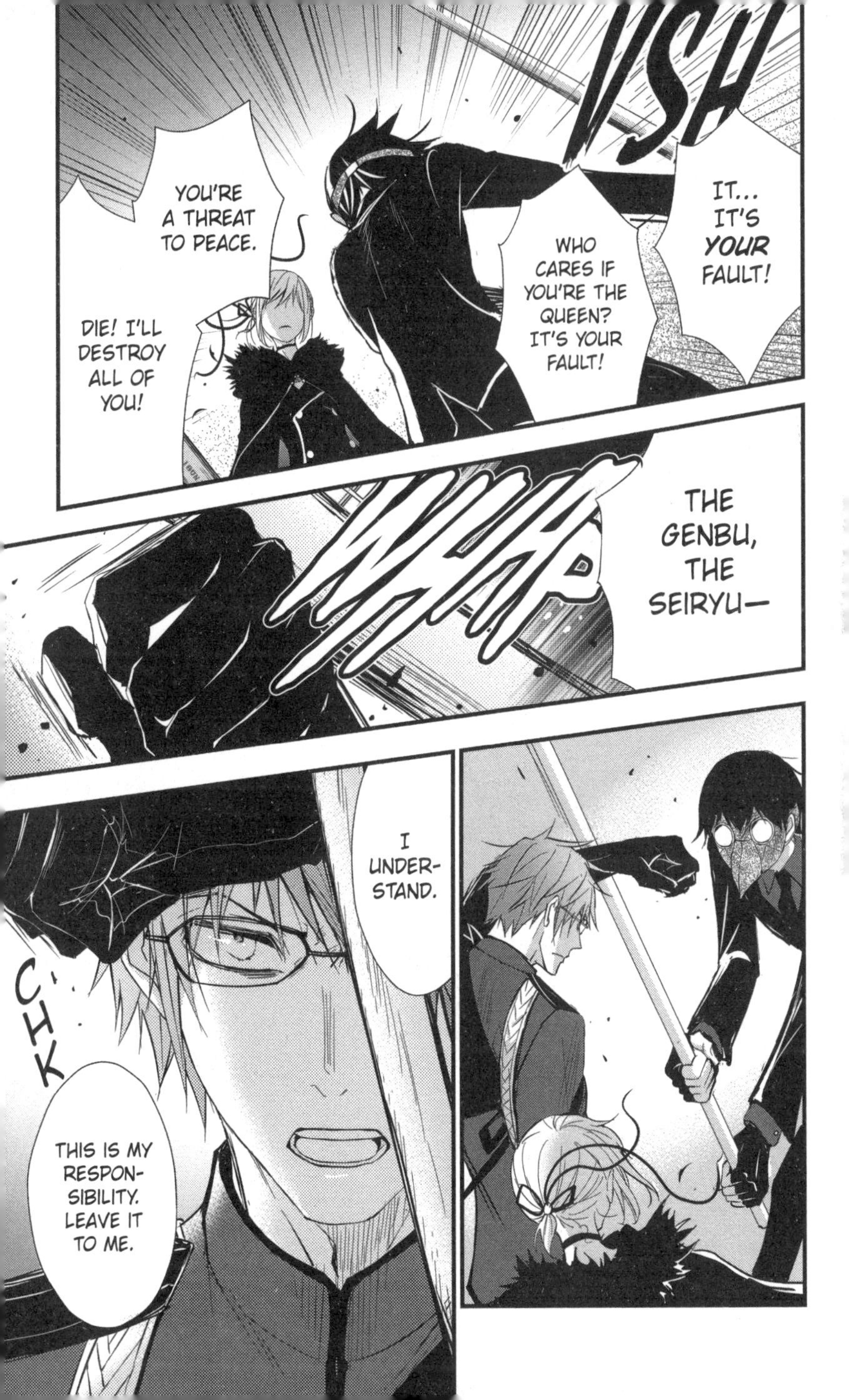
VSH
IT... IT'S YOUR FAULT!
WHO CARES IF YOU'RE THE QUEEN? IT'S YOUR FAULT!
YOU'RE A THREAT TO PEACE.
DIE! I'LL DESTROY ALL OF YOU!
THE GENBU, THE SEIRYU—
WHIP
I UNDER-STAND.
CHK
THIS IS MY RESPON-SIBILITY. LEAVE IT TO ME.

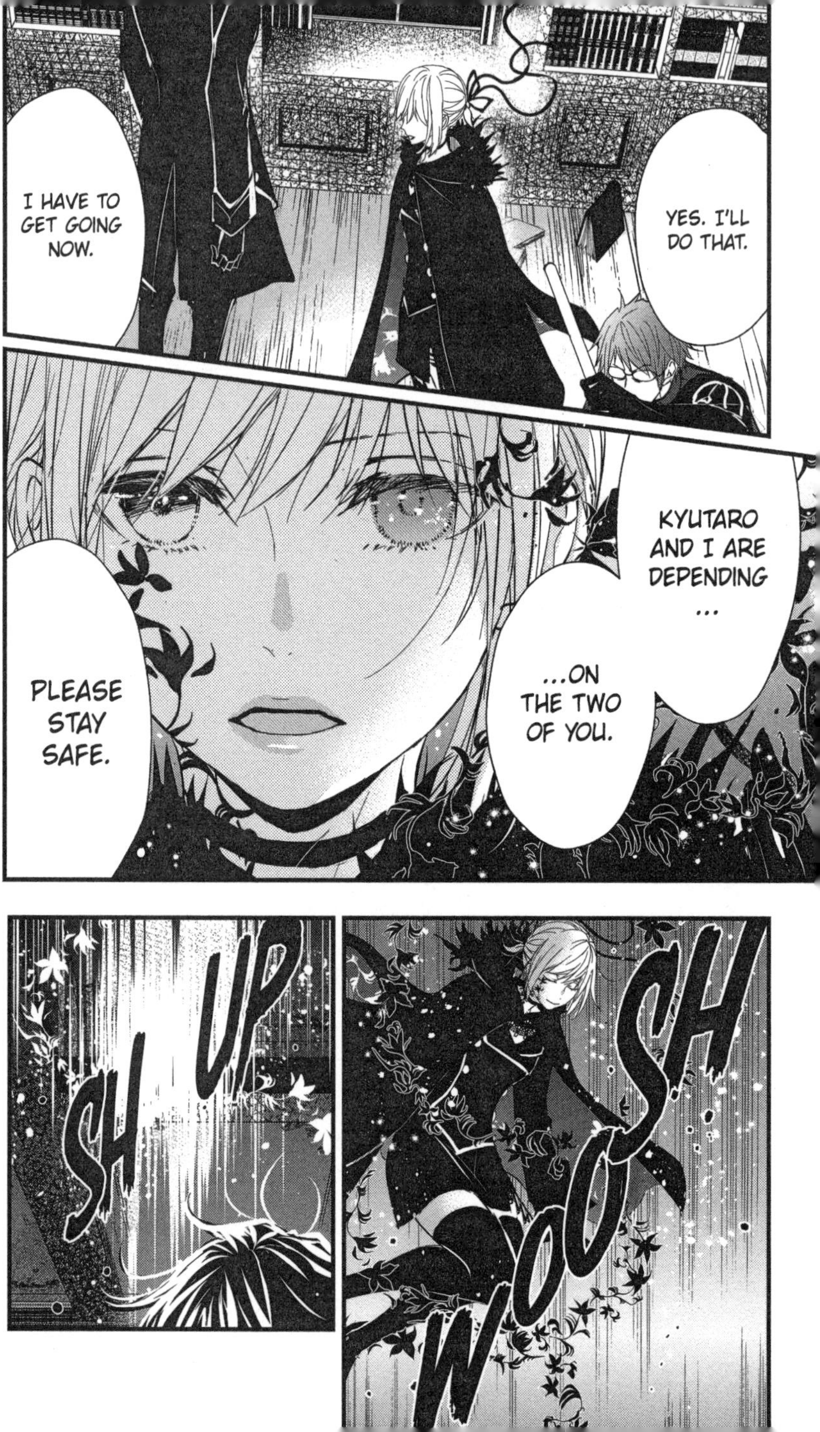
YES. I'LL DO THAT.
I HAVE TO GET GOING NOW.
KYUTARO AND I ARE DEPENDING...
...ON THE TWO OF YOU.
PLEASE STAY SAFE.
WOOOSH
SHUP

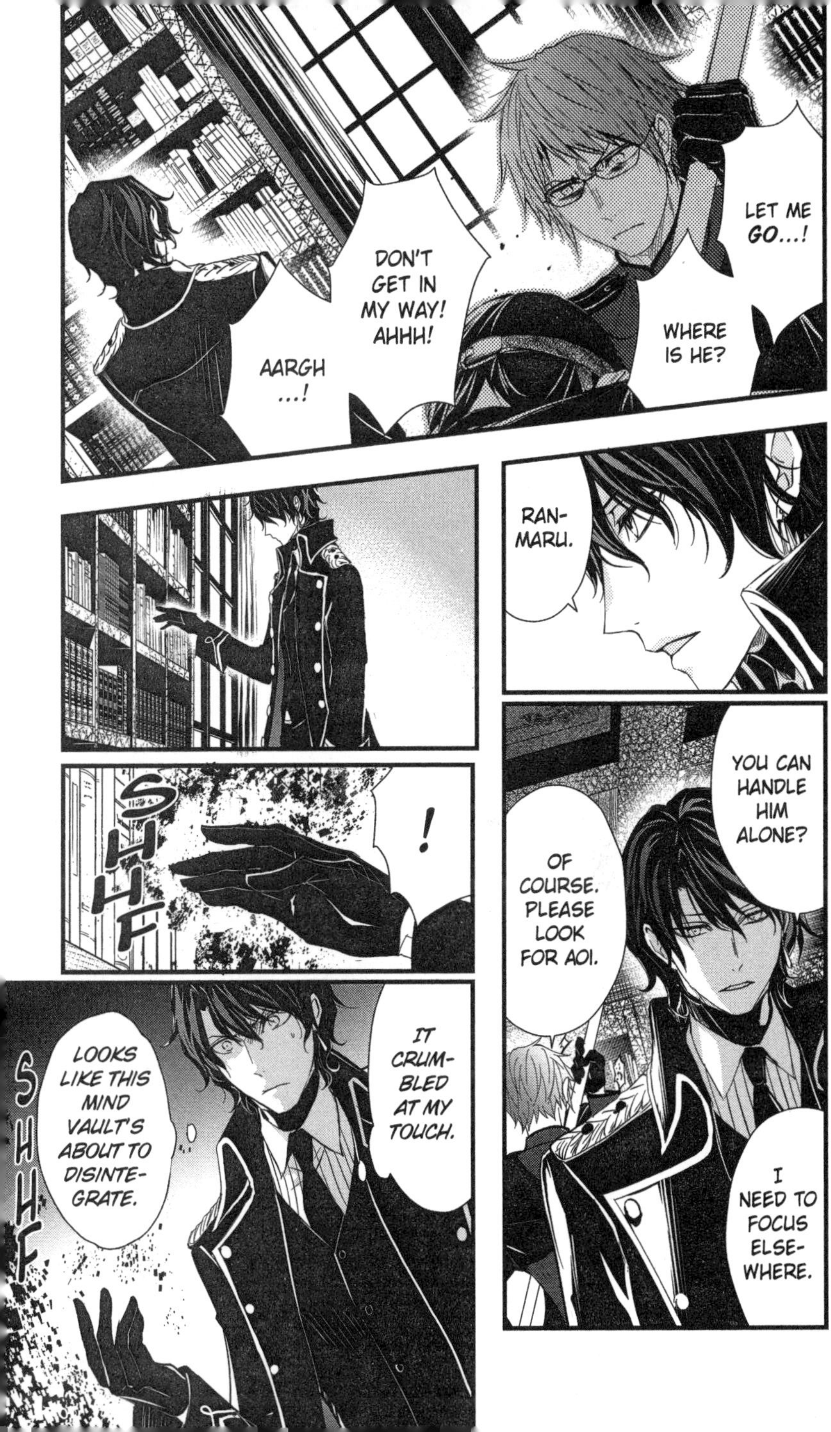
LET ME GO...!
WHERE IS HE?
DON'T GET IN MY WAY! AHHH!
AARGH ...!
RAN-MARU.
YOU CAN HANDLE HIM ALONE?
OF COURSE. PLEASE LOOK FOR AOI.
I NEED TO FOCUS ELSEWHERE.
!
SHHF
IT CRUMBLED AT MY TOUCH.
LOOKS LIKE THIS MIND VAULT'S ABOUT TO DISINTEGRATE.
SHHF

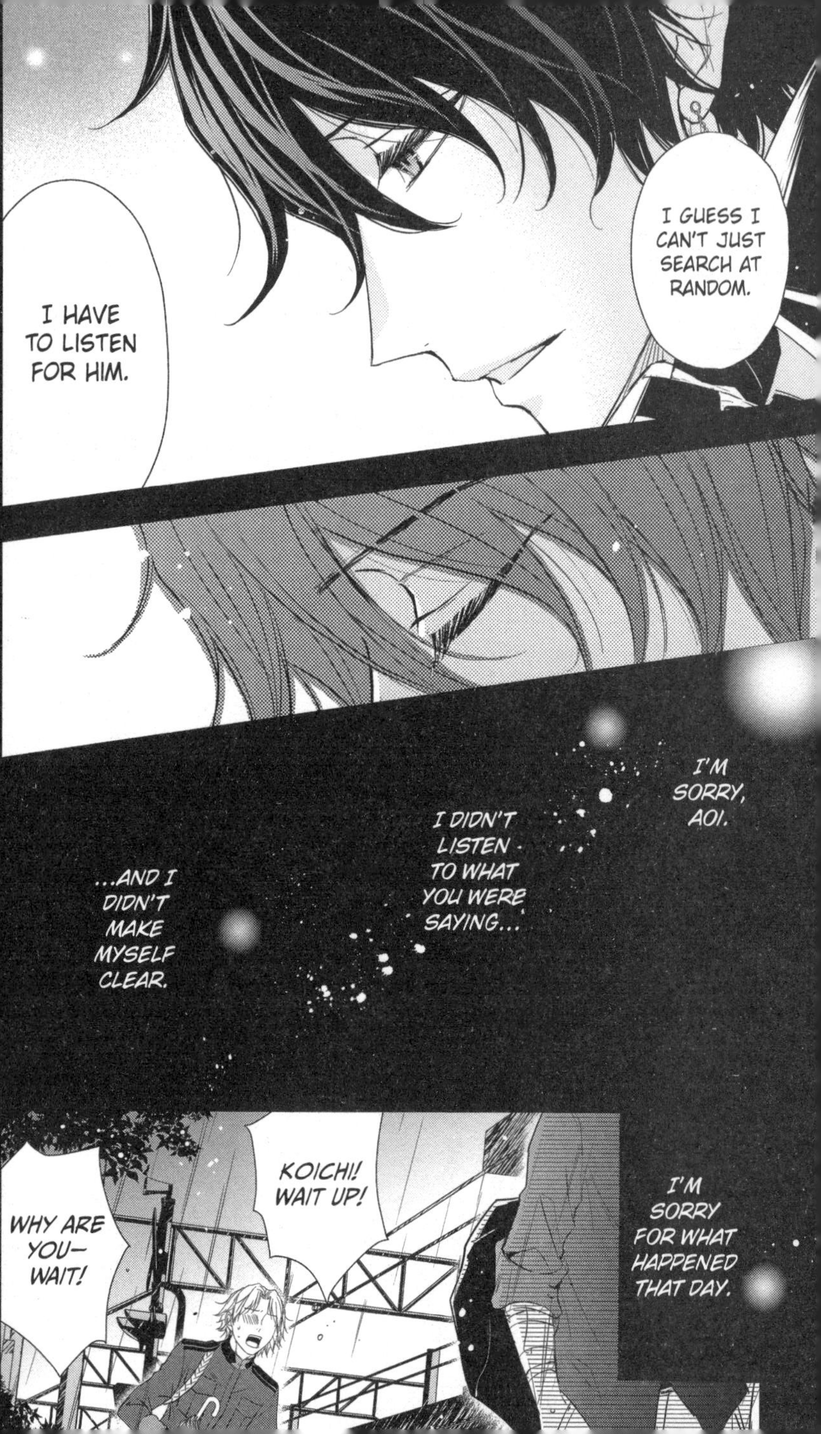
I GUESS I CAN'T JUST SEARCH AT RANDOM.
I HAVE TO LISTEN FOR HIM.
I'M SORRY, AOI.
I DIDN'T LISTEN TO WHAT YOU WERE SAYING...
...AND I DIDN'T MAKE MYSELF CLEAR.
I'M SORRY FOR WHAT HAPPENED THAT DAY.
KOICHI! WAIT UP!
WHY ARE YOU— WAIT!

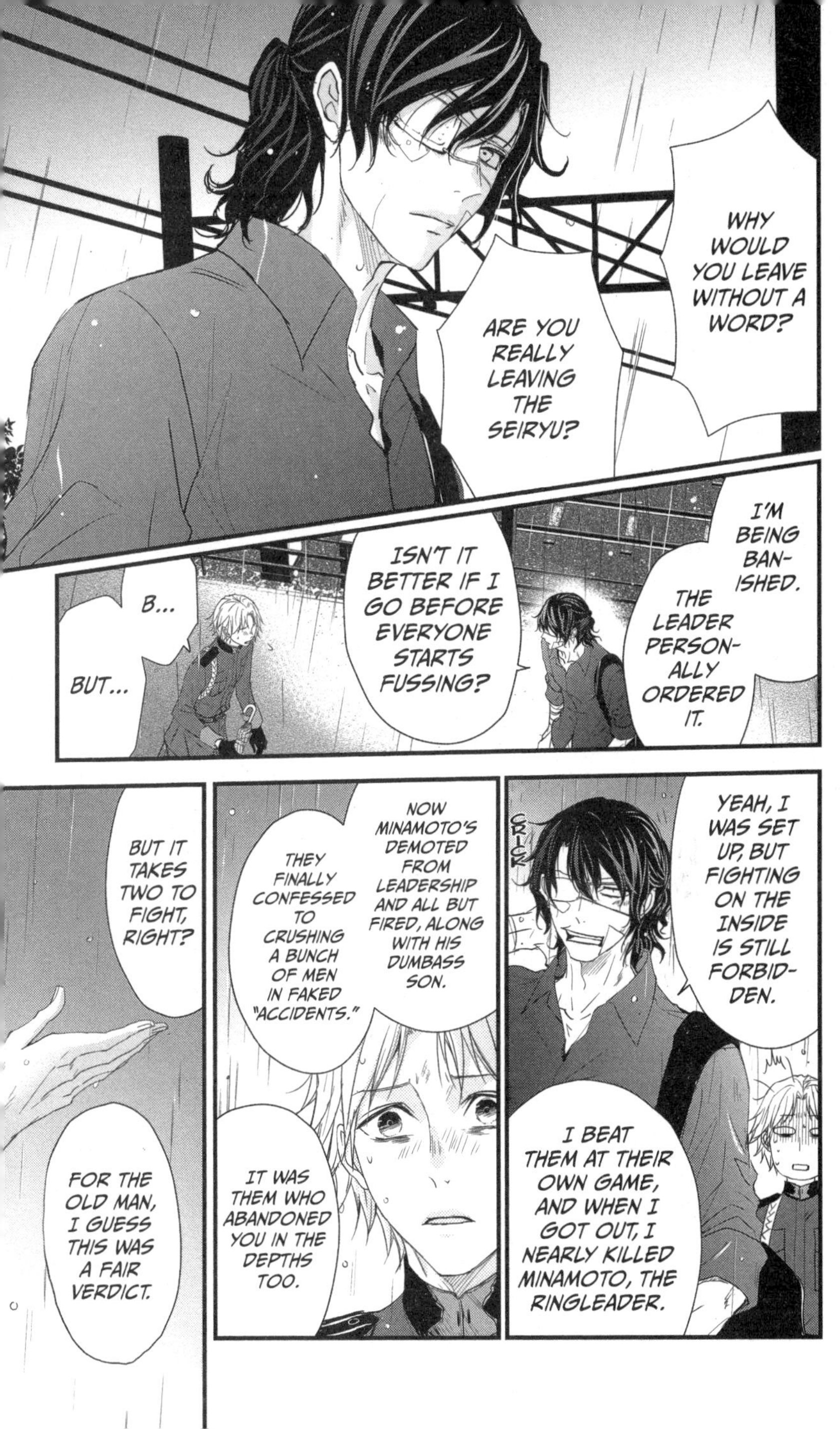

WHY WOULD YOU LEAVE WITHOUT A WORD?
ARE YOU REALLY LEAVING THE SEIRYU?
I'M BEING BAN-ISHED.
THE LEADER PERSON-ALLY ORDERED IT.
ISN'T IT BETTER IF I GO BEFORE EVERYONE STARTS FUSSING?
B...
BUT...
YEAH, I WAS SET UP, BUT FIGHTING ON THE INSIDE IS STILL FORBID-DEN.
CRICK
I BEAT THEM AT THEIR OWN GAME, AND WHEN I GOT OUT, I NEARLY KILLED MINAMOTO, THE RINGLEADER.
NOW MINAMOTO'S DEMOTED FROM LEADERSHIP AND ALL BUT FIRED, ALONG WITH HIS DUMBASS SON.
THEY FINALLY CONFESSED TO CRUSHING A BUNCH OF MEN IN FAKED "ACCIDENTS."
IT WAS THEM WHO ABANDONED YOU IN THE DEPTHS TOO.
BUT IT TAKES TWO TO FIGHT, RIGHT?
FOR THE OLD MAN, I GUESS THIS WAS A FAIR VERDICT.

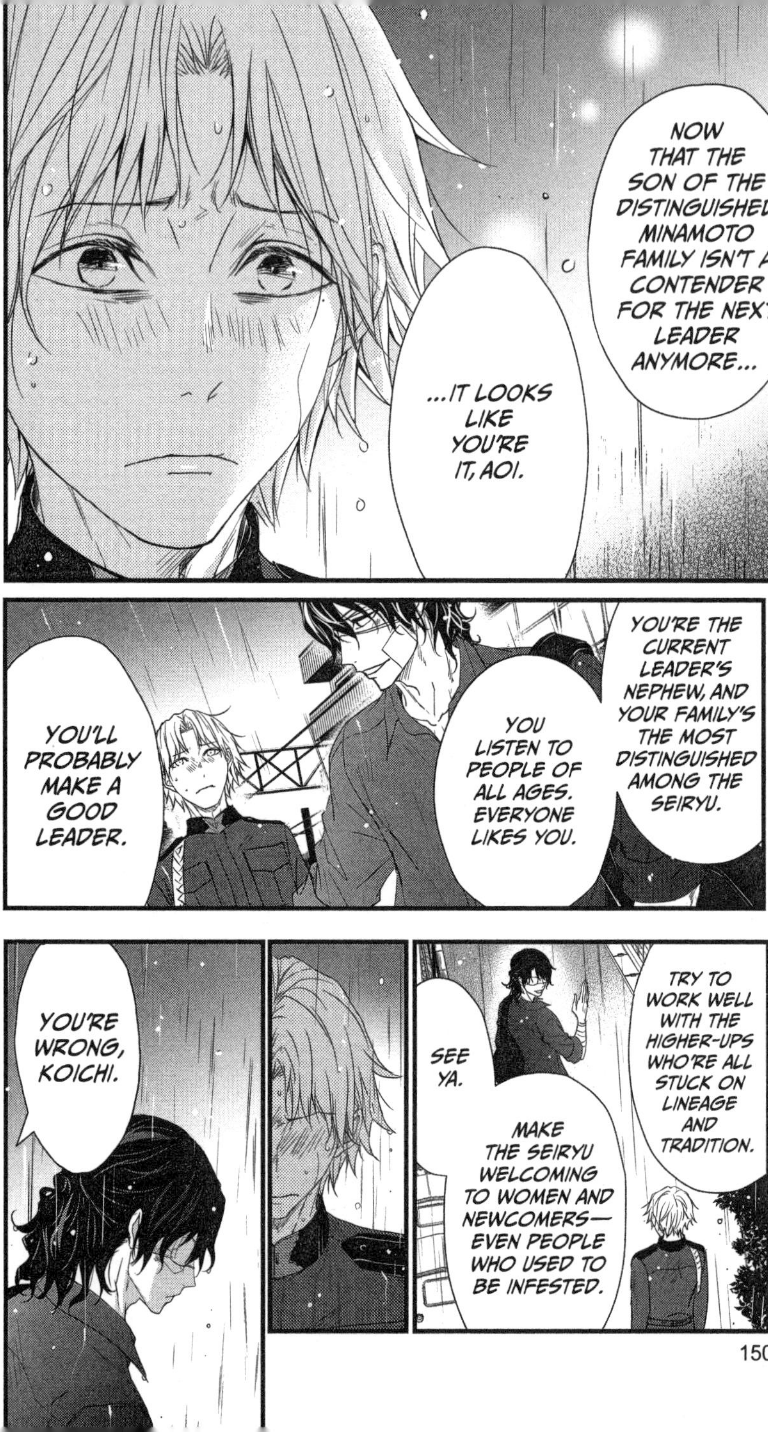
NOW THAT THE SON OF THE DISTINGUISHED MINAMOTO FAMILY ISN'T A CONTENDER FOR THE NEXT LEADER ANYMORE...
...IT LOOKS LIKE YOU'RE IT, AOI.
YOU'RE THE CURRENT LEADER'S NEPHEW, AND YOUR FAMILY'S THE MOST DISTINGUISHED AMONG THE SEIRYU.
YOU LISTEN TO PEOPLE OF ALL AGES. EVERYONE LIKES YOU.
YOU'LL PROBABLY MAKE A GOOD LEADER.
TRY TO WORK WELL WITH THE HIGHER-UPS WHO'RE ALL STUCK ON LINEAGE AND TRADITION.
MAKE THE SEIRYU WELCOMING TO WOMEN AND NEWCOMERS—EVEN PEOPLE WHO USED TO BE INFESTED.
SEE YA.
YOU'RE WRONG, KOICHI.

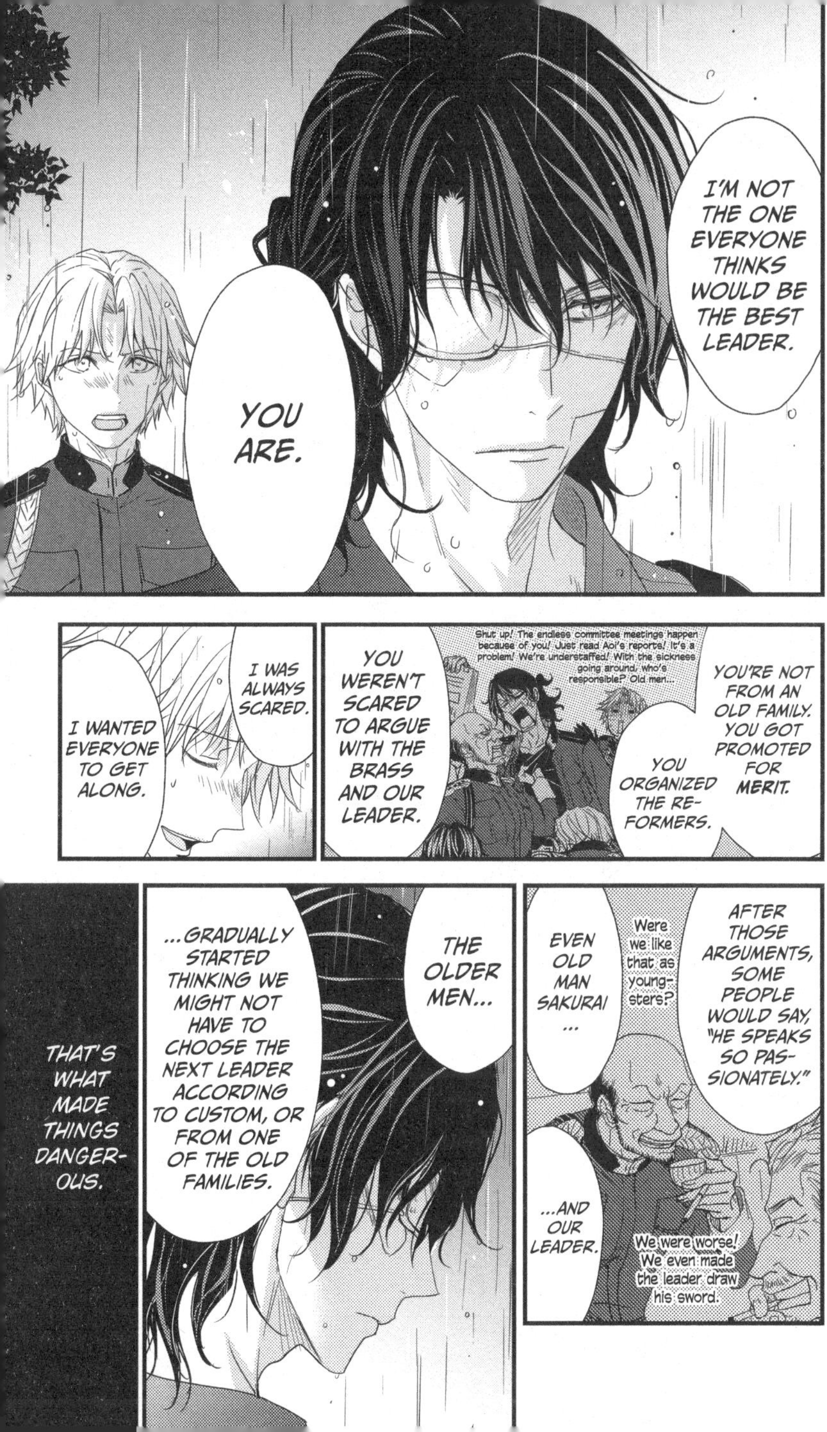
I'M NOT THE ONE EVERYONE THINKS WOULD BE THE BEST LEADER.
YOU ARE.
YOU'RE NOT FROM AN OLD FAMILY. YOU GOT PROMOTED FOR MERIT.
YOU ORGANIZED THE RE-FORMERS.
Shut up! The endless committee meetings happen because of you! Just read Aoi's reports! It's a problem! We're understaffed! With the sickness going around, who's responsible? Old men...
YOU WEREN'T SCARED TO ARGUE WITH THE BRASS AND OUR LEADER.
I WAS ALWAYS SCARED.
I WANTED EVERYONE TO GET ALONG.
AFTER THOSE ARGUMENTS, SOME PEOPLE WOULD SAY, "HE SPEAKS SO PAS-SIONATELY."
Were we like that as young-sters?
EVEN OLD MAN SAKURAI...
...AND OUR LEADER.
We were worse! We even made the leader draw his sword.
THE OLDER MEN...
...GRADUALLY STARTED THINKING WE MIGHT NOT HAVE TO CHOOSE THE NEXT LEADER ACCORDING TO CUSTOM, OR FROM ONE OF THE OLD FAMILIES.
THAT'S WHAT MADE THINGS DANGER-OUS.

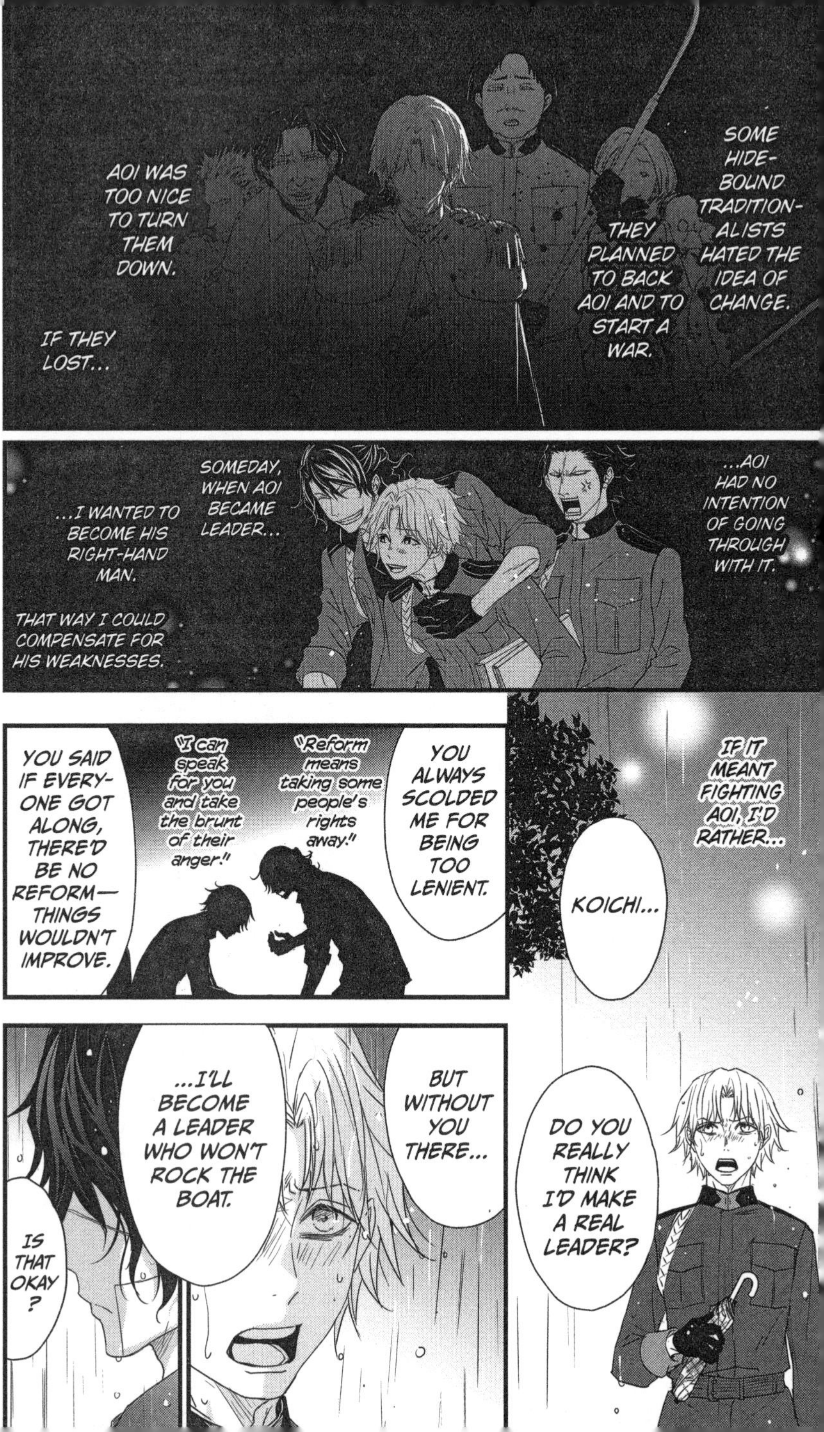
SOME HIDE-BOUND TRADITION-ALISTS HATED THE IDEA OF CHANGE.
THEY PLANNED TO BACK AOI AND TO START A WAR.
AOI WAS TOO NICE TO TURN THEM DOWN.
IF THEY LOST...
...AOI HAD NO INTENTION OF GOING THROUGH WITH IT.
SOMEDAY, WHEN AOI BECAME LEADER...
...I WANTED TO BECOME HIS RIGHT-HAND MAN.
THAT WAY I COULD COMPENSATE FOR HIS WEAKNESSES.
IF IT MEANT FIGHTING AOI, I'D RATHER...
KOICHI...
DO YOU REALLY THINK I'D MAKE A REAL LEADER?
YOU ALWAYS SCOLDED ME FOR BEING TOO LENIENT.
"Reform means taking some people's rights away."
"I can speak for you and take the brunt of their anger."
YOU SAID IF EVERYONE GOT ALONG, THERE'D BE NO REFORM—THINGS WOULDN'T IMPROVE.
BUT WITHOUT YOU THERE...
...I'LL BECOME A LEADER WHO WON'T ROCK THE BOAT.
IS THAT OKAY?

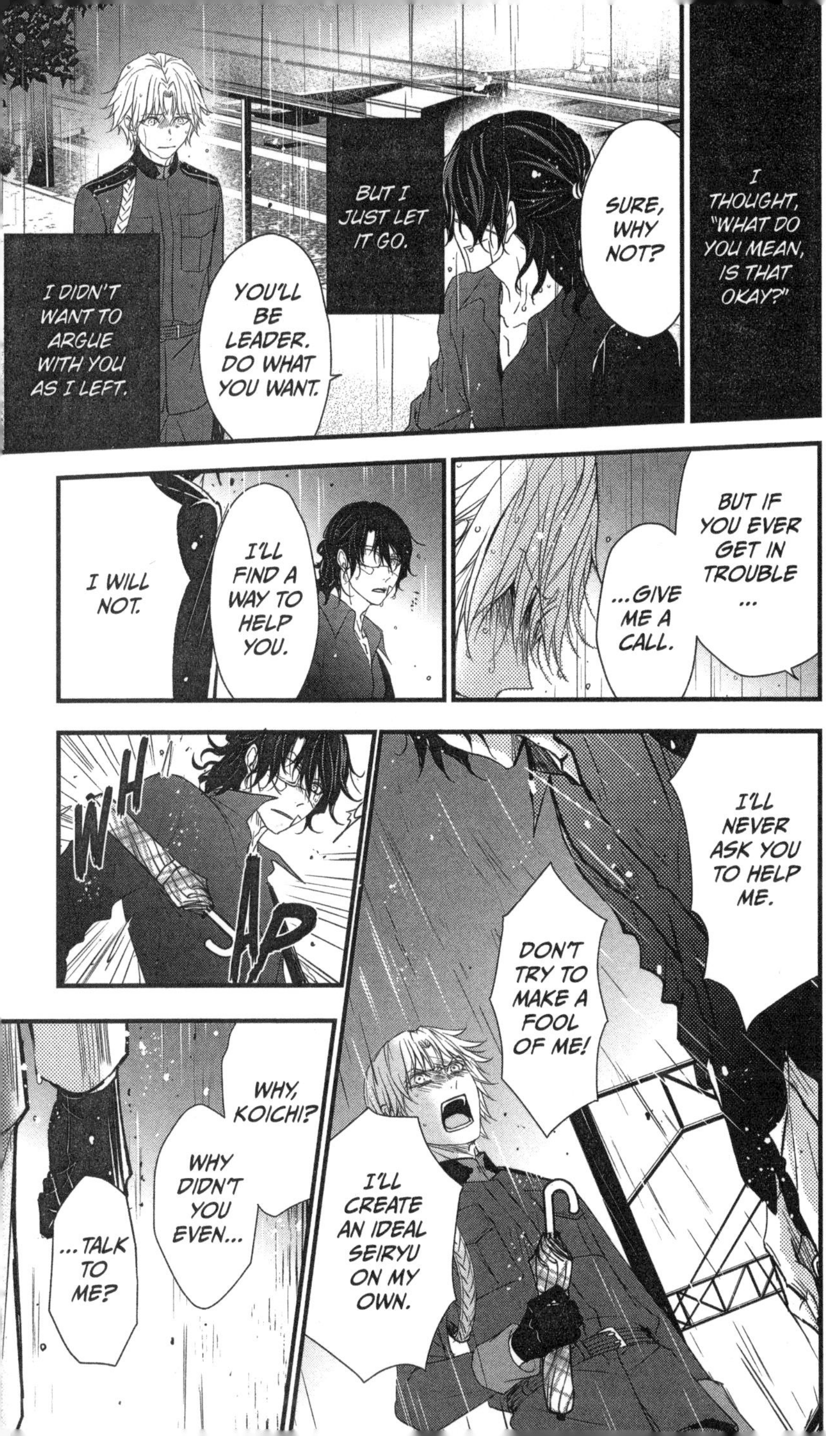
I THOUGHT, "WHAT DO YOU MEAN, IS THAT OKAY?"
SURE, WHY NOT?
BUT I JUST LET IT GO.
YOU'LL BE LEADER. DO WHAT YOU WANT.
I DIDN'T WANT TO ARGUE WITH YOU AS I LEFT.
BUT IF YOU EVER GET IN TROUBLE ...
...GIVE ME A CALL.
I'LL FIND A WAY TO HELP YOU.
I WILL NOT.
I'LL NEVER ASK YOU TO HELP ME.
DON'T TRY TO MAKE A FOOL OF ME!
I'LL CREATE AN IDEAL SEIRYU ON MY OWN.
WHAP
WHY, KOICHI?
WHY DIDN'T YOU EVEN...
...TALK TO ME?

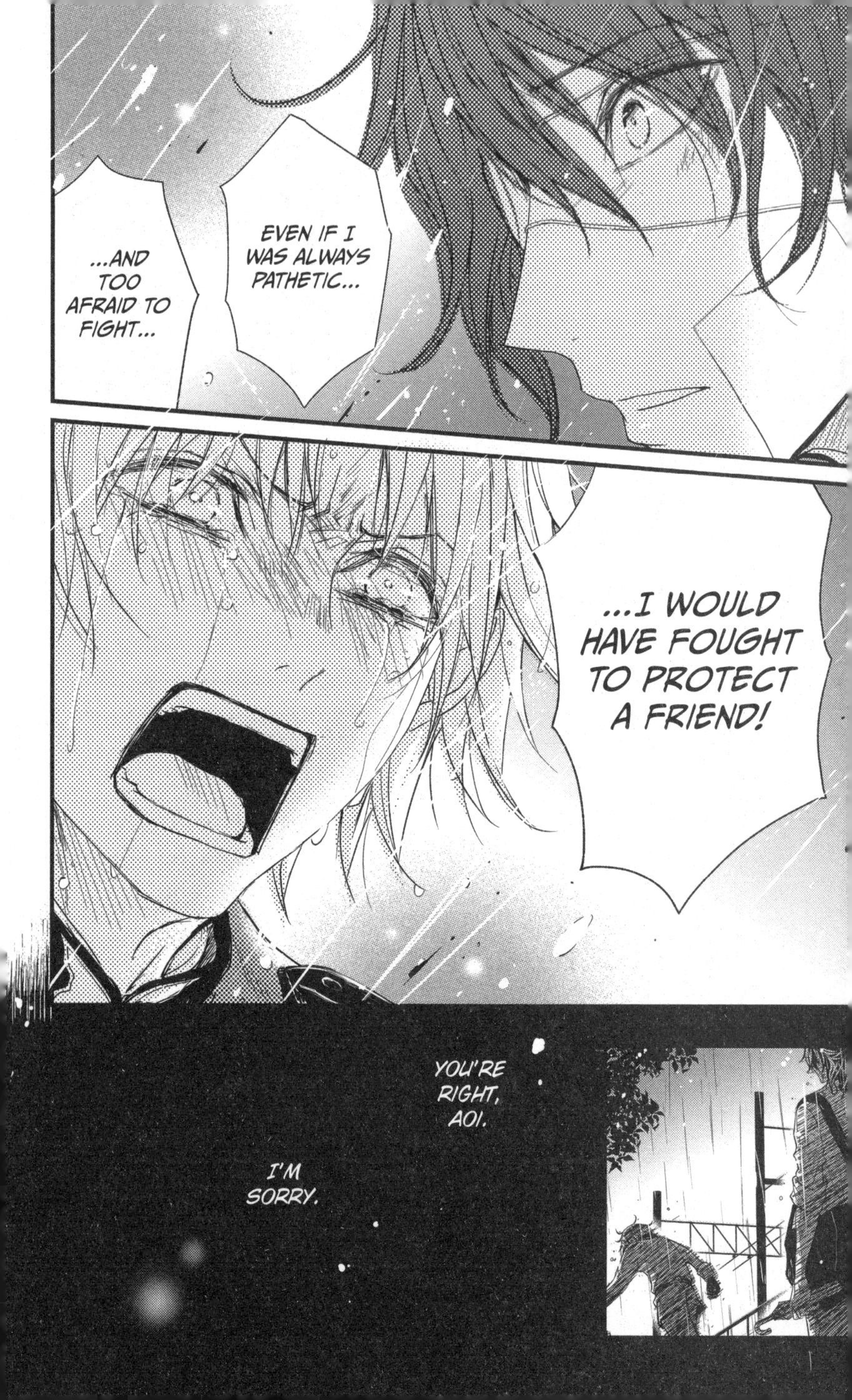
EVEN IF I WAS ALWAYS PATHETIC...
...AND TOO AFRAID TO FIGHT...
...I WOULD HAVE FOUGHT TO PROTECT A FRIEND!
YOU'RE RIGHT, AOI.
I'M SORRY.

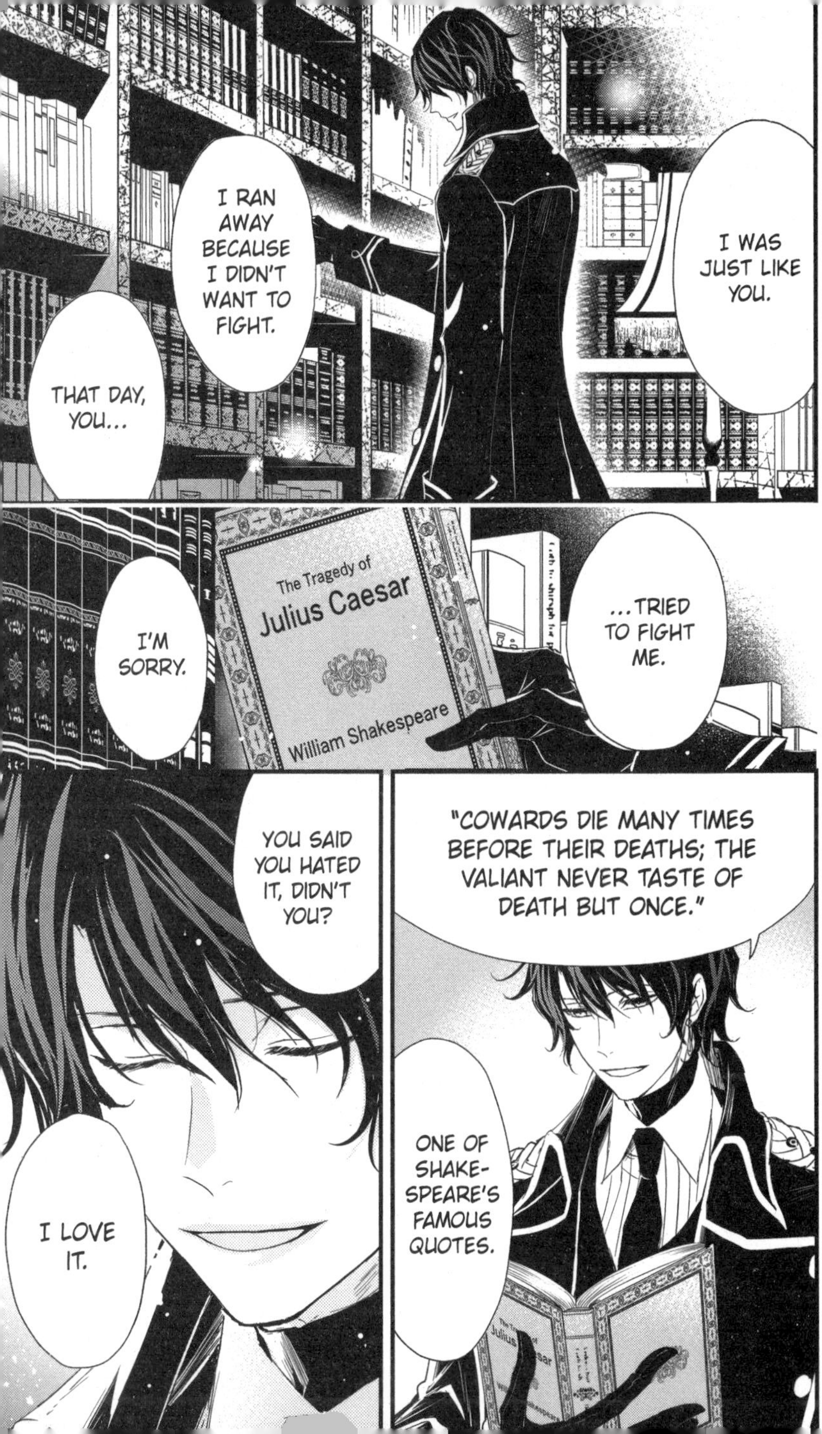
I WAS JUST LIKE YOU.
I RAN AWAY BECAUSE I DIDN'T WANT TO FIGHT.
THAT DAY, YOU...
...TRIED TO FIGHT ME.
The Tragedy of Julius Caesar William Shakespeare
I'M SORRY.
"COWARDS DIE MANY TIMES BEFORE THEIR DEATHS; THE VALIANT NEVER TASTE OF DEATH BUT ONCE."
ONE OF SHAKE-SPEARE'S FAMOUS QUOTES.
YOU SAID YOU HATED IT, DIDN'T YOU?
I LOVE IT.

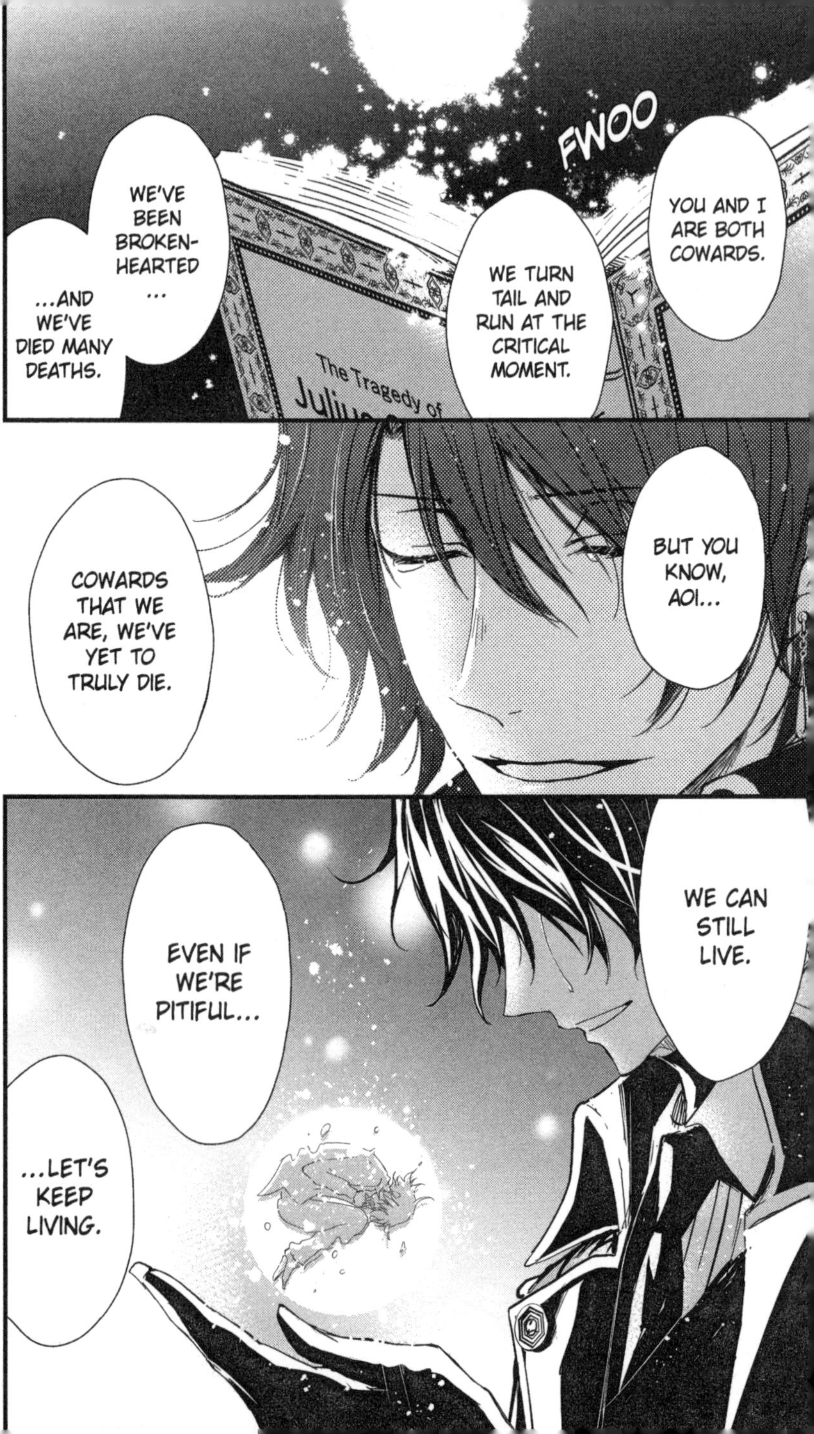
FWOO
YOU AND I ARE BOTH COWARDS.
WE TURN TAIL AND RUN AT THE CRITICAL MOMENT.
The Tragedy of
WE'VE BEEN BROKEN-HEARTED ...
...AND WE'VE DIED MANY DEATHS.
BUT YOU KNOW, AOI...
COWARDS THAT WE ARE, WE'VE YET TO TRULY DIE.
WE CAN STILL LIVE.
EVEN IF WE'RE PITIFUL...
...LET'S KEEP LIVING.

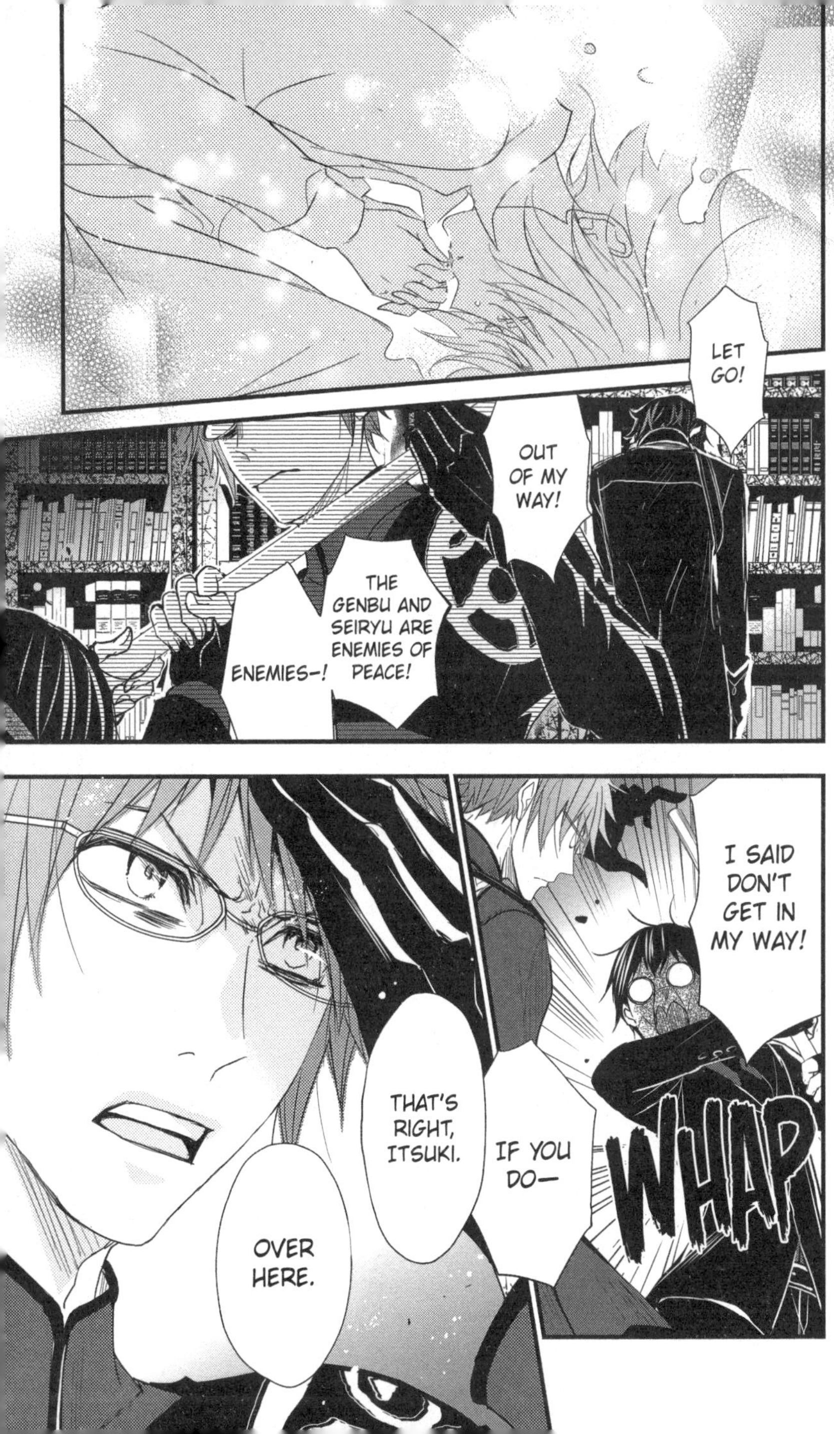
LET GO!
OUT OF MY WAY!
THE GENBU AND SEIRYU ARE ENEMIES OF PEACE!
ENEMIES—!
I SAID DON'T GET IN MY WAY!
IF YOU DO—
WHAP
THAT'S RIGHT, ITSUKI.
OVER HERE.

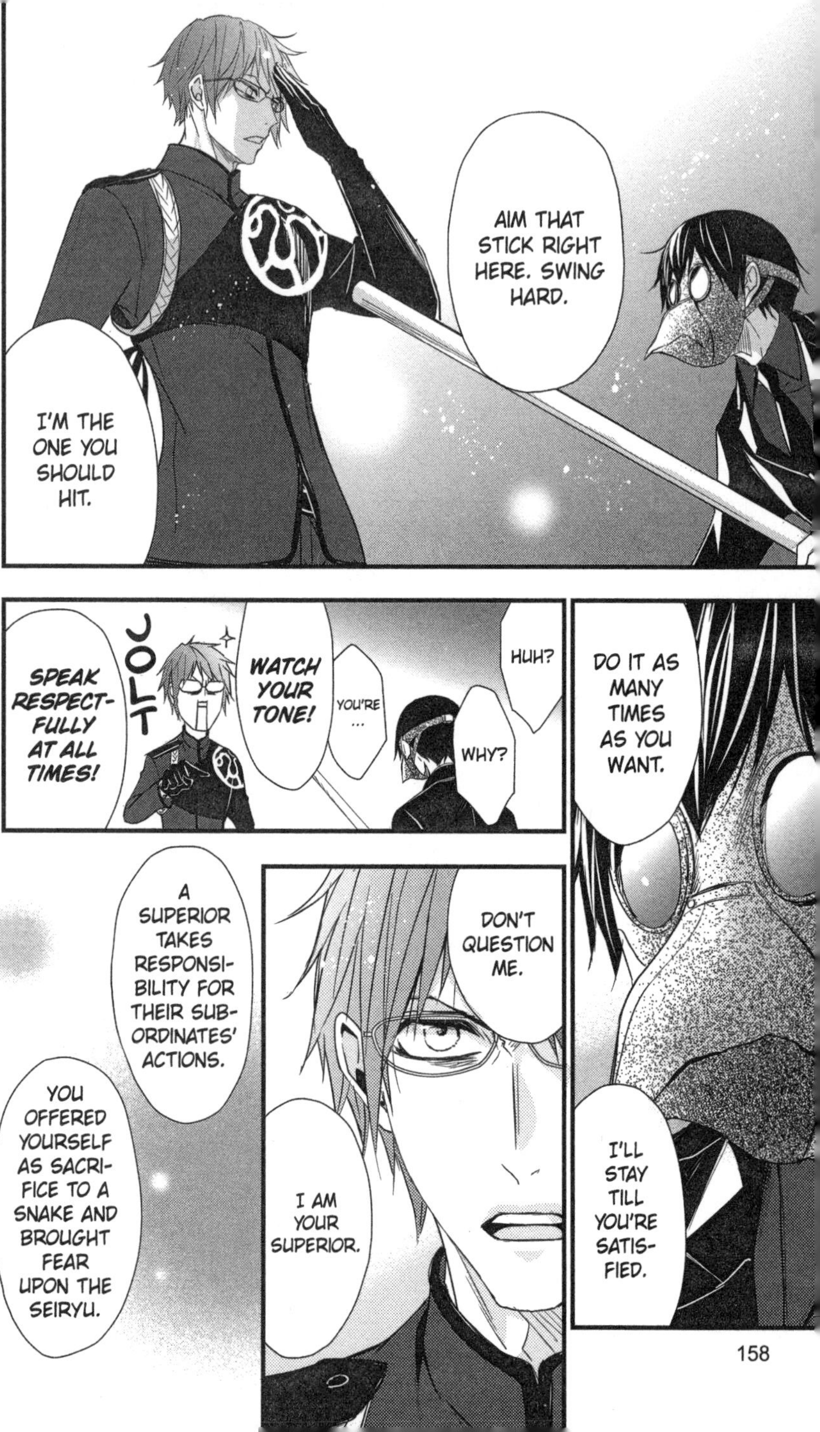
AIM THAT STICK RIGHT HERE. SWING HARD.
I'M THE ONE YOU SHOULD HIT.
DO IT AS MANY TIMES AS YOU WANT.
I'LL STAY TILL YOU'RE SATISFIED.
HUH?
WHY?
YOU'RE ...
WATCH YOUR TONE!
JOLT
SPEAK RESPECT-FULLY AT ALL TIMES!
DON'T QUESTION ME.
I AM YOUR SUPERIOR.
A SUPERIOR TAKES RESPONSI-BILITY FOR THEIR SUB-ORDINATES' ACTIONS.
YOU OFFERED YOURSELF AS SACRI-FICE TO A SNAKE AND BROUGHT FEAR UPON THE SEIRYU.

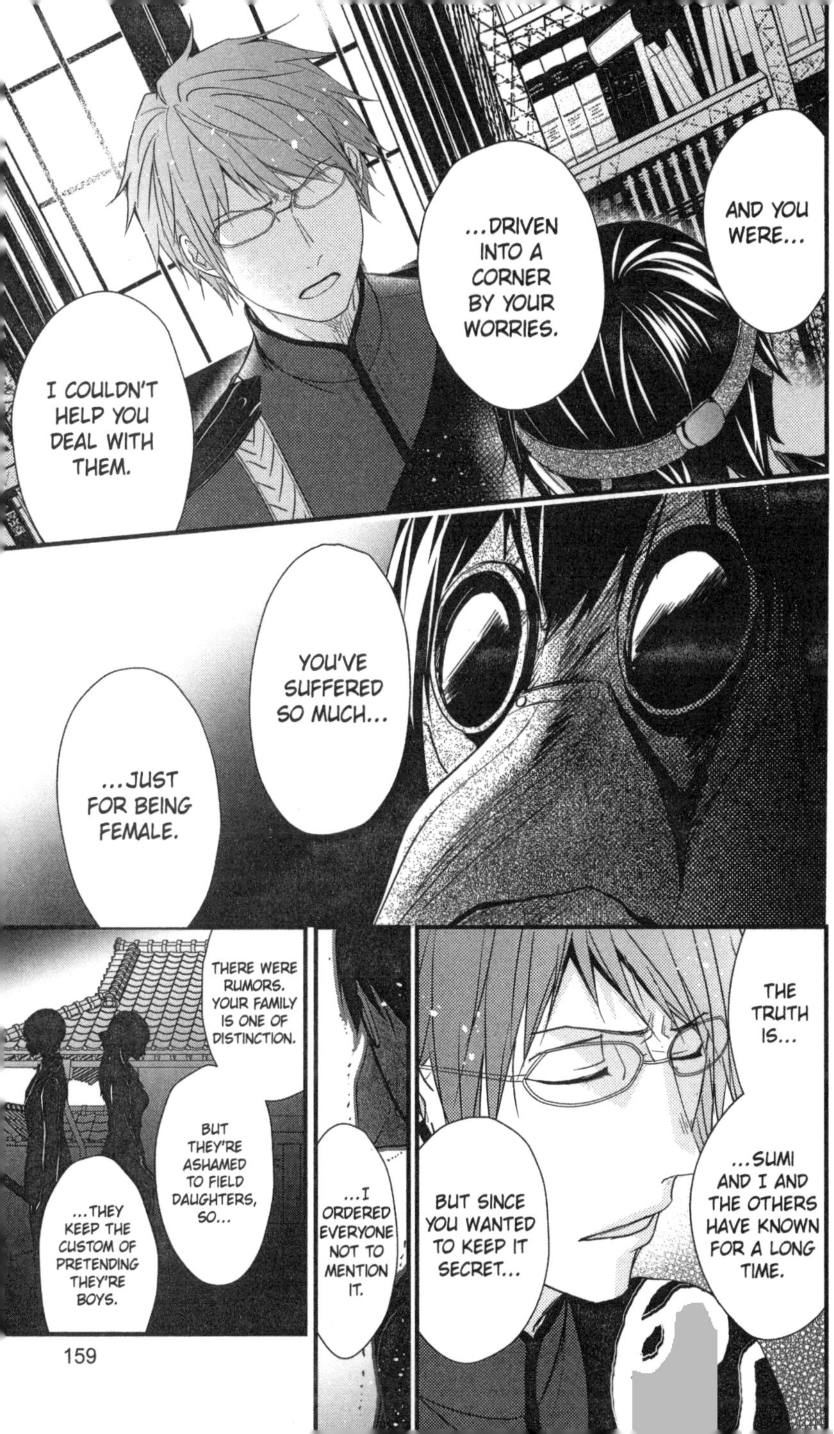
AND YOU WERE...
...DRIVEN INTO A CORNER BY YOUR WORRIES.
I COULDN'T HELP YOU DEAL WITH THEM.
YOU'VE SUFFERED SO MUCH...
...JUST FOR BEING FEMALE.
THE TRUTH IS...
...SUMI AND I AND THE OTHERS HAVE KNOWN FOR A LONG TIME.
BUT SINCE YOU WANTED TO KEEP IT SECRET...
...I ORDERED EVERYONE NOT TO MENTION IT.
THERE WERE RUMORS. YOUR FAMILY IS ONE OF DISTINCTION.
BUT THEY'RE ASHAMED TO FIELD DAUGHTERS, SO...
...THEY KEEP THE CUSTOM OF PRETENDING THEY'RE BOYS.

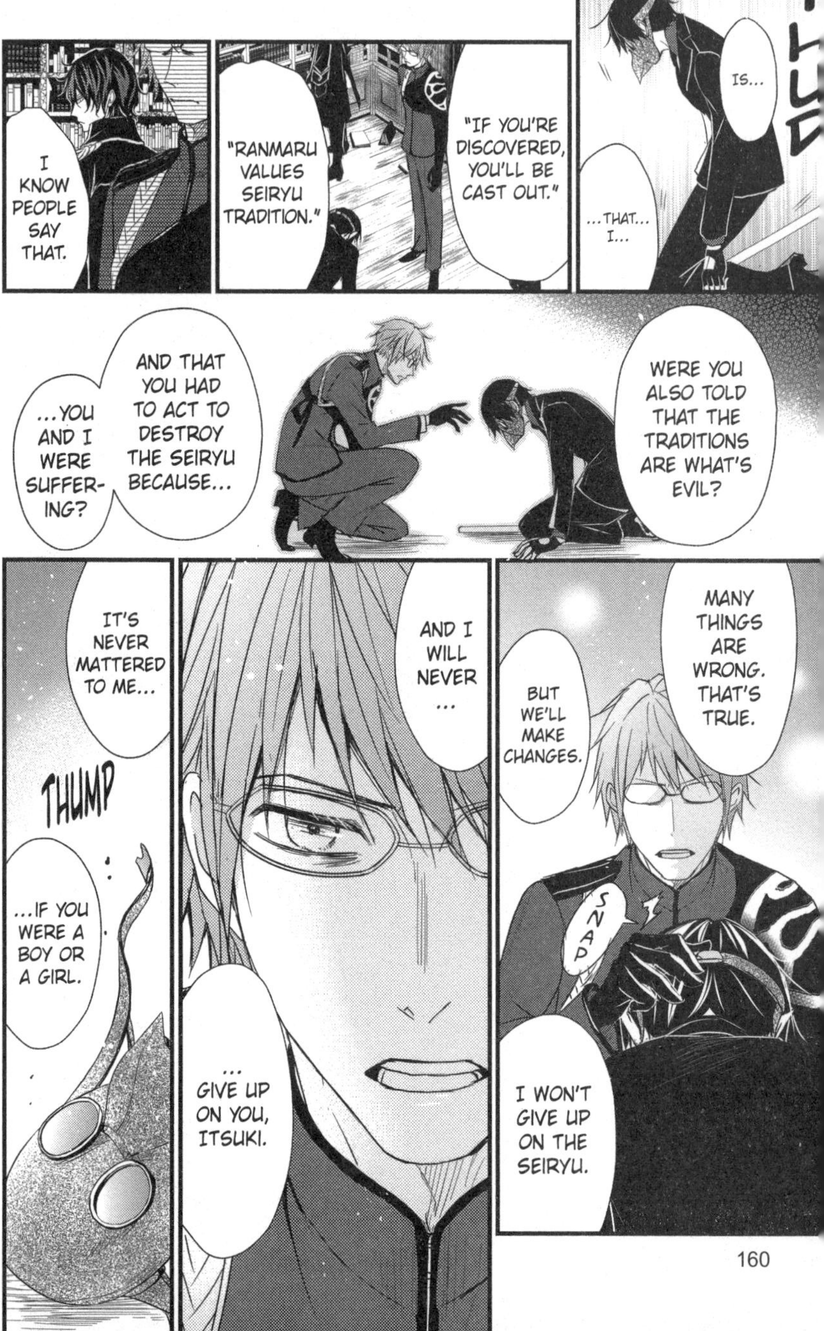
THUD
IS...
...THAT... I...
"IF YOU'RE DISCOVERED, YOU'LL BE CAST OUT."
"RANMARU VALUES SEIRYU TRADITION."
I KNOW PEOPLE SAY THAT.
WERE YOU ALSO TOLD THAT THE TRADITIONS ARE WHAT'S EVIL?
AND THAT YOU HAD TO ACT TO DESTROY THE SEIRYU BECAUSE...
...YOU AND I WERE SUFFER-ING?
MANY THINGS ARE WRONG. THAT'S TRUE.
BUT WE'LL MAKE CHANGES.
SNAP
I WON'T GIVE UP ON THE SEIRYU.
AND I WILL NEVER...
...GIVE UP ON YOU, ITSUKI.
IT'S NEVER MATTERED TO ME...
THUMP
...IF YOU WERE A BOY OR A GIRL.

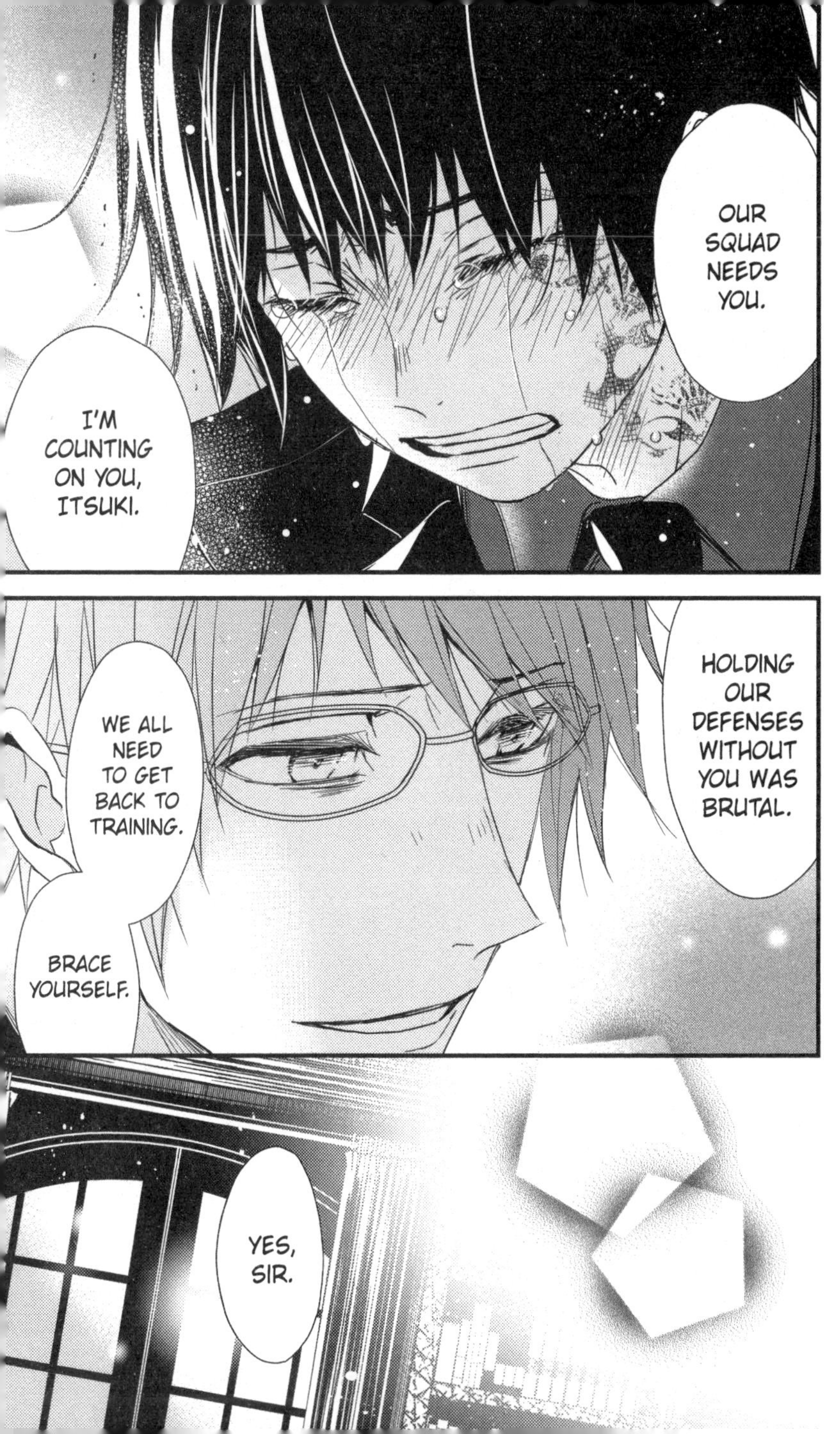
OUR SQUAD NEEDS YOU.
I'M COUNTING ON YOU, ITSUKI.
HOLDING OUR DEFENSES WITHOUT YOU WAS BRUTAL.
WE ALL NEED TO GET BACK TO TRAINING.
BRACE YOURSELF.
YES, SIR.

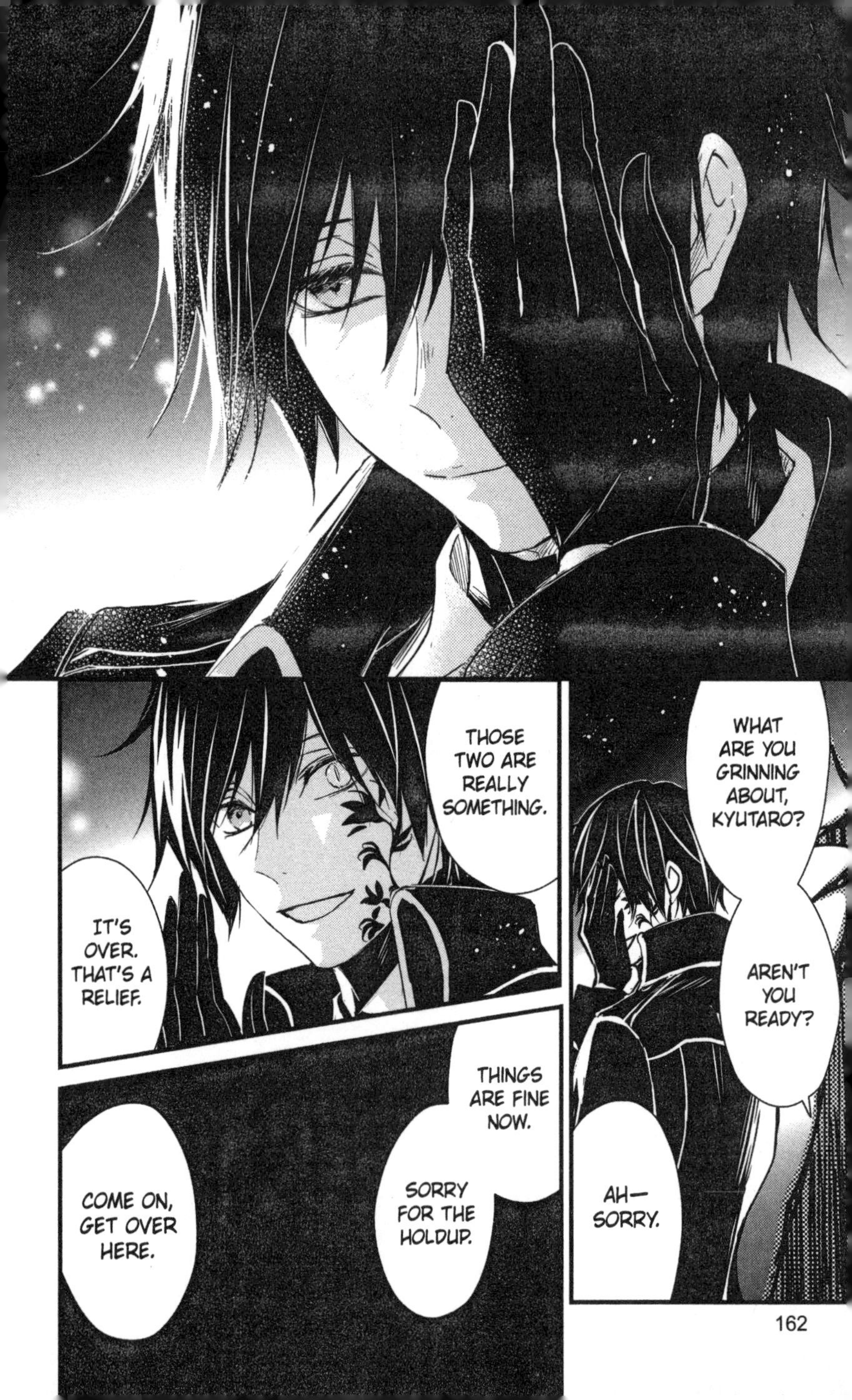
WHAT ARE YOU GRINNING ABOUT, KYUTARO?
AREN'T YOU READY?
AH— SORRY.
THOSE TWO ARE REALLY SOMETHING.
IT'S OVER. THAT'S A RELIEF.
THINGS ARE FINE NOW.
SORRY FOR THE HOLDUP.
COME ON, GET OVER HERE.

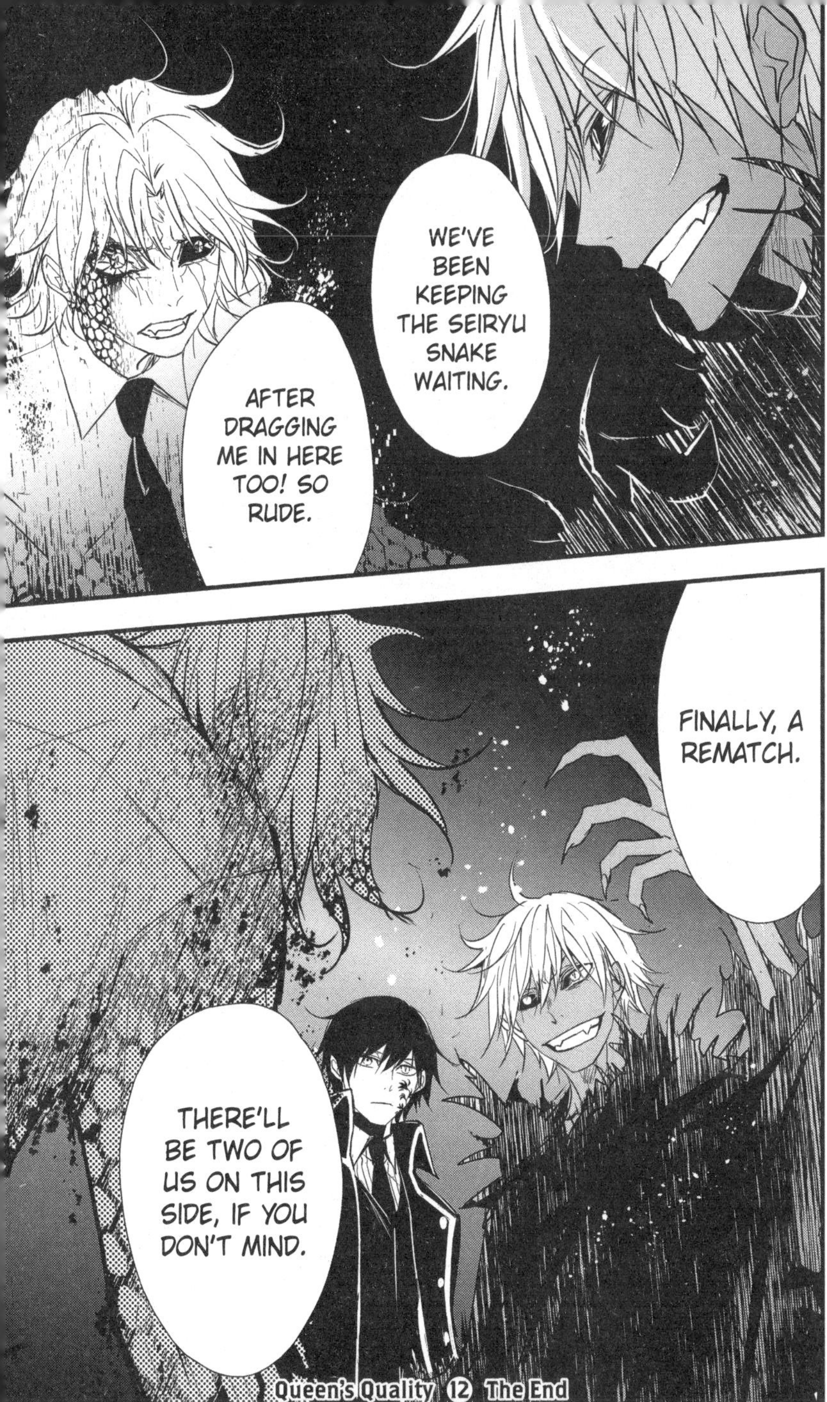
WE'VE BEEN KEEPING THE SEIRYU SNAKE WAITING.
AFTER DRAGGING ME IN HERE TOO! SO RUDE.
FINALLY, A REMATCH.
THERE'LL BE TWO OF US ON THIS SIDE, IF YOU DON'T MIND.
Queen's Quality 12 The End

Despite all the upheaval in the world, I have been well and continuing to draw manga. Kojiro is well too. It would make me so happy if you enjoy *Queen's Quality* volume 12.

—Kyousuke Motomi

Author Bio

Born on August 1, Kyousuke Motomi debuted in *Deluxe Betsucomi* with *Hetakuso Kyupiddo* (No Good Cupid) in 2002. She is the creator of *Dengeki Daisy*, *Beast Master* and *QQ Sweeper*, all available in North America from VIZ Media. Motomi enjoys sleeping, tea ceremonies and reading Haruki Murakami.

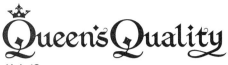

Queen's Quality

Vol. 12

Shojo Beat Edition

STORY AND ART BY

KYOUSUKE MOTOMI

QUEEN'S QUALITY Vol. 12
by Kyousuke MOTOMI

Original Japanese edition published by SHOGAKUKAN.
English translation rights in the United States of America, Canada, the United Kingdom, Ireland, Australia and New Zealand arranged with SHOGAKUKAN.

ORIGINAL DESIGN/Chie SATO+Bay Bridge Studio

English Adaptation/Ysabet Reinhardt MacFarlane
Translation/JN Productions
Touch-Up Art & Lettering/Rina Mapa
Design/Julian [JR] Robinson
Editor/Amy Yu

Printed in the U.S.A.

Published by VIZ Media, LLC
P.O. Box 77010
San Francisco, CA 94107

10 9 8 7 6 5 4 3 2 1
First printing, July 2021

VIZ MEDIA
viz.com

shojobeat.com

PARENTAL ADVISORY
QUEEN'S QUALITY is rated T for Teen and is recommended for ages 13 and up. This volume contains suggestive themes, partial nudity, spooky scenes and violence.

ratings.viz.com RATED T TEEN

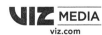

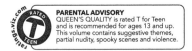

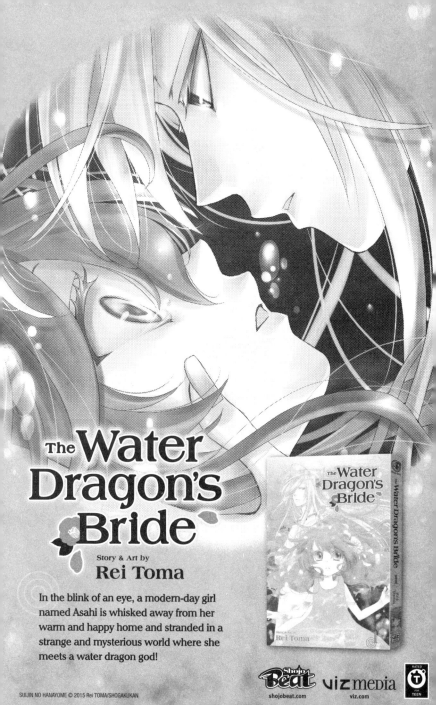

The Water Dragon's Bride

Story & Art by
Rei Toma

In the blink of an eye, a modern-day girl
named Asahi is whisked away from her
warm and happy home and stranded in a
strange and mysterious world where she
meets a water dragon god!

This is the Last Page!

It's true: In keeping with the original Japanese comic format, this book reads from right to left—so action, sound effects and word balloons are completely reversed. This preserves the orientation of the original artwork—plus, it's fun! Check out the diagram shown here to get the hang of things, and then turn to the other side of the book to get started!

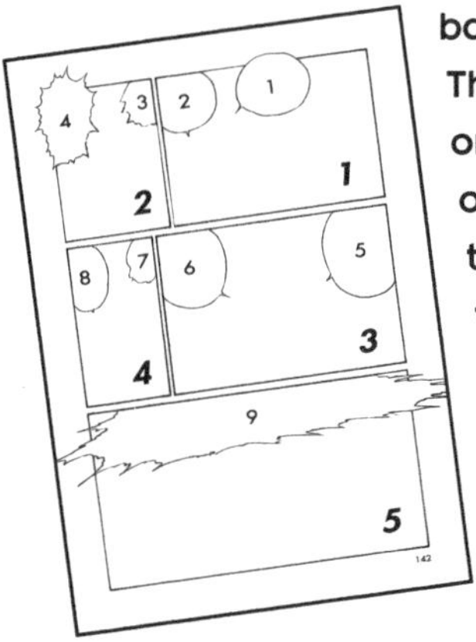
1
2
3
4
5
6
7
8
9
1
2
3
4
5
142

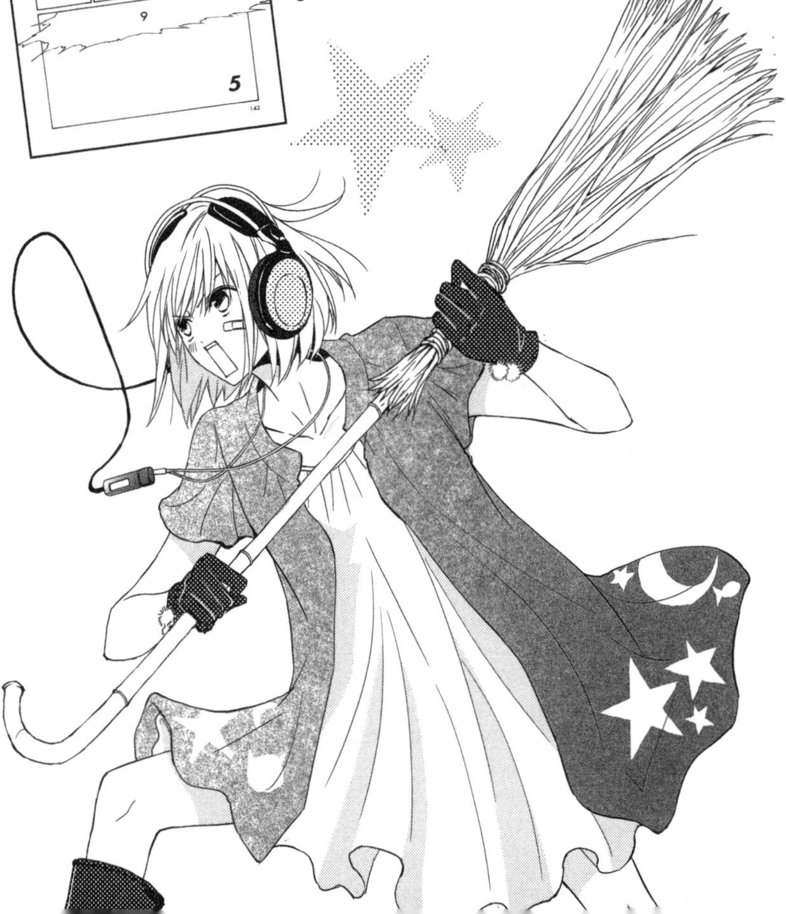